London
2017

A SELECTION
OF THE BEST
RESTAURANTS
& HOTELS

Contents

Where to **eat**

In Central London   32

Where to **stay**

In Central London   417

Lists of awards and features 16

In Greater London 298

▶ North-West 302

Archway • Belsize Park • Camden Town • Church End • Crouch End • Dartmouth Park • Kensal Green• Kentish Town • King's Cross St Pancras • Primrose Hill • Queens Park • Swiss Cottage • Tufnell Park • West Hampstead • Willesden Green

▶ North-East 320

Canonbury • Dalston • Hackney • Highbury • Hoxton • Islington • London Fields • Shoreditch • South Hackney • South Woodford • Stoke Newington • Wanstead

▶ South-East 350

Bethnal Green • Blackheath • Canary Wharf • East Dulwich • Forest Hill • Greenwich • Kennington • Peckham • Spitalfields • Stockwell • Vauxhall • Whitechapel

▶ South-West 372

Acton Green • Balham • Barnes • Battersea • Brixton • Chiswick • Clapham Common • Ealing • East Sheen • Fulham • Hammersmith • Kew • Putney • Richmond • Shepherd's Bush • South Ealing • Southfields • Teddington • Tooting • Twickenham • Wandsworth • Wimbledon

Index & Maps 474

The MICHELIN guide's commitments

Experienced in quality!

Whether they are in Japan, the USA, China or Europe, our inspectors apply the same criteria to judge the quality of each and every hotel and restaurant that they visit. The Michelin guide commands a worldwide reputation thanks to the commitments we make to our readers – and we reiterate these below:

→ Anonymous inspections

Our inspectors make regular and anonymous visits to hotels and restaurants to gauge the quality of products and services offered to an ordinary customer. They settle their own bill and may then introduce themselves and ask for more information about the establishment. Our readers' comments are also a valuable source of information, which we can follow up with a visit of our own.

→ Independence

To remain totally objective for our readers, the selection is made with complete independence. Entry into the guide is free. All decisions are discussed with the Editor and our highest awards are considered at a European level.

→ Selection & choice

The guide offers a selection of the best hotels and restaurants in every category of comfort and price. This is only possible because all the inspectors rigorously apply the same methods.

→ Annual updates

All the practical information, classifications and awards are revised and updated every year to give the most reliable information possible.

→ Consistency

The criteria for the classifications are the same in every country covered by the MICHELIN guide. The sole intention of Michelin is to make your travels safe and enjoyable.

Dear reader,

*W*e are delighted to present the 2017 edition of the MICHELIN Guide for London.

All the restaurants within this guide have been chosen first and foremost for the quality of their cooking. You'll find comprehensive information on over 600 dining establishments, ranging from gastropubs and neighbourhood brasseries to internationally renowned restaurants. The diverse and varied selection also bears testament to the rich and buoyant dining scene in London, with the city now enjoying a worldwide reputation for the quality and range of its restaurants.

You'll see that Michelin Stars are not our only awards – look out also for the Bib Gourmands. These are restaurants where the cooking is still carefully prepared but in a simpler style and, priced at under £28 for three courses, they represent excellent value for money.

To complement the selection of restaurants, our team of independent, full-time inspectors have also chosen 50 hotels. These carefully selected hotels represent the best that London has to offer, from the small and intimate to the grand and luxurious. All have been chosen for their individuality and personality.

We are committed to remaining at the forefront of the culinary world and to meeting the demands of our readers. As such, we are always very interested to hear your opinions on the establishments listed in our guide, as well as those you feel could be of interest for future editions. Please don't hesitate to contact us as your contributions are invaluable in directing our work and improving the quality of the information we provide.

Thank you for your support and happy travelling with the 2017 edition of the Michelin Guide for London.

Consult the Michelin Guide at www.viamichelin.co.uk
and write to us at themichelinguide-gbirl@michelin.com

How to use this guide...

Restaurants, classified according to comfort (particularly pleasant if in red)	✗ Quite comfortable	✗✗✗ Very comfortable	✗✗✗✗✗ Luxury in the traditional style
	✗✗ Comfortable	✗✗✗✗ Top class comfort	🍺 Pubs serving good food

Starred restaurants

Stars for excellent cooking

❀ to ❀❀❀

Cuisine type

London area or neighbourhood

Each area is colour coded:

■ Central London
■ Greater London

Birdy Nam-Nam

F u s i o n

98 War...
℘ 020 7...
www.ro...
⊖ To...
Closed 25...

Menu
🍴
🍷
📶

Notting Grill ❀❀

S e a f o o d   ▶ Plan XI

Court Road Lancaster St
SW1Y 4AN
℘ 020 7747 22 00
www.robscafe.com
⊖ Leicester Square

Closed Christmas-January,
Saturday lunch, Sunday,
Monday and bank holidays
– booking essential

Menu £14 (lunch)/25 – Carte £20/38   ✗✗✗✗

Practical information

Name, address and information about the establishment

Prices

Lowest/highest price for a set and à la carte menu

Restaurants symbols

🍳 Breakfast
🍽 Small plates
🌱 Vegetarian menu
🍷 Particularly interesting wine list
🍸 Notable cocktail list
🎭 Restaurants offering lower priced pre and/or post theatre menus
⇔ Private dining room

T...
T r...
98...
℘ ...
ww...
⊖...
Clos...

M...

🍴
🍷
📶

Emile Lepeletier

Linda House is a handsome four storey 18th century building in the heart of Soho. To gain entry, you ring the doorbell and you'll then be ushered into one of the two dining rooms. Regulars may have their favourite but there's little to choose between them – they're both warm and welcoming, although the first floor room is slightly larger than the ground floor.

There is something about being cosseted in a characterful house that makes dining here such a pleasure and it provides the perfect antidote for those feeling bruised and buffeted by the bigger, more boisterous places.

The cooking is modern in its approach and presentation but flavours are far more vigorous and full bodied than one expects and the marriages of various ingredients bear testament to real talent. Evidence of Bob's Welsh roots pops up here and there, from the laver bread to the Welsh cheeses and his homeland provides much of the produce. Tasting and Garden menus are available for those making it an occasion.

First Course	Main Course	Dessert
• Ravioli of shellfish with Champagne and chives	• Roast sea bass with black olives, baby squid and creamed fennel	• Lemongrass jelly with pineapple and coconut
• Loin of tuna rapped in basil with soy, avocado and a salad of radis	• Assiette of lamb with new season garlic, borlotti beans and rosemary	• Vanilla yoghurt parfait with blueberries

Sample menu for Starred restaurant

194

6

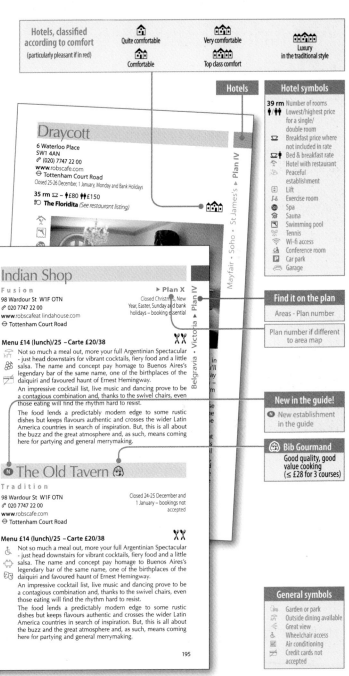

Hotels, classified according to comfort
(particularly pleasant if in red)

🏠 Quite comfortable

🏠 Comfortable

🏠🏠 Very comfortable

🏠🏠 Top class comfort

🏠🏠🏠 Luxury in the traditional style

Hotels

Hotel symbols

39 rm Number of rooms

🛉/🛉🛉 Lowest/highest price for a single/double room

🖙 Breakfast price where not included in rate

🖙🛉 Bed & breakfast rate

🕍 Hotel with restaurant

🌿 Peaceful establishment

🛗 Lift

🏋 Exercise room

💆 Spa

🏵 Sauna

🏊 Swimming pool

🎾 Tennis

📶 Wi-fi access

🛋 Conference room

🅿 Car park

🚗 Garage

Draycott

6 Waterloo Place
SW1 4AN
☎ (020) 7747 22 00
www.robscafe.com
⊖ Tottenham Court Road
Closed 25-26 December, 1 January, Monday and Bank Holidays

35 rm 🖙 – 🛉£80 🛉🛉£150
🕍 **The Floridita** (See restaurant listing)

🏠🏠

Mayfair · Soho · St James's ▶ Plan IV

Find it on the plan

Areas - Plan number

Plan number if different to area map

Indian Shop

F u s i o n   ▶ Plan X

98 Wardour St W1F OTN   Closed Christmas, New
☎ 020 7747 22 00   Year, Easter, Sunday and bank
www.robscafeat lindahouse.com holidays – booking essential
⊖ Tottenham Court Road

Belgravia · Victoria ▶ Plan IV

Menu £14 (lunch)/25 – Carte £20/38   ✗✗

🍸 Not so much a meal out, more your full Argentinian Spectacular
🎎 - just head downstairs for vibrant cocktails, fiery food and a little
📺 salsa. The name and concept pay homage to Buenos Aires's
legendary bar of the same name, one of the birthplaces of the
daiquiri and favoured haunt of Ernest Hemingway.

An impressive cocktail list, live music and dancing prove to be
a contagious combination and, thanks to the swivel chairs, even
those eating will find the rhythm hard to resist.

The food lends a predictably modern edge to some rustic
dishes but keeps flavours authentic and crosses the wider Latin
America countries in search of inspiration. But, this is all about
the buzz and the great atmosphere and, as such, means coming
here for partying and general merrymaking.

New in the guide!

🅝 New establishment in the guide

😊 Bib Gourmand
Good quality, good value cooking
(≤ £28 for 3 courses)

🅝 The Old Tavern 😊

T r a d i t i o n

98 Wardour St W1F OTN   Closed 24-25 December and
☎ 020 7747 22 00   1 January – bookings not
www.robscafe.com   accepted
⊖ Tottenham Court Road

Menu £14 (lunch)/25 – Carte £20/38   ✗✗

🦽 Not so much a meal out, more your full Argentinian Spectacular
🚡 - just head downstairs for vibrant cocktails, fiery food and a little
📺 salsa. The name and concept pay homage to Buenos Aires's
legendary bar of the same name, one of the birthplaces of the
daiquiri and favoured haunt of Ernest Hemingway.

An impressive cocktail list, live music and dancing prove to be
a contagious combination and, thanks to the swivel chairs, even
those eating will find the rhythm hard to resist.

The food lends a predictably modern edge to some rustic
dishes but keeps flavours authentic and crosses the wider Latin
America countries in search of inspiration. But, this is all about
the buzz and the great atmosphere and, as such, means coming
here for partying and general merrymaking.

195

General symbols

🌳 Garden or park

🍽 Outside dining available

🔭 Great view

♿ Wheelchair access

🆎 Air conditioning

🚫 Credit cards not accepted

A culinary history of London

London, influenced by worldwide produce arriving via the Thames, has always enjoyed a close association with its food, though most of the time the vast majority of its people have looked much closer to home for their sustenance.

Even as far back as the 2nd century AD, meat was on the menu: the profusion of wildlife in the woods and forests around London turned it into a carnivore's paradise, thereby setting the tone and the template. Large stoves were employed to cook everything from pork and beef to goose and deer. The Saxons added the likes of

C. Moirenc/hemis.fr

garlic, leeks, radishes and turnips to the pot, while eels became a popular staple in later years.

WHAT A LARK!

By the 13th century, the taste for fish had evolved to the more exotic porpoise, lamprey and sturgeon, with saffron and spices perking up the common-or-garden meat dish. Not that medieval tastes would have been considered mundane to the average 21st century diner: Londoners of the time would think nothing about devouring roasted thrush or lark from the cook's stalls dotted around the city streets. And you'd have been unlikely to hear the cry "Eat your greens!" In the 15th century, the vegetable diet, such as it was, seemed to run mainly to herbs such as rosemary, fennel, borage and thyme.

As commercial and maritime success burgeoned in the age of the Tudors, so tables began to groan under the weight of London's penchant for feasting. No excess was spared, as oxen, sheep, boars and pigs were put to the griddle; these would have been accompanied by newly arrived yams and sweet potatoes from America and 'washed down' with rhubarb from Asia. People on the streets could 'feast-lite': by the 17th century hawkers were offering all sorts of goodies on the hoof.

L. Klein/Cultúra Creative/Photononstop

FULL OF BEANS

All of this eating was of course accompanied by a lot of drinking. Though much of it took place in the alehouses and taverns - which ran into the thousands - by the 18th century coffee houses had become extraordinarily popular. These were places to do business as well as being convenient 'for passing evenings socially at a very small charge'.

Perhaps the biggest revolution in eating habits came midway through the 19th century when the first cavernous dining halls and restaurants appeared. These 'freed' diners from the communal benches of the cook-house and gave them, for the first time, the chance for a bit of seclusion at separate tables. This private dining experience was an egalitarian movement: plutocrats may have had their posh hotels, but the less well-off were buttering teacakes and scones served by 'nippies' at the local Lyons Corner House.

Influenced by post World War II flavours brought in by immigrants from Asia, the Caribbean and Africa – and, more recently, from Eastern Bloc Countries - Londoners now enjoy an unparalleled cuisine alive with global flavours. We're also more confident about waving the flag for Britain these days, with pop-ups, pubs and high end eateries helping us rediscover and celebrate our own culinary heritage.

Practical London

ARRIVAL/DEPARTURE

If you're coming to London from abroad, it's worth bearing in mind that the capital's airports are (with one exception), a long way from the city itself. The good news is that they're well-served by speedy express train services; the even better news is that if you travel by Eurostar you can go by train direct from the heart of Europe to the heart of London without having to worry about luggage limits, carousels and carbon footprints…

By air

Most people arrive via Heathrow – the UK's busiest airport – or Gatwick. You can catch the Heathrow Express rail service to Paddington every 15 minutes, and that's also about how long the journey takes. Another alternative is to board the Piccadilly line tube train: it's cheaper, but the drawn-out travelling time can make it seem as if you've spent most of your holiday just getting to the centre. Gatwick is further out, south of London's M25 ring road, and the quickest way into the city is via the Gatwick Express rail service, which takes half an hour to reach Victoria station. There are also frequent train services which connect with a host of central London stations, including London Bridge and King's Cross. The capital has three other airports: Stansted, 35 miles northeast of the city; Luton, 30 miles to the north; and London City Airport, which is nine miles to the east and connects to the centre via the Docklands Light Railway.

By train

The days of *having* to fly into London are long gone. Smart travellers from the Continent now jump on the Eurostar from Paris, Brussels or Lille, zip along at 186mph, and step onto the platform at St Pancras International in the time it takes to devour a coffee and a croissant (a big coffee, admittedly). From there, three tube lines from the adjoining King's Cross station whisk you into town. Book Eurostar far enough in advance (which isn't very far, by any means) and you can get tickets for just £69 return.

GETTING AROUND

The pearl that is Oyster

Single, return and day tickets (Travelcards) can be bought from machines and offices at tube, train and bus stations, or from London Travel Information Centres… but your best bet is to buy an Oyster card. This electronic smartcard is the fastest, easiest and cheapest way to pay for journeys around town; just zap it over a yellow reader to let you through the tube gates or onto a bus. Oysters are charged with a pre-paid amount of credit which can cover a week, a month

or be used to 'pay-as-you-go'. The deposit for a card is £5, which will be refunded upon its return, although the pay-as-you-go credit doesn't expire, so you can keep it to use on your next visit.

For details on fares, journey planners, service updates and more:

• visit the Transport for London website www.tfl.gov.uk

• call the 24-hour Travel Information Service on + 44(0) 343 222 1234

• or visit one of the London Travel Information Centres, which are based at Liverpool Street, Piccadilly Circus, King's Cross, Victoria, Euston, Paddington, Gatwick and Heathrow.

By Underground and Overground

First, the bad news: the tube can get hot and overcrowded and engineering works can close lines at weekends. But the good news? Generally speaking, the tube is by far the quickest way to get around town. There are 11 lines, plus the automated Docklands Light Railway (DLR); these cover pretty much the whole city and are all clearly shown on the free map you can pick up at any tube station. Trains run from 5am to just past midnight Monday-Saturday, with a reduced timetable on Sundays. There are also four Overground routes which operate across the city, running from Watford and Richmond in the north and south west to Croydon and Barking in the south and east.

By bus

They might move a bit slower than trains but when you ride on the top of a double-decker bus, you get the added bonus of an absorbing, tourist-friendly view. Many bus stops have live arrivals boards and you can pick up a handy central London bus map from a bus station. London buses do not accept cash – you can only pay with a Travelcard, an Oyster card or a UK-issued contactless payment card.

Look out for the updated version of the iconic 'Routemaster' that operates on several routes.

By car

The best advice is not to drive in central London, not if you want your sanity preserved anyway.

Roadworks and parking can be the stuff of nightmares, and that's before the Congestion Charge Zone is taken into consideration. This zone covers the central area and is clearly marked by red 'C' signs painted on the road. It's in operation Monday-Friday 7am-6pm (weekends and holidays are free) and you'll need to register the car's number plate on a database at tfl.gov.uk. If it all sounds too much of a headache, you always have the option of hailing a black cab – just stick out your hand when you see one with its 'taxi' light illuminated.

By bike

For short journeys, a greener alternative is the humble bike, and those aged 18 and above can hire a so-called 'Boris Bike' from one of the many Santander Cycle Hire docking points spread across the capital. There's no need to book ahead, they're available 24 hours a day, 7 days a week, and anyone 14 and over can ride. Simply pay the access fee (£2 for 24 hours) at a docking station terminal, using a credit or debit card. You are then charged for your usage but, as the scheme is designed for short journeys, the first 30 minutes are free and it's only £2 for the second 30 minutes. Simply return the bike to any docking station when you're done.

By boat

'Taking to the water' has become increasingly popular over the last few years: the Thames offers some little-seen views of London, and cutting through the open expanse of river can certainly be a most relaxing travel option. Most River Bus services operate every 20-60 minutes and there are piers all over the central area where you can jump on board, from Chelsea Harbour in the west to Woolwich Arsenal in the east. Pay with your Oyster card or at the pier ticket office.

By cable car

Launched in June 2012 for the London Olympics, the Emirates Air Line glides high over the Thames from the Royal Docks (near the Excel Centre) to North Greenwich (by The O2), and offers fantastic views of the Thames Barrier and Canary Wharf. It takes 5-10 minutes to make the crossing and each car can hold around 10 people. You can pay at the ticket office (presenting your Travelcard for a discount), or use your Oyster card at the gates.

LIVING LONDON LIFE

It almost goes without saying that visitors to the capital are spoilt for choice when it comes to having a good time. You could visit one of the city's 300 museums or galleries, many of which are free, or you could see for yourself why London's theatre scene is considered the best in the world. Come nightfall, choose from the vast number of globally-influenced restaurants or from one of 7,000 pubs and bars.

At the weekend, an interesting alternative to shopping or sports events is to browse one of the farmers' markets: on a Saturday, the best of the bunch can be found at Ealing, Notting Hill, Pimlico, Wimbledon and Twickenham. On Sundays, two of the favourites are in Marylebone and Blackheath, while, on the same day, the Columbia Road flower market, in the East End, is a wonderful place to while away the hours.

The more mainstream shopper might do well to steer clear of frenetic Oxford Street. Regent Street is a more alluring thoroughfare with its mid-priced fashion stores and hallowed names. If you're after a destination with a real touch of class, then nearby Jermyn Street is the place for bespoke men's clothing, but if your taste is for more outré threads, then Notting Hill or Camden are good bets. Back in the centre of town, Covent Garden is packed with speciality stores, quirky alleyways and – if you choose the wrong time to go – an awful lot of people!

Escape can always be found in the relative quiet of a good bookshop, and London is full of them. Still in Covent Garden, Stanford's is the city's number one travel bookshop, while not far away in Charing Cross Road, the legendary Foyles has relocated to bright new premises. But for the marriage of real elegance with a good read, head to Daunt Books in Marylebone High Street, which is set in an Edwardian building with long oak galleries and skylights; the bustle of London's streets will seem a million miles away.

Where to **eat**

Lists of awards and features

Starred restaurants

Within the selection, we have highlighted a number of restaurants for their excellent cooking. When awarding One, Two or Three Michelin Stars there are a number of factors we consider: the quality and compatibility of the ingredients, the technical skill and flair that goes into their preparation, the clarity and combination of flavours, the value for money and, above all, the taste. Equally important is the ability to produce excellent cooking not once but time and time again. Our inspectors make as many visits as necessary, so that you can be sure of the quality and consistency.

A Two Star restaurant has to offer something very special in its cuisine; a real element of creativity, originality or personality that sets it apart from the rest. Three Star – our highest award – are given to the very best.

Cuisines in any style and of any nationality are eligible for a Star; the decoration, service and comfort have no bearing on the award.

For every restaurant awarded a Star we include six specialities that are typical of their cooking style.

These specific dishes may not always be available but give an idea as to the type of cuisine you will find.

The awarding of a star is based solely on the quality of the cuisine.

N: highlights those establishments newly promoted to One, Two or Three stars.

✿✿✿
Exceptional cuisine, worth a special journey!
Our highest award is given for the superlative cooking of chefs at the peak of their profession. The ingredients are exemplary, the cooking is elevated to an art form and their dishes are often destined to become classics.

Alain Ducasse at The Dorchester	XxXxX	41
Gordon Ramsay	XxxX	273

✿✿
Excellent cooking, worth a detour!
The personality and talent of the chef and their team is evident in the expertly crafted dishes, which are refined, inspired and sometimes original.

Araki	XX	44	Ledbury	XxX	292
Dinner by Heston Blumenthal	XxX	269	Marcus	XxxX	144
Le Gavroche	XxxX	68	Sketch (The Lecture Room		
Greenhouse	XxX	70	and Library)	XxxX	104
Hélène Darroze			Umu	XxX	110
at The Connaught	XxxX	75			

✿
High quality cooking, worth a stop!
Using top quality ingredients, dishes with distinct flavours are carefully prepared to a consistently high standard.

Alyn Williams at The Westbury	XxxX	42	Kitchen Table at Bubbledogs	XX	192
Amaya	XxX	137	Kitchen W8	XX	291
Ametsa	XxX	138	Lima Fitzrovia	X	166
Angler	XX	217	Locanda Locatelli	XxX	167
L'Atelier de Joël Robuchon	X	119	Lyle's	X	344
Barrafina (Soho)	X	47	Murano	XxX	87
Benares	XxX	49	The Ninth N	X	194
Bonhams	XX	53	Outlaw's at The Capital	XX	279
Céleste N	XxxX	139	Pétrus	XxX	148
Chez Bruce	XX	413	Pidgin N	X	338
City Social	XxX	227	Pied à Terre	XxX	195
Clove Club	X	341	Pollen Street Social	XX	93
Club Gascon	XX	228	Portland	X	174
Dabbous	X	188	Quilon	XxX	149
Ellory N	X	336	Ritz Restaurant N	XxXxX	98
Fera at Claridge's	XxxX	65	River Café	XX	403
Five Fields N	XxX	271	St John	X	246
Galvin La Chapelle	XxX	365	Seven Park Place	XxX	101
Galvin at Windows	XxX	67	Social Eating House	X	105
The Glasshouse	XX	404	Story	XX	249
The Goring (Dining Room)	XxX	141	Tamarind	XxX	107
Gymkhana	XX	71	Texture	XX	179
Hakkasan Hanway Place	XX	190	Trinity N	XX	391
Hakkasan Mayfair	XX	72	Trishna	X	180
Harwood Arms	🍴	397	La Trompette	XX	388
Hedone	XX	385	Veeraswamy N	XX	112
HKK	XX	343	Yauatcha Soho	XX	114
Kai	XxX	79			

Bib Gourmand restaurants

😋 **Bib Gourmand: Good quality, good value cooking. 'Bibs' are awarded for simple yet skilful cooking for under £28**

L'Amorosa	X	400
Anchor and Hope	🍽	216
A. Wong	X	136
Azou	X	401
Bao **N**	X	45
Barbary **N**	X	185
Barnyard	X	186
Barrica	X	186
Bellanger **N**	XX	331
Bistro Union	X	387
Blixen	X	364
Brasserie Zédel	XX	54
Brawn	X	354
Cafe Spice Namaste	XX	370
Canton Arms	🍽	369
Charlotte's W5 **N**	X	393
Comptoir Gascon	X	229
Copita	X	60
Dehesa	X	63
Drapers Arms	🍽	332
Elliot's	X	230
Empress	🍽	347
Foley's **N**	X	164
Grain Store	X	314
Great Queen Street	X	189
Gunpowder **N**	X	366
Hereford Road	X	203
Honey and Co	X	191
Hoppers **N**	X	77
José	X	234
Kateh	X	203
Legs **N**	X	328
Market	X	309
Marksman **N**	🍽	355
Morito (Finsbury)	X	239
Newman Arms **N**	🍽	169
Opera Tavern	X	127
Padella **N**	X	242
Palomar	X	90
Paradise Garage **N**	X	356
Picture Fitzrovia	X	172
Polpetto	X	94
Primeur **N**	X	324
Provender	X	349
St John Bread and Wine	X	367
Salt Yard	X	197
Taberna do Mercado	X	368
Trullo	X	325
Upstairs (at Trinity) **N**	X	390
Vico **N**	X	131
Yipin China	X	335

Restaurants by cuisine type

Argentinian

Zoilo	✗	181

Asian

Bao	✗ ⊛	45
Bone Daddies	✗	52
Flesh and Buns	✗	189
Jinjuu	✗	78
XO	✗✗	308

Austrian

Fischer's	✗✗	163

Basque

Donostia	✗	163
Lurra	✗✗	168

Chinese

A. Wong	✗ ⊛	136
Baozi Inn	✗	46
Barshu	✗	46
Beijing Dumpling	✗	48
Bo Lang	✗	264
China Tang	✗✗✗	57
Duck and Rice	✗	63
Good Earth	✗✗	272
Grand Imperial	✗✗✗	142
Hakkasan Hanway Place	✗✗ ✿	190
Hakkasan Mayfair	✗✗ ✿	72
Haozhan	✗	73
HKK	✗✗ ✿	343
Imperial China	✗✗✗	78
Kai	✗✗✗ ✿	79
Manchurian Legends	✗	82
Min Jiang	✗✗✗	294
Park Chinois	✗✗✗	91
Plum Valley	✗✗	92
Royal China	✗✗	176
Royal China Club	✗✗	177
Shikumen (Ealing)	✗	394
Shikumen (Hammersmith)	✗✗	409
Toa Kitchen	✗✗	206
Yauatcha City	✗✗	255
Yauatcha Soho	✗✗ ✿	114
Yipin China	✗ ⊛	335

Classic cuisine

Ritz Restaurant	✗✗✗✗ ✿	98

Creative

Ametsa	✗✗✗ ✿	138
Archipelago	✗✗	158
Corner Room	✗	355
L'Etranger	✗✗	270
Flat Three	✗✗	289
Greenhouse	✗✗✗ ✿ ✿	70
Pied à Terre	✗✗✗ ✿	195
Pollen Street Social	✗✗ ✿	93
The Providores	✗✗	175
Texture	✗✗ ✿	179

Creative British

Anglo	✗	185
Dairy	✗	389
Fera at Claridge's	✗✗✗ ✿	65
The Manor	✗	389

Creative French

Céleste	✗✗✗ ✿	139

Fish and chips

Kerbisher and Malt	✗	393
Vintage Salt	✗	334

French

L'Absinthe	✗	315
Alain Ducasse at The Dorchester	✗✗✗✗ ✿ ✿ ✿	41
Angelus	✗✗	202
L'Atelier de Joël Robuchon	✗ ✿	119
Balcon	✗✗	45
Balthazar	✗✗	120
Bar Boulud	✗✗	262
Bellanger	✗✗ ⊛	331
Bibendum	✗✗✗	263
Bistro Aix	✗	310
Bistrotheque	✗	354
Blanchette	✗	50

Le Boudin Blanc	✗	52
Boulestin	✗✗	54
Boundary	✗✗✗	340
Brasserie Gustave	✗✗	265
Brasserie Zédel	✗✗ ⊛	54
Casse Croûte	✗	223
Chez Bruce	✗✗ ❀	413
Cigalon	✗✗	225
Clos Maggiore	✗✗	122
Club Gascon	✗✗ ❀	228
Colbert	✗✗	267
Le Colombier	✗✗	268
Comptoir Gascon	✗ ⊛	229
Les Deux Salons	✗✗	123
Galvin Bistrot de Luxe	✗✗	164
Galvin La Chapelle	✗✗✗ ❀	365
Garnier	✗✗	270
Gauthier - Soho	✗✗✗	66
Le Gavroche	✗✗✗✗ ❀ ❀	68
Gordon Ramsay	✗✗✗✗ ❀ ❀ ❀	273
The Grill	✗✗✗	69
High Road Brasserie	✗	386
Les 110 de Taillevent	✗✗	170
Little Social	✗	82
Lobster Pot	✗	363
Luc's Brasserie	✗✗	236
Marianne	✗✗	205
Mon Plaisir	✗✗	193
La Petite Maison	✗✗	91
Pétrus	✗✗✗ ❀	148
Piquet	✗✗	173
Le Pont de la Tour	✗✗✗	243
Provender	✗ ⊛	349
Rétro Bistrot	✗✗	411
Roux at the Landau	✗✗✗	176
Sauterelle	✗✗	247
Six Portland Road	✗	295
Sketch (The Lecture Room and Library)	✗✗✗✗ ❀ ❀	104
Soif	✗	383
The Square	✗✗✗✗	106
Le Vacherin	✗✗	376

Greek

Mazi	✗	293
Opso	✗	170
Retsina	✗	307

Indian

Amaya	✗✗✗ ❀	137
Babur	✗✗	361
Benares	✗✗✗ ❀	49
Bombay Brasserie	✗✗✗✗	264
Cafe Spice Namaste	✗✗ ⊛	370
Chutney Mary	✗✗✗	59
The Cinnamon Club	✗✗✗	140
Cinnamon Kitchen	✗✗	226
Cinnamon Soho	✗	59
Dishoom	✗	123
Gunpowder	✗ ⊛	366
Gymkhana	✗✗ ❀	71
Hazara	✗✗	307
Indian Zilla	✗✗	378
Indian Zing	✗✗	402
Kennington Tandoori	✗✗	362
Malabar	✗✗	293
Masala Grill	✗✗	276
Painted Heron	✗✗	280
Quilon	✗✗✗ ❀	149
Red Fort	✗✗✗	96
Shayona	✗	310
Swagat	✗	408
Talli Joe	✗	197
Tamarind	✗✗✗ ❀	107
Trishna	✗ ❀	180
Veeraswamy	✗✗ ❀	112
Zaika	✗✗	296
Zumbura	✗	392

Italian

500	✗	306
A Cena	✗✗	412
Al Duca	✗✗	40
Amaranto	✗✗✗	40
L'Amorosa	✗ ⊛	400
L'Anima	✗✗✗	339
L'Anima Café	✗✗	340
Antico	✗	216
Artusi	✗	363
Bernardi's	✗✗	159
Bibo	✗	405
Bocca di Lupo	✗	51
Cafe Murano (St James's)	✗✗	55
Cafe Murano (Strand and Covent Garden)	✗✗	121
Canonbury Kitchen	✗	324
Cantina Del Ponte	✗	222

Chucs Bar and Grill	XX	58
Enoteca Turi	XX	140
Franco's	XX	66
il trillo	XX	274
Lardo	X	337
Latium	XX	165
Locanda Locatelli	XxX ✿	167
Massimo	XX	143
Mele e Pere	X	85
Murano	XxX ✿	87
Olivo	X	145
Olivocarne	X	146
Osteria Dell' Angolo	XX	147
Ostuni	X	317
Padella	X ⊛	242
Polpetto	X ⊛	94
Polpo at Ape and Bird	X	196
Polpo Covent Garden	X	128
Polpo Smithfield	X	244
Polpo Soho	X	94
Riva	X	379
River Café	XX ✿	403
Rotorino	X	327
Santini	XxX	151
Sartoria	XxX	100
Spring	XX	129
Theo Randall	XX	108
Trullo	X ⊛	325
Union Street Café	XX	251
Vasco and Piero's Pavilion	XX	111
Vico	X ⊛	131
Zafferano	XxX	152

Japanese

Araki	XX ✿✿	44
Dinings	X	162
Jidori	X	326
Kiku	XX	80
Kiraku	X	394
Koji	X	398
Kouzu	X	143
Koya Bar	X	81
Kurobuta Marble Arch	X	204
Matsuba	X	407
Matsuri	XX	83
Nanban	X	384
Nobu	XX	88
Nobu Berkeley St	XX	88
Oliver Maki	X	89
Roka (Aldwych)	XX	128
Roka (Bloomsbury)	XX	196
Roka (Mayfair)	XX	97
Sake No Hana	XX	99
Shoryu	X	102
Sosharu	XX	248
Takahashi	X	415
Tokimeitē	XX	109
Tonkotsu	X	109
Umu	XxX ✿✿	110
UNI	XX	152
Yashin	XX	296
Yashin Ocean House	XX	283
Zuma	XX	283

Korean

Bibigo	X	50
Hana	X	381

Lebanese

Kenza	XX	235

Meats and grills

34	XxX	108
Barbecoa	XX	219
Beast	XX	159
Beef and Brew	X	312
Chicken Shop	X	313
Chop Shop	X	58
Cut	XxX	62
Electric Diner	X	288
Foxlow (Clerkenwell)	X	231
Goodman Mayfair	XX	69
Hawksmoor (City of London)	X	233
Hawksmoor (Knightsbridge)	XX	272
Hawksmoor (Mayfair)	XX	74
Hawksmoor (Spitalfields)	X	366
Hawksmoor (Strand and Covent Garden)	X	124
Hill and Szrok	X	335
MASH	XX	83
Maze Grill Mayfair	XX	85
Maze Grill Park Walk	XX	276
New St Grill	XX	240
Oblix	XX	240
Rib Room	XxX	281

Tramshed	X	346
Vivat Bacchus	X	253
Vivat Bacchus London Bridge	X	253
Zelman Meats	X	113

Mediterranean cuisine

Blixen	X ☺	364
Brackenbury	X	402
Dehesa	X ☺	63
Dock Kitchen	X	288
Duke of Sussex	🍺	376
Earl Spencer	🍺	410
Ember Yard	X	64
Empress	🍺 ☺	347
Garrison	🍺	232
Kateh	X ☺	203
Light House	X	414
Margaux	X	275
Market Cafe	X	337
May the Fifteenth	X	390
Moro	X	239
The Ninth	X ✿	194
Nopi	X	89
Opera Tavern	X ☺	127
The Orange	🍺	147
Ottolenghi (Islington)	X	333
Ottolenghi (Spitalfields)	X	367
Palmerston	🍺	360
Pizarro	X	243
Rivea	XX	281
Rosita	X	382
Sager + Wilde	X	356
Salt Yard	X ☺	197
Sardine	X	330
Social Wine and Tapas	X	178
Sonny's Kitchen	X	379
Terroirs	X	130
Wormwood	X	295

Mexican

Peyote	X	92

Modern British

45 Jermyn St	XX	64
The Alfred Tennyson	🍺	136
Almeida	XX	331
Anchor and Hope	🍺 ☺	216
Anglesea Arms	🍺	401
Berners Tavern	XX	160
Bistro Union	X ☺	387
Bluebird	XX	263
Brown Dog	🍺	377
Chiswell Street Dining Rooms	XX	225
Corrigan's Mayfair	XXX	61
Craft London	X	361
Dean Street Townhouse Restaurant	XX	62
Drapers Arms	🍺 ☺	332
Ealing Park Tavern	🍺	409
Ellory	X ✿	336
Fifteen London	X	329
Great Queen Street	X ☺	189
Harwood Arms	🍺 ✿	397
Keeper's House	XX	80
Legs	X ☺	328
Linnea	XX	405
London House	XX	381
Lyle's	X ✿	344
Magdalen	XX	237
Market	X ☺	309
Newman Arms	🍺 ☺	169
Oldroyd	X	333
Olympic Café + Dining Room	X	378
Paradise by way of Kensal Green	🍺	311
Parlour	🍺	312
Pharmacy 2	XX	370
Picture Fitzrovia	X ☺	172
Picture Marylebone	X	172
Pidgin	X ✿	338
Rabbit	X	280
Refuel	XX	97
Roast	XX	245
The Shed	X	294
sixtyone	XX	177
Tate Modern (Restaurant)	X	250
Tredwell's	X	130
La Trompette	XX ✿	388
Upstairs at The Guildford Arms	X	362
Upstairs (at Trinity)	X ☺	390
Victoria	🍺	395
The Wallace	XX	181
Well	🍺	254
The Woodford	XX	348

Modern cuisine

Butlers Wharf Chop House	✗	222
Canton Arms	⑂ 🏵	369
Colony Grill Room	✗✗	60
Crown	⑂	412
Dinner by Heston Blumenthal	✗✗✗ 🏵 🏵	269
Foxlow (Stoke Newington)	✗	348
Gilbert Scott	✗✗	314
The Goring (Dining Room)	✗✗✗ 🏵	141
Hereford Road	✗ 🏵	203
Hix (Soho)	✗✗	76
Hix Mayfair	✗✗✗	76
Hix Oyster and Chop House	✗	233
Ivy Chelsea Garden	✗✗	274
Ivy Market Grill	✗✗	125
The Ivy	✗✗✗	125
Jugged Hare	⑂	235
Lady Ottoline	⑂	191
Lamberts	✗	377
Light on the Common	✗	414
Marksman	⑂ 🏵	355
Mayfair Chippy	✗	84
Merchants Tavern	✗✗	342
Noble Rot	✗	193
Northall	✗✗✗	145
Paradise Garage	✗ 🏵	356
Paternoster Chop House	✗	242
Pig and Butcher	⑂	334
Princess of Shoreditch	⑂	345
Princess Victoria	⑂	408
Quality Chop House	✗	244
Quo Vadis	✗✗✗	96
Rex Whistler	✗✗	150
Rivington Grill	✗✗	346
Rules	✗✗	129
St John	✗ 🏵	246
St John Bread and Wine	✗ 🏵	367
St John Maltby	✗	247
Smokehouse	⑂	387
Tommy Tucker	⑂	400

Turkish

Oklava	✗	345

Vegetarian

Vanilla Black	✗✗	252

Vietnamese

Au Lac	✗	328
Cây Tre	✗	56
Viet Grill	✗	347

World cuisine

Arabica Bar and Kitchen	✗	218
Baltic	✗✗	219
Barbary	✗ 🏵	185
Caravan	✗	223
Chiltern Firehouse	✗✗	161
Foley's	✗ 🏵	164
Honey and Co	✗ 🏵	191
The Modern Pantry Clerkenwell	✗	238
The Modern Pantry Finsbury Square	✗✗	238
Palomar	✗ 🏵	90
Tandis	✗	308

Restaurants with outside dining

Restaurants with outside dining

Restaurants open for breakfast

45 Jermyn St	XX	64
L'Absinthe	X	315
Al Duca	XX	40
Andina	X	339
Aqua Shard	XX	218
Avenue	XX	43
Balcon	XX	45
Balthazar	XX	120
Bellanger	XX ⊛	331
Bernardi's	XX	159
Berners Tavern	XX	160
Bird of Smithfield	X	220
Blixen	X ⊛	364
Boulestin	XX	54
Boundary	XxX	340
Bread Street Kitchen	XX	221
Brumus	XX	55
Caravan	X	223
Chapters	XX	357
Charlotte's W5	X ⊛	393
Chiltern Firehouse	XX	161
Chucs Bar and Grill	XX	58
The Cinnamon Club	XxX	140
Clarke's	XX	287
Clerkenwell Kitchen	X	226
Colbert	XX	267
Colony Grill Room	XX	60
Dean Street Townhouse Restaurant	XX	62
Les Deux Salons	XX	123
Dickie Fitz	XX	162
Dishoom	X	123
Duck and Waffle	XX	229
Electric Diner	X	288
Fifteen London	X	329
Fischer's	XX	163
Franco's	XX	66
Garrison	⊡	232
Granger and Co. Clerkenwell	X	232
Granger and Co. King's Cross	X	315
Granger and Co. Notting Hill	X	289
The Grill	XxX	69
Ham Yard	XX	73
Hawksmoor (City of London)	X	233
Heddon Street Kitchen	XX	74
Honey and Co	X ⊛	191
Ivy Chelsea Garden	XX	274
Ivy Market Grill	XX	125
Jugged Hare	⊡	235
Koya Bar	X	81
Lardo	X	337
Light on the Common	X	414
The Magazine	XX	275
The Modern Pantry Clerkenwell	X	238
The Modern Pantry Finsbury Square	XX	238
Nopi	X	89
Olympic Café + Dining Room	X	378
Opso	X	170
The Orange	⊡	147
Ottolenghi (Islington)	X	333
Ottolenghi (Spitalfields)	X	367
Parlour	⊡	312
Percy and Founders	XX	171
Portrait	X	95
Provender	X ⊛	349
Quo Vadis	XxX	96
Riding House Café	X	175
Rivington Grill	XX	346
Roast	XX	245
St John Bread and Wine	X ⊛	367
Victoria	⊡	395
Village East	X	252
The Wolseley	XxX	111

Central London

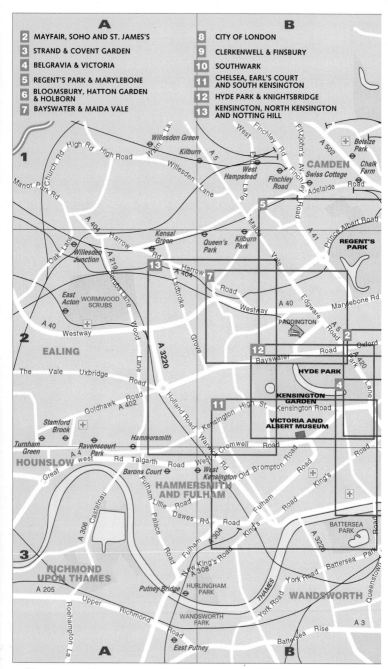

A

2	MAYFAIR, SOHO AND ST. JAMES'S
3	STRAND & COVENT GARDEN
4	BELGRAVIA & VICTORIA
5	REGENT'S PARK & MARYLEBONE
6	BLOOMSBURY, HATTON GARDEN & HOLBORN
7	BAYSWATER & MAIDA VALE

B

8	CITY OF LONDON
9	CLERKENWELL & FINSBURY
10	SOUTHWARK
11	CHELSEA, EARL'S COURT AND SOUTH KENSINGTON
12	HYDE PARK & KNIGHTSBRIDGE
13	KENSINGTON, NORTH KENSINGTON AND NOTTING HILL

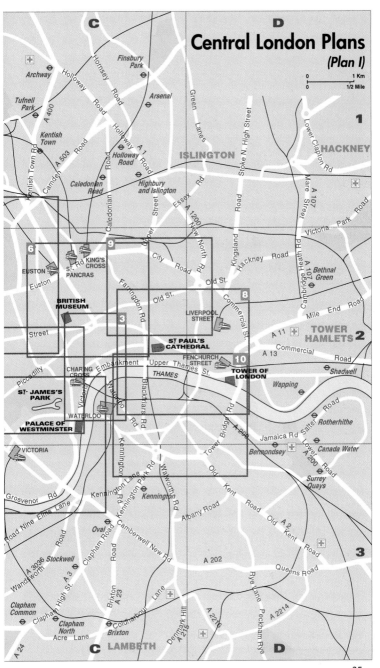

Central London Plans
(Plan I)

0   1 Km
0   1/2 Mile

C   **D**

Archway
Tufnell Park
Kentish Town
Finsbury Park
Arsenal
Hornsey Road
Holloway Road
Holloway Road
Caledonian Road
Highbury and Islington
ISLINGTON
Stoke N. High Street
Lower Clapton Rd
HACKNEY
1
Mare Street
Victoria Park Road
Green Lanes
Essex Rd
A 1200 New North Rd
Kingsland Road
Hackney Road
A 107
Cambridge Heath Rd
Bethnal Green
6
EUSTON
Euston
BRITISH MUSEUM
Street
9
ST. Rd KING'S CROSS
ST. PANCRAS
City Road
Old St.
Old St.
Farringdon Rd
3
St PAUL'S CATHEDRAL
8
LIVERPOOL STREET
Commercial St.
Mile End Road
TOWER HAMLETS
2
A 11
A 13 Commercial Road
CHARING CROSS
Embankment
Upper Thames St.
FENCHURCH STREET
10
TOWER OF LONDON
Shadwell
Wapping
St. JAMES'S PARK
WATERLOO
Victoria
Waterloo Rd
Blackfriars Rd
THAMES
Tower Bridge Rd
Lower Road
Jamaica Rd
Salter Road
Rotherhithe
Canada Water
PALACE OF WESTMINSTER
Piccadilly
VICTORIA
Bermondsey
A 200
Surrey Quays
Grosvenor Rd
Kennington Lane
Kennington Park Rd
Kennington
Walworth Rd
Old Kent Road
A 2
Nine Elms Lane
Oval
Clapham Road
Camberwell New Rd
Albany Road
A 2 Kent Road
Queens Road
Road
A 3036 Stockwell
Wandsworth
Brixton A 23
A 202
Rye Lane Peckham Rye
A 2214
Clapham Common
Clapham High A 3
Clapham North
Acre Lane
Brixton
Coldharbour Lane
Denmark Hill
A 215
A 216
C   **LAMBETH**   **D**
A 24

35

Mayfair · Soho · St James's

There's one elegant dividing line between Mayfair and Soho - the broad and imposing sweep of **Regent Street** - but mindsets and price tags keep them a world apart. It's usual to think of easterly Soho as the wild and sleazy half of these ill-matched twins, with Mayfair to the west the more sedate and sophisticated of the two. Sometimes, though, the natural order of things runs awry: why was rock's legendary wild man Jimi Hendrix, the embodiment of Soho decadence, living in the rarefied air of Mayfair's smart 23 Brook Street? And what induced Vivienne Westwood, punk queen and fashionista to the edgy, to settle her sewing machine in the uber-smart Conduit Street?

Mayfair has been synonymous with elegance for three and a half centuries, ever since the Berkeley and Grosvenor families bought up the local fields and turned them into posh real estate. The area is named after the annual May fair introduced in 1686, but suffice it to say that a raucous street celebration would be frowned upon big time by twenty-first century inhabitants. The grand residential boulevards can seem frosty and imposing, and even induce feelings of inadequacy to the humble passer-by but should he become the proud owner of a glistening gold card, then hey ho, doors will open wide. Claridge's is an art deco wonder, while **New Bond Street** is London's number one thoroughfare for the most chi-chi names in retailing. **Savile Row** may sound a little 'passé' these days, but it's still the place to go for the sharpest cut in town, before sashaying over to compact **Cork Street** to indulge in the purchase of a piece of art at one of its superb galleries. Science and music can also be found here, and at a relatively cheap price: the Faraday Museum in **Albemarle Street** explores 200 years of science, and Handel & Hendrix in Brook Street enables you not only to visit the beautifully presented home of the German composer and view his musical scores but also to explore the flat belonging to Hendrix, his 'future' next door neighbour, as it was in 1968-69.

Soho challenges the City as London's most famous square mile. It may not have the money of its brash easterly rival, but it sure has the buzz. It's always been fast and loose, since the days when hunters charged through with their cries of 'So-ho!' Its narrow jumbled streets throng with humanity, from the tourist to the tipsy, the libertine to the louche. A lot of the fun is centred round the streets just south of **Soho Square,** where area legends like The Coach & Horses ('Norman's Bar'), Ronnie Scott's and Bar Italia cluster in close proximity. There's 80s favourite, the Groucho Club. The tightest t-shirts in town are found in **Old Compton Street,** where the pink pound jangles the registers of gay-friendly bars and restaurants. To get a feel of the 'real' Soho, where old engraved signs enliven the shop fronts and the market stall cries echo back to the 1700s, a jaunt along **Berwick Street** is always in vogue, taking

P. Phipp/Travelshots / age fotostock

in a pint at the eternally popular Blue Posts, an unchanging street corner stalwart that still announces 'Watney's Ales' on its stencilled windows.

Not a lot of Watney's ale was ever drunk in **St James's;** not a lot of ale of any kind for that matter. Champagne and port is more the style here, in the hushed and reverential gentlemen's clubs where discretion is the key, and change is measured in centuries rather than years. The sheer class of the area is typified by **Pall Mall's** Reform Club, where Phileas Fogg wagered that he could zip round the world in eighty days, and the adjacent **St James's Square,** which was the most fashionable address in London in the late seventeenth century, when dukes and earls aplenty got their satin shoes under the silver bedecked tables.

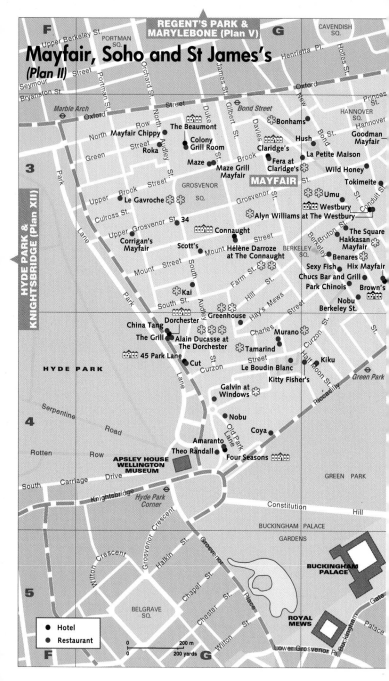

Mayfair, Soho and St James's
(Plan II)

REGENT'S PARK & MARYLEBONE (Plan V)

CAVENDISH SQ.

HYDE PARK & KNIGHTSBRIDGE (Plan XII)

Mayfair Chippy
The Beaumont
Bonhams
Hush
Goodman Mayfair
Roka
Colony Grill Room
Claridge's
La Petite Maison
Maze
Fera at Claridge's
Wild Honey
Maze Grill Mayfair
MAYFAIR
Tokimeite
Umu
Le Gavroche
Westbury
Alyn Williams at The Westbury
34
Connaught
The Square
Corrigan's Mayfair
Hakkasan Mayfair
Scott's
Hélène Darroze at The Connaught
Benares
Kai
Hix Mayfair
Sexy Fish
Chucs Bar and Grill
Park Chinois
Brown's
Greenhouse
Nobu Berkeley St.
China Tang
Dorchester
The Grill
Alain Ducasse at The Dorchester
Murano
45 Park Lane
Tamarind
Kiku
Cut
Le Boudin Blanc
HYDE PARK
Kitty Fisher's
Galvin at Windows
Nobu
Coya
Amaranto
Theo Randall
Four Seasons
APSLEY HOUSE WELLINGTON MUSEUM
GREEN PARK
BUCKINGHAM PALACE GARDENS
BUCKINGHAM PALACE
BELGRAVE SQ.
ROYAL MEWS

● Hotel
● Restaurant

0   200 m
0   200 yards

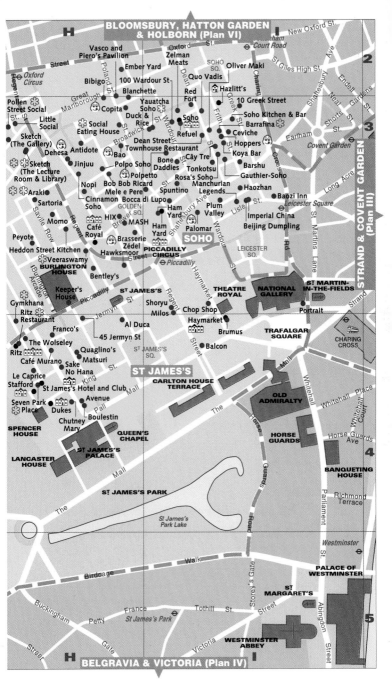

Oxford Circus

New Oxford St.

Oxford Street

Tottenham Court Road

St Giles High St.

Vasco and
Piero's Pavilion

Zelman
Meats

Oliver Maki

Ember Yard

SOHO
SQ.

Quo Vadis

Hazlitt's

Bibigo

100 Wardour St

Blanchette

Red
Fort

10 Greek Street

Pollen
Street Social

Copita

Yauatcha
Soho

Soho

Soho Kitchen & Bar

Barrafina

Little
Social

Social
Eating House

Duck &
Rice

Refuel

Ceviche

Sketch
(The Gallery)

Dehesa

Antidote

Dean Street
Townhouse Restaurant

Hoppers

Koya Bar

Bao

Câ y Tre

Barshu

Sketch
(The Lecture
Room & Library)

Jinjuu

Polpo Soho

Bone
Daddies

Tonkotsu

Gauthier-Soho

Nopi

Polpetto

Rosa's Soho

Manchurian
Legends

Haozhan

Araki

Bob Bob Ricard
Mele e Pere

Spuntino

Baozi Inn

Sartoria

Cinnamon Bocca di Lupo
Soho

Leicester Square

Momo

GOLDEN
SQ.

Ham
Yard

Plum
Valley

Imperial China

HIX

MASH

Peyote

Café
Royal

Beijing Dumpling

Ham
Yard

Palomar

Heddon Street Kitchen

Brasserie
Zédel

SOHO

Veeraswamy

Hawksmoor

Keeper's
House

Bentley's

PICCADILLY
CIRCUS

Piccadilly

LEICESTER
SQ.

Gymkhana

ST JAMES'S

Shoryu

THEATRE
ROYAL

NATIONAL
GALLERY

ST MARTIN-
IN-THE-FIELDS

Ritz
Restaurant

Milos

Chop Shop

Portrait

Franco's

Al Duca

Haymarket

Brumus

TRAFALGAR
SQUARE

45 Jermyn St

CHARING
CROSS

The Wolseley

Quaglino's

Balcon

Ritz

Café Murano

Matsuri

Sake
No Hana

ST JAMES'S
SQ.

Le Caprice

Stafford

St James's Hotel and Club

CARLTON HOUSE
TERRACE

Seven Park
Place

Avenue

Dukes

OLD
ADMIRALTY

Chutney
Mary

Boulestin

SPENCER
HOUSE

QUEEN'S
CHAPEL

HORSE
GUARDS

LANCASTER
HOUSE

ST JAMES'S
PALACE

BANQUETING
HOUSE

Richmond
Terrace

ST JAMES'S PARK

St James's
Park Lake

Westminster
St.

PALACE OF
WESTMINSTER

Birdcage
Walk

ST
MARGARET'S

Buckingham

Petty
France

St James's Park

Tothill St.

WESTMINSTER
ABBEY

STRAND & COVENT GARDEN (Plan III)

Covent Garden

Al Duca

I t a l i a n H4

4-5 Duke of York St ✉ SW1Y 6LA
✆ 020 7839 3090
www.alduca-restaurant.co.uk
⊖ Piccadilly Circus

Closed Easter, 25-26 December,
1 January, Sunday and bank
holidays

Menu £17/30 ✗✗

Al Duca has become as much a part of the fabric of St James's as many of the shirt makers who have made neighbouring Jermyn Street home over the years. It is also one of the those restaurants that manage the trick of appearing quiet one minute and full to the rafters the next without anyone noticing and this ensures that the atmosphere is never less than spirited. The serving team are a young, confident bunch and the manager knows who his regulars are. The menu is priced per course; there is plenty of choice and the cooking is crisp and confident, with plenty of well-priced bottles to match. The rib-eye with porcini mushrooms is a highlight. Prices are also pretty keen, especially for a restaurant in this neck of the woods.

Amaranto

I t a l i a n G4

Four Seasons Hotel,
Hamilton Pl, Park Ln ✉ W1J 7DR
✆ 020 7319 5206
www.fourseasons.com/london/dining
⊖ Hyde Park Corner

Carte £28/68 ✗✗✗

The Four Seasons hotel emerged from its huge refurbishment programme with a restaurant all about flexibility. Amaranto is a bar, a lounge and a dining room, and the idea is that you can have what you want, where you want it, from a largely Italian inspired menu that covers all bases. That means you can enjoy some crab cakes with your drink in the smart bar, share a plate of charcuterie with friends in the comfortable lounge or order a full 3 course meal with business clients in the handsome dining room. No expense was spared on the decoration – the space is full of the colours of the plant after which it is named and there's lots of lacquered wood. Unusually for hotels on Park Lane, there is also a fine terrace attached.

Alain Ducasse at The Dorchester ✿ ✿ ✿

French G4

Dorchester Hotel,
Park Ln ✉ W1K 1QA
℘ 020 7629 8866
www.alainducasse-dorchester.com
⊖ Hyde Park Corner

Closed 3 weeks August, first week
January, 26-30 December, Easter,
Saturday lunch, Sunday and
Monday – booking essential

Menu £60/95 ✗✗✗✗✗

Alain Ducasse at The Dorchester

Elegance, luxury and attention to detail are the hallmarks of Alain Ducasse's outpost at The Dorchester Hotel. Formality never crosses the line into starchiness however: service is attentive without being overbearing and the atmosphere warm and relaxed. The best tables are in the main part of the room, as those on the raised dais by the window can feel a little separate from the action; luminaries should plump for the 'Table Lumière' with its shimmering curtain for an opulent semi-private dining experience. The kitchen has seen a seamless change of chef, and continues to use the best seasonal produce, whether British or French, to create superbly crafted, visually striking dishes, including several which showcase the flavours of the South of France. Some of the dishes remain long in the memory, with the accompaniments adding to the experience, from the champagne trolley to the theatre of the rum baba and the preparation of a herbal infusion at the end of the meal. The wine list is exemplary, with a particularly impressive selection of Domaine de la Romanée Conti and Château d'Yquem.

First Course	Main Course	Dessert
• Dorset crab, celeriac and caviar.	• Simmered halibut with winkles, cockles and razor clams marinière.	• 'Baba like in Monte Carlo'.
• Preserved foie gras with white and black grapes.	• Veal medallion with sweetbreads and carrot.	• Hazelnut soufflé with pink grapefruit sorbet.

Alyn Williams at The Westbury ⬥

Modern cuisine H3

Westbury Hotel,
37 Conduit St ✉ W1S 2YF
📞 020 7183 6426
www.alynwilliams.com
⊖ Bond Street

Closed first 2 weeks January,
last 2 weeks August,
Sunday and Monday

Menu £30/65

Michelin

Peep inside this restaurant within the Westbury Hotel and the impression you get is one of considerable formality but the good news is that it's a long way from being one of those whispering shrines to gastronomy. Granted, it's a very comfortable room, with rosewood panelling and well-spaced, smartly laid tables but the reason the atmosphere never strays into terminal seriousness is largely down to the staff who exude a warmth and sincerity that one all too rarely sees these days. Their willingness to please can also take one by surprise – for instance, they'll willingly let you mix and match the à la carte with the weekend tasting menu. The other reason for its appeal is the relative value for money when one considers the quality of the ingredients and the skill of the kitchen. Alyn Williams is a man with an innate understanding of flavours; his dishes are colourful and quite elaborate constructions but the combinations of textures and tastes marry happily together. Sourcing of ingredients is key and he displays his foraged herbs in glass pots by the kitchen.

First Course

- Poached foie gras with smoked eel, dulse and mushroom broth.

- Roast langoustine with spring onion & herb risotto and preserved Périgord truffle.

Main Course

- Herdwick lamb with sweetbread kofta, pickled aubergine, feta and cucumber.

- Cornish turbot with ratatouille, rouille and bouillabaisse.

Dessert

- Caramelised Arctic roll, coffee and vanilla custard millefeuille.

- Raspberry pavlova with sweet cicely ice cream.

Antidote

Modern cuisine

12A Newburgh St ⊠ W1F 7RR
☏ 020 7287 8488
www.antidotewinebar.com
⊖ Oxford Circus

Closed Sunday –
booking advisable

Carte £30/41

Plates of cheese and charcuterie are the draw in the ground floor wine bar but it's in the upstairs dining room where some interesting things are happening. The French owners have created an appealing menu with the focus on prime, seasonal ingredients. The à la carte is a fluid thing as there are no starters or mains, rather a selection of dishes sized somewhere between the two – in terms of value, it's best to go for the Tasting menu, with wine pairings from their impressive list of organic and biodynamic wines. Dishes are never over-crowded and largely focus on two or three flavours – they appear quite earthy yet are light and easy to eat.

Avenue

Modern cuisine

7-9 St James's St. ⊠ SW1A 1EE
☏ 020 7321 2111
www.avenue-restaurant.co.uk
⊖ Green Park

Closed Sunday dinner
and bank holidays

Menu £25 (weekdays) – Carte dinner £32/49

If reinvention is the key to longevity then Avenue should be around for many years to come. In 2014 it went all American, with a new look from Russell Sage and a contemporary menu inspired by what's cooking in Manhattan. So in a street that once epitomised the very essence of Britishness, you can now enjoy a stack of buttermilk pancakes for breakfast, monkfish with Old Bay spice for lunch, and a shared Boston butt for dinner. As the cascading wine 'chandelier' suggests, wine has also been made more of a feature, with US and French wines fighting for supremacy – you can choose the winner by trying some great names by the glass. And as you'd expect from anywhere influenced by NYC, the cocktails at the long, lively bar are great.

Araki ✿✿

J a p a n e s e

12 New Burlington St ✉ **W1S 3BF**
✆ 020 7287 2481
www.the-araki.com
⊖ Oxford Circus

Closed 27 July-31 August,
Christmas- first week January and
Monday – booking essential
– (dinner only) – (tasting menu
only)

Menu £300

A/C

Araki

Mitsuhiro Araki is one of Japan's great Sushi Masters and his restaurant in Tokyo was one of the city's most celebrated. But he is also not a man to rest on his laurels so he closed it and moved his family to London – all because he wanted a fresh challenge. His greatest task has been in the sourcing of ingredients, as he set himself the task of using European fish and shellfish rather than importing it from Japan – the only item from home is the rice which is grown by his father-in-law. Different ingredients mean a different experience from Tokyo but what remains unchanged is the extraordinary deftness with which he prepares the Edomae sushi and, admittedly, the very high prices. Serving the counter from right to left, it is the different cuts of tuna which really stand out; the rice is also excellent, with each grain discernible in the mouth. Mayfair is a fair match for Ginza – he's found a nice little spot off Savile Row and fills the 10 seats with two sittings a night; the blond cypress counter – a gift from Ryuichi Sakamoto – is a thing of beauty.

First Course

- Sake-steamed abalone with grilled scallop.
- Clear sea bream and langoustine soup with yuzu.

Main Course

- Tuna tartare with truffle and wasabi.
- Welsh eel sushi.

Balcon

French 14

Sofitel London St James Hotel,
8 Pall Mall. ✉ SW1Y 4AN
℘ 020 7389 7820
www.thebalconlondon.com
⊖ Piccadilly Circus

Menu £20 (lunch) – Carte £25/45

 The increasingly ubiquitous Russell Sage was the designer charged with revamping this striking former banking hall and he's wrestled control of the room by installing vast chandeliers, upping the glamour and creating a balcony to house their impressive champagne 'cellar'. The room certainly has a grandeur that raises one's expectations but it needs to be near capacity to create an atmosphere. It's open from breakfast onwards and the classic brasserie menu is designed to appeal at any time of day. Dishes are rooted in French cuisine but most ingredients are British: snails are from Herefordshire, pork for the cassoulet is from Berkshire and their charcuterie, which is a feature, comes from Wales and France. A good value set menu changes weekly.

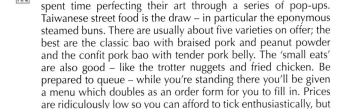

Ⓝ Bao 🏵

Asian H3

53 Lexington St ✉ W1F 9AS
℘ 020 3019 2200
www.baolondon.com
⊖ Tottenham Court Road

Closed Sunday –
bookings not accepted

Carte £17/27

AC Bao's instant success was no accident because the three founders spent time perfecting their art through a series of pop-ups. Taiwanese street food is the draw – in particular the eponymous steamed buns. There are usually about five varieties on offer; the best are the classic bao with braised pork and peanut powder and the confit pork bao with tender pork belly. The 'small eats' are also good – like the trotter nuggets and fried chicken. Be prepared to queue – while you're standing there you'll be given a menu which doubles as an order form for you to fill in. Prices are ridiculously low so you can afford to tick enthusiastically, but in the unlikely event that you realise you've under-ordered, extra dishes can be whipped up quite quickly. (There's another Bao in Windmill St.)

Baozi Inn

Chinese I3

25-26 Newport Court ✉ WC2H 7JS
☎ 020 7287 6877
⊖ Leicester Square

Closed 24-25 December
– bookings not accepted

Carte £15/22 ✗

It's camouflaged on the street by the humdrum and the ordinary, so blink and you'll miss this loud, buzzy little place that's great for a quick bite. Granted, the laminated photographs of the dishes in the window don't necessarily inspire confidence but if you like pork buns and big, steaming bowls of noodles along with a hit of Sichuan fire then you won't be disappointed. Only beer, water or tea is on offer but frankly that's all you need; tables are so close together they're almost communal and you can't order too much straight away – not because you won't be able to eat it, but because the dishes simply won't all fit on your table. But who cares? You'll leave feeling energised and rejuvenated without having spent much money.

Barshu

Chinese I3

28 Frith St. ✉ W1D 5LF
☎ 020 7287 8822
www.barshurestaurant.co.uk
⊖ Leicester Square

Closed 24-25 December
– booking advisable

Carte £27/69 ✗

Those who like their food with a kick won't be disappointed by Barshu as it features the fiery flavours of China's Sichuan province. The menu, which looks more like a brochure, features a photo of each dish along with a chilli rating – a useful aid, as the staff can be a little reluctant to engage with customers. But it's not all mouth-numbingly hot and some of the dishes do display a more subtle balance of flavours. The legendary chillies and peppers are imported directly from China and, with the chef coming from the province too, authenticity is assured, particularly with the 'Five colour appetiser platter', which includes duck tongues and pig intestines. Lots of carved wood and lanterns decorate the place; larger groups should head downstairs.

Barrafina ❀

S p a n i s h 13

54 Frith St. ✉ **W1D 3SL**
✆ 020 7440 1456
www.barrafina.co.uk
⊖ Tottenham Court Road

Closed bank holidays –
bookings not accepted

Carte £15/34   ✗

Michelin

The original Barrafina is still the best. Either join the queue before this tapas bar opens or chance your luck later in the hope that gaps will appear at the counter – and you'll find yourself enjoying wonderfully fresh ingredients and expert cooking that allows their natural flavours to shine. The seafood is often the highlight, whether that's the bonito or the squid, the sardines or the mackerel. Mind you, the meats are pretty damn good too, like the shoulder of rabbit or the succulent quail. The enthusiasm and pride of the staff behind the counter is palpable and the atmosphere is always terrific – you'll find yourself ordering more dishes when you glance over to see what your neighbour is having. When you can eat no more and finally drag yourself away, your first thought will be deciding when you can return. Be aware, though, that things will be changing at the end of 2016: everything will be packed up and shipped a street away when the restaurant is rehoused within the Hart brothers' Quo Vadis restaurant.

First Course	Main Course	Dessert
• Pimientos de padrón.	• Octopus with capers.	• Crema Catalana.
• Courgette flower filled with goat's cheese.	• Confit of rabbit shoulder with black onion aioli.	• Chocolate tart.

Beijing Dumpling

Chinese   I3

23 Lisle St. ⊠ WC2H 7BA
☏ 020 7287 6888
⊖ Leicester Square

Closed 24-25 December

Menu £18 – Carte £10/40

AC Flashing neon or hanging roast ducks in the window appear to be the popular Chinatown method of attracting passers-by; this little restaurant catches their attention by showing its chefs hard at work preparing dumplings. It's also a lot less frenzied than many of its more excitable neighbours and a cut above the norm with its food. It serves freshly prepared dumplings of both Beijing and Shanghai styles and, although the range is not quite as comprehensive as the restaurant's name would suggest, they are still the highlight, especially varieties of the famed Siu Lung Bao. The rest of the menu has a wide base but its worth exploring the specials which include the occasional Taiwanese offering like spicy chicken.

Bentley's

Seafood   H3

11-15 Swallow St. ⊠ W1B 4DG
☏ 020 7734 4756
www.bentleys.org
⊖ Piccadilly Circus

Closed 25 December, 1 January,
Saturday lunch and Sunday

Menu £25 (weekday lunch) – Carte £33/76

AC In 2016 this much-loved seafood institution celebrated the centenary of its founding and, under the aegis of Richard Corrigan, it remains as popular as ever. Upstairs is the Grill, a smartly dressed restaurant with formal service that's popular with the corporate-minded and those entertaining the in-laws. The menu is extensive and includes seafood classics and some grilled meats. On the ground floor is the Oyster Bar, where the atmosphere is a little more louche and considerably more fun. Here you'll find most of the regulars perched at the bar watching the white-jacketed staff shuck oysters; they also do a good fish pie. Bentley's familiar green neon sign looks set to shine brightly on Swallow Street for a few more years yet.

Benares ❀

Indian   H3

12a Berkeley Square House, Berkeley Sq.
✉ W1J 6BS
✆ 020 7629 8886
www.benaresrestaurant.com
⊖ Green Park

Closed 25 December,
1 January and Sunday lunch

Menu £35 (lunch and early dinner) – Carte £50/91   ✗✗✗

Benares

No Indian restaurant in London enjoys a more commanding location or expansive interior than Benares. You'll be greeted at the foot of the stairs before being escorted up past the flower-filled pool and busy bar into the cleverly textured and warmly lit main restaurant – you won't even notice the lack of windows. But what really sets this restaurant apart is the cooking. Atul Kochhar has lived in the east, north and south of India and his influences are many and varied. His use of British ingredients like Scottish scallops and New Forest venison is to be applauded and there is certainly no doubting his skill at spicing: flavours are judiciously layered and expertly balanced. Presentation isn't as elaborate or ornate as it once was and the dishes are all the better for it. The lunch menu offers good value and there is an evening tasting menu but the kitchen's strength lies with the à la carte. If you're coming in a large group consider booking the Chef's Table; its large window provides close-up views of all the action in the kitchen.

First Course	Main Course	Dessert
• Pan-seared scallops, broccoli couscous and cauliflower purée.	• Old Delhi style tandoori chicken, makhani sauce and spring salad.	• Dark chocolate mousse, passion fruit and hot chocolate sauce.
• Seekh kebab with sweetbread and mint & coriander chutney.	• Atlantic hake with curry leaf couscous and samphire pakoda.	• Strawberry tart, kalamansi parfait and elderflower jelly.

49

Bibigo

K o r e a n H2

58-59 Great Marlborough St ✉ **W1F 7JY**
✆ 020 7042 5225
www.bibigouk.com
⊖ Oxford Circus

Menu £13 – Carte £20/29 ✗

AC

Bibigo represents the first foray into the UK market from Korea's largest food company, 'CJ'. With a little help from Psy, Korea's other famous non-electronic export, their mission is to bring healthy staples such as bibimbap – bowls of rice, vegetables, seeds and nuts finished with a hot pepper paste (gochujang) – to a wider public. Start with a soju-based cocktail then watch the kitchen behind the glass send forth dishes such as kimchi, Bossam (simmered pork belly) and hot stone galbi (chargrilled short ribs). Dishes have been adapted slightly for western tastes and the place may feel a little chainy – you can even buy the sauces at reception on the way out – but it's enthusiastically run and won't break the bank.

Blanchette

F r e n c h H3

9 D'Arblay St ✉ **W1F 8DR**   Booking essential
✆ 020 7439 8100
www.blanchettesoho.co.uk
⊖ Oxford Circus

Menu £20 – Carte £14/22 ✗

AC

Opened by three frères – and named after their mother – Blanchette takes classic French bistro food and gives it the 'small plates' treatment. Start with a mini croque monsieur or some bite-sized cheese beignets and then try creamy smoked haddock Arnold Bennett or ox cheek Bourguignon which is made to mother Blanche's own recipe – this is the sort of food guaranteed to raise the spirits. The charcuterie is sliced in front of you; the veg section shouldn't be ignored and the wine list offers an interesting variety of styles and a decent selection by the carafe. There are just nine tables, one of which is communal, and the place has an appealing rustic look, with lots of tiles and exposed brick – the counter is a good place to sit.

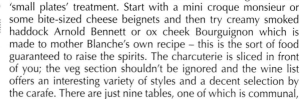

Mayfair • Soho • St James's ▶ Plan II

Bob Bob Ricard

Modern cuisine

1 Upper James St ⊠ W1F 9DF
☎ 020 3145 1000
www.bobbobricard.com
⊖ Oxford Circus

Carte £32/87

Everyone needs a little glamour now and again and Bob Bob Ricard is one place that can provide it. This is a restaurant where diners still dress up a little and there's a feeling of exclusivity in the air. Start with a cocktail in their terrific basement bar then snare one of the booths in the restaurant. The room may be quite small but it clearly sees itself as a grand salon and is shiny, plush and elegant – you even get a button to push if you require more champagne. The menu is all encompassing, although the presence of caviar and vodka are clues as to the owner's nationality. For lighter eaters there are oysters, salads and grilled fish; those with heartier appetites can choose beef Wellington, a venison burger or chicken Kiev.

Bocca di Lupo

Italian

12 Archer St ⊠ W1D 7BB
☎ 020 7734 2223
www.boccadilupo.com
⊖ Piccadilly Circus

Closed 25 December and
1 January – booking essential

Carte £15/58

Deservedly busy from the day it opened, Bocca di Lupo is one of the best things to have arrived in Soho since the espresso bar. But be sure to sit at the marble counter in front of the chefs rather than at one of the faux-distressed tables at the back – not only is the atmosphere here more fun but the food is often better as it hasn't hung around the waiters' station waiting to be delivered. Each item has its region of origin within Italy noted on the menu and is available in a large or smaller size. The flavours don't hang back and over-ordering in all the excitement is very hard to resist. Highlights include the veal and pork agnolotti, the poussin in bread, and the tripe; leave room for dessert or visit their gelato shop opposite.

Bone Daddies

A s i a n 13

31 Peter St ✉ W1F OAR
✆ 020 7287 8581
www.bonedaddies.com
⊖ Piccadilly Circus

Closed 25 December –
bookings not accepted

Carte £16/24

[A/C] Maybe ramen is the new rock 'n' roll. Bone Daddies' charismatic young Aussie chef-owner feels that we've only just begun to appreciate the potential of this Japanese speciality; he believes that anything can go into these warming, comforting bowls and that the combinations are endless. Along with the ramen, you'll find other dishes, such as yellowtail sashimi with ponzu and chilli, that owe their influence to the time he spent at Nobu. The staff are a confident, hospitable bunch and the shared tables add to the community spirit. You may have to queue but throughput is apparently quicker than at some of the top floor services offered close by. Those over 30, who probably don't like standing in line, at least get to recognise the music.

Le Boudin Blanc

F r e n c h G4

5 Trebeck St ✉ W1J 7LT
✆ 020 7499 3292
www.boudinblanc.co.uk
⊖ Green Park

Closed 24-26 December and
1 January

Menu £15 (lunch and early dinner) – Carte £28/53

   Cries of "Bonjour!" and "Bon appétit!" will soon alert even the most limited linguist that they've wandered into a little bit of France here in Shepherd Market. The terrific atmosphere hits you as soon as you sit down – it's warm, lively and contagious, thanks largely to the ebullient service team, and is also helped by the closeness of the tables – but do ask for the ground floor rather than upstairs. The large menu is unapologetically classical and very comforting; French onion soup, steak frites and of course boudin blanc are omnipresent, while daily fish or game specials are chalked up on the blackboard. Even the most nationalistic of customers will find it hard not to be swept along by the very Frenchness of it all.

Bonhams

Modern cuisine

H3

101 New Bond St (lower ground floor) (For
dinner entrance via Haunch of
Venison Yard off Brook St) ✉ W1S 1SR
☎ 020 7468 5868
www.bonhams.com
⊖ Bond Street

Closed 2 weeks August,
24 December-2 January,
Saturday-Sunday, dinner Monday-
Tuesday and bank holidays
– booking advisable

Menu £60 (dinner) – Carte £38/68

✂ ✂

Mayfair • Soho • St James's ▶ Plan II

♿

A/C

⍾

Bonhams

Established in 1793, Bonhams is one of the world's largest
auctioneers of fine art and antiques. Following a recent £30m
renovation, it now includes this modern, crisply decorated
restaurant with floor to ceiling windows, which is tucked away
at the back of the building. The succinct lunch menu with four
choices per course is an appealing document governed by what's
in season. The dishes are elegantly presented and quite delicate
in appearance yet there's real clarity to the flavours thanks to
their French base being combined with Scandic-style simplicity.
The menu is accompanied by a very thoughtful wine list, which
is no surprise when you find that it is compiled by Bonhams'
own wine department. It includes some terrific older vintages
and some of the finest wines at quite generous prices, including
by the glass and carafe. Service is assured and professional and
while the restaurant can get busy on sales days, it provides a
relaxing environment. It's now also open for 3 dinners a
week, when it offers a set menu.

First Course	Main Course	Dessert
• Pertuis asparagus with soft-boiled egg, confit lemon and trout eggs. • Red mullet with Italian artichoke, peas and bouillabaisse sauce.	• Roast Cornish brill with cauliflower couscous and curried mussels. • Guinea fowl with charred onions, leeks, baby carrots and albufera sauce.	• Floating island with sour cherry purée, pistachio anglaise and bitter chocolate sorbet. • Coconut, mango and passion fruit.

Mayfair • Soho • St James's ▸ Plan II

Boulestin

French   H4

✉ SW1A 1EF
☏ 020 7930 2030
www.boulestin.com
⊖ Green Park

Closed Sunday and bank holidays

Menu £25 – Carte £33/60   ✕✕

St James's is one of the most elegant and distinguished parts of London and Boulestin is a perfect fit for the neighbourhood. Nearly a century after Xavier Marcel Boulestin opened his eponymous restaurant showcasing 'Simple French Cooking for English Homes', his spirit was resurrected by another name synonymous with the capital's dining scene – Joel Kissin. Behind the 17C bay windows, you'll find an elegant, light-filled brasserie with mirrors and antique lighting, which just oozes fin de siècle French charm. It also comes with a lovely courtyard terrace. The seasonal menu of classic, unfussy and flavoursome dishes like oeuf en gelée, duck confit and crème brulée pays homage to M. Boulestin's original offerings.

Brasserie Zédel

French   H3

20 Sherwood St ✉ W1F 7ED
☏ 020 7734 4888
www.brasseriezedel.com
⊖ Piccadilly Circus

Closed 24-25 December and
1 January – booking advisable

Menu £13/20 – Carte £19/41   ✕✕

In many cities, the closer one gets to its centre, the more elusive good value restaurants become. Bucking this trend in London is this grand French brasserie, courtesy of Chris Corbin and Jeremy King – its prices are almost ridiculously friendly, especially for somewhere that can provide such a glamorous night out just a few paces from Piccadilly Circus. The bustling subterranean space has been restored to its original art deco splendour and the large menu includes all the classic French dishes you'd want to find, from cassoulet and boudin noir to Îles flottantes and tarte au citron – the 'formule' menu is a real steal. There's also a bar, a cabaret theatre and, on the ground floor, a small café.

Brumus

Modern cuisine 14

Haymarket Hotel,
1 Suffolk Pl ✉ SW1Y 4HX
☎ 020 7470 4000
www.haymarkethotel.com
⊖ Piccadilly Circus

Menu £20 – Carte £25/61

Brumus has always benefitted from its great location – pre-theatre dining is an altogether less frenzied activity when you can actually see the theatre from your table – but it also makes genuine efforts to appeal to a wide variety of customer. It's a modern yet elegant space, with switched-on staff adding to the appeal. It's also open from breakfast until late and usually has something to suit the time of day whether that's a shepherd's pie, burger or Dover sole. If you veer away from the set menus, prices can start to rise quite quickly – although the 'dish of the day' on the à la carte is often the way to go, followed by one of their sundaes. Alternatively, you can share a platter in the busy bar.

Cafe Murano

Italian H4

33 St. James's St ✉ SW1A 1HD
☎ 020 3371 5559
www.cafemurano.co.uk
⊖ Green Park

Closed Sunday dinner –
booking essential

Menu £19 (weekdays)/23 – Carte £25/64

  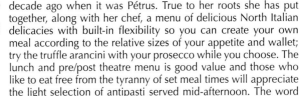

How satisfying it must have been for Angela Hartnett when she took over this site, considering she worked here over a decade ago when it was Pétrus. True to her roots she has put together, along with her chef, a menu of delicious North Italian delicacies with built-in flexibility so you can create your own meal according to the relative sizes of your appetite and wallet; try the truffle arancini with your prosecco while you choose. The lunch and pre/post theatre menu is good value and those who like to eat free from the tyranny of set meal times will appreciate the light selection of antipasti served mid-afternoon. The word 'café' was presumably adopted to imply accessibility but the place has proved so popular that pre-booking is essential.

Le Caprice

Modern cuisine H4

Arlington House, Arlington St. ⊠ SW1A 1RJ
☎ 020 7629 2239
www.le-caprice.co.uk
⊖ Green Park

Closed 24-26 December

Menu £20 (weekday lunch) – Carte £32/65

There are two types of customer at Le Caprice: those who are regulars and others who wish they were. This is one of those glamorous restaurants where the atmosphere is effortlessly sophisticated; the live pianist brings a bygone elegance to proceedings and the clientele are confident and urbane. The kitchen is well-practised and capable and the menu has something for everyone, whether that's a salad, their famous burger or a more ambitious offering like a well-judged game dish or Asian-spiced fish. From the moment you call to make a reservation to the time they bid you goodbye, the suited staff are reassuringly efficient – and it's not hard to see why this has been one of the capital's busiest restaurants for more than 35 years.

Câ.y Tre

Vietnamese I3

42-43 Dean St ⊠ W1D 4PZ
☎ 020 7317 9118
www.caytresoho.co.uk
⊖ Tottenham Court Road

Booking advisable

Menu £15 (lunch)/23 – Carte £19/30

The West End could do with having plenty more Vietnamese restaurants, so hopefully others will follow the lead of Cây Tre. The bright and sleek surroundings of this Soho branch are smarter than the original in Hoxton and the bustling environment provides plenty of atmosphere. Staff know their menu and go about their business with determined efficiency. Dishes are made for sharing and influences cover all points from north to south. Standouts include Cha La lot (spicy ground pork wrapped in betel leaves) and the fragrant slow-cooked Mekong catfish, with its well-judged sweet and spicy sauce. Pho (noodle soup) is available in six different versions and represents good value; the set menu is a great starting point for neophytes.

Ceviche Soho

Peruvian　　　　　　　　　　　　　　　　**I3**

17 Frith St ✉ W1D 4RG　　　　　　　　Booking essential
✆ 020 7292 2040
www.cevicheuk.com/soho
⊖ Tottenham Court Road

Carte £16/27　　　　　　　　　　　　　　

Based on a Lima Pisco bar, Ceviche is as loud as it is fun and a great place to pop into for cocktails with a difference and some light dishes to share with friends. The long narrow room has a busy bar specialising in deliriously addictive drinks based on the Peruvian spirit Pisco, a grape brandy, and beyond it you'll find tightly packed tables, posters and photos of 1950s Peru, and waiting staff struggling to keep up. As the name suggests, ceviche, marinated in lime and chilli, is the star of the show, whether that's the sea bass or the Alianza Lima – a mix of prawns, squid and octopus. 3 dishes per person plus perhaps an anticuchos skewer should be enough; they arrive in a random order so ask if you want the ceviche before any hot dish.

China Tang

Chinese　　　　　　　　　　　　　　　　**G4**

Dorchester Hotel,　　　　　　　　　Closed 24-25 December
Park Ln ✉ W1K 1QA
✆ 020 7629 9988
www.chinatanglondon.co.uk
⊖ Hyde Park Corner

Menu £30 (lunch) – Carte £28/79　　

Sir David Tang's atmospheric, art deco inspired Chinese restaurant at The Dorchester Hotel is always a blur of activity, with noise spilling out from the large tables in the centre; regulars head for the library side, from where one can take in the whole room. In contrast to the sleek and decorative surroundings, the kitchen is a model of conservatism and rightly sticks to what it does best, namely classic Cantonese cooking. Peking duck and roasted meats are the highlights, but check out the chef's recommendations at the back of the menu too. The standard is good considering the numbers of customers and you can even have the full menu in the striking bar at lunch or dinner. Apart from the set lunch menu, it may not be cheap – but it is fun.

Chop Shop

Meats and grills I3

66 Haymarket ✉ SW1Y 4RF
✆ 020 7842 8501
www.chopshopuk.com
⊖ Piccadilly Circus

Menu £19/35 – Carte £24/41

 Things are changing down at Haymarket – a huge redevelopment is underway which will allow new restaurants to give the established chains a run for their money. First off the mark was Chop Shop from New York's Altamarea Group. Spread over two floors and using reclaimed materials for that ersatz-industrial look, it would not look out of place in Manhattan's Meatpacking district. The menu too takes its influences from both sides of the Atlantic: start with 'jars' of mousses, 'crocks' of meatballs or 'planks' of cheese; or simply order one of their house cocktails and then head straight for the main event: the steaks and chops. Perfectly matured meats from Cumbria, along with Creekstone USDA steak, are expertly cooked and hit the spot.

Chucs Bar and Grill

Italian H3

30b Dover St. ✉ W1S 4NB
✆ 020 3763 2013
www.chucsrestaurant.com
⊖ Green Park

Closed 25-26 and dinner 24 and
31 December, 1 January and bank
holidays – booking essential

Carte £38/59

Rather like the clothes shop to which it is attached, Chucs Bar and Grill caters for those who know their way around the Riviera and are not afraid of showing it. The interior, with just 6 tables and some seats at the bar, is decked out like a yacht, with blond wood, brass handrails and navy banquettes; there are also sepia pictures of Positano on the walls and Murano glass chandeliers above. While there is something a little disconcerting about sitting in a restaurant where all your fellow diners seem to know each other, the staff – kitted out in linen mess jackets – have a charming swagger that makes you feel included. The succinct and not inexpensive menu offers satisfying, classic Mediterranean dishes with a focus on flavour.

Chutney Mary

I n d i a n H4

73 St James's St ✉ SW1A 1PH Closed Sunday
✆ 020 7629 6688
www.chutneymary.com
⊖ Green Park

Menu £30 (weekday lunch) – Carte £35/60

After 25 years in Chelsea, one of London's pioneering Indian restaurants has been busy establishing itself in a more central position here in St James's. It has been helped in this regard by the welcoming and attentive service team, as well as the elegant surroundings with its bold art, smart bar and period features. The menu suffers a little from having too many headings, which include Indian grills, slow-cooked dishes, and small plates which are actually just starters by another name, but there's no denying the cooking is good. There is a subtlety to the spicing; the classics are done well; and some of the regional dishes have been successfully updated – the 'Silver Crescent' with Calcutta prawns is well worth ordering.

Cinnamon Soho

I n d i a n H3

5 Kingly St ✉ W1B 5PF Closed 1 January
✆ 020 7437 1664
www.cinnamonsoho.com
⊖ Oxford Circus

Carte £16/33

Don't be put off by the slightly branded feel of the place because this younger sister to the more formal Cinnamon Club in Victoria is good fun and offers a great selection of classic and contemporary Indian dishes. Let the very charming staff guide you through the meal – they run the place really well and cope effortlessly with the numbers. Along with the familiar dishes like king prawns with coconut come more quirky offerings like Rogan Josh shepherd's pie and their signature dish 'Balls!': deep-fried balls of various flavours which could include crab, quail or lamb – these are good to share. High Chai is offered in the afternoon and their pre-theatre menu is a steal. Just avoid the lower floor where the acoustics are hellish.

Colony Grill Room

T r a d i t i o n a l   B r i t i s h   **G3**

The Beaumont Hotel,   Booking essential
Brown Hart Gdns. ✉ W1K 6TF
☎ 020 7499 9499
www.colonygrillroom.com
⊖ Bond Street

Carte £27/79

When restaurateurs Chris Corbin and Jeremy King opened The Beaumont, their first hotel, it was always going to include a restaurant where everyone wants to get a table. Based on traditional 1920s grills seen in London and New York, it comes with perfectly burnished leather booths, striking age-of-speed art deco murals and clever lighting so that you hardly notice the absence of windows. Ironically, by making the room and style of service so defiantly old fashioned, they have created somewhere effortlessly chic. The wide-ranging menu criss-crosses the Atlantic, offering shrimp cocktail alongside Omelette Arnold Bennett, a pastrami Reubens next to shepherd's pie, and trifle along with sundaes – satisfying food without fuss or fanfare.

Copita

S p a n i s h   **H3**

27 D'Arblay St ✉ W1F 8EP   Closed Sunday and bank holidays
☎ 020 7287 7797   – bookings not accepted
www.copita.co.uk
⊖ Oxford Circus

Carte £15/30

It may not occupy a prime Soho spot but that hasn't stopped this tapas bar, a sister to Barrica, from being packed most nights. A no bookings policy means your best bet is to come before 7pm or else try your luck at lunch when there are fewer drinkers; then simply perch yourself on one of the high stools or stay standing and get stuck in. The daily menu offers a colourful array of diminutive dishes like pea and cheese croquettes, crab and spinach tart, and pumpkin and sage ravioli and you'll find it hard to stop ordering – even the delicate custard tart is delightfully moreish. Staff add to the lively atmosphere and everything on the thoughtfully compiled Spanish wine list is available by the glass or copita.

Veuve Clicquot

■ REIMS FRANCE ■

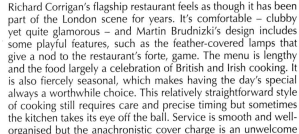

Corrigan's Mayfair

Modern British   G3

28 Upper Grosvenor St. ⊠ W1K 7EH
☏ 020 7499 9943
www.corrigansmayfair.com
⊖ Marble Arch

Closed 25-30 December,
Saturday lunch and bank holidays

Menu £25 (weekday lunch) – Carte £32/79

Richard Corrigan's flagship restaurant feels as though it has been part of the London scene for years. It's comfortable – clubby yet quite glamorous – and Martin Brudnizki's design includes some playful features, such as the feather-covered lamps that give a nod to the restaurant's forte, game. The menu is lengthy and the food largely a celebration of British and Irish cooking. It is also fiercely seasonal, which makes having the day's special always a worthwhile choice. This relatively straightforward style of cooking still requires care and precise timing but sometimes the kitchen takes its eye off the ball. Service is smooth and well-organised but the anachronistic cover charge is an unwelcome sight.

Coya

Peruvian   G4

118 Piccadilly ⊠ W1J 7NW
☏ 020 7042 7118
www.coyarestaurant.com
⊖ Hyde Park Corner

Closed 24-26 December and
1 January – booking advisable

Menu £21 (weekday lunch) – Carte £33/57

It didn't take long for the people behind Roka and Zuma to act upon the realisation that the Next Big Thing on the London restaurant scene was Peruvian food. Their loud and enthusiastically run basement restaurant on Piccadilly provides a lively spot in which to discover this fresh and zesty cuisine. Add in the live music at weekends and it also represents a great night out, especially when fuelled by the deliriously addictive Pisco Sours. Prepared in one of the three kitchens – the main room, the charcoal grill or the ceviche bar – the food is a mix of the authentic, the refined and the more contemporary; ordering a sharp, refreshing ceviche is a must and consider too the huge tiger prawns cooked in the Josper oven.

Cut

Meats and grills G4

45 Park Lane Hotel,
45 Park Ln ✉ W1K 1PN
℘ 020 7493 4545
www.45parklane.com
⊖ Hyde Park Corner

Booking essential

Menu £29 (weekday lunch) – Carte £51/176

Cut is the first European venture from Wolfgang Puck, the US-based Austrian chef whose level of celebrity makes our lot look positively anonymous. Teaming up with the Dorchester's 45 Park Lane hotel, he has created a slick, stylish and sexy room where glamorous people come to eat meat. The steaks – from Kansas, Chile, Australia and Devon – are first presented raw with a few words about their heritage and then cooked over hardwood and charcoal and finished off in a broiler. Sides are as good as the steaks, especially the fries and the macaroni cheese. Artery hardening continues with dessert which eschews the much-needed citrus in favour of lots of cream. You'll leave eminently satisfied, if slightly heavier in weight and lighter in pocket.

Dean Street Townhouse Restaurant

Modern British I3

Dean Street Townhouse Hotel,
69-71 Dean St. ✉ W1D 3SE
℘ 020 7434 1775
www.deanstreettownhouse.com
⊖ Piccadilly Circus

Booking essential

Menu £29 – Carte £29/44

A restaurant for every occasion – even shouty ones, as you're hit by a cacophony of sound as soon as you open the heavy door of this attractive Georgian house. It's also a place to be seen, or perhaps not – a ban on flash photography means it's ideal for illicit trysts too. The classic brasserie aesthetic makes it look like it's been here for years and the heartwarming British comfort food fits these surroundings well. There's Dover sole and Porterhouse steaks but also plenty more proletariat fare on offer, like faggots with cabbage or mince and potatoes. The salads such as trout with truffled potato or smoked pigeon with scotch egg are noteworthy and who can resist kipper pâté for afternoon tea?

Dehesa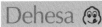

Mediterranean cuisine H3

25 Ganton St ✉ W1F 9BP Closed 25 December
✆ 020 7494 4170
www.dehesa.co.uk
⊖ Oxford Circus

Carte £14/36

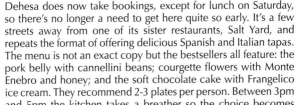 Dehesa does now take bookings, except for lunch on Saturday, so there's no longer a need to get here quite so early. It's a few streets away from one of its sister restaurants, Salt Yard, and repeats the format of offering delicious Spanish and Italian tapas. The menu is not an exact copy but the bestsellers all feature: the pork belly with cannellini beans; courgette flowers with Monte Enebro and honey; and the soft chocolate cake with Frangelico ice cream. They recommend 2-3 plates per person. Between 3pm and 5pm the kitchen takes a breather so the choice becomes ham on or off the bone, charcuterie and cheese. The drinks list is worthy of a visit in itself. Dehesa is a wooded area of Spain and home to Ibérico pigs who produce such great ham.

Duck & Rice

Chinese I3

90 Berwick St ✉ WIF 0QB
✆ 020 3327 7888
www.theduckandrice.com
⊖ Tottenham Court Road

Carte approx. £38

 Alan Yau is one of the most innovative restaurateurs around and with Duck & Rice he has once again created something a little different – a converted pub with a Chinese kitchen. The ground floor is the most 'pubby' part of the operation – the clue is in the four huge copper tanks of Pilsner Urquell – where the snacks and nibbles are served to complement your beer rather than the other way round. The real action, though, takes place in an intimate space upstairs which has a vague Victorian vibe thanks to the booths and fireplaces. Here the menu focuses on Chinese favourites and comforting classics such as Kung Po chicken and crispy shredded beef. The duck is, appropriately enough, the standout – whether crispy aromatic or Cantonese roast.

Ember Yard

Mediterranean cuisine H2

60 Berwick St ✉ W1F 8DX
☎ 020 7439 8057
www.emberyard.co.uk
⊖ Oxford Circus

Closed 25-26 December and
1 January – booking advisable

Carte £20/33 🍴

Those familiar with the Salt Yard Group will recognise the Spanish and Italian themed menus at this fun and sprightly restaurant spread over two floors. But, as the name suggests, there is one major difference between this and the other three outlets – and that's the focus on cooking over charcoal or wood which imparts such an individual flavour to each dish. Start with the terrific smoked chorizo skewers, then share hot-smoked Gloucester Old Spot pork belly or chargrilled Cornish mackerel – even a gratin of root vegetables comes with some smoked ricotta. It's not just the ingredients that are seasonal – the wood, which could be hazel or silver birch, changes over the year – and even some of the cocktails come with a seductive smokiness.

45 Jermyn St

Modern British H4

45 Jermyn St. ✉ SW1 6DN
☎ 020 7205 4545
www.45jermynst.com
⊖ Piccadilly Circus

Closed 25-26 December

Carte £26/66 🍴🍴

In 2015 Fortnum & Mason bade farewell to their 60-year old Fountain restaurant and, in its stead, created this contemporary brasserie for the modern age. The art deco inspired room is bright and colourful – most customers want the booths but others are happy to perch at the long marble-topped bar. Its previous incarnation isn't forgotten as tribute is paid in the form of sodas, coupes and floats, while the main menu has a strong British element running through it, with several dishes being modern interpretations of classics. Prices can get a little steep – and not just when you opt for their caviar – but, in contrast, the well-chosen wine list comes with very restrained mark-ups and offers some great value.

Fera at Claridge's ❀

C r e a t i v e   B r i t i s h   **G3**

Claridge's Hotel,   Booking advisable
Brook St ✉ W1K 4HR
☎ 020 7107 8888
www.feraatclaridges.co.uk
⊖ Bond Street

Menu £39/110 – Carte £53/85   ✗✗✗✗

Michelin

The most eagerly anticipated restaurant opening of 2014 didn't disappoint. Earth-father, forager supreme, farmstead owner and gastronomic alchemist Simon Rogan came down from the boondocks of Cumbria and shook up that bastion of British propriety – Claridge's hotel. The 'wild' of Fera may refer to the influence of nature but this is intricately planned and highly refined cuisine. There's a purity and a natural, unforced style to the cooking that is evident on the plate, yet the wonderfully well-balanced and textured dishes deliver multi-dimensional layers of flavours. The tasting menu is perhaps the best way to go and the wine list offers an intelligent mix of the classic and the more esoteric. For their part, the hotel did a magnificent job in transforming this room into a thing of beauty. The muted tones of green give it an almost herbaceous feel which is juxtaposed by touches of art deco and magnificent detailing, yet the grandeur of the room is tempered by the refreshing lack of pomposity or mannered formality in the service.

First Course	Main Course	Dessert
• Rose veal tartare with oyster and kohlrabi.	• Turbot in pine oil, Jerusalem artichoke, oyster mushroom and spring herbs.	• Meadowsweet cake, celeriac, apple and burnt honey.
• Portland crab with green tomato, fennel and pickled seaweed.	• Goosnargh duck with roast radish, turnip, rhubarb and oxalis.	• Frozen white chocolate with dill, cucumber and apple.

Franco's

Italian H4

61 Jermyn St ⊠ SW1Y 6LX
☎ 020 7499 2211
www.francoslondon.com
⊖ Green Park

Closed Sunday and bank holidays
– booking essential

Menu £26 – Carte £30/60 ✗✗

There can be few things more English than afternoon tea or the sound of Alan Bennett reading from The Wind in the Willows and, surprisingly enough, both can be enjoyed here at Franco's, one of London's oldest Italian restaurants that was relaunched in the mid-noughties. Open from breakfast onwards, it attracts a largely well-groomed clientele as befits its Jermyn Street address and boasts a clubby feel. Indeed, if you're not a regular visitor, you may find yourself with time to admire the service being enjoyed by other tables. The chef hails from Northern Italy but his menu covers all parts. There is a popular grill section, along with classics like beef Rossini – ideal accompaniment for one of those big Tuscan reds on the wine list.

Gauthier - Soho

French I3

21 Romilly St ⊠ W1D 5AF
☎ 020 7494 3111
www.gauthiersoho.co.uk
⊖ Leicester Square

Closed Monday lunch,
Sunday and bank holidays except
Good Friday

Menu £18 (lunch)/75 ✗✗✗

Alexis Gauthier's restaurant occupies a charming Georgian townhouse that seems at odds with Soho's increasingly rowdy reputation. Dining is spread over three floors, with the ground floor often the most animated, the first floor used more for the special occasion diner and the top floor consisting of two private dining rooms. The main menu allows you to virtually construct your own meal: it's divided into five sections or 'plats' and you can order any combination of meat, fish or vegetarian dishes that suits you. The cooking is skilled and the kitchen is not afraid of adding some innovative touches to classic combinations. The enthusiastic sommeliers, in turn, also come up with some refreshingly original recommendations.

Galvin at Windows ✿

M o d e r n   c u i s i n e   **G4**

London Hilton Hotel, 22 Park Ln (28th floor)
✉ W1K 1BE
✆ 020 7208 4021
www.galvinatwindows.com
⊖ Hyde Park Corner

Closed Saturday lunch and
Sunday dinner

Menu £33/70   ✗✗✗

Galvin at Windows

The lift may take time to drop off its cargo of Hilton Hotel residents as it makes its way up to the 28th floor but the wait will be worth it as the views from up here are spectacular – and it's certainly worth arriving early for a drink in the busy adjacent bar. The restaurant has been cleverly laid out to make the most of the three sides of views and, if you can't secure a window table, the elevated section in the middle of the room is a good compromise. Service is relaxed and friendly which softens some of the formality of the room, although a little more passion would dispel some of the corporate blandness that pervades the atmosphere. It is the food, however, that provides worthy competition to the views. British ingredients like Cornish lamb, Cumbrian beef and Dorset crab proudly feature on the various menus on offer – the Menu du Jour draws in plenty of customers at lunch as it's a steal for this postcode. There's a classical base to the boldly flavoured dishes, which come with a pleasing degree of flair and innovation.

First Course

- French asparagus with organic egg and a praline & chickpea tuile.

- Marinated Ibérico pork with cucumber salad, soybeans and chilli paste.

Main Course

- Roast fillet of halibut with pommes purée, shiitake mushrooms, prawn & dashi broth.

- Rump of lamb with crispy spiced shoulder, couscous, aubergine and harissa jus.

Dessert

- Nougat parfait with banana, muscovado meringues and black pepper ice cream.

- Passion fruit and white chocolate soufflé with pistachio ice cream.

Le Gavroche ❀❀

French G3

43 Upper Brook St ✉ W1K 7QR
☎ 020 7408 0881
www.le-gavroche.co.uk
⊖ Marble Arch

Closed Christmas–January,
Saturday lunch, Sunday,
Monday and bank holidays
– booking essential

Menu £57/128 – Carte £67/165 ✗✗✗✗

A/C

Michelin

A little indulgence never did anyone any harm and Le Gavroche is all about indulgence. Michel Roux and head chef Rachel Humphrey's unapologetically extravagant French dishes are an exhilarating riposte to all those hectoring health-conscious calorie-counters. The menu is a roll-call of luxury ingredients, the sauces are sublime and the cooking is accompanied by one of London's best wine lists. There are oohs and aahs as trolleys are brought forward and carving knives sharpened; regulars mingle with newcomers and the atmosphere is refreshingly unstuffy, helped along by there being more of a female presence to the service these days. Anyone with an interest in Britain's post-war culinary adventures should be aware of Le Gavroche's significance, not just because of its celebration of, and dedication to, the art of French cuisine but also because of all those chefs who have benefitted from passing through its kitchen. Just avoid sitting too close to the stairs by asking for a table in the main body of this historic restaurant.

First Course

- Mousseline de homard au champagne et caviar.
- Tête de porc pressée, escargots braisés persil et citron.

Main Course

- Côte de veau rôtie, morilles et ail sauvage.
- Darne de turbot, Kalamata olives, asperges blanches et beurre blanc.

Dessert

- Omelette Rothschild.
- Assiette de deux chocolate, banane et rhum.

Goodman Mayfair

26 Maddox St ✉ **W1S 1QH**
☎ 020 7499 3776
www.goodmanrestaurants.com
⊖ Oxford Circus

Closed Sunday and bank holidays
– booking essential

Mayfair · Soho · St James's ▶ Plan II

Carte £28/103   ✗✗

A/C Goodman is a Russian-owned New York steakhouse in Mayfair, which sounds like a sketch from the UN's Christmas party. Wood and leather give it an authentic feel and it has captured that macho swagger that often seems to accompany the eating of red meat. Tables are usually full of guffawing men, with their jackets thrown over the back of their chairs and their sleeves rolled up. The American and Irish beef is mostly grain-fed and either dry or wet aged in-house – Australian beef is an option at lunch. It is cooked in a Josper oven using a blend of three types of charcoal and offered with a choice of four sauces. While the steaks, especially the rib-eye, are certainly worth coming for, side dishes tend to be more variable in quality.

The Grill

Dorchester Hotel,
Park Ln ✉ **W1S 2XG**
☎ 020 7659 4500
www.dorchestercollection.com
⊖ Hyde Park Corner

Booking advisable

Menu £39 (weekday lunch) – Carte £43/89   ✗✗✗

A/C

In a hotel as magnificent as The Dorchester, a restaurant needs to be able to hold its own, and there are no doubts that the Grill can do just that. With a hand-blown Murano glass chandelier as its striking centrepiece, strips of reflective gold on the walls, leather banquettes and an abundance of copperware on display, it has all the glitz and glamour one would expect. Such surroundings could easily lead to stuffiness, but the bar, the well-spaced tables and an agreeable team adept at putting diners at ease mean that the atmosphere is far from formal. Grill favourites sit alongside modern day classics on the menu; sharing dishes are a good choice, as are the speciality soufflés which get a section all to themselves.

Greenhouse ಣಣ ಣಣ

27a Hay's Mews ✉ W1J 5NY
☎ 020 7499 3331
www.greenhouserestaurant.co.uk
⊖ Hyde Park Corner

Closed Saturday lunch,
Sunday and bank holidays

Menu £40/95   ✗ ✗ ✗

Michelin

One of the many charms of The Greenhouse is its setting. You enter via the Mews, through a little bamboo garden, and this pastoral theme continues inside with a pale green colour scheme and leaf-etched glass; it's bright and airy during the day, and warm and intimate by night. Chef Arnaud Bignon offers a set lunch menu, a 6 course tasting menu, a 'Discovery' menu for those who don't mind surprises, and the main à la carte; descriptions are fashionably pithy so don't be afraid to seek help from the staff. He has sourced terrific produce from the UK – seafood from Scotland, fish from Cornwall, and lamb and venison from Wales, although he will look to Europe for certain ingredients. His cooking is highly innovative, light, balanced and rendered with exceptional skill – he's a chef who not only understands flavour but knows when to back off. The wine list features the good and the great and the breadth of vintages is exceptional: Château Lafite back to 1870, Château Latour to 1900, Château Haut Brion to 1945, 15 vintages of La Tâche and 37 of Penfolds Grange.

First Course	Main Course	Dessert
• Orkney scallop with sea urchin, fennel and clementine.	• Monkfish with onion, banana, kaffir lime and dukkah.	• Mananka chocolate with kumquat and coriander.
• Foie gras with cherry, anise and cocoa.	• Limousin veal with provola, peas and tamarind.	• Raspberry with verbena and milk.

Gymkhana

Indian

42 Albemarle St ✉ W1S 4JH
☎ 020 3011 5900
www.gymkhanalondon.com
⊖ Green Park

Closed 1-3 January,
25-27 December and Sunday
– booking essential

Mayfair • Soho • St James's ▶ Plan II

Menu £25 (lunch and early dinner)/80 – Carte £25/61 ✗✗

Michelin

If you enjoy Trishna then you'll love Karam Sethi's Gymkhana – that's if you can get a table. Inspired by Colonial India's gymkhana clubs, the interior is full of wonderful detail and plenty of wry touches, from the hunting trophies and ceiling fans to the glass wall lamps and Grandma Sethi's barometer. If you're on the ground floor ask for one of the booths but it's worth a little persistence to ensure you're seated downstairs where the beaten brass topped tables, leather banquettes and the dimmest of lighting add to the intimate atmosphere. In such charming surroundings it would be easy for the food to play second fiddle but, far from it. There's an array of dishes inspired by the flavours of North India – don't procrastinate, just go straight for the 6 courser; included could be wild tiger prawns that show what a charcoal grill can do; kid goat methi keema with a pleasing richness and well-judged spicing; suckling pig vindaloo with complex flavours; or wild muntjac biryani, a triumph of flaky pastry.

First Course	Main Course	Dessert
• Kid goat methi keema, salli and pao.	• Wild muntjac biryani, pomegranate and mint raita.	• Cardamom and strawberry kheer.
• Soft shell crab with poha masala.	• Black pepper fish tikka with lasooni tomato chutney.	• Saffron and carrot halwa.

Hakkasan Mayfair 🏵

C h i n e s e **H3**

17 Bruton St ✉ W1J 6QB
✆ 020 7907 1888
www.hakkasan.com
⊖ Green Park

Closed 24-25 December
– booking essential

Menu £38 (lunch and early dinner) – Carte £34/101

Hakkasan Mayfair

This is less a copy, more a sister to the original Hakkasan; a sister who's just as fun and glamorous but simply lives in a far nicer part of town. As with many of the best addresses, it doesn't draw attention to itself – you could easily walk past the entrance without knowing, and that adds to the appeal. The biggest difference is that this Hakkasan has a funky, more casual ground floor to go with the downstairs dining room; but it's still worth booking for the lower level, as a walk down the stairs will heighten the sense of occasion and add a little mystery. The menu of Cantonese treats is an appealing tome; dim sum must surely be the only way to go at lunch, while the signature dishes, such as silver cod with champagne and honey, and Jasmine tea smoked chicken, can be saved for dinner. Desserts are unashamedly tailored towards European tastes but there's a fine range of speciality teas, as well as an impressive selection of cocktails. The staff, dressed in black – what else? – know their menu backwards, so are more than willing to help those seeking guidance.

First Course	Main Course	Dessert
• Jasmine tea smoked organic pork ribs.	• Roast silver cod with champagne and honey.	• Jivara bomb.
• Morel mushroom and vegetable spring roll.	• Sanpei chicken claypot with sweet basil, chilli and spring onion.	• Apple and vanilla crème brûlée with calvados, crème fraîche and crystallised fennel.

Ham Yard

Modern cuisine I3

Ham Yard Hotel,
1 Ham Yard, ✉ W1D 7DT
☎ 020 3642 1007
www.firmdalehotels.com
⊖ Piccadilly Circus

Menu £20 (dinner) – Carte £28/46 ✗✗

At Ham Yard's stylish and exuberantly decorated restaurant, you might not even make it past the pewter-topped bar: the bitters, syrups, even the tonic water are homemade using herbs grown in the hotel's rooftop garden and the cocktails are as good as the range of little nibbles they serve. The room comes with bright colours and bold patterns; there are kilim prints from India and silk-lined walls; and the tables are all immaculately laid. The menu moves with the seasons and the kitchen has the confidence to keep the cooking appealingly simple. If it's a nice day the smart money is outside on the courtyard terrace – it may be a thoroughfare but the mature trees and parasols bring a continental air rarely seen in this part of town.

Haozhan

Chinese I3

8 Gerrard St ✉ W1D 5PJ   Closed 24-25 December
☎ 020 7434 3838
www.haozhan.co.uk
⊖ Leicester Square

Menu £14 – Carte £15/43 ✗

A plethora of Chinatown restaurants vie for your attention by offering special deals or just brightening their neon. Haozhan adopts the more worthy policy of serving food that's a cut above the norm. Inside the somewhat garish looking menu is not the usual vast list but rather an interesting collection of dishes that owe more to a fusion style, with mostly Cantonese but other Asian influences too; head straight for the specialities, such as jasmine ribs or wasabi prawns. You'll find there's a freshness to the ingredients that also marks this restaurant out – try the Tom Yum prawns in their pancake cones and leave room for the egg custard buns. Appropriately enough, the name Haozhan translates as "a good place to eat".

Hawksmoor

Meats and grills

H3

5a Air St ✉ W1J 0AD
☎ 020 7406 3980
www.thehawksmoor.com
⊖ Piccadilly Circus

Closed 24-26 December
– booking advisable

Menu £28 (lunch and early dinner) – Carte £23/59

For the fourth, and possibly the best Hawksmoor they took over the old L'Odeon restaurant and gave it a great little art deco makeover; there are mirrors down one side and the famous arched windows have been frosted and stained. As with the other branches, the sourcing of British beef is top-notch – the 35-day aged Longhorn beef comes with a charred exterior and a juicy centre – but the difference is that here they also offer great seafood, with charcoal-grilled turbot, Dover sole and monkfish proving popular. The prices are 'Mayfair' but not extreme; there's an excellent Express Menu at lunch and very early evening, and staff are a delightful and well organised lot. Soak up the boisterous atmosphere by first having a cocktail in the bar.

Heddon Street Kitchen

Modern cuisine

H3

3-9 Heddon St ✉ W1B 4BE
☎ 020 7592 1212
www.gordonramsayrestaurants.com/heddon-street-kitchen/
⊖ Oxford Circus

Closed 25 December

Menu £27 (lunch and early dinner) – Carte £30/53

There was once a time when the only person you'd see in Heddon Street would be a David Bowie fan paying homage to the place where the Ziggy Stardust album cover was shot. These days the street looks far less shadowy and indeed plays host to a number of restaurants, including Gordon Ramsay's follow up to his Bread Street Kitchen. The place is spread over two floors but the ground floor is the more fun, helped along by – or perhaps entirely due to – the fact that there is where the cocktail bar is positioned. This is all-day dining at its best: breakfast covers all tastes, there's brunch at weekends, and the à la carte offers an appealing range of largely European dishes, all executed with a palpable degree of care and precision.

Hélène Darroze at The Connaught ✿ ✿

Modern cuisine | G3

Connaught Hotel,
Carlos Pl. ✉ W1K 2AL
☎ 020 7107 8880
www.the-connaught.co.uk
⊖ Bond Street

Booking essential

Menu £52/92

XXXX

Michelin

When it's time to choose what you're going to eat you'll be handed a Solitaire board featuring 13 marbles, each bearing the name of a single ingredient – you choose 5, 7 or 9 (courses). The board is accompanied by a menu showing the other components of the dishes in question which are delivered in any order you wish. Some will love this game, others will hate it, but at least it highlights the fact that the dishes are built around a stunning main ingredient and it also allows Hélène Darroze to shine a light on her wonderful French and British suppliers. Her cooking is largely informed by her homeland but she's not averse to using the occasional unexpected flavour, be it Asian or Indian, if she feels it brings something to the dish; she is also aware of the modern diners' preference for a lighter, less elaborate style of cooking. The wood-panelled room is comfortable and elegant and considerable credit must go to the service team who keep the atmosphere light, relaxed and never overbearingly formal.

First Course

- Scallop, tandoori spices, carrot, citrus and coriander.
- Wild garlic with snails, Bigorre Black ham and ricotta.

Main Course

- Pigeon with beetroot and foie gras.
- Sweetbread with asparagus, morels, broad beans and lime.

Dessert

- Savarin Armagnac, rhubarb and ginger.
- Raspberry with Greek yogurt, Espelette pepper and lemongrass.

Mayfair · Soho · St James's ▶ Plan II

Hix

Traditional British H3

66-70 Brewer St. ✉ W1F 9UP
✆ 020 7292 3518
www.hixsoho.co.uk
⊖ Piccadilly Circus

Closed 25-26 December

Menu £20 (weekday lunch) – Carte £27/65 ✗✗

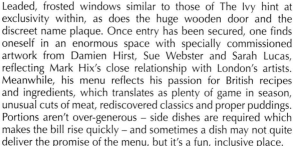

Leaded, frosted windows similar to those of The Ivy hint at exclusivity within, as does the huge wooden door and the discreet name plaque. Once entry has been secured, one finds oneself in an enormous space with specially commissioned artwork from Damien Hirst, Sue Webster and Sarah Lucas, reflecting Mark Hix's close relationship with London's artists. Meanwhile, his menu reflects his passion for British recipes and ingredients, which translates as plenty of game in season, unusual cuts of meat, rediscovered classics and proper puddings. Portions aren't over-generous – side dishes are required which makes the bill rise quickly – and sometimes a dish may not quite deliver the promise of the menu, but it's a fun, inclusive place.

Hix Mayfair

Traditional British H3

Brown's Hotel,
33 Albemarle St ✉ W1S 4BP
✆ 020 7518 4004
www.hixmayfair.com
⊖ Green Park

Menu £28 (dinner) – Carte £33/65 ✗✗✗

Brown's is a thoroughly British hotel with a long history so it makes sense for its restaurant to celebrate Britain's own culinary traditions. Mark Hix – one of London's busier restaurateurs – was the man entrusted with the task and he has put together an appealing looking menu that's big on seasonality and provenance. Good use is made of ingredients from across the UK, such as Portland crab, Morecambe Bay shrimps and Aberdeenshire beef and there's also a daily roast for lunch, served from the trolley. The traditional feel of the wood-panelled dining room is enlivened by works from leading contemporary British artists, which ensure that the atmosphere never gets too solemn.

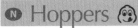 **Hoppers**

South Indian   I3

49 Frith St ✉ W1D 4SG
✆ 020 3011 1021
www.hopperslondon.com
⊖ Tottenham Court Road

Closed 1-3 January and
24-31 December. –
bookings not accepted

Carte £13/27   ✗

Having made their name with Trishna and cemented their reputation with Gymkhana, the Sethi family then turned their attention to street food inspired by the flavours of Tamil Nadu, in the south of India, and Sri Lanka. This diminutive restaurant takes its name from the bowl-shaped pancakes made from fermented rice and coconut milk that are the perfect accompaniment to their creamy 'karis' such as lamb or guinea fowl. But this is far from a single-dish restaurant – there are plenty of other great dishes for sharing, from the delicious 'short eats' like bone marrow varuval, to the Spit chicken served with Gotu Kola sambol. Add in some great cocktails and terrific prices and it's no wonder there are customers queuing outside.

Hush

Modern cuisine   H3

8 Lancashire Ct., Brook St. ✉ W1S 1EY
✆ 020 7659 1500
www.hush.co.uk
⊖ Bond Street

Closed 25 December and
1 January – booking essential

Carte £28/61   ✗✗

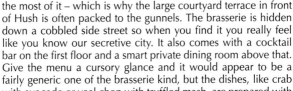

No one is more grateful for a bit of summer warmth than us Brits – and certainly no one could ever accuse us of not making the most of it – which is why the large courtyard terrace in front of Hush is often packed to the gunnels. The brasserie is hidden down a cobbled side street so when you find it you really feel like you know our secretive city. It also comes with a cocktail bar on the first floor and a smart private dining room above that. Give the menu a cursory glance and it would appear to be a fairly generic one of the brasserie kind, but the dishes, like crab with avocado or veal chop with truffled mash, are prepared with considerably more care than one expects. Service too is bright and enthusiastic.

Imperial China

C h i n e s e I3

White Bear Yard, 25a Lisle St ✉ WC2H 7BA
☎ 020 7734 3388
www.imperialchina-london.com
⊖ Leicester Square

Closed 25 December –
booking advisable

Menu £20/36 – Carte £16/96

 Heave open the heavy smoked-glass double doors, cross the bamboo bridge and you'll be transported to a calm oasis that seems a world away from the bustle outside. Sharp, well-organised service and comfortable surroundings are not the only things that set this restaurant apart: the Cantonese cooking exudes freshness and vitality, whether that's the steamed dumplings or the XO minced pork with fine beans. Indeed, they pride themselves on seafood and their 'lobster feasts' are very popular - the personable staff are also more than happy to offer recommendations. There are eight private rooms of various sizes available upstairs and these are often in full swing. The owners also run Beijing Dumpling a few doors down.

Jinjuu

A s i a n H3

15 Kingly St ✉ W1B 5PS
☎ 020 8181 8887
www.jinjuu.com
⊖ Oxford Circus

Closed 25 December

Menu £15 (weekday lunch)/42 – Carte £26/86

 American-born TV chef Judy Joo's first restaurant celebrates her Korean heritage, and it's not only great fun but also the perfect spot for those who think Korean food just means barbecue. The place has an industrial feel and is spread over two floors – the ground floor bar offers a great selection of cocktails, many of which use Korean's famous spirit, soju, as a base, but the heart of the operation is downstairs, with its small open kitchen. Much of the menu is designed for sharing, especially the Ssam platters and the Tong Dak, their signature whole chicken dish. The Bibimbap bowls burst with flavour and there are some dishes, like the Sae-woo pops and the prawn cakes, that you won't want to give up without a fight.

Kai ✿

C h i n e s e   G3

65 South Audley St ✉ W1K 2QU
℘ 020 7493 8988
www.kaimayfair.co.uk
⊖ Hyde Park Corner

Closed 25-26 December and
1 January – booking essential

Carte £39/136   ✗✗✗

Kai

Traditionalists will find a few familiar classics on the menu but Chef Alex Chow's strengths are his modern creations and re-workings of traditional Chinese recipes. There are Cantonese, Shanghainese, Hunanese and Sichuanese influences but he also uses the occasional flavour from other Asian countries. The resulting dishes have real depth, use superb ingredients and are wonderfully balanced. Vegetarians are well catered for and desserts are given a bigger billing than one usually sees. The lunch menu offers further proof that this isn't your typical Chinese restaurant: instead of dim sum, they call their smaller versions of the dinner specialities 'little plates of loveliness'. The service team in their silk jackets expertly anticipate their customers' needs, whether that's demonstrating how to construct a pork pancake, expertly filleting sea bass or offering jasmine tea to those awaiting a soufflé. The clientele is international and the interior unashamedly glitzy, with the only discordant note being the incongruously clubby music.

First Course	Main Course	Dessert
• Halibut with ginger, spring onions and soy.	• Kagoshima Wagyu with 7 spice salt and rice balls.	• Durian and vanilla soufflé with salted caramel.
• Roast abalone mushroom with black bean, pickled chillies and soy.	• Tiger prawns with crisp curry leaves, lime and chilli dressing.	• Chocolate and mandarin fondant with orange & kumquat confit.

Keeper's House

Modern British H3

Royal Academy of Arts, Burlington House,
Piccadilly ✉ W1J 0BD
☎ 020 7300 5881
www.keepershouse.org.uk
⊖ Green Park

Closed 25-26 December and
Sunday

Menu £21/26 – Carte £27/44

The Keeper's House, built in the 1860s and fully restored, sits in the corner of the courtyard of Burlington House and acts as a members' club for Royal Academicians and Friends of the RA. In the evenings, though, it's open to all of us – to find it, look for the Tracey Emin neon 'Keep me safe' above the door. The two intimate, interconnecting rooms come with low ceilings and walls lined with green baize and hung with architectural casts; there's also a modern bar which leads out into a hidden garden. The menu is appealingly concise and the emphasis is on seasonality, freshness and contrasts in textures and flavours. The kitchen strives for a certain amount of originality and, when the dishes work, they work very well.

Kiku

Japanese H4

17 Half Moon St. ✉ W1J 7BE
☎ 020 7499 4208
www.kikurestaurant.co.uk
⊖ Green Park

Closed 25-27 December,
1 January and lunch Sunday and
bank holidays

Menu £24 (weekday lunch) – Carte £23/78

It's not just the fact that it's family owned and has been here for over 35 years that makes Kiku unlike most Mayfair restaurants – this Japanese restaurant is also very sweet. There's an authentic simplicity to its decoration and a pleasing earnestness to the service; most evenings the majority of diners appear to be homesick Japanese. Virtually every style of Japanese cuisine is on offer, from shabu shabu to sukiyaki, yakitori to teriyaki and if you want to try something a little different, like sliced squid and guts or salmon zosui (rice soup), then here's your chance. The extensive à la carte menu is supplemented by a number of set menus and these are worth exploring if you want an all-round experience.

Kitty Fisher's

Modern cuisine H4

10 Shepherd Mkt ✉ W1J 7QF
📞 020 3302 1661
www.kittyfishers.com
🚇 Green Park

Closed Christmas,
New Year, Easter, Sunday and
bank holidays – booking essential

Menu £30 (weekday lunch) – Carte £33/54

Named after an 18C courtesan, presumably in honour of the profession for which Shepherd Market was once known, Kitty Fisher's is a small, intimate and refreshingly unpretentious restaurant. Its best seats are downstairs, in a room which has something of a Dickensian feel and from where you can see into the kitchen – be sure to ask for the 'Lord's Table', the best seat in the house. Service is relaxed and friendly, with the cheerful owner on hand to oversee things. The menu changes twice a day and is ingredient-led; the cooking is rustic, unfussy and all about flavour. The star of the show is undoubtedly the wood grill which gives the dishes depth and character – don't miss the chargrilled bread with burnt onion butter.

Koya Bar

Japanese I3

50 Frith St ✉ W1D 4SQ
📞 020 7433 4463
www.koyabar.co.uk
🚇 Tottenham Court Road

Closed 24-25 December and
1 January – bookings not
accepted

Carte £10/23

Those suffering udon noodle withdrawal symptoms by the closure of Koya will find Koya Bar a more than suitable replacement. Their udon noodles are made fresh each morning and cooked to order; choose hot or cold ones to go with your flavoursome broth which is finished with onions and includes a choice of beef, chicken or duck amongst others. Extra toppings allow you to create your own bespoke bowl, and there are small dishes also available such as tofu, pickles and tempura. It's a simple spot with counter seats looking into the kitchen – bookings aren't taken so there'll probably be a queue but it moves quite quickly. Service is sweet and polite and staff are happy to make recommendations to novice slurpers.

Little Social

French   H3

5 Pollen St ✉ W1S 1NE
✆ 020 7870 3730
www.littlesocial.co.uk
⊖ Oxford Circus

Closed Sunday and bank holidays
– booking essential

Menu £25 (weekday lunch) – Carte £33/58

Jason Atherton wisely decided that keeping an eye on your growing restaurant empire is easier when you have two restaurants in the same street. In contrast with the more formal Pollen Street Social, Little Social is a lively French bistro with a clubby, masculine feel and an appealing, deliberately worn look. The best seats are the discreet leather booths at the back; avoid the bar as you can get crowded out by those having a pre-prandial drink. Service is bright, breezy and capable and the French food is fairly classic, with the occasional modern twist. The menu constantly evolves and the choice is enhanced by daily specials; the soups and steaks are winners but there are also some more interesting options like pork head terrine or ox cheeks.

Manchurian Legends

Chinese   I3

16 Lisle St ✉ WC2H 7BE
✆ 020 7287 6606
www.manchurianlegends.com
⊖ Leicester Square

Closed Christmas

Menu £16/25 – Carte £20/38

There's a bewildering choice of Chinese restaurants in these parts so look out for a chef behind the window making the dumplings, which are one of the specialities at this simple yet authentic spot. Also available are specialities from the northeast corner of China – the Dongbei region. They battle the long winters out there with stews and BBQ dishes, along with heartening soups like rib and lotus root. The chillies beside each dish on the menu warn of their relative heat – ignore these at your peril – although the chef cleverly balances the heat with herbs and various other spices. There are ingredients like gizzards, intestines and tripe for the more adventurous eater and it's worth starting with some of the street snacks.

MASH

Meats and grills

77 Brewer St ⊠ W1F 9ZN
☎ 020 7734 2608
www.mashsteak.co.uk
⊖ Piccadilly Circus

Closed 24-26 December and
Sunday lunch

Menu £25 – Carte £30/94

It took a brave team to take on the daunting task of raising the old Titanic restaurant from the depths of Brewer Street but that is what a group of experienced Copenhagen restaurateurs did back in 2012. In restoring many of the original art deco features and combining them with contemporary fittings, they created a striking 350-seater restaurant. Instead of showcasing Danish cuisine, they went for a 'Modern American Steak House'. They offer mostly Danish prime and corn-fed Nebraskan and Uruguayan beef and it's clear the kitchen knows what it's doing. Starters are equally robust and include charcuterie and foie gras. Add in a great cocktail bar, slick service and an impressive wine list and you have a seriously grown up restaurant.

Matsuri

Japanese

15 Bury St. ⊠ SW1Y 6AL
☎ 020 7839 1101
www.matsuri-restaurant.com
⊖ Green Park

Closed 25 December and
1 January

Carte £30/169

While there is a separate sushi counter at this longstanding Japanese restaurant, go for what they do best – teppanyaki. You'll get to enjoy a bit of skilled knife work along with the top-notch ingredients, many of which are imported from Japan. The beef is excellent, although it comes at a price, and the style of cooking allows natural flavours to shine through. The last refurbishment refreshed the large space; there's a bar on the ground floor while all the dining is done downstairs. Staff are charming and discreet and the restaurant is a worthy counterpoint to all those establishments offering their own modern interpretations of Japanese food. It's especially popular with those entertaining business clients.

Mayfair Chippy

Traditional British   **G3**

14 North Audley St ✉ W1K 6WE
☎ 020 7741 2233
www.eatbrit.com
⊖ Marble Arch

Closed 25 December and
1 January

Carte £20/35

  Any roll call of classic British institutions would have to include the local chippy, as fish and chips rank alongside a full English breakfast and afternoon tea as our most celebrated contributions to world cuisine. When the local area is Mayfair, however, things start to look a little different – indeed, The Mayfair Chippy is unlike any other. For a start, it serves cocktails and wine, and also provides starters and desserts – it even has reserved seating. However, any fears that this isn't a real chippy are assuaged by the sight of the 'Mayfair Classic' – fried cod or haddock, with chips, tartar sauce, mushy peas and curry sauce. For those who like doing things in a more traditional way, there is a takeaway service available.

Maze

Modern cuisine   **G3**

10-13 Grosvenor Sq ✉ W1K 6JP
☎ 020 7107 0000
www.gordonramsayrestaurants.com/maze
⊖ Bond Street

Menu £30 (weekday lunch) – Carte £44/76

  This Gordon Ramsay restaurant still offers a glamorous night out, thanks to its great cocktails, effervescent atmosphere and easy-to-eat food. The lower level is best if you want to feel part of the action, while the upper level offers greater intimacy; if you're part of a group consider the 'Maze View' private dining room with views into the kitchen. The style of the menu, with its smaller plates and Asian influences, has changed little over the years; three or four dishes per person are about the going rate, especially as they're not really built for sharing, despite what the serving team may say. What has changed is that some of the precision has gone out of the cooking, caused perhaps by regular changes in kitchen personnel.

Maze Grill Mayfair

Meats and grills

London Marriott Hotel Grosvenor Square, 10-
13 Grosvenor Sq ⊠ W1K 6JP
☎ 020 7495 2211
www.gordonramsayrestaurants.com/
maze-grill-mayfair
⊖ Bond Street

Menu £27 (lunch) – Carte £29/88 𝗫𝗫

Maze Grill is the more down to earth sibling to next door Maze and steak is its thing. Expect a good range of properly aged meat, including Aberdeen Angus (28 days), Dedham Vale (31), USDA Prime (36) and Wagyu 9th Grade (49). Cooked on the Josper grill and properly rested, the steaks are presented on wooden boards, which means they lose their temperature quite quickly but which at least ensures the Laguiole knives stay sharp. A choice of seven sauces is offered alongside assorted sides which can pump up the bill quite rapidly. There's also sushi available for less committed carnivores. If you enter from the Marriott hotel the staff can seem taken by surprise so you're better off using the main entrance on Grosvenor Square.

Mele e Pere

Italian I3

46 Brewer St ⊠ W1F 9TF
☎ 020 7096 2096
www.meleepere.co.uk
⊖ Piccadilly Circus

Closed 25-26 December and
1 January

Menu £23 (dinner) – Carte £23/43 𝗫

Faced with a wall of Murano glass apples and pears as colourful as the street you're standing in, you'd be forgiven for thinking this is a gallery. But head downstairs – the 'apple and pears'? – and you'll find yourself in a vaulted room in the style of a homely Italian kitchen, and one that happens to have an appealing Vermouth bar attached. The owner-chef worked in some decent London kitchens over a number of years but as he hails from Verona you can expect a selection of gutsy Italian dishes, like rabbit with olives, shoulder of lamb, and tripe with grated Parmigiano. Main courses come with a side dish that you get to choose and puds are excellent, especially the panna cotta.

Milos

S e a f o o d I4

1 Regent St ⊠ SW1Y 4NR
☏ 020 7839 2080
www.milos.ca
⊖ Piccadilly Circus

Closed 25 December and Sunday

Menu £29/49 – Carte £58/130 ✗✗✗

London's branch of this international group of Greek seafood estiatorios takes full advantage of the grand listed building it occupies – this was originally British Columbia House. The ceiling's so high there's a mezzanine floor and a staggering amount of white marble has been used. The menu is almost more of a guideline – for the main event you wander over to the impressive display of fish flown in daily from Greek waters to choose what you fancy; it's then weighed to calculate the price while you discuss your preferred method of preparation. There's no denying it's expensive, but that doesn't seem to bother the clientele who give the impression that, when they venture down to the Greek Islands, they do so in their own vessel.

Momo

M o r o c c a n H3

25 Heddon St. ⊠ W1B 4BH
☏ 020 7434 4040
www.momoresto.com
⊖ Oxford Circus

Closed 25 December and
1 January

Menu £20 (weekday lunch) – Carte £28/51 ✗✗

Whether you're a couple looking to rekindle that Marrakech magic or just out with a group of friends, Momo and its Moroccan food should fit the bill. For one thing, there's depth and authenticity to the decoration here, with antiques, kilim rugs, Berber artwork, bright fabrics and lanterns; even the open kitchen adds to the feeling that you're dining close to the souk – shut your eyes and you can imagine Jemaa el Fna Square just outside the door. When it comes to the food, the classics are the highlights: zaalouk, briouats, pigeon pastilla and all manner of tagines accompanied by mountains of fluffy couscous; be sure to have the milk pastilla for dessert. If you want to experience a slightly more relaxed pace, then try the weekend brunches.

Murano ✿

Italian **G4**

20 Queen St ✉ W1J 5PP
✆ 020 7495 1127
www.muranolondon.com
⊖ Green Park

Closed Christmas and Sunday

Menu £33/65

XXX

♿ A/C

Michelin

For some chefs, attaining a certain level of success means they can all but abandon their stoves for the more glitzy existence of TV and travel. Not so Angela Hartnett, who is very much in evidence at her restaurants and none more so than at her flagship, Murano: the elegant yet understated restaurant named after the famous Venetian glassware. Seasonal, Italian-inspired dishes – like baked potato gnocchi with homemade coppa and curly kale or Carnaroli risotto with Cornish crab – have their roots in the love of food and cooking engendered by her Italian grandparents, who came from Bardi in the heart of Emilia-Romagna. Angela's cooking exhibits an appealing lightness of touch; dishes are uncluttered and balanced and flavours, assured and defined. The menu is divided into 5 sections and diners can choose however many dishes they want, with 3 or 4 being the ideal number. This relaxed approach is reflected in both the décor and the service, with staff striking the right balance between friendliness and formality.

First Course

- Crab tortellini & bisque with cucumber, turnip and spring onion.
- Rabbit with baby carrots, radish, orange, quail eggs and pancetta.

Main Course

- Smoked pigeon with orange purée, fennel, pine nuts and pancetta.
- Halibut with honey-soused tomatoes, razor clams, cucumber and peas.

Dessert

- Pistachio soufflé with hot chocolate sauce.
- Vanilla panna cotta with roasted raspberry ice cream and shortbread.

Nobu

Japanese G4

Metropolitan Hotel, 19 Old Park Ln ✉ W1Y 1LB
☎ 020 7447 4747
www.noburestaurants.com
⊖ Hyde Park Corner

Booking essential

Menu £30 – Carte £24/73

These days there are Nobu restaurants stretching from Malibu to Moscow and Beijing to Budapest but back in 1997 when Europe's first branch opened here at the Metropolitan hotel it sent shockwaves through the city. Not only did it add serious sparkle and bags of glamour to the dining out scene but also its innovative cuisine – an intriguing mix of Japanese cuisine and South American ingredients – was unlike anything else at the time. Nobu's heyday may have slipped past but the restaurant remains buzzy and fun, and if you need proof of the influence it has had then simply check out the menus of some of its competitors and imitators and you'll see plenty of evidence of some pretty shameless culinary plagiarism.

Nobu Berkeley St

Japanese H3

15 Berkeley St. ✉ W1J 8DY
☎ 020 7290 9222
www.noburestaurants.com
⊖ Green Park

Closed 25 December and
Sunday lunch except December
– booking essential

Menu £40 (lunch) – Carte £30/92

The cries of "irasshaimase" may not be quite as heartfelt as they once were and the food may be lacking some of the lustre of previous years but this branch of the international chain can still provide a glamorous night out. That night out does not come cheap but you do get a huge menu of specialities blending Japanese cuisine with South American influences so everyone will find something they want. Be sure to get some dishes from the wood-fired oven – and you can't go too wrong if you order some of the classics. This branch has always been more of a party animal than its elder sibling at The Metropolitan so get in the mood with cocktails in the downstairs bar - or come at lunch for a less frenzied experience.

Nopi

Mediterranean cuisine H3

21-22 Warwick St. ✉ W1B 5NE Closed 25-26 December
☏ 020 7494 9584
www.nopi-restaurant.com
⊖ Piccadilly Circus

Carte £34/48 ✗

   There isn't an Aga in the country that doesn't share kitchen space with a few of his cookbooks and his terrific delis are now much copied – so it's no surprise that Yotam Ottolenghi's restaurant is a great success too. It's cleverly designed because you'd think those white walls would make it stark and cold but it actually feels warm and soothing – and the brass lamps and marble add a hint of the exotic. The flavours take in the Med, the Middle East and Asia and whether you share a few smaller dishes or plough your own furrow, you'll find the food refreshing and vibrant and will feel healthy just eating it. This is a relaxed, informal all-day restaurant that is genuinely well run – the staff really make an effort to ensure you enjoy yourself.

Oliver Maki

Japanese I3

33 Dean St ✉ W1D 4PW
☏ 020 7734 0408
www.olivermaki.co.uk
⊖ Leicester Square

Carte £38/56 ✗

 This small restaurant group has branches in Bahrain and Kuwait so it's perhaps surprising that their first European outpost is a small corner restaurant in Soho and not somewhere big and shiny in Mayfair. What London is certainly used to is modern interpretations of Japanese food, but few restaurants have pushed the fusion element quite so much – even the soy dipping sauce is mixed with olive oil. Purists, however, will find themselves charmed and reassured by the eagerness of the staff and the obvious quality of the produce. Not every dish works but the kitchen has an undeniable confidence and clearly understands the importance of textures and temperatures. The upstairs room is the nicer of the two.

100 Wardour St

Modern cuisine I3

100 Wardour St ⊠ W1F 0TN
℘ 020 7314 4000
www.100wardourst.com
⊖ Tottenham Court Road

Closed 25-26 December

Menu £30 (weekday dinner) – Carte £17/57

AC
Cocktails, food and live music usually equal a fun night out so if
you've got friends from out of town looking for a bit of glamour
think about bringing them to the vast 100 Wardour St. This was
the site of the original Marquee Club; some will remember the
space as Mezzo restaurant, others as Cuban-influenced Floridita.
At night you want to be downstairs – for music and a menu that's
an amalgam of all that is contemporary, with its Japanese and
South American influences, its use of the robata grill and its
dishes designed for sharing. During daylight hours everything
happens at ground level, with a simpler, all-day menu; here
you'll also find a bar, a billiards table and a pop-in/plug-in lounge
popular with itinerant bloggers.

Palomar

World cuisine I3

34 Rupert St ⊠ W1D 6DN
℘ 020 7439 8777
www.thepalomar.co.uk
⊖ Piccadilly Circus

Closed 25-26 December
and Sunday dinner
– booking advisable

Carte £23/42

AC

Run by a brother and sister team who used to own a nightclub,
Palomar brings a hip slice of modern-day Jerusalem to the heart
of theatreland. Inside it's a bit of a squeeze, with a zinc kitchen
counter running back to an intimate, wood-panelled dining
room, but the limited space, its propensity to get packed and
the proximity to the animated chefs make for a high-energy
buzz. Like the atmosphere, the food here is fresh and vibrant,
with contemporary Middle Eastern cooking taking a tour round
Southern Spain and Italy, through North Africa and to the Levant.
Starters come from the raw bar, unless you choose the 'Daily
6' assorted mezze, while main dishes come from the stove, the
Josper or the plancha and are designed for sharing.

Park Chinois

C h i n e s e

17 Berkeley St ✉ W1J 8EA
☎ 020 3327 8888
www.parkchinois.com
⊖ Green Park

Booking essential

Carte £40/107

XXX

A/C

Alan Yau, one of the UK's most influential restaurateurs, has again created something original and spectacular. His flair, imagination and renowned eye for detail are all evident here at his exquisitely decorated restaurant. The inspiration comes from 1920s Shanghai – it's about glamour, good food and live music. The restaurant comes in two parts: the richly furnished ground floor is about comfort and luxury; downstairs has more of a nocturnal, mischievous feel. An army of white-jacketed waiters deliver the dishes of Chinese food course by course instead of all together. Two specialities of note are roast duck served with caviar, and carbonara with Inaniwa udon and sea urchin. Lunchtime dim sum and afternoon tea are also served.

La Petite Maison

F r e n c h

54 Brooks Mews ✉ W1K 4EG
☎ 020 7495 4774
www.lpmlondon.co.uk
⊖ Bond Street

Closed Christmas-New Year
– booking essential

Carte £30/70 s

XX

A/C

A little piece of southern France and Ligurian Italy in Mayfair. The sister operation to the Nice original has a great, buzzy feel which is almost as enticing as the aromas from the kitchen. There's more than a soupçon of glamour and the staff, in their aprons and bow ties, give the impression that nothing ever fazes them. Simply reading the menus will improve your tan: there are over 20 starters and mains and you can expect lots of healthy olive oil, artichokes, peppers, lemons and tomatoes. There's a fresh pasta of the day, seafood is popular and the whole chicken or gigot of lamb for two are worth ordering. This is a proper neighbourhood restaurant – but as that neighbourhood happens to be Mayfair, don't expect down-to-earth prices.

Peyote

Mexican   H3

13 Cork St ⊠ W1S 3NS
☏ 020 7409 1300
www.peyoterestaurant.com
⊖ Green Park

Closed Saturday lunch and
Sunday – booking essential

Menu £24 (weekdays) – Carte £30/60

 An energetic and moodily lit Mexican restaurant which comes from the same stable as Zuma and Roka, so expect it to be full of youthful, well-heeled diners who look good and know a decent Margarita when they taste one. It has the slight feel of a glamorous private members club and music thumps out from the DJ's decks at the end of the week. The kitchen offers a 'refined interpretation of Mexican cuisine' which means that the dishes, which are designed for sharing, are well-judged, use good ingredients and come with an exhilarating freshness. Start with the terrific guacamole and don't miss the cactus salad or the tostados nopales; the lime-driven ceviche is very refreshing; quesadillas are satisfying and you just have to end with churros.

Plum Valley

Chinese   I3

20 Gerrard St. ⊠ W1D 6JQ
☏ 020 7494 4366
⊖ Leicester Square

Closed 23-24 December

Menu £38 – Carte £19/37

 Is Chinatown finally casting off its tourist-trap reputation? Plum Valley is the latest venture with genuine aspirations in Gerrard Street and its contemporary styling gives the street a much-needed boost. The striking black façade makes it easy to notice, while flattering lighting and layered walls give the interior a dash of sophistication. The chef is from Chiu Chow, a region near Guangdong, and his menu is largely based on Cantonese cooking, with occasional forays into Vietnam and Thailand as well as the odd nod towards contemporary presentation. Dim sum is his kitchen's main strength which fits nicely with the all-day opening of the restaurant. If only those doing the service could muster the same levels of enthusiasm.

Pollen Street Social ✿✿

Creative H3

8-10 Pollen St ⊠ W1S 1NQ
☎ 020 7290 7600
www.pollenstreetsocial.com
⊖ Oxford Circus

Closed Sunday and bank holidays
– booking essential

Menu £32 (lunch) – Carte £60/70

Pollen Street Social

One could argue whether Jason Atherton now has enough restaurants to classify as an 'empire' but what is certain is that he must be gathering air-miles at a very healthy lick. Pollen Street Social is where it all started for him when he went solo and it's clear he still takes great pride in the place. Fortunately, he has a strong pool of culinary talent to support his ambitions and between them they have kept his flagship restaurant buzzing along nicely. Top quality British produce lies at the heart of a menu which offers a hugely appealing selection of modern, innovative dishes that are always very easy to eat. The cooking is clearly undertaken with great care, whether that's the squid cooked in cauliflower or the perfectly roasted squab pigeon; and dessert is always worth saving room for, with its modern takes on old favourites like cheesecake or Eton mess. The à la carte prices can get a little dizzying but there's a decent value lunch menu. The wine list has impressive breadth and is rooted in the classic regions.

First Course	Main Course	Dessert
• Crab salad with apple, coriander, black garlic, lemon purée and brown crab on toast.	• Loin and braised neck of lamb with roast artichoke, Merguez sausage, curds & whey.	• Bitter chocolate pavé with olive biscuit and chocolate ice cream.
• Pine-smoked quail 'English breakfast'.	• John Dory with crayfish, artichoke and shellfish broth.	• Beetroot and blood orange sorbet with hibiscus, apple and candied beetroot.

93

Polpetto

Italian

I3

11 Berwick St ⊠ W1F 0PL
☎ 020 7439 8627
www.polpetto.co.uk
⊖ Tottenham Court Road

Closed Sunday – (bookings not accepted at dinner)

Carte £12/18

𝄃𝄃

Following its short stint above the French House, restaurateur Russell Norman spent quite some time finding and decorating new premises for Polpetto – but the wait was worth it. It's almost three times the size of its former incarnation and set over two floors; and it manages the trick of being all new but looking lived-in. Waiting for a table is still an inevitability as bookings aren't accepted at dinner but your odds improve if you don't mind eating at the bar. The style of food chimes perfectly with the appealingly relaxed environment: the small, seasonally inspired Italian dishes are uncomplicated, appealingly priced and deliver great flavours; order a few and they arrive when ready but at an even pace.

Polpo Soho

Italian

H3

41 Beak St ⊠ W1F 9SB
☎ 020 7734 4479
www.polpo.co.uk
⊖ Oxford Circus

(bookings not accepted at dinner)

Menu £25 – Carte £12/21

𝄃𝄃

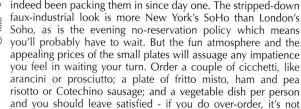

Opening a Venetian bacaro in an 18C townhouse where Canaletto once lodged does seem providential and Polpo has indeed been packing them in since day one. The stripped-down faux-industrial look is more New York's SoHo than London's Soho, as is the evening no-reservation policy which means you'll probably have to wait. But the fun atmosphere and the appealing prices of the small plates will assuage any impatience you feel in waiting your turn. Order a couple of cicchetti, like arancini or prosciutto; a plate of fritto misto, ham and pea risotto or Cotechino sausage; and a vegetable dish per person and you should leave satisfied - if you do over-order, it's not going to break the bank. Venetian wines, available by the carafe, complete the picture.

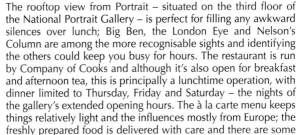

Portrait

M o d e r n   c u i s i n e 13

National Portrait Gallery (3rd floor), St Martin's
Pl. ✉ WC2H 0HE
℡ 020 7312 2490
www.npg.org.uk/portraitrestaurant
⊖ Charing Cross

Closed 24-26 December
– booking essential – (lunch only
and dinner Thursday-Saturday)

Menu £27 – Carte £34/49 ✗

The rooftop view from Portrait – situated on the third floor of the National Portrait Gallery – is perfect for filling any awkward silences over lunch; Big Ben, the London Eye and Nelson's Column are among the more recognisable sights and identifying the others could keep you busy for hours. The restaurant is run by Company of Cooks and although it's also open for breakfast and afternoon tea, this is principally a lunchtime operation, with dinner limited to Thursday, Friday and Saturday – the nights of the gallery's extended opening hours. The à la carte menu keeps things relatively light and the influences mostly from Europe; the freshly prepared food is delivered with care and there are some good value pre-theatre and weekend set menus.

Quaglino's

M o d e r n   c u i s i n e H4

16 Bury St ✉ SW1Y 6AJ
℡ 020 7930 6767
www.quaglinos-restaurant.co.uk
⊖ Green Park

Closed Easter Monday and
Sunday dinner

Menu £20 (weekdays)/30 – Carte £36/66 ✗✗

The old girl may have been around for a while now but she can still shake it like the best of them if you're looking for a fun night out. This vast, glamorous and colourful restaurant may be synonymous with the '90s but an updated look and the creation of the central Q Bar have added some much needed sultriness and energy, as has the live music on Fridays and Saturdays – there's also music in the bar. The kitchen specialises in contemporary brasserie-style food with an extensive à la carte menu that includes a grill section and some dishes that are available to share. The restaurant also serves brunch with an appealing bottomless fizz offer, as well as afternoon teas, which should help bring back the crowds.

Mayfair · Soho · St James's ▶ Plan II

Quo Vadis

Traditional British 13

26-29 Dean St ✉ W1D 3LL
☎ 020 7437 9585
www.quovadissoho.co.uk
⊖ Tottenham Court Road

Closed 25-26 December,
1 January and bank holidays

Menu £20 – Carte £33/48

Few restaurants in London are as synonymous with their neighbourhood as Quo Vadis. There's been a restaurant at this address since 1926 and its neon sign is a famous Soho landmark; you may even spot tourists peering up at the first floor because it was once home to Karl Marx. At the end of 2016 there will be some changes to this institution: the restaurant will be a little smaller as space will be made on the ground floor to accommodate Barrafina, the Hart Brother's tapas bar. To compensate, chef Jeremy Lee will also have a second restaurant upstairs, which will be for the exclusive use of QV members. What will remain the same is the food – classic British dishes prepared with obvious pride, and with game a highlight.

Red Fort

Indian 13

77 Dean St. ✉ W1D 3SH
☎ 020 7437 2525
www.redfort.co.uk
⊖ Tottenham Court Road

Closed Sunday – bookings
advisable at dinner

Menu £15/59 – Carte £32/65

Soho now boasts one of London's most buoyant restaurant scenes but that wasn't the case back in 1983 when Red Fort opened its doors on Dean Street. Its longevity is down to the professionalism with which it is run, the fact that it keeps on top of its looks and, of course, the ability and ambition of the kitchen. Inside is bigger than you think and the smart, stylish and contemporary decoration pays homage to Lal Quila, Delhi's Red Fort. The cooking also takes its cue from the Mughal Court while making good use of produce from the UK like Welsh lamb and Scottish lobster. The tandoor oven is used to good effect, especially with the breads, and you can expect to see more unusual ingredients like rabbit. Zenna is its intimate basement bar.

Refuel

M o d e r n   B r i t i s h 13

Soho Hotel,
4 Richmond Mews ✉ W1D 3DH
☎ 020 7559 3007
www.sohohotel.com
⊖ Tottenham Court Road

Menu £21/25 – Carte £31/54   ✗✗

It comes as no surprise that a hotel as fashionable as The Soho has a restaurant as cool as Refuel. A large part of the room is given over to a slick cocktail bar and the lively atmosphere here tends to seep through into the restaurant through osmosis. Service in the hotel is one of its great strengths and the serving team here are a bright and enthusiastic bunch who are always ready with a smile. The menu is all about ease of eating and includes a popular section of grilled dishes, which could range from Dover sole to a burger, as well as assorted pasta dishes and salads for the image-conscious. Side dishes are needed but can leave you with a sizeable bill so it's worth considering the better value set menu.

Roka

J a p a n e s e G3

30 North Audley St ✉ W1K 6HP   Closed Christmas-New Year
☎ 020 7305 5644
www.rokarestaurant.com
⊖ Bond Street

Carte £24/116   ✗✗

Rainer Becker and Arjun Waney's empire now stretches to all parts of the globe but London was where it all began and is where they continue to open new restaurants. For the capital's third Roka they ventured into the rarefied surroundings of Mayfair and the restaurant's sultry, seductive looks prove a good fit. Tempting aromas fill the air as once again the robata grill takes centre stage – quite literally if you haven't booked and find yourself seated at the Indonesian elm counter that surrounds it. All the favourites from their modern Japanese repertoire are on show here; the tasting menu is often the best way of getting a good all round experience and the dessert platter really is a sight. Even the doggy bags look good.

Ritz Restaurant ✿

Mayfair • Soho • St James's ► Plan II

Ritz Hotel,
150 Piccadilly ✉ W1J 9BR
☎ 020 7300 2370
www.theritzlondon.com
⊖ Green Park

Menu £49 (weekday lunch) – Carte £72/103

XXXXX

Michelin

The world may be considerably less formal these days but one of the reasons why London is such an exciting and dynamic city is its variety of restaurants. Thanks to the lavishness of its Louis XVI decoration, there is nowhere grander or more opulent than The Ritz – this is the place for the most special of special occasions, so it's hardly surprising they insist on a jacket and tie. To match the luxurious surroundings comes classic cuisine using the most extravagant of ingredients, but where the kitchen has been clever is in adopting subtle contemporary elements and techniques to lift those dishes to new heights, while still respecting their spirit and heritage. This new vitality is not just in the cooking – the service is also unrecognisable from what it was. There may be more ranks than your average ship's company but a younger breed of staff have brought greater enthusiasm and more personality to proceedings. The Ritz may have been here for over a century but it has probably never been better.

First Course	Main Course	Dessert
• Langoustine with broad beans and mint.	• Loin of lamb with pommes Anna and shallot & herb crust.	• Custard tart with poached rhubarb and ginger ice cream.
• Veal sweetbread with parsnip and Périgord truffle.	• Turbot with leeks and caviar.	• Blackcurrant soufflé with oat crumble and yoghurt ice cream.

Rosa's Soho

Thai   I3

48 Dean St ✉ W1D 5BF   Closed 25-26 December
☎ 020 7494 1638   – booking advisable
www.rosasthaicafe.com
⊖ Leicester Square

Menu £20 – Carte £19/25

Those instinctively suspicious of anywhere too shiny and flashy
will find Rosa's worn-in appearance suitably reassuring. The
simple, pared down look of this authentic Thai café also adds
to its intimate feel; the waitresses, in bright red T-shirts to match
the colour of the façade, provide cheerful and swift service. The
menu is appealing and wide-ranging and the relative heat levels
of each dish are indicated. The chef may be from Chiang Mai but
his cooking is influenced by all parts of the country. Signature
dishes include warm minced chicken salad and a sweet pumpkin
red curry; while squid, prawns, mussels and scallops all go into
their seafood Pad Cha. The refreshing Tom Yam soup comes with
a lovely balance of sweet, sour and spice.

Sake No Hana

Japanese   H4

23 St James's ✉ SW1A 1HA   Closed 25 December and Sunday
☎ 020 7925 8988
www.sakenohana.com
⊖ Green Park

Menu £31 – Carte £22/69

 The Grade II listed former offices of The Economist now play
host to this modern Japanese restaurant and the '60s edifice
needed an awful lot of cedar wood and bamboo to soften its
appearance. The escalator remains, which doesn't really add a
great deal to the experience, but you'll receive a warm welcome
and feel well looked after. There's a huge number of dishes on
offer and the food is certainly best shared with a group, although
as prices fluctuate fairly wildly it may be worth appointing
someone in your party the designated bill monitor before starting
on their excellent cocktails. The sashimi is worthy of addition, as
are the very good kamameshi or rice pot dishes, like black cod.
There's a separate sushi bar on the ground floor.

Sartoria

Italian H3

20 Savile Row ✉ W1S 3PR
☎ 020 7534 7000
www.sartoria-restaurant.co.uk
⊖ Oxford Circus

Closed 25-26 December, Saturday
lunch, Sunday and bank holidays

Menu £27 (weekday lunch) – Carte £26/58

Competition is hotting up in this little district west of Regent Street so everyone's been busy raising their game. Sartoria has long been a well-dressed feature on Savile Row but is now looking considerably more dapper and a great deal sharper. That wasn't the only change in 2015 – Francesco Mazzei, formerly of L'Anima restaurant, hooked up with D&D to take the kitchen reins and the place feels more energised because of it. While there is evidence of Francesco's Calabrian roots with ingredients like 'nduja and liquorice, the menu covers all regions of Italy and keeps things fairly classic. The dishes for two prove very popular, whether that's risotto, the salt-crusted sea bass, veal Milanese or the wonderfully rich zabaglione.

Scott's

Seafood G3

20 Mount St ✉ W1K 2HE
☎ 020 7495 7309
www.scotts-restaurant.com
⊖ Bond Street

Closed 25-26 December

Carte £37/57

When a restaurant is considered an 'institution', one usually assumes its best days are in the past. Scott's proves that a restaurant can have a long, proud history but can still be glamorous, relevant and fashionable. It is the clubby feel of the place that is particularly appealing: sit at the counter – which dominates the room and must surely be the most comfortable one in London – and you immediately feel part of a club as you'll be surrounded by regulars on all sides. The seafood is of prime quality and there's enough choice for everyone, whether you just want oysters and simply grilled fish, or something more adventurous with Asian influences. Prices may be high but you'll remember the experience – this is Scott's, after all.

Seven Park Place ✤

Modern cuisine

St James's Hotel and Club,
7-8 Park Pl ✉ SW1A 1LS
☎ 020 7316 1615
www.stjameshotelandclub.com
⊖ Green Park

Michelin

Not every chef chases TV fame or product endorsements – William Drabble is happiest when he's in his kitchen, here at St James's Hotel and Club. He describes his cooking as being "all about the ingredients" and his food provides an object lesson in the importance of using the best quality produce available. He eschews alchemy or elaborate experimentation and instead focuses on clarity and precision which in turn allows the natural flavours of the ingredients to shine. He forged a close relationship with his butcher in the Lake District when he worked in that part of the world and their loyalty to each other clearly pays off – both know what each animal has been fed and where it has eaten it. Barbon Fell venison and Lune Valley lamb feature regularly and are a must but you can also expect supremely fresh seafood – his scallops are particularly good. The diminutive, secreted restaurant is in a curious spot as you have to slither past the bar stools in the hotel brasserie to reach it. It's divided into two areas; try to secure one of the three tables in the gilded back room.

First Course

- Poached native lobster tail with asparagus and champagne hollandaise.
- Roast quail and veal sweetbreads with orange and hazelnut dressing.

Main Course

- Griddled fillet of sea bass with salt-baked celeriac, apple and truffle.
- Pot-roast squab pigeon with sweetcorn, crispy bacon and Madeira.

Dessert

- Victoria pineapple confit with vanilla and coconut sorbet.
- Assiette of coffee.

H4

Closed Sunday and Monday
– booking essential

Mayfair • Soho • St James's ▶ Plan II

Menu £32 (weekday lunch)/63

XX

Sexy Fish

S e a f o o d H3

Berkeley Sq. ⊠ W1J 6BR
☏ 020 3764 2000
www.sexyfish.com
⊖ Green Park

Closed 25 December

Carte £33/90

Everyone will have their own opinion about the name but what is indisputable is that this is a very good-looking restaurant. Works by Frank Gehry and Damien Hirst decorate the large, grand room which was, unsurprisingly, once a bank; the ceiling, designed by Michael Roberts, is a thing of beauty and the private dining room has two live coral reef tanks. The restaurant quickly became the glitterati's de facto HQ yet the pleasant staff exude none of that too-cool-for-school attitude which blights similar places. The large Asian-influenced menu is heavily weighted towards seafood; dishes are meant for sharing and those from the robata grill are often the highlight – but don't ignore the meat dishes like the beef rib skewers.

 Shoryu

J a p a n e s e I3

9 Regent St. ⊠ SW1Y 4LR
www.shoryuramen.com
⊖ Piccadilly Circus

Closed 25 December and
1 January – bookings not
accepted

Carte £20/40

The restorative powers of ramen are so great it should be prescribed on the NHS. Shoryu is owned by the Japan Centre opposite and specialises in Hakata tonkotsu ramen, which originated in Kyushu in the south and is the most popular style of ramen in Japan. At its base is a milky broth made from pork bones; to this is added springy hosomen noodles made in-house; nitamago (the boiled, marinated egg – an important element); sesame, and extra toppings of your choice; if you want a more robust flavour try a miso-based ramen. The surprisingly large menu includes other items with their roots in Chinese cooking, such as gyoza dumplings. If the queue is too long, try one of the two larger branches in Soho.

Sketch (The Gallery)

Modern cuisine H3

9 Conduit St ⊠ W1S 2XG
✆ 020 7659 4500
www.sketch.london
⊖ Oxford Circus

Closed 25 December – booking
essential – (dinner only)

Carte £37/80

It's been the HQ of RIBA, a safe house for the suffragette movement and an atelier of Christian Dior, but it's as a nesting place for London's art, fashion and culinary cognoscenti that this striking Georgian house really shines. Reinvention has always been key here and The Gallery's most recent look is from India Mahdavi and comes with artwork from Turner Prize nominated David Shrigley. At dinner the room transmogrifies from art gallery to restaurant when it suddenly reverberates to the rattle of the barman's cocktail shaker and the buzz of contented diners. The menu is a mix of the classic, the modern and the esoteric – beef burger with foie gras, fish and chips with a twist, sweet and sour snails – which suits the surroundings perfectly.

Spuntino

North American I3

61 Rupert St. ⊠ W1D 7PW
www.spuntino.co.uk
⊖ Piccadilly Circus

Closed dinner 24 December, 25-
26, 31 December and 1 January
– bookings not accepted

Carte £14/22

Despite its Italian name – meaning 'snack'– Spuntino draws its influences from Downtown New York and is so convincing you feel you could be on Clinton Street. It has the so-discreet-you-walk-straight-past-it entrance, a no-reservations policy (not even a phone number) and an interior that more than hints at a former industrial life – this was once a dairy. Just grab, or wait for, a space at the counter and, from the brown paper menu, go for the more American dishes such as mac 'n' cheese, soft-shell crab, farmhouse cheddar grits or 'sliders'. The peanut butter and jelly sandwiches for dessert will be always on your mind. The staff, who look like they could also fix your car, really add to the fun.

Sketch (The Lecture Room & Library) 🕸 🕸

F r e n c h   **H3**

9 Conduit St (1st floor) ✉ W1S 2XG
☏ 020 7659 4500
www.sketch.london
⊖ Oxford Circus

Closed 25 December, 1 January,
2 weeks late August/ Early
September, Saturday lunch,
Sunday and Monday

Menu £35/120 – Carte £112/140   ✕✕✕✕

A/C
🕩
🍇

Michelin

We all need a little luxury in our lives from time to time – so praise be for Mourad Mazouz and Pierre Gagnaire's 18C funhouse. As you're whisked past the braided rope and up the stairs to the Lecture Room & Library, you'll feel your expectations rise with every step. The room is lavishly decorated in a kaleidoscope of colours and the impeccably set tables are so far apart they're virtually in different postcodes. The staff are unfailingly polite and professional and it appears that nothing is too much trouble. The French cooking bears all the Pierre Gagnaire hallmarks: the main 'plate' comes surrounded by a number of complementary dishes and at first you don't quite know what to focus on – now is the time to relax into that comfortable armchair and just enjoy the variety of textures and tastes, the complexity and depth of flavours and the quality of the ingredients. The wine list is a tome of epic proportions; take the sommeliers advice, they know what they're talking about. And do make sure you order the array of treats that make up the 'grand dessert' – pudding it ain't.

First Course	Main Course	Dessert
• Pike soufflé with watercress poached trout and frogs' legs.	• Organic rack of pork with sage, mango vinegar and seasonal fruit.	• Pierre Gagnaire's 'grand dessert'.
• Ballotine of French rabbit & foie gras with black olives, rocket and pine nuts.	• Pavé of turbot with lemon thyme and roast chicken jus.	• Dark chocolate biscuit soufflé with aged rum ganache and pistachio parfait.

Social Eating House ⇌

M o d e r n   c u i s i n e   **H3**

58 Poland St ✉ W1F 7NR
✆ 020 7993 3251
www.socialeatinghouse.com
⊖ Oxford Circus

Closed Christmas,
Sunday and bank holidays
– booking advisable

Menu £21 (lunch and early dinner) – Carte £39/57

Michelin

If you're looking for somewhere with terrific food that represents all that is great about this dynamic part of town then this Jason Atherton restaurant is it – it's huge fun, noisy and gloriously unstuffy. The low-ceilinged speakeasy-style bar upstairs is a great place to have in your address book, while the restaurant, with its bare bricks and raw plastered walls has something of Brooklyn about it. They've certainly made the best use of the available room as virtually every space is set for dining, including the counter of the bar and in the kitchen where the 'pass' would be. The menu makes an eminently good read but while you do so be sure to order a cocktail – those in the know ask for the more comprehensive list from upstairs. Kick things off on the food front by sharing one or two of their 'jars' – something like ham hock terrine or smoked hummus, before ordering robustly flavoured dishes like the ever-popular wild mushrooms on toast with cep purée, or hake with smoked celeriac mousseline.

First Course	Main Course	Dessert
• Smoked Lincolnshire eel with salt & vinegar potatoes, macadamia and rock samphire.	• Rack of Herdwick lamb with confit neck, peas and sheep's ricotta.	• Chocolate crémeux with salted caramel, mascarpone and almond biscotti.
• Confit rabbit, chicken and leek terrine with celeriac, almond and truffle.	• Wild Cornish turbot, with cockles, celeriac, mussel ketchup and sea vegetables.	• Caramelised milk and brown sugar tart with ginger wine and fromage frais sorbet.

The Square

French   H3

6-10 Bruton St. ⊠ W1J 6PU
☎ 020 7495 7100
www.squarerestaurant.com
⊖ Green Park

Closed 24-26 December and
Sunday lunch

Menu £40/95

It was all change in 2016 at this landmark Mayfair restaurant –
Philip Howard, the chef who had been at the helm for 25 years,
stepped down and the restaurant itself also changed hands. It now
belongs to Marlon Abela's portfolio of international restaurants,
which include Umu and The Greenhouse in London. A period
of transition naturally follows but what seems certain is that the
restaurant will continue to offer French-influenced, sophisticated
cuisine in these comfortable and bright surroundings, along
with service that is detailed and formally structured. Scores of
talented chefs have passed through the kitchens of this important
restaurant over the years, so let's hope the standard of cuisine
returns to its previous heights.

10 Greek Street

Modern cuisine   I3

10 Greek St ⊠ W1D 4DH
☎ 020 7734 4677
www.10greekstreet.com
⊖ Tottenham Court Road

Closed Christmas,
Easter and Sunday

Carte £29/67

With just 28 seats and a dozen more at the counter, the first
challenge is getting a table at this modishly sparse-looking bistro
– you can book at lunch but dinner is first-come-first-served.
You'll then worry that those at the next table are too close for
comfort but soon you'll find yourself caught up with the general
bonhomie and start relaxing. The chef-owner's menu is chalked
up on a couple of blackboards each day and his cooking comes
with Anglo, Mediterranean and Middle Eastern elements. Start
with some small plates – maybe burrata or sand eels – then try
crab rigatoni or Cornish hake with dates; and it's worth choosing
a dish for two, like leg of lamb. Wine is the passion of the other
owner and the list is constantly evolving.

Tamarind

20 Queen St. ✉ W1J 5PR
☎ 020 7629 3561
www.tamarindrestaurant.com
⊖ Green Park

Closed 25-26 December,
1 January and Saturday lunch

Mayfair • Soho • St James's ▶ Plan II

Menu £22/75 – Carte £36/69   ✗✗✗

Michelin

Tamarind is a perpetually busy restaurant so you need to book; when you do so, ask for a table around the edge of the room as it can feel a little like Piccadilly Circus in the middle section with the army of staff all buzzing around. The reason for this restaurant's enduring popularity is less to do with its looks – although the gilded pillars and smoked mirrors do make the most of the basement location – and everything to do with the assured Indian cuisine. Despite the chef being from the south, the menu remains largely influenced by the traditional Moghul cuisine of Northern India, so don't expect showy or elaborate dishes but do think delicate spicing and balanced flavours. The kebabs are a favourite and the tandoor oven – a definite influence from the Northwest – is used to good effect. The Hyderabadi lamb shank is another highlight, as are the well-judged vegetable dishes such as saag aloo and bhindi do pyaza. The 6 course tasting menu is a good way to try a cross-section of dishes in smaller portions.

First Course

- Spiced chickpeas with wheat crisps, yoghurt and tamarind chutney.
- Chicken kebab with cheese, spices and mixed peppers.

Main Course

- Lamb simmered with shallots and pickling spices.
- Tiger prawns with sautéed onions, chilli, fenugreek seeds and coconut.

Dessert

- Cardamom flavoured hung yoghurt.
- Mango kulfi.

Theo Randall

I t a l i a n   **G4**

InterContinental London Park Lane, 1 Hamilton
Pl, Park Ln ✉ W1J 7QY
☏ 020 7318 8747
www.theorandall.com
⊖ Hyde Park Corner

Closed Christmas, Easter,
Saturday lunch, Sunday dinner
and bank holidays

Menu £27/33 – Carte £40/65

A lighter, fresher and less formal look to the room was unveiled
in 2016 to celebrate Theo's 10 years of residency here at the
InterContinental hotel. The lack of windows and the corporate
nature of the hotel have never done the room any favours but at
least there is now greater synergy between its look and the type
of food being served – and from some tables you get tantalising
glimpses into the kitchen. That food is rustic Italian, with the
appealing dishes featuring top quality ingredients sourced from
Italy or the British Isles or sometimes both, like Devon Crab with
Sardinian bottarga, or Hereford beef with fritto misto. The pasta
dishes are always a highlight and for dessert look no further than
the Amalfi lemon tart.

34

M e a t s   a n d   g r i l l s   **G3**

34 Grosvenor Sq (entrance on South Audley St)
✉ W1K 2HD
☏ 020 3350 3434
www.34-restaurant.co.uk
⊖ Marble Arch

Closed 25-26 December, dinner
24 December and lunch 1 January

Menu £28 (weekday lunch) – Carte £34/60

Caprice Holdings' restaurants are all about glamour and
exclusivity and 34 is no exception. Both its main culinary
influences and intended customer base are announced by the
flying of the Union Flag and the Stars and Stripes above the door.
Inside is a wonderful mix of art deco styling and Edwardian
warmth – it feels like a classic brasserie that's been around for
years, but in a good way. The star is the parrilla, an Argentinian
charcoal grill used for the cooking of Dover sole and brochettes
as well as the meat, choose from Scottish dry-aged, US prime,
organic Argentinian and Australian Wagyu; good quality game
also features and they do a decent weekend brunch. It may not
come cheap but then glitz never does.

Tokimeitē

Japanese H3

23 Conduit St ⊠ W1S 2XS
☏ 020 3826 4411
www.tokimeite.com
⊖ Oxford Circus

Closed 25 December
and Sunday dinner

right margin
Mayfair · Soho · St James's ▶ Plan II

Carte £28/136

XX

Yoshihiro Murata is one of Japan's most celebrated chefs but Chrysan, his first London restaurant, never bedded in. For his second attempt he has teamed up with the Zen-Noh group, an arm of Japan's largest agricultural cooperative. Their aim is to promote Wagyu beef in the UK and Europe so, naturally enough, it features heavily on the menu – in everything from tartare to sukiyaki and teriyaki – with the kitchen using A4 quality. It's certainly worth ordering and proves more successful than other choices like the sushi and tempura. The handsome restaurant is spread over two floors, with sparkling golden lights and lots of wood that you find you want to occasionally stroke. It's worth coming at lunch for a well-priced bento or donburi.

Tonkotsu

Japanese I3

63 Dean St ⊠ W1D 4QG
☏ 020 7437 0071
www.tonkotsu.co.uk
⊖ Tottenham Court Road

Bookings not accepted

Carte £17/26

X

If you want to see why ramen is all the rage in various cities around the world then stand in line and wait for a table at this simple Soho stop. Good ramen is all about the base stock and here 18 hours goes into its preparation to ensure the bowls of soup and homemade wheat-based noodles reach a depth of flavour that seems to nourish one's very soul. Tonkotsu is named after the pork bone broth favoured in southern Japan; you can also try the soy based Tokyo ramen or go for a little northern Japanese influence with the miso base ramen – and when it arrives, with its seasoned egg and assorted toppings like pork belly and bamboo shoots, don't forget to slurp. While you wait for your ramen, share some of the gyoza – handmade Japanese dumplings.

109

Umu ✿✿

Japanese H3

14-16 Bruton Pl. ✉ W1J 6LX
☎ 020 7499 8881
www.umurestaurant.com
⊖ Bond Street

Closed Christmas, New Year,
Saturday lunch, Sunday and bank
holidays

Menu £35/155 – Carte £57/158

Umu

The kaiseki menu is the best way to truly experience chef Yoshinori Ishii's cuisine – he trained at Kitcho in Kyoto, a bastion of tradition where the central tenets and philosophy of kaiseki are preserved and celebrated. Here at Umu he has steadily been shifting the food away from a Western idea of Japanese food to a more authentic base, which means that flavours are more delicate and subtle than many expect. It hasn't always been easy: to get hold of fish in the right condition he went out with Cornish fishermen himself to teach them the method of ikejime for killing fish – and you'll see the benefit in the firmer texture of the tsukuri. But that's not to say he's trying to replicate what happens in Kyoto – he wisely acknowledges that this is a London restaurant by incorporating the best of the UK's larder as well as dropping in an occasional playfulness – how many Japanese are familiar with a scotch egg? Instead of tatami rooms there's a neatly laid out restaurant which makes good use of warm woods and natural materials.

First Course	Main Course	Dessert
• Cornish line-caught squid with Exmoor caviar.	• Grade 11 Japanese Wagyu smoked à la minute.	• Caramel custard with fuki.
• Chargrilled Welsh eel with sweet soy sauce.	• Red clam & bottarga with tiger prawn, abalone and nori.	• Spring berry mousse with sparkling sakura sake.

Vasco and Piero's Pavilion

Mayfair · Soho · St James's ▶ Plan II

Italian   H2/3

15 Poland St ✉ W1F 8QE
✆ 020 7437 8774
www.vascosfood.com
⊖ Oxford Circus

Closed Saturday lunch,
Sunday and bank holidays
– booking essential at lunch

Menu £18 (lunch and early dinner) – Carte £25/55

Not only does Vasco still oversee the kitchen – he keeps a particularly keen eye on the pasta making – but he also likes to help out in the restaurant so he can keep in touch with his regulars, for it is they who have ensured that this institution is still going strong after 40 years. The simply decorated room, closely set tables and matter-of-fact service blend nicely together and there's usually a good mix of customer, including a few tourists, who, by luck or judgement, have stumbled into the right place. The twice daily changing menu is made up of comforting Italian classics but its heart and soul is firmly in Umbria. The presence of Vasco's son will hopefully ensure the future is looking bright for another 40 years.

The Wolseley

Modern cuisine   H4

160 Piccadilly ✉ W1J 9EB
✆ 020 7499 6996
www.thewolseley.com
⊖ Green Park

Closed dinner 24 December
– booking essential

Carte £22/68

The Wolseley didn't take long to earn iconic status, thanks to its stylish décor and celebrity following. Its owners, Chris Corbin and Jeremy King, created a restaurant in the style of a grand European café: all pillars, arches and marble. Open from breakfast until late, the flexible menu offers everything from Austrian and French classics to British staples, so the daily special could be coq au vin or Lancashire hotpot. Pastries come from the Viennoiserie and lunch merges into afternoon tea – so one table could be tucking into Beluga caviar or a dozen oysters while their neighbours enjoy a salt beef sandwich or eggs Benedict. The large clock and swift service are reminders that there are probably people waiting for your table.

Veeraswamy ⌘

I n d i a n H3

Victory House, 99 Regent St (Entrance on
Swallow St.) ✉ W1B 4RS
☎ 020 7734 1401
www.veeraswamy.com
⊖ Piccadilly Circus

Menu £30 (lunch and early dinner) – Carte £40/55 ✗✗

Michelin

If anyone needs an example of somewhere that has never rested
on its laurels, they need look no further than Veeraswamy.
London's oldest surviving Indian restaurant opened in 1926
yet it continues to go from strength to strength, even after 90
years. It's not unreasonable to expect that a restaurant with this
sort of heritage might be a little old-fashioned but it's actually
awash with colour and full of life – as soon as you get out of
the lift, you're aware of the bustle and the vitality. It is also run
with enormous charm by a committed and enthusiastic team –
even when there's a mass exodus in the early evening by those
heading to the theatres they display a reassuring calmness and
control. The really significant improvements, however, have
been in the food. The menu's main focus is on updated classic
dishes from across the country and the genuine care taken by
the kitchen is palpable, whether that's in the freshly made crab
cakes, the succulent lamb chops with a pistachio and almond
crust, or the rich Keralan prawn curry.

First Course	Main Course	Dessert
• Wild tiger prawns, coriander, mint and chilli.	• Pistachio and almond crusted lamb chops.	• Caramelised banana kulfi.
• Smoked chicken tikka with garam masala and mace.	• Steamed fillet of sea bass with lime.	• Almond halwa tart.

Wild Honey

M o d e r n   c u i s i n e   H3

12 St George St. ✉ W1S 2FB
℘ 020 7758 9160
www.wildhoneyrestaurant.co.uk
⊖ Oxford Circus

Closed 25-26 December,
1 January and Sunday

Menu £35 (lunch and early dinner) – Carte £39/60   ✗✗

 Elegant wood panelling, immaculately kept leather seating, ornate plasterwork and a handsome hand-blown chandelier all tell you this is a classic Mayfair institution. There is nothing crusty or old fashioned about it however, because the customers and the personable service team combine to keep the atmosphere enjoyably light and easy-going. The style of food remains the same: the kitchen uses good quality British ingredients and a French base but is not afraid of adding the occasional international flavour; what has become more elusive is the precision with which those dishes are prepared. There are a number of menus available, including a weekend Tasting Menu – the set menu offered represents very good value.

ⓝ Zelman Meats

M e a t s   a n d   g r i l l s   I2

2 St Anne's Ct ✉ W1F 0AZ
℘ 020 7437 0566
www.zelmanmeats.com
⊖ Tottenham Court Rd

Closed bank holidays, dinner
Sunday and lunch Monday

Carte £35/49

You don't build up a couple of successful restaurant chains without recognising an opportunity when you see it. Those clever people behind Goodman and Burger & Lobster noticed a lack of fun, affordable steakhouses and so created Zelman Meats, named after the company boss. It serves three cuts of beef, priced per 100g: picanha (from the rump) and chateaubriand, which are cooked in the open kitchen over charcoal and served sliced, and a wonderfully smoky short rib. Start with oysters or a lovely red prawn ceviche and bear in mind that the side dishes are big enough to share. The prices are certainly reasonable and there are plenty of booths to be had in the dimly lit, semi-industrial space. Two traditional roasts are offered on Sundays.

Yauatcha Soho ✿

Chinese

15 Broadwick St ✉ W1F 0DL
☎ 020 7494 8888
www.yauatcha.com
⊖ Tottenham Court Road

Closed 25 December

Menu £29 (weekday lunch) – Carte £18/61

Yauatcha Soho

No cuisine or style of eating is immune from revolution, due largely to the changing ways we all live our lives. Go to Hong Kong and you'll see that even dim sum is evolving and has come to mean so much more than merely snacks to accompany the daytime drinking of tea. For over 10 years, Yauatcha has always been at the heart of this change and its success is not hard to understand. The food is so good and the surroundings so slick and stylish that customers found it hard to be in and out in their allotted time – so now you can keep hold of your table for a couple of hours. There is also a bar on the ground floor which means you can wait for your table in a little more comfort. Three dim sum per person followed by some noodles or a stir-fry should be enough. Stand-out dishes are the scallop shui mai, prawn cheung fun, the wonderfully light baked venison puff and the Kung Po chicken. Those who prefer something sweet to accompany their Silver Needle white tea can also come for cakes, tarts and pastries during the day. There's now another Yauatcha in The City.

First Course	Main Course	Dessert
• Scallop shui mai.	• Kung pao chicken with cashew nut.	• Chocolate 'pebble'.
• Mushroom spring roll with truffle.	• Steamed Dover sole with black bean sauce.	• Strawberry meringue.

Strand · Covent Garden

It's fitting that Manet's world famous painting 'Bar at the Folies Bergère' should hang in the **Strand** within a champagne cork's throw of theatreland and Covent Garden. This is the area perhaps more than any other which draws in the ticket-buying tourist, eager to grab a good deal on one of the many shows on offer, or eat and drink at fabled landmarks like J.Sheekey or Rules. It's here the names already up in lights shine down on their potential usurpers: celeb wannabes heading for The Ivy, West Street's perennially fashionable restaurant. It's here, too, that Nell Gwyn set up home under the patronage of Charles II, while Oscar Wilde revelled in his success by taking rooms at the Savoy.

The hub of the whole area is the piazza at **Covent Garden,** created by Inigo Jones four hundred years ago. It was given a brash new lease of life in the 1980s after its famed fruit and veg market was pulled up by the roots and re-sown in Battersea. Council bigwigs realised then that 'what we have we hold', and any further redevelopment of the area is banned. Where everyone heads is the impressive covered market, within which a colourful jumble of arts and crafts shops gels with al fresco cafés and classical performers proffering Paganini with your cappuccino. Outside, under the portico of St Paul's church, every type of street performer does a turn for the tourist trade. The best shops in Covent Garden, though, are a few streets north of the market melee,

emanating out like bicycle spokes from Seven Dials.

For those after a more highbrow experience, one of London's best attractions is a hop, skip and *grand jeté* from the market. Around the corner in **Bow Street** is the city's famed home for opera and ballet, where fire – as well as show-stopping performances – has been known to bring the house down. The **Royal Opera House** is now in its third incarnation, and it gets more impressive with each rebuild. The handsome, glass-roofed Paul Hamlyn Hall is a must-see, so enjoy a drink in the Champagne Bar before curtain up or during the interval. At the other end of the Strand the **London Coliseum** offers more opera, this time all performed in English. Down by Waterloo Bridge, art lovers are strongly advised to stop at **Somerset House** and take in one of London's most sublime collections of art at the Courtauld Gallery. This is where you can get up close and personal to Manet's barmaid, as well as an astonishing array of Impressionist masters and twentieth century greats. The icing on the cake is the compact and accessible eighteenth century building that houses the collection: real icing on a real cake can be found in a super little hidden-away café downstairs.

Of a different order altogether is the huge **National Gallery** at Trafalgar Square which houses more than two thousand Western European pieces (it started off with 38). A visit to the modern Sainsbury Wing is rewarded with some

AGE / Photononstop

unmissable works from the Renaissance. It can get just as crowded in the capital's largest Gallery as in the square outside, so a good idea is to wander down **Villiers Street** next to Charing Cross station and breathe the Thames air along the Victoria Embankment. Behind you is the grand Savoy Hotel; for a better view of it, you can head even further away from the crowds on a boat trip from the **Embankment,** complete with on-board entertainment. And if the glory of travel in the capital, albeit on the water, has whetted your appetite for more, then pop into the impressively renovated Transport Museum in Covent Garden piazza, where gloriously preserved tubes, buses and trains from the past put you in a positive frame of mind for the real live working version you'll very probably be tackling later in the day.

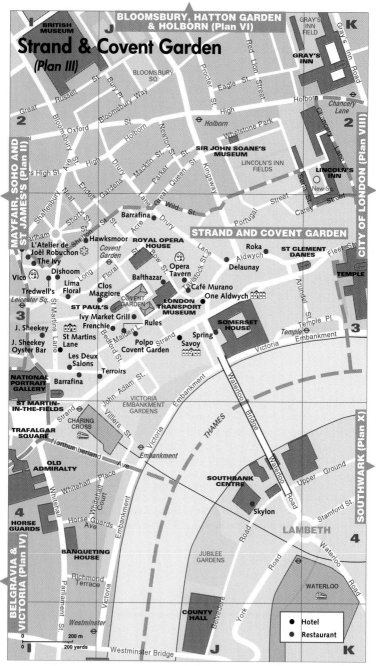

Strand & Covent Garden
(Plan III)

BLOOMSBURY, HATTON GARDEN & HOLBORN (Plan VI)

BRITISH MUSEUM

GRAY'S INN FIELD

GRAY'S INN

BLOOMSBURY SQ.

MAYFAIR, SOHO AND ST JAMES'S (Plan II)

Holborn

Chancery Lane

CITY OF LONDON (Plan VIII)

SIR JOHN SOANE'S MUSEUM

LINCOLN'S INN FIELDS

LINCOLN'S INN

New Sq.

Barrafina

STRAND AND COVENT GARDEN

Hawksmoor

ROYAL OPERA HOUSE

Roka

ST CLEMENT DANES

TEMPLE

L'Atelier de Joël Robuchon

Covent Garden

Delaunay

The Ivy

Opera Tavern

Vico

Dishoom

Balthazar

Café Murano

Lima Floral

Clos Maggiore

One Aldwych

Tredwell's

Leicester Sq.

ST PAUL'S

COVENT GARDEN

LONDON TRANSPORT MUSEUM

SOMERSET HOUSE

Temple Pl.

Temple

Ivy Market Grill

Rules

J. Sheekey

Polpo Covent Garden

Spring

Savoy

J. Sheekey Oyster Bar

St Martins Lane

Les Deux Salons

Terroirs

NATIONAL PORTRAIT GALLERY

Barrafina

VICTORIA EMBANKMENT GARDENS

THAMES

ST MARTIN-IN-THE-FIELDS

CHARING CROSS

TRAFALGAR SQUARE

OLD ADMIRALTY

Embankment

SOUTHBANK CENTRE

LAMBETH

SOUTHWARK (Plan X)

BELGRAVIA & VICTORIA (Plan IV)

HORSE GUARDS

BANQUETING HOUSE

Skylon

WATERLOO

JUBILEE GARDENS

COUNTY HALL

Westminster

Westminster Bridge

● Hotel
● Restaurant

0   200 m
0   200 yards

118

L'Atelier de Joël Robuchon £3

French

13-15 West St. ✉ **WC2H 9NE**
✆ 020 7010 8600
www.joelrobuchon.co.uk
⊖ Leicester Square

Closed 25-26 December,1 January
and August bank holiday Monday

Menu £38 (lunch and early dinner) – Carte £40/90

Michelin

London's L'Atelier de Joël Robuchon differs from his other 'branches' dotted around the world's culinary hotspots by being two restaurants under one roof: on the ground floor is L'Atelier itself, with an open kitchen and large counter; upstairs is the monochrome La Cuisine, a slightly more structured, sleek and brightly-lit affair with table seating. Apart from a few wood-fired dishes upstairs, the menus are largely similar. The cooking is artistic, creative and occasionally playful; it is also technically accomplished and highly labour intensive – there are over thirty chefs in the building – but it is never overworked, and each dish is nicely balanced and its flavours true. French is the predominant influence, with an emphasis on the Mediterranean; ordering a number of smaller dishes is the best way to fully appreciate Robuchon's craft and vision, although your final bill can quite quickly get pretty lofty. Service is well-timed and confident and sitting at the counter will give you further insight into this polished operation.

First Course	Main Course	Dessert
• Egg cocotte carbonara style with black truffle.	• Pyrenean milk-fed lamb cutlets with fresh thyme.	• Praline custard with hazelnut and white coffee ice cream.
• Hot chicken broth with foie gras ravioli and spicy whipped cream.	• John Dory with wild asparagus, tandoori lime emulsion and Timut pepper.	• Chocolate sphere with hazelnut ice cream.

Balthazar

French J3

4-6 Russell St. ✉ WC2B 5HZ
☎ 020 3301 1155
www.balthazarlondon.com
⊖ Covent Garden

Closed 25 December
– booking essential

Menu £18 (weekday lunch) – Carte £27/56

It's not just musicals and plays that transfer between London and New York – the world's two greatest cities now trade in restaurants as well. Balthazar has long been a landmark in Manhattan's SoHo district but now there's a London version occupying the old Theatre Museum in Covent Garden which, thanks to its red leather seats, mosaic floor, mirrors and flattering lighting, will seem uncannily familiar to anyone who knows the original. This being a London copy of a New York copy of a classic Parisian brasserie means that the Franglais menu plays it safe and focuses on reassuringly familiar dishes like moules frites, coq au vin and duck confit. It's open from breakfast onwards; the cocktails are great; and the atmosphere lively and excitable.

Barrafina

Spanish I3

10 Adelaide St ✉ WC2N 4HZ
☎ 020 7440 1456
www.barrafina.co.uk
⊖ Charing Cross

Closed Christmas,
New Year and bank holidays
– bookings not accepted

Carte £14/34

The second Barrafina is not only brighter than the Frith Street original, it's also bigger and, although that doesn't mean the queues are shorter, it does mean you can wait inside with a drink for a couple of the 29 counter seats to become available. Once safely ensconced, order a glass of Manzanilla and some plump olives and set about choosing your tapas. Don't fill up with pan con tomate, good though it is; instead, go for the wonderful crab on toast and try more unusual offerings like ortiguillas, crispy sea anemone, or succulent meats like the suckling pig or the herb-crusted rabbit shoulder. The kitchen's deft touch is also much in evidence with specialities like frit Mallorquin and the crisp monkfish cheeks.

PRACTISE THE ART
of FINE FOOD.

Live in Italian

View the story on youtube.com/SanPellegrinoTV

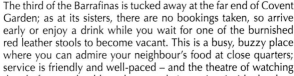

Barrafina

S p a n i s h

43 Drury Ln ✉ WC2B 5AJ
☎ 020 7440 1456
www.barrafina.co.uk
⊖ Covent Garden

Closed bank holidays
– bookings not accepted

Strand • Covent Garden ▶ Plan III

Carte £24/47 🍴

The third of the Barrafinas is tucked away at the far end of Covent Garden; as at its sisters, there are no bookings taken, so arrive early or enjoy a drink while you wait for one of the burnished red leather stools to become vacant. This is a busy, buzzy place where you can admire your neighbour's food at close quarters; service is friendly and well-paced – and the theatre of watching the chefs at work adds to the appeal. A seat just inside the door affords a view of the seafood counter – fresh, vibrantly flavoured fish and shellfish dishes like octopus with paprika and capers or lemon sole cooked on the chargrill are a real highlight here. The menu covers all bases but the tortillas y huevos are another special feature.

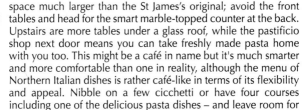

Cafe Murano

I t a l i a n

36 Tavistock St ✉ WC2E 7PB
☎ 020 7240 3654
www.cafemurano.co.uk
⊖ Charing Cross

Closed Sunday dinner

Menu £17 – Carte £31/49 🍴🍴

The second Café Murano is in the heart of Covent Garden, in a space much larger than the St James's original; avoid the front tables and head for the smart marble-topped counter at the back. Upstairs are more tables under a glass roof, while the pastificio shop next door means you can take freshly made pasta home with you too. This might be a café in name but it's much smarter and more comfortable than one in reality, although the menu of Northern Italian dishes is rather café-like in terms of its flexibility and appeal. Nibble on a few cicchetti or have four courses including one of the delicious pasta dishes – and leave room for the Muscavado tart! Everything sounds tempting and it'll only be your purse or your appetite that holds you back.

Clos Maggiore

French J3

33 King St ✉ WC2E 8JD
℡ 020 7379 9696
www.closmaggiore.com
⊖ Leicester Square

Closed 24-25 December

Menu £23 (weekday lunch)/38 – Carte £37/66

A/C

Any West End restaurateurs still half-hearted about pre and post theatre dining should come to Clos Maggiore to see how it can be done: the menu represents excellent value, the kitchen is well organised and the staff get on with the serving, which means the theatregoer doesn't have to keep checking the time. Clos Maggiore is also one of the most romantic restaurants around – just be sure to ask for the table in the enchanting conservatory at the back, with its retractable roof. The chef is from Provence and you can almost smell the lavender when reading his menu. The French dishes are sophisticated in their make-up while the ingredients come mostly from the British Isles. The wine list has great depth and reflects the owner's passion.

Delaunay

Modern cuisine J3

55 Aldwych ✉ WC2B 4BB
℡ 020 7499 8558
www.thedelaunay.com
⊖ Temple

Closed dinner 24 December and
25 December – booking essential

Carte £27/64

A/C

Just like The Wolseley, its hugely successful older sibling, The Delaunay was inspired by the grand cafés of Europe and boasts a similar celebrity clientele, yet this is more than a mere replica. It may have opened in 2011, but the 150-seater dining room manages to evoke the 1920s with all its wood panelling, brass and leather. The menu is also more mittel-European, with great schnitzels and wieners featuring prominently. Daily specials could include daube of beef or fish stew, or you could just come for some eggs or a salad – it's that sort of place. There's a nostalgic element too; you'll find Black Forest gateau, banana split, and even a cover charge. The staff are engaging and swift but never make you feel rushed.

Les Deux Salons

French I3

40-42 William IV St ✉ **WC2N 4DD**
☎ 020 7420 2050
www.lesdeuxsalons.co.uk
⊖ Charing Cross

Closed 25-26 December and
1 January

Menu £17 (early dinner) – Carte £26/70

Sir Terence Conran, a man whose contribution to London's restaurant scene is incalculable, shows no signs of slowing down. Together with his business partner Peter Prescott, he took over this handily-placed site in 2015 and injected a tidy sum into its redesign. The ground floor now comes with a café, bistro, bar and épicerie; while upstairs is home to a more formal restaurant. The influence of the Parisian brasseries and bistros is writ large on the menu, with snails, soups and charcuterie sitting alongside bavette and boudin noir. Upstairs, the ingredients become more luxurious, the service more formal and the prices predictably higher. If you're here early evening, sit in the bistro to take advantage of their great value pre-theatre menu.

Dishoom

Indian I3

12 Upper St Martin's Ln ✉ **WC2H 9FB**
☎ 020 7420 9320
www.dishoom.com
⊖ Leicester Square

Closed 24 December dinner,
25-26 December and 1-2 January
– booking advisable

Carte £13/30

Dishoom is a facsimile of the sort of café that populated Bombay in the early 20th century. They were opened by Persian immigrants and served snacks and specialities that merged the two countries, along with other dishes displaying some colonial influences; and, because they were classless and casteless, they appealed to everyone. That same inclusiveness is evident here in Covent Garden: the place is usually full of everyone from couples to business-types enjoying a table of shared dishes. It's all about ordering as little or as much as you want, whether that's a full breakfast; some baked roti rolls with chai; vada pav – Bombay's version of the chip butty; a curry; or meats cooked on the grill in the open kitchen.

Frenchie

Modern cuisine J3

16 Henrietta St ✉ WC2E 8QH
☏ 020 7836 4422
www.frenchiecoventgarden.com
⊖ Covent Garden

Closed 25-26 December and
1 January – booking advisable

Menu £28 (weekday lunch) – Carte £33/47

The eponymous Frenchie is chef-owner Greg Marchand – the nickname was given to him by Jamie Oliver when he was head chef at Fifteen and is also the name of his original restaurant in Paris' 2nd arrondissement. This time round, the modern-day bistro is in the heart of Covent Garden and split over two levels: the basement, home to the open kitchen, is the more intimate space, but the ground floor, which is dominated by a handsome white marble bar counter, is the better place to sit. Marchand's cooking is informed by his extensive travels, so expect to see ingredients like yuzu, Madras spices and preserved lemons featuring alongside Yorkshire rhubarb and Cornish clotted cream in the adventurous, ambitious dishes.

Hawksmoor

Meats and grills I3

11 Langley St ✉ WC2H 9JG
☏ 020 7420 9390
www.thehawksmoor.com
⊖ Covent Garden

Closed 24-26 December

Menu £25 (weekdays)/28 – Carte £22/60

Impressive renovation work from those clever Hawksmoor people turned this former brewery cellar into a very atmospheric restaurant whose primary function is the serving and eating of red meat – a suitably apt activity as one of the brewery's 18C owners used to host a steak club. You'll get a friendly greeting at the bottom of the stairs and can either eat in the bar or in the large and bustling dining room with its ersatz industrial look. Steaks from Longhorn cattle lovingly reared in North Yorkshire and dry-aged for at least 35 days are the stars of the show. A blackboard shows availability and meat is priced per 100g. But beware as side orders and competitive over-ordering on the size of the cut can push up the final bill.

The Ivy

T r a d i t i o n a l   B r i t i s h I3

9 West St ✉ WC2H 9NE
✆ 020 7836 4751
www.the-ivy.co.uk
⊖ Leicester Square

Closed 25 December

Menu £23 (weekday lunch) – Carte £30/65

The Ivy once had a virtual monopoly as a celebrity hangout but competition is a lot fiercer these days. Add in the fact that the owners had started rolling out Ivy Grills and it was clear something needed to be done with 'head office'. So it closed, everything from its signs to its front doors was sold off as a clever PR stunt, and it re-emerged with a new look in time for its centenary in 2017. The biggest difference is that there's now an oval bar in the centre of the room and gone are the 'Siberia' tables. The menu has also evolved: you can still find the old classics, but now they're accompanied by a few more international choices. The service, from a bevy of personable staff, is as on-the-button as ever.

Ivy Market Grill

T r a d i t i o n a l   B r i t i s h J3

1 Henrietta St ✉ WC2E 8PS
✆ 020 3301 0200
www.theivymarketgrill.com
⊖ Leicester Square

Menu £21 (early dinner) – Carte £25/54

Its heyday may have been in the 1990s but, for us mere mortals, The Ivy is still one of the hardest restaurants at which to get a table. Thanks to the largesse or, more likely, the business acumen of Caprice Holdings, far more people can now share in that Ivy experience by eating here at Ivy Market Grill. The look is smart brasserie de luxe, with a few decorative touches that pay homage to the original. The menu keeps things mostly British with a roll-call of classics; there's also a large Grill section. Breakfast and a roaring trade in afternoon tea keep it busy all day - and as well as a decently priced pre-theatre menu, they also offer shepherd's pie and champagne when the show finishes. There's another even busier branch in Chelsea.

J.Sheekey

S e a f o o d

28-32 St Martin's Ct, ✉ **WC2N 4AL**
✆ 020 7240 2565
www.j-sheekey.co.uk
⊖ Leicester Square

Closed 25-26 December
– booking essential

Menu £24 – Carte £33/69

 XX

Named after the restaurant's first chef who cooked for its then owner Lord Salisbury, J. Sheekey proves that longevity and tradition need not mean old and crusty. It is as fashionable now as it was in 1896 and remains one of the first choices for the theatrical world and those whose business is show. The wood panelling and silver on the tables add to the timeless British feel and service is as charming and efficient as ever. Fish and seafood are handled deftly: the Arbroath smokie and potted shrimps are permanent fixtures and the fish pie and lemon sole are rightly renowned. Avoiding pre and post-theatre times will shorten the odds of your getting a table; ask for 'dining room 4' which is the largest of the five rooms.

J. Sheekey Oyster Bar

S e a f o o d I3

33-34 St Martin's Ct. ✉ **WC2 4AL**
✆ 020 7240 2565
www.j-sheekey.co.uk
⊖ Leicester Square

Closed 25-26 December

Carte £25/41

 Y

 And you can't even see the join. When the opportunity arose for J. Sheekey to expand next door, the obvious decision would have been to extend the restaurant which has, after all, been working well since 1896. Instead, they decided to create this terrific oyster bar – and for that we should all be grateful. There are four or five tables but you're much better off sitting at the bar as you can chat with the chaps behind it and, if you're on the far side, watch the chefs in action. The tablemat doubles as a menu, which offers the same high quality seafood as next door but at slightly lower prices. Along with favourites like oysters and the fish pie, come dishes designed for sharing such as the fruits de mer.

Lima Floral

Peruvian I3

14 Garrick St ✉ **WC2E 9BJ**
✆ 020 7240 5778
www.limalondongroup.com/floral
⊖ Leicester Square

Closed 26-27 December,
2 January, bank holiday Mondays

Menu £18 (weekdays) – Carte £32/48

When your second branch is located this close to the original it needs to do something a little different – and that's what Lima Floral does. For a start, it has a terrific basement Pisco Bar which serves piqueos, or Peruvian tapas, along with an impressive array of cocktails and infusions to get your heart pumping. The colourful restaurant is a little smaller than the original but manages to feel light and airy at lunch and cosy and intimate at dinner. The cooking is also a little different – dishes are a little less refined but more substantial in size, bringing in more regional Peruvian flavours and vibrancy. Don't ignore the side dishes – the cusco corn cake is worth the price of admission alone – or desserts, which are rich and comforting.

Opera Tavern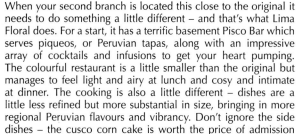

Mediterranean cuisine J3

23 Catherine St. ✉ **WC2B 5JS**
✆ 020 7836 3680
www.operatavern.co.uk
⊖ Covent Garden

Closed 25 December and
1 January

Carte £14/25

That many of its more touristy areas now boast some decent restaurants is testament to London's maturing dining scene. Opera Tavern shares the same appealing concept of small plates of Spanish and Italian delicacies as its sisters, Salt Yard and Dehesa, and occupies a converted old pub dating from 1879, albeit one that's had a complete makeover. If you haven't booked a table in the upstairs dining room then try your luck on the lively ground floor; order 2 or 3 dishes per person and be prepared to share – stand-outs are the Ibérico ham, chorizo with piquillo pepper and crispy squid. The wine list also swings between Spain and Italy and includes some rare and ancient grape varieties. The staff are all reassuringly confident and clued up.

Polpo Covent Garden

I t a l i a n J3

6 Maiden Ln. ✉ WC2E 7NA
✆ 020 7836 8448
www.polpo.co.uk
⊖ Leicester Square

Closed 25-26 December
– (bookings not accepted at
dinner)

Carte £12/21

 After sewing up Soho with their first three restaurants, this clever little group then turned its attention to neighbouring Covent Garden to open this Venetian bacaro. Behind the delicately embroidered linen screens is another shrewdly designed spot, with a tin ceiling imported from New York and church pews contrasting with the ersatz industrial look. It covers two floors – the ground floor is best. Over-ordering is easy, as the small plates are surprisingly filling, with delights such as the wonderfully fresh flavours of white anchovy pizzette vying with fennel and almond salad, fritto misto competing with spaghettini and meatballs. A no-bookings policy after 5.30pm means that there will be queues but turnover is naturally quick.

Roka

J a p a n e s e J3

71 Aldwych ✉ WC2B 4HN
✆ 020 7294 7636
www.rokarestaurant.com
⊖ Temple

Closed 25 December

Menu £27 – Carte £32/58

 The 10th anniversary of the original Roka in Charlotte Street was marked with the opening of this fourth branch, the largest in the group, which sits in the strip of town that separates the West End from The City. The smart interior features a sleek black marble counter running around the robata grill, stained grey timbers on the walls and soft leather seating. All the signature dishes are here, along with a few that are unique to this branch, such as the langoustine and cod cheek skewers, the Wagyu beef tartare and the Hokkaido-style cheesecake. Service is unfailingly attentive – to such a degree that you may have to ask them to slow down the delivery of dishes. Consider the better value tasting menu as it gives you a good all-round experience.

Rules

T r a d i t i o n a l   B r i t i s h   **J3**

35 Maiden Ln ✉ WC2E 7LB
✆ 020 7836 5314
www.rules.co.uk
⊖ Leicester Square

Closed 25-26 December
– booking essential

Carte £36/71

 Some restaurants don't even last 1798 days but Rules opened in 1798, at a time when the French were still revolting, and it has been a bastion of Britishness ever since. Virtually every inch of wall is covered with a cartoon or painting and everyone from Charles Dickens to Buster Keaton has passed through its doors. The first floor is now a bar; time it right and you'll spot some modern-day theatrical luminaries who use it as a Green Room. The hardest decision is whether to choose the game, which comes from their own estate in the Pennines, or one of their celebrated homemade pies. Be sure to leave room for their proper puddings, which come with lashings of custard - no wonder John Bull was such a stout fellow. It makes you proud.

Spring

I t a l i a n   **J3**

New Wing, Somerset House, Strand (Entrance
on Lancaster Pl) ✉ WC2R 1LA
✆ 020 3011 0115
www.springrestaurant.co.uk
⊖ Temple

Closed Sunday dinner
– booking advisable

Menu £28 (lunch)/32 – Carte £40/67

 Spring occupies the 'new wing' of Somerset House which for many years was inhabited by the Inland Revenue – it's hard to believe that this is where taxes were once calculated. The bright room, with its Doric columns, ornate cornicing and arched windows looking towards Waterloo Bridge, now comes with an appealingly feminine feel which is appropriate as the whole operation is under the aegis of Australian-born chef Skye Gyngell, previously of Petersham Nurseries. Her cooking is Italian influenced and led by the ingredients, albeit largely luxury ingredients that come at a price; her menu is written daily and the dishes are without fuss and adornment, which allows the flavours to be the focus.

129

Terroirs

J3

5 William IV St ✉ **WC2N 4DW**
☎ 020 7036 0660
www.terroirswinebar.com
⊖ Charing Cross

Closed 25-26 December,
1 January, Sunday and bank
holidays

Carte £24/37 ✗

Eat in the lively ground floor bistro/wine bar or head down to the more intimate cellar with its bare brick walls and counter; it's the same menu throughout although they also have a blackboard menu downstairs offering sharing dishes like rib of beef for two. Tables down here are a little bigger which makes sharing easier and, despite being two floors down, it is more atmospheric. The flavoursome and satisfying French cooking has added Italian and Spanish influences and the wine list is thoughtfully compiled, varied and well-priced, with many organic and biodynamic choices from artisan producers. Service remains a mixed bag and can be of the headless chicken variety, but the slightly chaotic feel adds to the charm.

Tredwell's

I3

4a Upper St Martin's Ln ✉ **WC2H 9EF**
☎ 020 3764 0840
www.tredwells.com
⊖ Leicester Square

Closed 25-26 December,
1 January and Easter Monday

Menu £25 (lunch and early dinner) – Carte £26/51 ✗

Considering its central location, it's a surprise that Seven Dials hasn't been awash with good restaurants for years – but at least it now has Tredwell's, a modern brasserie courtesy of Marcus Wareing. It's named after the butler in Agatha Christie's 'The Seven Dials Mystery' and one could argue that the dark, sleek look of the place does evoke the art deco period during which the book was written. Cooking is best described as modern English, although the robata grill gets a good workout with steaks from the Lake District and Wales and there is an occasional Mediterranean note too. As you would expect from this stable, dishes show a degree of refinement and a commendable amount of thought has gone into addressing allergen issues.

Ⓝ Vico

Italian   I3

1 Cambridge Circus ✉ WC2H 8PA   Closed 25 December and
☎ 020 7379 0303   1 January
www.eatvico.com
⊖ Leicester Square

Carte £23/40   ✗

    Sister to Bocca di Luppo is this relaxed modern-day trattoria,
    popular with theatregoers, tourists, families and office workers
    alike. Fashioned as an indoor piazza, it has a fountain at its
    centre, cavernous ceilings strung with Edison bulbs and an
    authentic Gelupo ice cream bar which is guaranteed to plaster
    a grin on the face of your inner child. The menu champions
    the cuisine of the Appian Way – the Roman road connecting
    Rome to Brindisi in the heart of southern Italy – and uses the best
    Italian ingredients. This is sunshine food: simply cooked, super-
    fresh and seasonal; generous of portion and vibrant in colour
    and flavour. The all-Italian wine list is nicely priced, with house
    wines available on-tap by the glass, half litre or carafe.

Good quality cooking
at a great price?
Look out for the Bib
Gourmand ⊛.

Belgravia · Victoria

The well-worn cliché 'an area of contrasts' certainly applies to these ill-matched neighbours. To the west, Belgravia equates to fashionable status and elegant, residential calm; to the east, Victoria is a chaotic jumble of backpackers, milling commuters and cheap-and-not-always-so-cheerful hotels. At first sight, you might think there's little to no common ground, but the umbilical cord that unites them is, strange to say, diplomacy and politics. Belgravia's embassies are dotted all around the environs of **Belgrave Square,** while at the furthest end of bustling Victoria Street stands **Parliament Square.**

Belgravia – named after 'beautiful grove' in French - was developed during the nineteenth century by Richard Grosvenor, the second Marquess of Westminster, who employed top architect Thomas Cubitt to come up with something rather fetching for the upper echelons of society. The grandeur of the classical designs has survived for the best part of two centuries, evident in the broad streets and elegant squares, where the rich rub shoulders with the uber-rich beneath the stylish balconies of a consulate or outside a high-end antiques emporium. You can still sample an atmosphere of the village it once was, as long as your idea of a village includes exclusive designer boutiques and even more exclusive mews cottages.

By any stretch of the imagination you'd have trouble thinking of **Victoria** as a village. Its local railway station is one of London's

major hubs and its Coach station brings in visitors from not only all corners of Britain, but Europe too. Its main 'church', concealed behind office blocks, could hardly be described as humble, either: **Westminster Cathedral** is a grand concoction based on Istanbul's Hagia Sophia, with a view from the top of the bell tower which is breathtaking. From there you can pick out other hidden charms of the area: the dramatic headquarters of Channel 4 TV, the revolving sign famously leading into New Scotland Yard, and the neat little Christchurch Gardens, burial site of Colonel Blood, last man to try and steal the Crown Jewels. Slightly easier for the eye to locate are the grand designs of **Westminster Abbey,** crowning glory and resting place of most of England's kings and queens, and the neo-gothic pile of the **Houses of Parliament.** Victoria may be an eclectic mix of people and architectural styles, but its handy position as a kind of epicentre of the Westminster Village makes it a great place for political chit-chat. And the place to go for that is The Speaker, a pub in Great Peter Street, named after the Commons' centuries-old peacekeeper and 'referee'. It's a backstreet gem, where it's not unknown for a big cheese from the House to be filmed over a pint.

Winston Churchill is someone who would have been quite at home holding forth at The Speaker, and half a mile away in King Charles Street, based within the **Cabinet War Rooms** – the secret under-

M. Rellini/Sime/Photononstop

ground HQ of the war effort - is the Churchill Museum, stuffed full of all things Churchillian. However, if your passion is more the easel and the brush, then head down to the river where another great institution of the area, **Tate Britain,** gazes out over the Thames. Standing where the grizzly Millbank Penitentiary once festered, it offers, after the National Gallery, the best collection of historical art in London. There's loads of space for the likes of Turner and Constable, while Hogarth, Gainsborough and Blake are well represented, too. Artists from the modern era are also here, with Freud and Hockney on show, and there are regular installations showcasing upwardly mobile British talent. All of which may give you the taste for a trip east along the river to Tate Modern; this can be done every forty minutes courtesy of the Tate to Tate boat service.

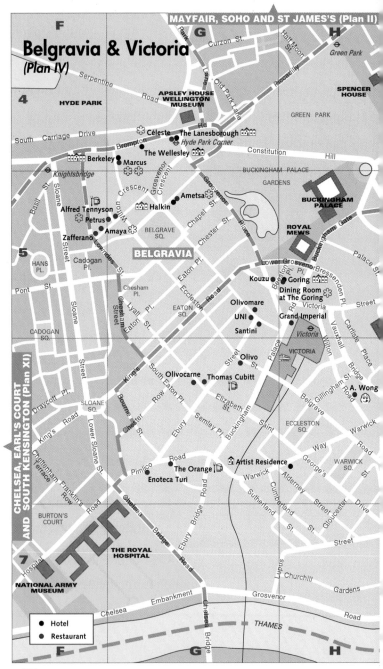

Belgravia & Victoria
(Plan IV)

HYDE PARK

APSLEY HOUSE
WELLINGTON
MUSEUM

SPENCER
HOUSE

GREEN PARK

Céleste   The Lanesborough

Hyde Park Corner

The Wellesley

Berkeley   Marcus

Constitution   Hill

BUCKINGHAM PALACE
GARDENS

BUCKINGHAM
PALACE

Ametsa

Alfred Tennyson
Petrus   Halkin

ROYAL
MEWS

Zafferano

Amaya

BELGRAVE
SQ.

BELGRAVIA

HANS
PL.

Cadogan
Pl.

Chesham
Pl.

Eaton Pl.

Lower Grosvenor Pl.

Kouzu   Goring

Dining Room
at The Goring

Eccleston

Olivomare

UNI

Victoria

Santini

Grand Imperial

VICTORIA

Olivo

EATON
SQ.

Olivocarne   Thomas Cubitt

A. Wong

SLOANE
SQ.

Elizabeth
St.

ECCLESTON
SQ.

WARWICK
SQ.

Artist Residence

The Orange

Enoteca Turi

BURTON'S
COURT

THE ROYAL
HOSPITAL

NATIONAL ARMY
MUSEUM

Chelsea   Embankment

Grosvenor

THAMES

CHELSEA, EARL'S COURT
AND SOUTH KENSINGTON (Plan XI)

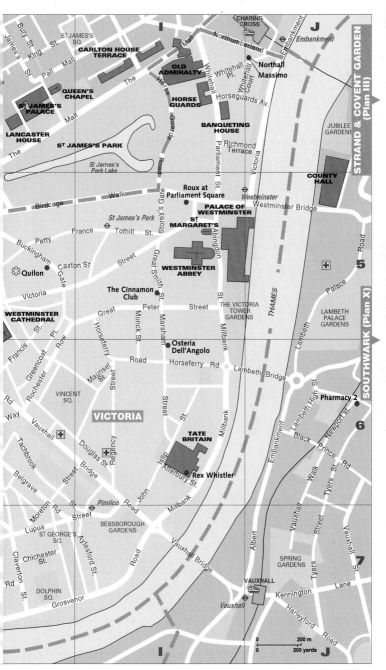

CHARING CROSS

ST JAMES'S SQ.

CARLTON HOUSE TERRACE

Bury St.
James's
King
St.

OLD ADMIRALTY

Pall Mall

The Mall

QUEEN'S CHAPEL

ST JAMES'S PALACE

LANCASTER HOUSE

The Mall

HORSE GUARDS

Horse Guards Road

ST JAMES'S PARK

St James's Park Lake

Northumberland

Whitehall Pl.

Whitehall

Whitehall Court

Northall Massimo

Horseguards Av.

BANQUETING HOUSE

Richmond Terrace

Parliament St.

Victoria

STRAND & COVENT GARDEN (Plan III)

JUBILEE GARDENS

COUNTY HALL

Birdcage Walk

St James's Park

Storey's Gate

Roux at Parliament Square

Westminster

Westminster Bridge

Petty France

Tothill St.

PALACE OF WESTMINSTER

ST MARGARET'S

Abingdon

Buckingham Gate

Caxton St.

Great Smith St.

WESTMINSTER ABBEY

St.

Victoria

Quilon

WESTMINSTER CATHEDRAL

The Cinnamon Club

Great

Peter Street

THE VICTORIA TOWER GARDENS

THAMES

Palace

LAMBETH PALACE GARDENS

5

SOUTHWARK (Plan X)

Francis St.

Greencoat Row

Rochester

Horseferry Row

Monck St.

Marsham

Osteria Dell'Angolo

Horseferry Rd.

Lambeth Bridge

Lambeth

Maunsel St.

Road

Millbank

Vauxhall
Way
Rd

VINCENT SQ.

Street

Street

VICTORIA

St.

Lambeth High St.

Pharmacy 2

Embankment

Newport St.

Black Prince Rd.

6

Tachbrook

Belgrave

Moreton Rd.

Douglas St.

Regency St.

TATE BRITAIN

Islip

Atterbury St.

Millbank

Walk

Tyers St.

Rex Whistler

Lupus

ST GEORGE'S SQ.

Aylesford St.

Pimlico Road

John

Street

Millbank

Vauxhall Bridge

Chichester St.

Clayton

Rd

DOLPHIN SQ.

Grosvenor

BESSBOROUGH GARDENS

Vauxhall Road

Albert Embankment

SPRING GARDENS

Tyers Street

Vauxhall St.

7

VAUXHALL

Vauxhall

Kennington Lane

Harleyford Road

0 ———— 200 m
0 ———— 200 yards

I J

A. Wong

Chinese H6

70 Wilton Rd ⊠ SW1V 1DE
𝒞 020 7828 8931
www.awong.co.uk
⊖ Victoria

Closed 23 December-4 January,
Sunday and Monday lunch
– booking essential

Menu £14 (weekday lunch) – Carte £22/33 ✗

Before taking over the family business, Andrew Wong spent many months travelling through the provinces of China, garnering ideas for his menus. This was obviously time well spent as the restaurant has a huge local following and is regularly packed with people wanting to taste his light, fresh and well-balanced cooking. Lunchtime dim sum is very popular – try the Shanghai steamed dumpling with ginger-infused vinegar. The main menu features all your favourites but if you want the full-on experience then opt for the modern 10 course Taste of China menu; a three hour journey around China, with a focus on the 14 countries that border it. Service is keen, as are the prices. Sit at the counter if you want to see the chefs in action.

The Alfred Tennyson

Modern British G5

10 Motcomb St ⊠ SW1X 8LA
𝒞 020 7730 6074
www.thealfredtennyson.co.uk
⊖ Knightsbridge.

Closed 25 December
– booking advisable

Carte £29/50

What used to be The Pantechnicon is now The Alfred Tennyson; the esteemed Victorian poet who wrote 'The Charge of the Light Brigade' used to live nearby and you feel he would have approved of the parquet floor and leather armchairs that give this cosy pub its clubby feel – although it's a moot point whether he'd enjoy seeing quotations from his work on the backs of the toilet doors! The ground floor is crammed with tables and works on a first-come-first-served basis; upstairs you'll find a more formal, Georgian-style dining room and there's even a top floor cocktail bar – this is Belgravia after all. Classic dishes have light, modern touches, so expect potted smoked mackerel to come with a rhubarb purée or Scottish scallops with a chorizo dressing.

Amaya

I n d i a n   F5

Halkin Arcade, 19 Motcomb St ⊠ SW1X 8JT
✆ 020 7823 1166
www.amaya.biz
⊖ Knightsbridge

Menu £24 (weekday lunch) – Carte £34/70   ✗✗✗

Amaya

Amaya loosely translates as 'without boundaries' and this reflects
both the Indian restaurant's open layout – the kitchen forms part
of the main room – and its desire to attract all types of diner, from
families and friends to business-types and couples. It is this mix
of customer that lends the room its lively atmosphere, helped
along by the noise and aroma of the chefs working on the tawa,
tandoor and sigri grills. Bring an appetite with you and order a
couple of small plates from the first two sections of the menu,
then a main course each and some breads; and don't ignore the
excellent vegetable dishes like calabrese and sweetcorn. The
menu changes regularly but certain popular dishes like grilled
lamb chops, griddled scallops and tandoori black pepper chicken
rarely come off it. Dishes taste as good as they look – and they
look very good indeed. The kitchen takes care to ensure your
meal is nicely paced and vegetarians are equally well looked
after. The waiting staff are helpful and enthusiastic and if you
haven't booked, try the long, communal table.

First Course	Main Course	Dessert
• Flash-grilled rock oysters with coconut and ginger.	• Slow-roasted leg of baby lamb, cumin and garam masala.	• 'Passion in chocolate'.
• Duck tikka with tandoori plum chutney.	• Griddled fillet of sea bass with coconut and herb crust.	• Pistachio and almond kulfi.

Ametsa ❀

Halkin Hotel,
5 Halkin St ✉ SW1X 7DJ
☎ 020 7333 1234
www.comohotels.com/thehalkin
⊖ Hyde Park Corner

Closed 24-26 December,
lunch 31 December, Sunday and
lunch Monday

Menu £28/110 – Carte £58/85   ✗✗✗

A/C

Michelin

Ametsa has matured considerably since opening on the ground
floor of the Halkin hotel in 2013. Service not only comes with
warmth and personality but the staff also display a willingness
to engage with their customers, which is especially important
considering the menu descriptions vary from the economical
to the nebulous. The restaurant's confidence is reflected in
the cooking, with the kitchen secure in its own identity. Juan
Mari and Elena Arzak are behind the restaurant and whilst they
come over regularly to advise and assist, they have always been
keen for Ametsa to find its own feet and not be a facsimile or a
clone of their iconic San Sebastián restaurant. Apart from items
like the Ibérico hams, most of the ingredients used are sourced
from within the British Isles but the flavours, combinations
and colours are typically Basque. There is a wonderful vitality
to the cooking and, whilst the techniques are clever and the
presentation striking, the dishes are very easy to eat and always
manage to satisfy.

First Course	Main Course	Dessert
• Scallops 'at home'.	• Beef fillet with green tomato.	• Orange French toast and spinach.
• Langoustine on bamboo.	• Cod with garlic.	• Roast apple with floral candy.

 ⓝ Céleste ❀

Creative French   G4

The Lanesborough Hotel,
Hyde Park Corner ✉ SW1X 7TA
☏ 020 7259 5599
www.lanesborough.com
⊖ Hyde Park Corner

Menu £29 (lunch) – Carte £42/88   ✗✗✗✗

Michelin

While most restaurants are paring back their interior decoration, the multi-million pound refurbishment of the Lanesborough Hotel gave its light-filled, glass-roofed restaurant a luxurious Regency look, with mirrors, portraits, vast chandeliers, Wedgwood blue friezes and fluted columns. Well-spaced tables are dressed with thick linen; deep armchairs cosset diners, and an army of staff deliver formal, attentive service of the kind you'd expect in a hotel of this stature. Chef Florian Favario is a protégé of Eric Fréchon – head chef of Le Bristol in Paris – who oversees the restaurant. His classic French cuisine is delivered in an original, modern style and the richness of dishes like venison smoked on juniper wood with a civet sauce or chocolate soufflé with pistachio ice cream reflect the opulence of the décor. Ingredients are top-class, cooking well-executed and flavours nicely pronounced. À la carte and tasting menus offer plenty of choice, and vegetarians are well catered for too.

First Course	Main Course	Dessert
• Pan-fried langoustine with wild grains and basil-infused broth.	• Pigeon, petits pois à la Française and potato soufflé.	• Guanaja chocolate with caramelised cashew nut praline and coffee bean ice cream.
• Grilled avocado with spiced guacamole and marinated yellowfin tuna.	• Roast John Dory with spiced green zebra tomatoes and green olives.	• Sugar strawberry with Gariguette mousse and sorbet.

The Cinnamon Club

Indian I5

30-32 Great Smith St ✉ SW1P 3BU
☎ 020 7222 2555
www.cinnamonclub.com
⊖ St James's Park

Closed bank holidays

Menu £26 (lunch) – Carte £31/68

Tourists and locals, politicians and business people – The Cinnamon Club attracts all sorts, which explains why you'll be greeted by that appealing wall of noise enjoyed by many successful restaurants. It certainly makes good use of its surroundings, the listed former Westminster library. You'll be faced with quite a few menus; grab the drinks one first as you'll need time to decide what to eat. The style is quite different from most Indian restaurants, with the somewhat elaborately constructed dishes arriving fully garnished and a separate section of the menu dedicated to sharing plates. Spicing is quite subtle – in fact, any watering of eyes is more likely to be caused by some of the prices. Service is supervised by lots of managers in suits.

Enoteca Turi

Italian G6

87 Pimlico Rd ✉ SW1W 8PU
☎ 020 7730 3663
www.enotecaturi.com
⊖ Sloane Square

Closed 25-26 December,
1 January, Sunday and bank
holiday lunch

Menu £26 (lunch) – Carte £32/54

In 2016 Putney's loss was Pimlico's gain when, after 25 years, Guiseppe and Pamela Turi were forced to find a new home for their Italian restaurant. They took over the site previously home to Tinello, also an Italian restaurant, made it a little lighter and wisely brought their manager Cesare with them – he does an admirable job of looking after all diners, both old and new. The chef has introduced a broader range of influences, with each dish signalling the particular region from which it comes, but what hasn't changed is the classic style of preparation in accord with the principles of the Italian kitchen. The other thing that everyone should be delighted they brought with them is their superb wine list.

Dining Room at The Goring ✿

Traditional British

Goring Hotel,
15 Beeston Pl ✉ SW1W 0JW
✆ 020 7396 9000
www.thegoring.com
⊖ Victoria

Closed Saturday lunch

Menu £45/57

XXX

The Goring

If you've ever wondered what the difference is between a restaurant and a dining room then book a table here. The Goring hotel is a model of British style and understatement and its ground floor dining room the epitome of grace and decorum. Designed by Viscount Linley, it appeals to those who 'like things done properly' and is one of the few places in London for which everyone appears to dress up – but don't come thinking it's going to be stuffy in any way. It is supremely well run; even those who decry tradition will be charmed by the well-choreographed service team and the earnestness with which they undertake their duties. Chef Shay Cooper's menu shows respect for the hotel's reputation for classic British food while also acknowledging that tastes and techniques move on, so there are more modern, lighter options available alongside recognisable old favourites. All the dishes are prepared with equal care and equally superb ingredients, and the skilful kitchen displays an impressive understanding of balance, flavour and texture.

First Course	Main Course	Dessert
• Broth of Cornish squid, plaice and red prawn with roast garlic and saffron.	• Fallow deer with parsnip, mushroom duxelle, glazed faggot and pine nut.	• Caramel cream with sea buckthorn jelly, mandarin sorbet and fresh orange.
• Confit egg yolk with crispy chicken wings, caramelised cauliflower and Ibérico ham.	• Roast cod with deep fried oyster, horseradish, cucumber and parsley oil.	• Eccles cake with Beauvale cheese and apple vinegar.

Grand Imperial

Chinese   **H5**

Grosvenor Hotel, 101 Buckingham Palace Rd

✉ SW1W OSJ

☎ 020 7821 8898

www.grandimperiallondon.com

⊖ Victoria

Closed 25-26 December

Menu £30/60 – Carte £20/71

 ♿
 🅰️🅲

Grand it most certainly is, as this elegant Chinese restaurant is to be found in the impressive surroundings of The Grosvenor Hotel's former ballroom. In fact, in between the pillars and the ornate ceiling, the only indication that this is a Chinese restaurant is the calligraphy on the walls. The Grand Imperial is a collaboration between the hotel owners and a Malaysian restaurant company and specialises in Cantonese cuisine, particularly the version found in Hong Kong. Techniques of steaming and frying are used to great effect with such signature dishes as diced beef steak with black pepper sauce and steamed lobster with Chinese wine and egg white. There is no fusion food here; just authentic flavours and quality ingredients.

The sun's out?
Enjoy eating outside
on the terrace: 🌁.

Kouzu

Belgravia • Victoria ▶ Plan IV

J a p a n e s e   **G5**

21 Grosvenor Gdns ✉ SW1 0BD
📞 020 7730 7043
www.kouzu.co.uk
⊖ Victoria

Closed 24-25 December,
1 January, Saturday lunch and
Sunday

Menu £20 (lunch)/85 – Carte £27/111

 Occupying two floors of an attractive Grade II listed building dating from the 1850s is this modern Japanese restaurant – and you don't have to dig too deep to see where its influences come from. Anyone who has eaten in Zuma or Nobu will not only recognise the style and much of the content of the menu but will also find the fashionable surroundings and gilded, youthful clientele quite familiar. Using a mix of European and Japanese ingredients, the kitchen carefully prepares 'new stream' sashimi, tempura and assorted sushi – although the latter is priced individually and enthusiastic orderers will find their bill soaring northwards. Don't ignore the dishes whose providence is more home-grown, like the lamb chops with spicy miso and the desserts.

Massimo

I t a l i a n   **J4**

Corinthia Hotel,
10 Northumberland Ave. ✉ WC2N 5AE
📞 020 7321 3156
www.corinthia.com/london
⊖ Embankment

Closed Sunday

Menu £30 – Carte £28/57

 David Collins has been responsible for designing some of London's most striking restaurants but few can match the grandeur of Massimo. The huge room is dominated by vast, striped Corinthian columns; beautiful mosaics and plenty of marble augment the feeling of unrelenting luxury, while leather-covered booths add some warmth and comfort to proceedings. Taking up the challenge provided by these surroundings is a kitchen specialising in seafood and while the menu may be written in Italian, the cooking could be considered largely Mediterranean. Dishes are kept fairly classical in influence and relatively simple in make-up, and although the food may not always live up to the splendour of the room, the prices do.

Marcus ✿ ✿

Modern cuisine

Berkeley Hotel,
Wilton Pl ✉ **SW1X 7RL**
☎ 020 7235 1200
www.marcus-wareing.com
⊖ Knightsbridge

Closed Sunday

Menu £49/85

XXXX

Marcus

Anticipation builds as you approach the glamorous Berkeley Hotel, the setting of Marcus Wareing's eponymous flagship. Once inside those expectations are met, if not surpassed, as the restaurant is elegant, stylish and eminently comfortable, with a relaxed feel and professional yet engaging staff – who seem to be hired as much for their personality as their experience and know-how. The man himself also puts in regular appearances and these seem to be much appreciated by his diners, keen to meet one of the judges of MasterChef. Wareing's media profile may have risen over the last few years but it hasn't been at the detriment of his restaurant. Dishes like 'salmon, langoustine, buttermilk and quince' and 'Herdwick lamb, onion and anchovy' are sophisticated and interesting yet come with a refreshing lack of complication; relying on excellent quality ingredients and accurate techniques to deliver intense, well-defined flavours. While the tasting menu showcases the kitchen's talents, the à la carte menu comes with in-built flexibility allowing you to choose 2, 3 or 4 courses.

First Course	Main Course	Dessert
• Salmon with langoustine, buttermilk and quince.	• Herdwick lamb with onion and anchovy.	• Pumpkin custard, maple syrup and passion fruit.
• Roast baby gem with girolles and truffle honey.	• Turbot with wild garlic and shellfish.	• Peanut parfait with raspberry and salted caramel.

Northall

Traditional British J4

Corinthia Hotel,
Whitehall Pl. ✉ WC2N 5AE
℘ 020 7321 3100
www.thenorthall.co.uk
⊖ Embankment

Menu £24/75 – Carte £26/73

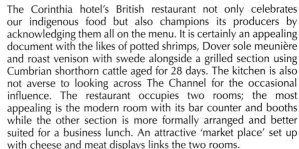

The Corinthia hotel's British restaurant not only celebrates our indigenous food but also champions its producers by acknowledging them all on the menu. It is certainly an appealing document with the likes of potted shrimps, Dover sole meunière and roast venison with swede alongside a grilled section using Cumbrian shorthorn cattle aged for 28 days. The kitchen is also not averse to looking across The Channel for the occasional influence. The restaurant occupies two rooms; the most appealing is the modern room with its bar counter and booths while the other section is more formally arranged and better suited for a business lunch. An attractive 'market place' set up with cheese and meat displays links the two rooms.

Olivo

Italian G6

21 Eccleston St ✉ SW1W 9LX
℘ 020 7730 2505
www.olivorestaurants.com
⊖ Victoria

Closed lunch Saturday-
Sunday and bank holidays
– booking essential

Menu £25 (weekday lunch) – Carte £31/46

The cooking at Olivo has always been highly capable and reassuringly reliable, which does tend to make up for the service, which is never quite as engaging as you hope it will be. Nevertheless this is a popular, pleasant and relaxed little neighbourhood Italian, with vivid blues and yellows, rough wooden floorboards and intimate lighting. The menu showcases the robust flavours of Sardinia and changes fortnightly, although some dishes, such as spaghetti bottarga and linguine with crab, remain permanent features. There are normally a few daily specials – designed with the regulars in mind – and dishes are clearly prepared with care. Desserts continue the regional theme; try sebada, a traditional Sardinian cheese fritter.

Olivocarne

I t a l i a n   **G6**

61 Elizabeth St ✉ SW1W 9PP
☎ 020 7730 7997
www.olivorestaurants.com
⊖ Sloane Square

Menu £25 (weekday lunch) – Carte £30/54

 Mauro Sanno seems to have this part of town sewn up – and here the focus is on meat dishes. This place is smarter, chicer and larger than his others; head up the steps to the brighter section which has a striking mural themed around Sardinian folklore. Regulars at his other establishments will be familiar with the range of tasty, rustic dishes, but here meat is the principle ingredient, from suckling pig to oxtail, and there's a whole section of the menu dedicated to beef. The dishes are delicious and satisfying; none more so than the roast bone marrow with Mirto salt and crostini. Classic Sardinian pasta dishes like lorighittas with duck sauce are also much in demand. Head upstairs first, for a cocktail in Joe's bar.

Olivomare

S e a f o o d   **G5**

10 Lower Belgrave St ✉ SW1W 0LJ   Closed bank holidays
☎ 020 7730 9022
www.olivorestaurants.com
⊖ Victoria

Carte £33/44

 Italian seafood, particularly Sardinian seafood, is celebrated here at Olivomare, a bright and lively restaurant whose design owes as much to Barbarella as it does M.C. Escher. Bottarga naturally features and not just with spaghetti – it also comes with Sardinian artichokes and even burrata. The stews are terrific as are the couscous soups; the octopus, whether in a salad, a stew or just roasted is always worth ordering. For pud the 'gelato allo yoghurt' is good and is just one of the items that can also be bought from their well-stocked deli next door. The wine list is a little limited by the glass but otherwise this is a very warmly run and understandably popular local, where freshness and simplicity combine to great effect.

The Orange

M e d i t e r r a n e a n   c u i s i n e   G6

37 Pimlico Rd ✉ SW1W 8NE
☎ 020 7881 9844
www.theorange.co.uk
⊖ Sloane Square.

Carte £28/40

 The former home of the Orange Brewery is a handsome pub that's as charming as its stucco-fronted façade suggests. The locals will no doubt have filled the bar, where the wood-burning oven is quite a feature, but it's still worth trying your luck to get one of the tables here or in the adjacent room; if you book ahead you'll be upstairs which is just as pleasantly decorated but a little more sedate. There's a clear Mediterranean bias to the menu which also includes plenty of salads along with spelt or wheat-based pizzas which come with some original toppings; there are also roasts on a Sunday and pies for the traditionalists. Unusually for a London pub, there are bedrooms upstairs: these are stylish and comfortable.

Osteria Dell' Angolo

I t a l i a n   I6

47 Marsham St ✉ SW1P 3DR
☎ 020 3268 1077
www.osteriadellangolo.co.uk
⊖ St James's Park

Closed 1-4 January, Easter,
24-28 December, Saturday
lunch, Sunday and bank holidays
– booking essential at lunch

Carte £32/45   ✗✗

 The name may suggest a simple little neighbourhood trattoria but this is, in fact, a rather smart, conscientiously run restaurant offering some authentic, carefully prepared Italian food. As it's opposite the Home Office, lunch is quite a busy time and regulars, who include the odd MP, tend to get the tables on the raised section at the back rather than the less comfortable area by the bar where the Johnny-come-latelys get seated. The kitchen team, visible behind the glass, offer a fairly comprehensive culinary tour of the country's regions and their dishes deliver reassuringly emphatic flavours. There's also a decent selection of wines by the glass for anyone who fears the ignominy of having their expense claims examined.

Pétrus ✿

1 Kinnerton St ✉ SW1X 8EA
✆ 020 7592 1609
www.gordonramsayrestaurants.com/petrus
⊖ Knightsbridge

Closed 21-27 December,
1 January and Sunday

Menu £38/95

Michelin

A seamless transition to a new chef means that the cooking at Pétrus remains as reliable as ever. Regulars, though, will notice a few differences, not least the fact that the dishes are now a little more generously proportioned. The kitchen's influences also occasionally come from slightly further afield, although the cooking still has its roots very much in classical French techniques. What hasn't changed is the wide choice available – as well as the extensive and nicely balanced main menu, there are also tasting and vegetarian options. For anyone who wants to see how it is all done, there's a Chef's Table downstairs in the kitchen facing the pass. For the rest of us, there's a smart, sophisticated and well-dressed room, at the centre of which is a striking circular wine store. Its contents are highly prized as the wine list is superb and includes, appropriately enough, Château Pétrus going back to 1928. Meanwhile, the service is undertaken by a courteous and highly professional team who you'll find are as well groomed as your fellow diners.

First Course	Main Course	Dessert
• Seared Orkney scallop with braised kombu and bacon & egg sabayon.	• Rack of Herdwick lamb with pommes purée, artichoke and wild garlic.	• Coconut parfait with dark chocolate and lime.
• Sautéed foie gras with mead, elderflower and puffed rice.	• Fillet of Brixham turbot with Jersey Royals, morels and wild garlic.	• Gariguette strawberries with pistachio, basil and strawberry ice cream.

Quilon ⍟

St James' Court Hotel,
41 Buckingham Gate ✉ SW1E 6AF
✆ 020 7821 1899
www.quilon.co.uk
⊖ St James's Park

Closed 25 December

Menu £31/60 – Carte £34/67   ✗✗✗

Quilon

Anyone jaded by the generic fare found in many a local Indian restaurant could do with a visit to Quilon – the experience will remind them how fresh, vibrant, colourful and indeed healthy, Indian food can be. This restaurant's great strength is that it focuses largely on just one region of the country, namely the southwest coast. That means lots of fish and a cooking style that eschews oil and butter – a style which, in turn, makes the dishes lighter and easier to eat. That's not to say they don't pack a punch as Chef Sriram Aylur and his team understand how to get the best out of their prime produce and they add their own modern and original touches. They also put equal care into the vegetable dishes: the baby aubergines are excellent and okra, that most maligned of vegetables, is served wonderfully crisp. The set menu, rather than the à la carte, will give you the best and most rounded experience; pescatarians can go for the wholly seafood set menu. The restaurant itself is stylish and comfortable and the service team are bright and enthusiastic.

First Course	Main Course	Dessert
• Lotus stem and colocasia chop with mango and mint.	• Braised lamb shank with freshly ground herbs.	• Creamy vermicelli kheer with rose ice cream.
• Crispy-fried cauliflower with yoghurt, green chilli and curry leaves.	• Lobster with butter, pepper and garlic.	• Baked yoghurt with confit orange, mango and lychee.

Rex Whistler

Traditional British 16

Tate Britain, Millbank ⊠ SW1P 4RG
☎ 020 7887 8825
www.tate.org.uk
⊖ Pimlico

Closed 24-26 December
– (lunch only)

Menu £31

When Tate Britain reopened after its £45million renovation, it wasn't just fans of British art who were pleased to see the return of this Victorian landmark. Its restaurant, Rex Whistler, also benefitted from a facelift – but one that remained loyal to its original look. The most striking element remains Whistler's mural, 'The Expedition in Pursuit of Rare Meats', which envelops the room and was painstakingly restored. A 'food historian' works with the chef to produce a monthly menu that is stoutly British and influenced to a degree by the 1920s, the decade in which the restaurant first opened. However, it is the terrific wine list that really leaves an impression: some of the prices are remarkable and the 'half bottle' selection is unrivalled.

Roux at Parliament Square

Modern cuisine 15

Royal Institution of Chartered Surveyors,
Parliament Sq. ⊠ SW1P 3AD
☎ 020 7334 3737
www.rouxatparliamentsquare.co.uk
⊖ Westminster

Closed Saturday, Sunday and bank
holidays – bookings advisable
at lunch

Menu £35 (weekday lunch)/59

The offices of the Royal Institute of Chartered Surveyors play host to this attractive Westminster restaurant. It's really a Compass-run operation, in conjunction with Michel Roux of Le Gavroche fame. However, instead of the classical French cuisine for which M. Roux is known, here the food is more contemporary in style and adopts some modern techniques. Dishes are still carefully crafted but occasionally you can find some interesting combinations of flavours. The decoration is cool and comfortable, with plenty of natural light flooding through the Georgian windows. Service, from a well-trained team, comes with personality and there is a particularly attractive private dining room in the library.

Santini

Italian G5

29 Ebury St ✉ SW1W 0NZ
✆ 020 7730 4094
www.santinirestaurant.com
⊖ Victoria

Closed 23-26 December,
1 January and Easter

Carte £30/67 ✕✕✕

Despite the high prices within, and the economic challenges without, Santini's loyal and immaculately coiffured customers continue to eschew cheaper alternatives and instead turn up here with impressive regularity. Indeed, it is by looking after its regulars so well for over 30 years that the restaurant has managed to remain largely unruffled by the winds of recession. The menu of classic Italian dishes, broadly Venetian in style, is supplemented by daily specials; the cooking is reliable and confident, while pasta dishes and desserts remain the standout courses. If you are one of the regulars, you'll find yourself not only charmed by the flattery you'll receive, but you'll also be offered their excellent Carasau bread.

Thomas Cubitt

Modern cuisine G6

✉ SW1W 9PA
✆ 020 7730 6060
www.thethomascubitt.co.uk
⊖ Sloane Square.

Booking essential

Carte £29/44

Thomas Cubitt was the master builder behind Eaton and Belgrave Squares so it's appropriate that the pub bearing his name is an unquestionably handsome establishment. Regency and Georgian styles have been combined to good effect, especially in the discreet and surprisingly genteel upstairs dining room, where you'll find an impeccably behaved clientele enjoying a sophisticated menu of quite elaborate constructions that are British at their core. The ground floor, where bookings aren't taken, is more relaxed, more fun and distinctly louder, although on sunny days when the French windows are thrown open, it's hard to get a table. The menu here is more accessible, both in content and price, although some dishes are served on both floors.

UNI

J a p a n e s e

18a Ebury St ✉ SW1W 0LU
☎ 020 7730 9267
www.restaurantuni.com
⊖ Victoria

Carte £27/75

A/C It takes a brave soul to open a restaurant emulating a world-renowned concept like Nobu, but the owner of this sweet little place has done just that. UNI may not have the celebrities or the attendant paparazzi but it does have flavoursome Nikkei cuisine, which fuses the flavours of Japan and Peru; delivering some of the excitement of Nobu but without the high prices. It's small but stylish and is spread across three levels: sit at a table, at the counter or in a cosy cellar alcove. The menu offers everything from gyoza dumplings to ceviche and tiradito, with some excellent tempura, nigiri and maki. The robata grill is used to good effect in fiery dishes like octopus with aji amarillo salsa – and uni unsurprisingly appears on the menu in several forms.

Zafferano

I t a l i a n F5

15 Lowndes St ✉ SW1X 9EY
☎ 020 7235 5800
www.zafferanorestaurant.co.uk
⊖ Knightsbridge

Closed 25 December
– booking essential

Carte £36/79

  It's hard to believe that Zafferano once felt like an intimate little Italian restaurant – over the years it has steadily been expanded and extended and now it's something of a colossus. Fortunately, it all seems to work, proof being in the high number of impeccably dressed regulars that continue to support it. Large tables are easily absorbed without dominating the space; the atmosphere positively hums along; and an army of staff is on hand to ensure no one has to wait too long for their food. The menu concentrates on recognisable, easy-to-eat classics from all parts of Italy and the portions are quite generous, which is just as well because the prices can be pretty steep – even for Belgravia.

Regent's Park · Marylebone

The neighbourhood north of chaotic Oxford Street is actually a rather refined place where shoppers like to venture for the smart boutiques, and where idlers like to saunter for the graceful parkland acres full of rose gardens and quiet corners. In fact, Marylebone and Regent's Park go rather well together, a moneyed village with a wonderful park for its back garden.

Marylebone may now exude a fashionable status, but its history tells a very different tale. Thousands used to come here to watch executions at Tyburn gallows, a six hundred year spectacle that stopped in the late eighteenth century. Tyburn stream was covered over, and the area's modern name came into being as a contraction of St Mary by the Bourne, the parish church. Nowadays the people who flock here come to gaze at less ghoulish sights, though some of the inhabitants of the eternally popular Madame Tussauds deserved no better fate than the gallows. South across the busy Marylebone Road, the preponderance of swish restaurants and snazzy specialist shops announces your arrival at **Marylebone High Street.** There are patisseries, chocolatiers, cheese shops and butchers at every turn, nestling alongside smart places to eat and drink. At St Marylebone Church, each Saturday heralds a posh market called Cabbages & Frocks, where artisan food meets designer clothing in a charming garden. Further down, the century old Daunt Books has been described as London's most beautiful bookshop: it has long oak galleries beneath graceful conservatory skylights. Close by, the quaintly winding Marylebone Lane boasts some truly unique shops like tiny emporium The Button Queen, which sells original Art Deco, Victorian and Edwardian buttons. In complete contrast, just down the road from here is the mighty **Wigmore Hall,** an art nouveau gem with great acoustics and an unerringly top-notch classical agenda that can be appreciated at rock-bottom prices. Meanwhile, art lovers can indulge an eclectic fix at the **Wallace Collection** in **Manchester Square,** where paintings by the likes of Titian and Velazquez rub shoulders with Sevres porcelain and grand Louis XIV furniture.

Regent's Park – an idyllic Georgian oasis stretching off into London's northern suburbs - celebrated its two hundredth birthday in 2011. Before architect John Nash and his sponsor The Prince Regent gave it its much-loved geometric makeover, it had been farming land, and prior to that, one of Henry VIII's hunting grounds. His spirit lives on, in the sense that various activities are catered for, from tennis courts to a running track. And there are animals too, albeit not roaming free, at **London Zoo,** in the park's northerly section. Most people, though, come here to while away an hour or two around the boating lake or amble the Inner Circle which

C. Eymenier / MICHELIN

contains **Queen Mary's Gardens** and their enchanting bowers of fragrant roses. Others come for a summer sojourn to the Open Air Theatre where taking in a performance of 'A Midsummer Night's Dream' is very much *de rigueur*. The Regent's Canal provides another fascinating element to the park. You can follow its peaceful waters along a splendid walk from the **Little Venice** houseboats in the west, past the golden dome of the **London Central Mosque,** and on into the north-west confines of Regent's Park as it snakes through London Zoo, before it heads off towards Camden Lock. On the other side of Prince Albert Road, across from the zoo, the scenic glory takes on another dimension with a climb up Primrose Hill. Named after the grassy promontory that sets it apart from its surrounds, to visitors this is a hill with one of the best panoramas in the whole of London; to locals (ie, actors, pop stars, media darlings and the city set) it's an ultra fashionable place to live with pretty Victorian terraces and accordingly sky-high prices. Either way you look at it (or from it), it's a great place to be on a sunny day with the breeze in your hair.

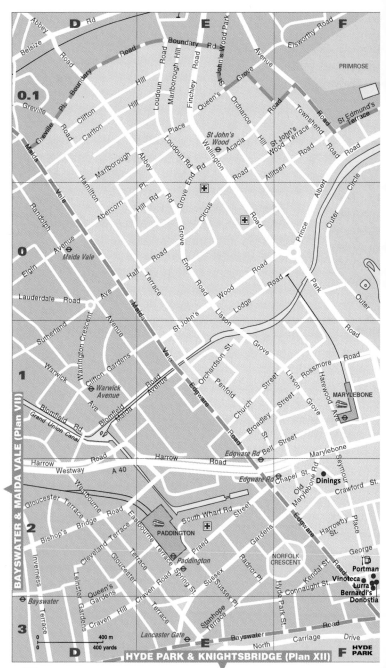

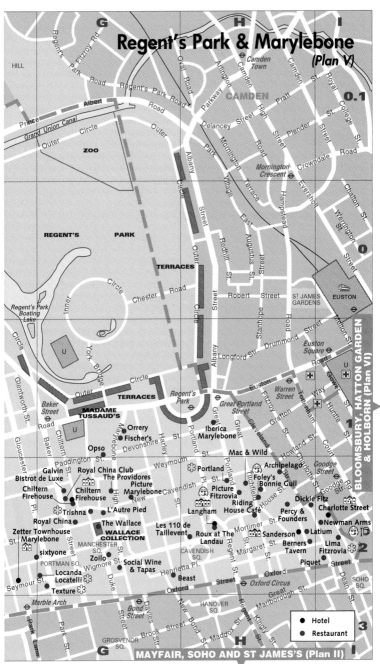

Regent's Park & Marylebone
(Plan V)

HILL

Fitzroy Rd

Regent's Park Road

Albert Road

Prince Albert Road

Grand Union Canal

Outer Circle

ZOO

REGENT'S PARK

TERRACES

Outer Circle

Inner Circle

Chester Road

Regent's Park Boating Lake

York Bridge

Circle

Outer Circle

TERRACES

Circle

Glentworth St.

Baker Street

MADAME TUSSAUD'S

Marylebone Road

Baker Street

Gloucester Place

Chiltern St.

Paddington St.

Orrery's
● Fischer's
Opso

Devonshire St.

Harley St.

Weymouth St.

Galvin Bistrot de Luxe

Royal China Club
The Providores

Chiltern Firehouse

Chiltern Firehouse

Picture Marylebone

New Cavendish St.

Trishna

L'Autre Pied

Royal China

The Wallace

WALLACE COLLECTION

Zetter Townhouse Marylebone

sixtyone

Marylebone Lane

Manchester St.

MANCHESTER SQ.

PORTMAN SQ.

Locanda Locatelli

Zoilo

Wigmore St.

Texture

Social Wine & Tapas

Duke St.

Henrietta Pl.

Beast

Seymour St.

Marble Arch

Bond Street

Davies St.

New Bond Street

GROSVENOR SQ.

Park Lane

Park St.

Brook Str.

HANOVER SQ.

Maddox St.

Iberica Marylebone

Mac & Wild

Portland Pl.

Portland St.

Portland St.

Cleveland St.

Cavendish Pl.

Picture Fitzrovia

Langham

Riding House Café

Les 110 de Taillevent

Roux at The Landau

Mortimer St.

Sanderson

Margaret St.

Regent St.

CAVENDISH SQ.

Oxford Circus

Oxford Street

Great Marlborough St.

Kingly St.

Regent St.

SOHO SQ.

Dean St.

Camden Town

CAMDEN

Parkway

Delancey Street

Mornington Crescent

Arlington Road

Camden High Street

Pratt St.

Plender Street

Crowndale Road

Royal College St.

St. Pancras Way

Mornington Terrace

Park Village East

Albany Street

Redhill St.

Augustus St.

Robert Street

Stanhope St.

Hampstead Road

Drummond Str.

ST JAMES GARDENS

EUSTON

Euston Road

Eversholt Street

Chalton St.

Werrington St.

Euston Square

Gower St.

Warren Street

Grafton Way

Tottenham Court Road

Huntley St.

Great Portland Street

Portland St.

Howland St.

Goodge Street

Goodge St.

Archipelago

Foley's
Bonnie Gull

Charlotte St.

Dickie Fitz

Charlotte Street

Percy & Founders

Newman Arms

Berners St.

Berners Tavern

Latium

Lima Fitzrovia

Piquet

Eastcastle Street

BLOOMSBURY, HATTON GARDEN & HOLBORN (Plan VI)

MAYFAIR, SOHO AND ST JAMES'S (Plan II)

	Legend
●	Hotel
●	Restaurant

Archipelago

Creative H2

53 Cleveland St ⊠ W1T 4JJ
☏ 020 7637 9611
www.archipelago-restaurant.co.uk
⊖ Goodge Street

Closed 24-28 December, Saturday
lunch, Sunday and bank holidays

Carte £32/46

The gloriously oddball Archipelago is unlike any other restaurant in London – its exuberant decoration makes you feel as if you're eating in an eccentric Oriental bazaar which is running out of space and, food wise, it pushes boundaries to the point where tales of your meal could be used to frighten small children. 'Exploring the exotic' is their slogan although 'eating the exotic' would be more exact: with choices like crocodile wrapped in vine leaves, pan-fried chermoula crickets and sweet chilli smoked python carpaccio, the menu reads like an inventory at a safari park. Several dishes are given an Asian twist and side dishes include the 'love-bug salad' made with locusts and crickets – which makes for a memorable experience.

L'Autre Pied

Modern cuisine G2

5-7 Blandford St. ⊠ W1U 3DB
☏ 020 7486 9696
www.lautrepied.co.uk
⊖ Bond Street

Closed 4 days Christmas,
1 January and Sunday dinner

Menu £29/50

It's been a quick 10 years since David Moore opened this more relaxed sibling to his Pied à Terre restaurant, and back in 2007 it was one of the restaurants that helped establish this part of town as a destination for those looking for a night out. This sense of neighbourhood has always been one of its most appealing features, coupled with the easy going atmosphere – ask for one of the window tables around the corner if you want to enjoy this local feel. The European-influenced cooking has always managed to feel contemporary yet without becoming too innovative and unfamiliar. There are a number of menus on offer, including some good value choices at lunch.

Beast

Meats and grills G2

3 Chapel Pl ✉ W1G 0BG
☎ 020 7495 1816
www.beastrestaurant.co.uk
⊖ Bond Street

Closed Sunday, lunch Monday-
Wednesday and bank holidays
– (tasting menu only)

Carte £60/100 ✗✗

  ♿

From the Goodman people, who previously brought us 'Burger and Lobster', comes 'Steak and Crab' – otherwise known as Beast. A full-sized bear welcomes you in; you then head down to an underground banquet hall furnished with three exceedingly long tables set for communal dining. There's a chiller full of USDA imported beef, hung for 30 days, and numerous tanks teeming with live male Norwegian King crabs. Put your bib on (you'll need it) before tucking into starters like Mersea oysters, shrimp tempura or Volzhenka sturgeon caviar. Mains could be a perfectly cooked rib-eye steak or a large platter of succulent, warm King crab – besides which, sides and puddings seem superfluous. Bring a big appetite and a fat wallet.

Bernardi's

Italian F2

62 Seymour St ✉ W1H 5BN
☎ 020 3826 7940
www.bernardis.co.uk
⊖ Marble Arch

Menu £18 (weekday lunch) – Carte £30/42 ✗✗

This modern Italian offers all you might ask of a neighbourhood restaurant: it's chic yet relaxed, with a friendly atmosphere and a firm belief that tables should always be held back for locals; food is fresh and unfussy, and is served all day and all week, so you can pop in for pizzette and prosecco at the sparkly cocktail bar, catch up with a friend over breakfast, or linger over a three course dinner. Brothers Gabriel and Marcello Bernardi are the brains behind the operation and have hired a twice Roux scholarship finalist to run the kitchen. Everything is homemade, using the best quality ingredients possible and dishes like pappardelle with veal and fennel sausage are vibrantly flavoured, with a lightness of touch.

Berners Tavern

Modern British   **H2**

The London Edition Hotel,
10 Berners St ⊠ W1T 3NP
☏ 020 7908 7979
www.bernerstavern.com
⊖ Tottenham Court Road

Menu £25 (lunch) – Carte £34/67   ✗✗

There's nothing like a bit of glamour to see off the monochrome days of austerity and Berners Tavern is certainly one of the most beautiful rooms in London – just don't turn up thinking it's a pub. It's like a grand salon and was the original ballroom of the Berners hotel which has been transformed by Ian Schrager in conjunction with Marriott into the London Edition. Every inch of wall is filled with gilt-framed prints, oils and photographs while the vast ceiling, ornate plasterwork and opulent chandeliers keep many pairs of eyes raised towards the heavens. Jason Atherton, whose empire is expanding faster than a trencherman's waistline, has put together an appealing and accessible menu and the cooking is satisfying and assured.

Bonnie Gull

Seafood   **H2**

21a Foley St ⊠ W1W 6DS   Closed 25 December-2 January
☏ 020 7436 0921   – booking essential
www.bonniegull.com
⊖ Goodge Street

Carte £22/44   ✗

The very sweet Bonnie Gull calls itself a 'seafood shack' – a reference perhaps to its modest beginnings as a pop-up before it docked permanently here in the West End. It's kitted out in a pretty fishing-village kind of way and the tables are packed into the small room in an appropriately sardine-like manner. There's a decent raw bar to kick things off, offering oysters and cockles, winkles and whelks. The main menu is a mix of traditional favourites and more ambitious dishes, although the kitchen appears to be more adept at the former. Many go for the fish and chips but you can also get a decent Cullen skink and a huge Devon cock crab; it's also worth getting a side order of chunky chips cooked in beef dripping.

Chiltern Firehouse

World cuisine   G2

Chiltern Firehouse Hotel,
1 Chiltern St ✉ WIU 7PA
℘ 020 7073 7676
www.chilternfirehouse.com
⊖ Baker Street

Carte £37/65

What could be more appropriate than one of the hottest tickets in town being a converted fire station? Everyone from Prime Ministers to pop stars have been papped on their way into this New York style brasserie, their smiles revealing the relief they feel in having secured a reservation. A wall of sound hits you as you enter and the room positively bursts with energy, but what makes this celebrity hangout unusual is that the food is good. The kitchen is overseen by Nuno Mendes and he has used all his experience working in North and South America to create a clever menu full of vibrant and flavoursome dishes. If you're more interested in checking out the cooking rather than your fellow diners, ask to sit at the kitchen counter.

Good quality cooking
at a great price?
Look out for the Bib
Gourmand ⊛.

Dickie Fitz

M o d e r n   c u i s i n e H2

48 Newman St ✉ W1T 1QQ
✆ 020 3667 1445
www.dickiefitz.co.uk
⊖ Goodge Street

Closed Sunday dinner and bank
holiday mondays

Carte £25/46

What was 48 Newman Street has become Dickie Fitz; its memorable moniker coming courtesy of the owner, Richard Fulford-Smith, and the area in which the restaurant is situated (Fitzrovia). In its previous guise, this was a classic Victorian corner pub; now its light-filled interior is brightly decorated, with granite-topped tables, canary-yellow banquettes and a striking glass-panelled, art deco inspired staircase. Cooking is full of flavour and originality, with a subtle mix of Australian, Pacific and Asian influences. Menus take you through from breakfast until dinner, with bottomless weekend brunches proving popular. Service manages to be laid-back yet also consummately professional; ask staff to recommend one of their Aussie cocktails.

Dinings

J a p a n e s e F2

22 Harcourt St. ✉ W1H 4HH
✆ 020 7723 0666
www.dinings.co.uk
⊖ Edgware Road

Closed Christmas
– booking essential

Carte £24/57

In Tokyo the hanging sign outside would be considered positively flamboyant but in London it's the very definition of discretion, making this sweet little place easy to miss. There are half a dozen seats at the counter on the ground floor and a few tables downstairs in the somewhat claustrophobic basement; but wherever you sit, it's hard not to be charmed by it all. The menu is a very extensive document, supplemented by blackboard specials, and takes many of its influences from the style of Japanese food found at Nobu, the owner's alma mater: accordingly, highlights are the more creative dishes like the 'sashimi four ways'. The temptation is to order plenty to share but beware because the prices can make this an expensive activity.

Donostia

B a s q u e F2

10 Seymour Pl ✉ W1H 7ND
📞 020 3620 1845
www.donostia.co.uk
⊖ Marble Arch

Closed Christmas, Easter and
Monday lunch

Carte £10/37 ✗

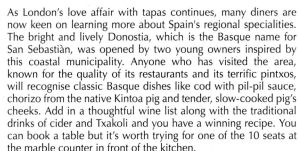 As London's love affair with tapas continues, many diners are now keen on learning more about Spain's regional specialities. The bright and lively Donostia, which is the Basque name for San Sebastiàn, was opened by two young owners inspired by this coastal municipality. Anyone who has visited the area, known for the quality of its restaurants and its terrific pintxos, will recognise classic Basque dishes like cod with pil-pil sauce, chorizo from the native Kintoa pig and tender, slow-cooked pig's cheeks. Add in a thoughtful wine list along with the traditional drinks of cider and Txakoli and you have a winning recipe. You can book a table but it's worth trying for one of the 10 seats at the marble counter in front of the kitchen.

Fischer's

 A u s t r i a n G1

50 Marylebone High St ✉ W1U 5HN
📞 020 7466 5501
www.fischers.co.uk
⊖ Baker Street

Closed 24-25 December and
1 January

Carte £29/47 ✗✗

 There appears to be no end to the number of restaurants being opened by Chris Corbin and Jeremy King. Following the success of The Wolseley et al, they took over a site in Marylebone where others have recently struggled, and opened a stylish Austrian café and konditorei that summons up the spirit of old Vienna. It stays open from 8 until late, with breakfast possibly being the best time to visit – the Viennoiserie are made in-house and are as good as they look. The main menu is a comprehensive document, supplemented by a mittel-European wine list with an impressive choice available by the glass. The schnitzels are first rate – do upgrade to a Holstein – and save room for desserts like the poppy seed parfait.

N Foley's

World cuisine   **H2**

23 Foley St ☒ W1W 6DU
☏ 020 3137 1302
www.foleysrestaurant.co.uk
⊖ Goodge Street

Closed Sunday
– booking advisable

Carte £23/30   ✗

Mitz Vora, former sous chef at Palomar, has brought his vibrant, original cooking to foodie Fitzrovia. Cosy up in one of the intimate ground floor booths or head downstairs to the engine room of this lively restaurant, with its busy open kitchen and counter seating, and its barrel-vaulted caves for six. The fresh, flavourful small plates reflect the international spice trail so your sweet potato fritters come with grilled pineapple, jalapeño yoghurt and saffron coconut sauce and your pork belly with tamarind, apple, green papaya, red onions and cashews. Although you will want to order more, 3 or 4 dishes will suffice – but hold back, because desserts include baklava cheesecake, and homemade spiced milk chocolate with banana doughnuts.

Galvin Bistrot de Luxe

French   **G2**

66 Baker St. ☒ W1U 7DJ
☏ 020 7935 4007
www.galvinrestaurants.com
⊖ Baker Street

Closed dinner 24 December-
26 December and 1 January

Menu £22/24 (weekdays) – Carte £33/55   ✗✗

Despite the great success of Galvin La Chapelle in The City, brothers Chris and Jeff Galvin have never taken their eyes off the ball here at their eponymous Bistrot de Luxe. Regulars still flock here for the clubby, relaxed atmosphere and the traditional French food, which may look simple on the plate but is carefully constructed behind the scenes. The emphasis is very much on flavour; the kitchen's understanding and appreciation of ingredients, and the classic combinations in which they are used, really come through. The menu has enough variety to satisfy those happy to indulge but those with one eye on the cost should come for lunch or before 7pm to take advantage of the fixed price menu. An elegant basement cocktail bar adds to the comfy feel.

Iberica Marylebone

Spanish H1

195 Great Portland St ✉ W1W 5PS
☏ 020 7636 8650
www.ibericarestaurants.com
⊖ Great Portland Street

Closed 24-26 December, Sunday
dinner and bank holidays

Menu £22 (weekday dinner) – Carte £14/46

 The original Iberica at the top end of Great Portland Street is a sizeable space spread over two floors and comes divided into assorted areas, so instead of taking the table you're offered, politely ask if you can wander around first – some prefer the intimacy and the sedate pace of upstairs, others the bustle of the ground floor with its bar and deli. Along with an impressive array of Iberico hams, cured meats and cheeses are plenty of tapas style dishes to share. Highlights include the more filling dishes such as glossy black rice with cuttlefish and prawns and a slowly braised beef cheek; if you go for the speciality Spanish omelette, you'll be asked if you'd prefer it medium or well done! Charming young staff are on hand to offer advice.

Latium

Italian H2

21 Berners St. ✉ W1T 3LP
☏ 020 7323 9123
www.latiumrestaurant.com
⊖ Oxford Circus

Closed 25-26 December,
1 January and lunch Saturday-
Sunday

Menu £21 (weekdays) – Carte £28/42

 This Italian stalwart is tucked away discreetly in foodie Fitzrovia; still with a loyal following, but lighter and less formal than in previous years – and all the better for it. Tables by the entrance are given away first but it's worth asking to be seated further in; you'll almost certainly be accommodated as staff are a friendly and considerate bunch. The menu focuses on Lazio but travels the length of Italy for inspiration. A generous welcome comes in the form of freshly baked focaccia, carta di musica, cheese and olives; 'fatto a casa' is their motto and fresh pasta, their speciality. There's a window into the kitchen for those who like to know where their food comes from, and a chef's table for those who want to watch them at it.

Lima Fitzrovia ✿

31 Rathbone Pl ✉ W1T 1JH
✆ 020 3002 2640
www.limalondongroup.com/fitzrovia
⊖ Goodge Street

Closed Monday lunch
and bank holidays

Menu £25 (lunch and early dinner) – Carte £41/53   ✗

Michelin

Lima Fitzrovia is one of those restaurants that just makes you feel good about life – and that's even without the Pisco Sours which, to be honest, will get you in the mood for anything. Peruvian food is the ideal antidote to times of austerity: it's full of punchy, invigorating flavours and fantastically vivid colours. Virgilio Martinez, who runs the acclaimed 'Central' restaurant in Lima, has created somewhere intimate, informal and fun in which to enjoy his refreshing and exciting cuisine. The menu may be awash with unfamiliar ingredients like tiger's milk and sacha inchi oil but the staff are more than willing to offer help. Most ingredients are from the UK but some are from small suppliers in Peru such as potatoes 4000 metres' (a reference to the altitude rather than the depth at which these tubers are grown). Tiradito and its cousin ceviche are popular starters (the former being a slightly punchier version) and there is plenty of originality throughout the menu along with some playfulness, but there's also great skill.

First Course	Main Course	Dessert
• Braised octopus with purple corn and Botija olives.	• Beef with yellow potato purée and cow's milk.	• Dulce de leche ice cream with bee pollen.
• Artichoke with red potato, avocado, passion fruit, achiote and crazy pea.	• Seared black cod with camu camu, Cuzco corn and palm heart.	• Chirimoya parfait with Amazonian chocolate and blue potato crisps.

Locanda Locatelli

I t a l i a n   **G2**

8 Seymour St. ⊠ W1H 7JZ
✆ 020 7935 9088
www.locandalocatelli.com
⊖ Marble Arch

Closed 25-26 December
and 1 January

Carte £37/63   XXX

Michelin

A few minutes in the company of Giorgio Locatelli, whether face
to face or through the medium of television, reveals a man who
is passionate about Italian food and it is that very passion that
has kept Locanda Locatelli at the top for so long. The restaurant
may be into its second decade but, despite having to close for a
few months in 2015 following a gas explosion in the kitchen, it
still looks as dapper as ever and remains in the premier league
of London's most fashionable addresses. The layout and style
of the room were clearly designed with conviviality in mind
and this is further helped along by service that is smooth but
never intrusive. The other reason for its enduring popularity is
the great food and the consistency that the kitchen maintains.
The hugely appealing menu covers many of the regions of Italy
and provides plenty of choice for everyone including coeliacs,
as the terrific pasta dishes available include gluten-free options.
Unfussy presentation and superlative ingredients allow natural
flavours to shine through.

First Course	Main Course	Dessert
• Pan-fried scallops with celeriac purée and saffron vinaigrette.	• Cornish red mullet wrapped in Parma ham with fennel and tomato sauce.	• Gorgonzola panna cotta, chocolate crumble, pear foam and honey ice cream.
• Orecchiette with peas and pork belly.	• Roast breast of guinea fowl, glazed carrots, liver crostino and black truffle.	• Cannoli with orange sauce.

Lurra

B a s q u e   **F2**

9 Seymour Pl ✉ W1H 5BA
☎ 020 7724 4545
www.lurra.co.uk
⊖ Marble Arch

Closed Monday lunch
and Sunday dinner

Carte £25/65   ✗✗

🏠
A/C
≣

Sister to Donostia just over the road, comes Lurra – again inspired
by its owners' love of the Basque Country; its name meaning
'land' to reflect their use of the freshest produce, cooked over
the sort of charcoal grill that's common in the region. There's
an open kitchen with counter dining; an über-cool, Scandic-
style room which opens onto a courtyard – and a buzz of
contentment throughout. They have gained a reputation for the
quality of their beef – 14 year old Galician cow aged for at least
45 days – and sell it by weight, as they do their whole grilled
turbot. Slow-cooked shoulder of lamb completes the triumvirate
of large sharing plates; the rest of the dishes are mostly 'picoteo'
or nibbles, with the fries with paprika and aioli a must-try.

Is breakfast
included? If it is,
the cup symbol ☕
appears after the
number of rooms.

Mac & Wild

Scottish

H2

65 Great Tichfield St ✉ W1W 7PS

Closed Sunday dinner

℘ 020 7637 0510

www.macandwild.com

⊖ Oxford Circus

Carte £23/50

✗

[A/C] The warm welcome, the upbeat soundtrack and the rustic-looking interior all make this one of those restaurants where you instantly feel that you're in for a good time. The owner is the son of a Highland butcher and after selling his family's produce in London, had a few 'pop-ups' before setting up home here. He's called it a 'Highland restaurant' which makes complete sense when you see the menu – it is all about their wild venison and top quality game and seafood from Scotland, with the provenance of all produce listed, including the names of the fishermen's boats! Don't miss the 'wee plates' like the deliriously addictive haggis pops. There's also a choice of over 100 whiskies, along with suggested whisky pairings for each dish.

 Newman Arms

Modern British

I2

23 Rathbone St ✉ W1T 1NG

Closed 24-26 December

℘ 020 3643 6285

and bank holidays

www.newmanarmspub.com

⊖ Goodge St

Menu £15 (weekday lunch) – Carte £26/39

Matt Chatfield, a farmer's son from Launceston, is fiercely proud of all the wonderful produce his home county has to offer and has spent several years creating a network to supply some of the best restaurants in London; in turn, creating jobs for Cornish folk. This charming Georgian pub – a one-time haunt of Dylan Thomas – is the latest to benefit, and this time it's Matt himself who's the owner. Downstairs is a real boozer, great for a pie and a pint, but the quaint wood-panelled upstairs room is where most of the eating happens; ask for one of the window tables. The menu may be short but every ingredient is super-fresh, often arriving from the sea or field within 24 hours. Beef and lamb are the stars – along with fish from the day boats.

ⓃLes 110 de Taillevent

French H2

16 Cavendish Sq ✉ W1G 9DD
☏ 020 3141 6016
www.les-110-taillevent-london.com
⊖ Oxford Circus

Closed 7-29 August, 25 December
and 1 January

Menu £30 – Carte £35/67

Les 110 de Taillevent is the latest restaurant to bring a slice of Paris to London; the original, named after the 14C chef believed by many to have written the first cookbook, is somewhat of an institution. 110 refers to the number of wines they offer by the glass; that is, 4 different wine pairings for each dish on the menu, in 4 different price brackets. With choices like pâté en croûte, turbot meunière or rib of beef with béarnaise sauce, dishes are firmly in the French vein; they don't serve bread unless you ask for it and mains come unadorned so you will need to buy a side dish or two. Bottle green furnishings reflect the brasserie's raison d'être, and ornate high ceilings combine with deep green banquettes to create a stylish, elegant space.

Opso

Greek G1

10 Paddington St ✉ W1U 5QL
☏ 020 7487 5088
www.opso.co.uk
⊖ Baker Street

Closed 23 December-3 January
and Sunday dinner

Menu £15 (weekday lunch) – Carte £17/45

Andreas, a Greek national, created this modern Greek restaurant with a little help from the team behind Athens' Funky Gourmet restaurant. It has proved a good fit for the neighbourhood – and not just because it's around the corner from the Hellenic Centre. You can start the day here with cakes or granola yoghurt before enjoying what they describe as 'social style dining': small sharing plates that mix the modern with the traditional. Many of the ingredients are imported from Greece and the vividly coloured dishes are satisfying and easy to eat. The narrow room is bright and intimate, and a young team keep the atmosphere animated; if you're coming in a larger group ask for one of the semi-private booths downstairs.

Orrery

Modern cuisine   **G1**

55 Marylebone High St ✉ W1U 5RB   Booking essential
𝄞 020 7616 8000
www.orrery-restaurant.co.uk
⊖ Regent's Park

Menu £30/55   XXX

Enthusiastic post-prandial shopping can be a perilously expensive pastime – the danger is doubled here as Orrery is perched temptingly above a Conran shop. These are actually converted stables from the 19C but, such is the elegance and style of the building, you'd never know. What is sure is the long, narrow restaurant looks its best when the daylight floods in; on warm days make time to have a drink on the terrific rooftop terrace. To complement these charming surroundings you'll be offered a bewildering array of menus, all of which feature quite elaborate, modern European cooking. Dishes are strong on presentation and there is the occasional twist but it's usually done with some meaning rather than merely straining for effect.

Percy & Founders

Modern cuisine   **H2**

1 Pearson Sq, (off Mortimer St) ✉ W1T 3BF
𝄞 020 3761 0200
www.percyandfounders.co.uk
⊖ Goodge Street

Carte £25/49   XX

Where Middlesex hospital once stood is now a residential development that includes this all-day operation which is regarded by its owners as the prototype for a new breed of pub. Named after Hugh Percy, the architect of the former teaching hospital, it is a distinctly smart affair but in looks it's perhaps more akin to a modern brasserie, with a comfortable cocktail lounge attached. The menu is kept quite short and seasonal and the kitchen brings quite a refined touch, although it also likes to inject a little playfulness now and then. It all kick-offs first thing with breakfast, and bar snacks are served in the lounge during the day. As the neighbourhood develops this could become a useful local dining spot.

Picture Fitzrovia

Modern British H2

110 Great Portland St. ✉ W1W 6PQ
☎ 020 7637 7892
www.picturerestaurant.co.uk
⊖ Oxford Circus

Closed Sunday and bank holidays

Menu £45 – Carte £24/37 🍴

Two chefs and a manager, who all made their reputations at Arbutus and Wild Honey, set out on their own in 2013 and opened this terrific place in an underdeveloped part of Central London. The look may be a little stark – there's a large counter at the front fashioned out of recycled flooring and tables at the back beneath a skylight – but the service team add enormous warmth to the place and their enthusiasm is palpable. What was saved on the decoration was clearly spent on the shiny kitchen downstairs, and it's paying dividends for these very skilful chefs. The small plates are vibrant, fresh and colourful; the flavours are assured and the contrasting textures a delight. And at these prices, Picture deserves success.

Picture Marylebone

Modern British G2

19 New Cavendish St ✉ W1G 9TZ
☎ 020 7935 0058
www.picturerestaurant.co.uk
⊖ Bond Street

Closed Sunday and bank holidays

Menu £22 (lunch) – Carte £27/37 🍴

Three years after launching their first restaurant, this young trio decided it was time to create a second. The two places might only be five minutes apart but following the success of their first venture, this smaller sister hit the ground running. The great value lunch menu changes daily and offers a choice of 3 or 4 courses, and there's a cleverly created à la carte of small plates which are divided into 3 vegetable, 3 fish and 3 meat choices, followed by 3 desserts – choose one from each section. Dishes are full of flavour and may include ravioli of caramelised onions with peas, broad beans and lettuce, cod with corn, chorizo and Paris brown mushrooms or warm almond cake with apricot and frozen lemon and thyme yoghurt.

Piquet

92-94 Newman St ✉ **W1T 3EZ**
✆ 020 3826 4500
www.piquet-restaurant.co.uk
⊖ Tottenham Court Rd

Closed 25-26 December,
1-2 January and Sunday dinner

Menu £24 – Carte £29/59

Elegantly dressed, with dark wood panelling, parquet flooring and vintage chairs, this basement bistro feels as if it's been here for years, and betrays no hint of its former life as a subterranean garage. Enjoy a pre-prandial cocktail or two upstairs in the Fir Room, where a Dameon Priestly painting evokes the area's promiscuous heritage. France meets Britain on the appealing daily menu, with classic French dishes made from the finest British produce, including much from Kent; snails for the pithivier come from Littlebourne, the oysters are from Colchester – and the berries may even have been foraged by the chef. Don't be fooled by the understated descriptions: portions are generous and pack a flavoursome punch.

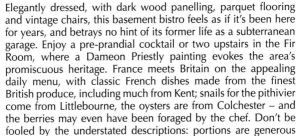 Portman

M o d e r n   c u i s i n e   F2

51 Upper Berkeley St ✉ **W1H 7QW**
✆ 020 7723 8996
www.theportmanmarylebone.com
⊖ Marble Arch.

Carte £25/48

When it went by the name of The Masons Arms this pub was widely known for its gruesome history. It was here that the condemned, on their way to Tyburn Tree gallows, would take their last drink, which purportedly led to the phrase "one for the road". Reincarnated as the Portman, the pub these days boasts a less disreputable clientele who are more attracted by the quality of the cooking. Food is served all day and you can choose to eat in the busy ground floor bar or in the unexpectedly formal upstairs dining room, all thick-pile carpet and starched tablecloths. Fortunately, the style of food remains thoroughly down-to-earth and satisfying and is accompanied by a well-organised wine list and an interesting selection of cocktails.

Portland ✿

113 Great Portland St ✉ W1W 6QQ
℘ 020 7436 3261
www.portlandrestaurant.co.uk
⊖ Great Portland Street

Closed Sunday
– booking essential

Carte £35/52   ✗

Portland

Two friends, Will Lander – co-owner of Quality Chop House – and Daniel Morgenthau of 10 Greek Street fame, have created one of those restaurants that you warm to immediately because its exudes honesty. The look of the room may be somewhere between pared down and austere but the open kitchen adds some colour and the atmosphere is welcoming and intimate. Their young chef, who came from In De Wulf restaurant in Belgium, proves to be the perfect fit. One glance at his daily menu and you know you're in for a good meal – the combinations of ingredients just sound right together. Start with snacks like wonderfully crisp pig's head croquette, before diving into perfectly cooked venison with pearl barley or turbot with white asparagus. The food is unfussy yet there is depth and real understanding here – quite an achievement for such a young team; the concise wine list and its 'single bottle' list contains some real gems. The economics of running such a relatively small restaurant mean that you're not encouraged to linger too long at your table, but you'll want to return soon anyway.

First Course	Main Course	Dessert
• Celeriac and grain risotto, scorched cod cheek and nettle sauce.	• Cornish monkfish with courgette, preserved lemon and almond.	• Steamed chocolate & ale cake, beer caramel and barley ice cream.
• Chargrilled duck hearts with girolles and sweet corn.	• Middle White pig with charred baby onions and peach.	• Raspberry, crème fraîche, lychee and meringue.

The Providores

Creative G2

109 Marylebone High St. ✉ W1U 4RX Closed 25-26 December
✆ 020 7935 6175
www.theprovidores.co.uk
⊖ Bond Street

Menu £34 (dinner) – Carte £35/49

'Marylebone Village' offers so many restaurants and cafés that it's becoming a destination in itself. Included in the roll call is this fusion restaurant within a former Edwardian pub. The warmth of the staff and the general buzz hit you immediately in the ground floor Tapa Room, where tables and tapas are shared. Upstairs is a slightly more sedate room but the staff are equally charming. Here all dishes come in starter size to "minimise food envy" and allow for sharing; three courses plus a dessert should suffice. There is no doubting the originality or the quality of the ingredients, but sometimes there's a flavour or two too many on the plate. The wine list champions New Zealand. Bookings are needed upstairs; downstairs, it's first-come-first-served.

Riding House Café

Modern cuisine H2

43-51 Great Titchfield St ✉ W1W 7PQ Closed 25-26 December
✆ 020 7927 0840
www.ridinghousecafe.co.uk
⊖ Oxford Circus

Carte £23/41

For their third project, the owners of The Garrison and Village East ventured uptown, albeit to an area hitherto untroubled by the presence of decent restaurants. It's less a café, more an all-day Manhattan-style brasserie and cocktail bar, with some charming touches of quirky design. You turn left for the restaurant but it's more fun in the main section where you can't book – either at a counter facing the kitchen or on a large refectory table where you rub shoulders with strangers. It's the same menu throughout, starting with breakfast and followed by a choice of small plates, along with more straightforward main courses like steaks or burgers. Stick with the small plates, which have a bit more zing to them, but be careful not to over-order.

Roux at The Landau

French H2

Langham Hotel,
1c Portland Pl., Regent St. ✉ W1B 1JA
☎ 020 7636 1000
www.rouxatthelandau.com
⊖ Oxford Circus

Closed Saturday lunch and
Sunday

Menu £39 – Carte £43/79

It does have its own street entrance but it's best to enter this grand, oval-shaped restaurant from the hotel, as you don't often get the chance to walk through a 'wine corridor'. The hotel brought in the considerable experience of the Roux organisation – which means Albert and Michel Jr – to add vigour and ambition to the operation. Classical, French-influenced cooking is the order of the day but one can detect the emergence of a lighter style of cuisine with the odd twist. The restaurant is also sensible enough to keep its more traditionally minded regulars happy by ensuring that their favourites, like grilled Dover Sole, remain constants. The daily special from the trolley goes down well with the busy lunchtime corporates.

Royal China

Chinese G2

24-26 Baker St ✉ W1U 7AB
☎ 020 7487 4688
www.royalchinagroup.co.uk
⊖ Baker Street

Menu £30 (lunch)/38 – Carte £20/74

It could be just as at home in Hong Kong's Wanchai or Central districts but, as it is, Royal China sits very comfortably in Baker Street. The large kitchen is staffed exclusively by Chinese chefs, including the early rising dim sum chef, who is responsible for the specialities served between midday and 5pm each day. The Cantonese dishes are strong on aroma and colour and, while the restaurant does not sell a great deal of seafood due to a lack of tank space, the lobster dishes remain some of the more popular choices. However, it is the barbecued meats, assorted soups, stir-fries and the choice of over 40 different types of dim sum that draw the large groups and ensure that this branch of the Royal China group remains as bustling as ever.

Royal China Club

Chinese G2

40-42 Baker St ✉ W1U 7AJ
☎ 020 7486 3898
www.royalchinagroup.co.uk
⊖ Baker Street

Closed 25-27 December

Regent's Park • Marylebone ▶ Plan V

Carte £32/70

'The Club' is the glittering bauble in the Royal China chain but along with the luxurious feel of the room comes an appealing sense of intimacy and calm. The service helps in this regard, as the staff are personable, offer sound advice and seem able to anticipate their customers' needs. At first glance the menu appears similar to the other branches but it soon becomes apparent that the ingredients here are from the luxurious end of the spectrum, especially when it comes to seafood – just check out the large tanks, holding everything from crabs and lobsters to eels and sea bass. The best time to come is for lunch and their very good dim sum. At dinner, look out for the Cantonese dishes and the chef's seasonal specials.

sixtyone

Modern British G2

Montcalm Hotel, 61 Upper Berkeley St ✉ W1H 7TW
☎ 020 7958 3222
www.montcalm.co.uk
⊖ Marble Arch

Closed Sunday and Monday

Menu £25 (lunch and early dinner) – Carte £33/84

A joint venture between chef Arnaud Stevens and Searcy's and occupying space leased from the Montcalm hotel, sixtyone is a modern, smoothly run operation in a useful central location. The light-filled, crisply furnished room, with its mirrored columns and eye-catching ceiling display of hanging copper tubes, comes with a certain style and a degree of elegance. The interesting modern menu is British in base and clearly much thought went into its construction; it also gives the impression that it was designed to allow the kitchen to show off its full repertoire of techniques and its lightness of touch. Dishes like mackerel with pickled vegetables or pork belly with wasabi and smoked rib broth show originality and are at times quite playful.

Social Wine & Tapas

Mediterranean cuisine   **G2**

39 James St ✉ W1U 1DL
✆ 020 7993 3257
www.socialwineandtapas.com
⊖ Bond Street

Closed bank holidays
– bookings not accepted

Menu £20 (lunch) – Carte £15/36

The word 'social' lets you know that this is a Jason Atherton venture; the rest of the name tells you what it does. There's wine – lots of it – stored on-view over the two floors, with sommeliers on hand to guide your choices. And then there's tapas to accompany your wine: a mix of Spanish and Mediterranean dishes with some Atherton classics for good measure; sent out by the chefs behind the counter, as and when they're ready. They get very busy and don't take bookings so arrive either at 6pm before the rush or at 9pm after it, and head for the cosy, moodily lit basement. 3 or 4 dishes per person, plus a ham or cheese platter is about the right amount – and make sure you save room for a dessert, like their rather tasty version of a crema Catalana.

Vinoteca

Modern cuisine   **F2**

15 Seymour Pl. ✉ W1H 5BD
✆ 020 7724 7288
www.vinoteca.co.uk
⊖ Marble Arch

Closed Christmas, bank holidays
and Sunday dinner
– booking advisable

Menu £16 (weekday lunch) – Carte £21/36

They transferred the winning formula from their Clerkenwell original, so expect a great selection of wines, gutsy and wholesome cooking, young and enthusiastic staff and almost certainly a wait for a table. One side of the room is given over to shelves of wine; not only is the selection immeasurably appealing but the staff display both a knowledge and, more importantly, enormous enthusiasm when giving advice - there is even a daily wine tasting. The daily changing menu takes its cue from the sunnier parts of Europe and includes thoughtfully compiled salads and good charcuterie. There are also some firmly British dishes too, like mutton and oyster pie, and each one comes with a suggested wine pairing.

Texture ✿

C r e a t i v e   **G2**

34 Portman St ✉ **W1H 7BY**
☎ 020 7224 0028
www.texture-restaurant.co.uk
⊖ **Marble Arch**

Closed first 2 weeks August,
1 week Easter, Christmas-New
Year, Sunday and Monday

Menu £29/85 – Carte £50/84   ✕✕

Texture

Chef-owner Agnar Sverrisson has steadily gone about creating an exceedingly good restaurant. The Champagne Bar at the front has become a destination in itself and is separated from the restaurant by a large cabinet so you never feel too detached from it. The high ceilings add a little grandeur to the place and the service is very pleasant, with staff all willing and ready with a smile. Agnar's cooking is a little less showy than when Texture opened in 2007 and is all the better for that; you feel he's now cooking the food he wants to cook rather than the food he thought he should be cooking. Iceland is his country of birth so it is no surprise to find lamb, cod (whose crisp skin is served with drinks), langoustine and skyr, the dairy product that nourished the Vikings; the bread, and the olive oils, are very good too. There's considerable technical skill and depth to the cooking but dishes still appear light and refreshing and, since the use of cream and butter is largely restricted to the desserts, you even feel they're doing you good.

First Course	Main Course	Dessert
• Norwegian King crab with coconut, ginger, lime leaf and lemongrass.	• Black Angus rib-eye with ox cheek, horseradish and olive oil béarnaise.	• Icelandic skyr with vanilla ice cream, rye breadcrumbs and Yorkshire rhubarb.
• Quail with sweetcorn, bacon popcorn and red wine essence.	• Lightly salted Icelandic cod with avocado, tomatoes and chorizo.	• White chocolate with dill and cucumber.

Trishna

I n d i a n   **G2**

15-17 Blandford St. ✉ W1U 3DG
☎ 020 7935 5624
www.trishnalondon.com
⊖ Baker Street

Closed 25-27 December and
1-3 January

Menu £35 (lunch) – Carte £26/46

Trishna

They may have opened Gymkhana but the owners haven't
forgotten about Trishna, their first restaurant. It is dressed in
an elegant, understated style, with the coast of southwest India
providing the kitchen with most of its influences. The menu is
full of appealing dishes, ranging from the playful – try their own
mini version of 'fish and chips' as a starter – to the original; the
succulent guinea fowl comes with lentils, fennel seed and star
anise. However, the undoubted star of the show is a version
of the dish made famous by the original Trishna in Mumbai:
brown crab, in this case from Dorset, comes with lots of butter
and a little kick of wild garlic; it is so wondrously rich no man
alone can finish a bowl, and you'll be licking your lips for days
afterwards. The various tasting menus offered often provide the
most rounded experience but all the dishes are as fresh tasting as
they are colourful. Wine is taken seriously too and much thought
has gone into matching wines, with recommendations next to
each dish.

First Course

- Aloo shakarkandi chaat.
- Baby squid with raw rice, coconut and lemongrass.

Main Course

- Bream with green chilli, coriander and smoked tomato kachumber.
- Guinea fowl seekh kebab with curry leaf oil and sprout chaat.

Dessert

- Kheer with cardamom, fig, raisin and pistachio.
- Baked yoghurt with kumquats and pepper biscuit.

The Wallace

Modern British

Hertford House, Manchester Sq ✉ W1U 3BN
✆ 020 7563 9505
www.peytonandbyrne.co.uk/the-wallace-restaurant/index.html
⊖ Bond Street

Closed 24-26 December – (lunch only and dinner Friday-Saturday)

Menu £23 – Carte £31/48 ✗✗

The Wallace Collection of 18 and 19C decorative art is one of London's finest, if lesser known museums and is found within Sir Richard and Lady Wallace's former home, Hertford House. Go through the French windows in what was once the dining room of this imposing mansion and you'll find yourself in a vast, glass-roofed courtyard. Turn left into the café for healthy salads and home-baked cakes; head right into the restaurant for a menu of modern British dishes like pan-fried lemon sole with shrimps and caper butter or roasted rump of lamb with celery, feta and onion. With its indoor trees and comfy sofas, there's a sedate, restful feel to the restaurant, and service remains smooth and unruffled, even when the crowds descend.

Zoilo

Argentinian G2

9 Duke St. ✉ W1U 3EG
✆ 020 7486 9699
www.zoilo.co.uk
⊖ Bond Street

Menu £10 (weekdays) – Carte £20/46 ✗

Zoilo focuses on Argentina's regional specialities; it's also all about sharing so plonk yourself down at the counter and order away. Typical dishes include braised pig head croquettes with apricot jam or grilled scallops with sweet potato, caramelised pork belly and chorizo. The beef is predictably good but why not try grilled sweetbreads with lemon instead? The ground floor is the livelier of the two but if you want to know how it's all done then sit downstairs in front of the open kitchen. Throw in an appealing all-Argentinian wine list and it's easy to see why London is in the grip of a South American love affair.

Bloomsbury ·
Hatton Garden · Holborn

A real sense of history pervades this central chunk of London. From the great collection of antiquities in the British Museum to the barristers who swarm around the Royal Courts of Justice and Lincoln's Inn; from the haunts of Charles Dickens to the oldest Catholic church in Britain, the streets here are dotted with rich reminders of the past. Hatton Garden's fame as the city's diamond and jewellery centre goes back to Elizabethan times while, of a more recent vintage, Bloomsbury was home to the notorious Group (or Set) who, championed by Virginia Woolf, took on the world of art and literature in the 1920s.

A full-on encounter with **Holborn** is, initially, a shock to the system. Coming up from the tube, you'll find this is where main traffic arteries collide and a rugby scrum regularly ensues. Fear not, though; the relative calm of London's largest square, part-flanked by two quirky and intriguing museums, is just round the corner. The square is **Lincoln's Inn Fields,** which boasts a canopy of characterful oak trees and a set of tennis courts. On its north side is **Sir John Soane's Museum,** a gloriously eccentric place with over forty thousand exhibits where the walls open out like cabinets to reveal paintings by Turner and Canaletto. On its south side, the Hunterian Museum, is a fascinating repository of medical bits and pieces. Visitors with a Damien Hirst take on life will revel in the likes of animal digestive systems in formaldehyde, or perhaps the sight of half of mathematician Charles Babbage's brain. Others not so fascinated by the gory might flee to the haunting silence of **St Etheldreda's church** in Ely Place, the only surviving example of thirteenth-century Gothic architecture in London. It survived the Great Fire of 1666, and Latin is still the language of choice.

Contemplation of a different kind takes centre stage in the adjacent **Hatton Garden.** This involves eager-eyed couples gazing at the glittering displays of rings and jewellery that have been lighting up the shop fronts here for many generations, ever since the leafy lane and its smart garden environs took the fancy of Sir Christopher Hatton, a favourite of Elizabeth I. After gawping at the baubles, there's liquid refreshment on hand at one of London's most atmospheric old pubs, the tiny Ye Old Mitre hidden down a narrow passageway. The preserved trunk of a cherry tree stands in the front bar, and, by all accounts, Elizabeth I danced the maypole round it (a legend that always seems more believable after the second pint).

Bloomsbury has intellectual connotations, and not just because of the writers and artists who frequented its townhouses in the twenties. This is where the University of London has its headquarters, and it's also home to the **British Museum,** the vast treasure trove of international artefacts that

C. Eymenier / MICHELIN

attracts visitors in even vaster numbers. As if the exhibits themselves weren't lure enough, there's also the fantastic glass-roofed Great Court, opened to much fanfare at the start of the Millennium, which lays claim to being the largest covered public square in Europe. To the north of here by the Euston Road is the **British Library,** a rather stark red brick building that holds over 150 million items and is one of the greatest centres of knowledge in the world. Meanwhile, Dickens fans should make for the north east corner of Bloomsbury for the great man's museum in **Doughty Street:** this is one of many London houses in which he lived, but it's the only one still standing. He lived here for three years, and it proved a fruitful base, resulting in Nicholas Nickleby and Oliver Twist. The museum holds manuscripts, letters and Dickens' writing desk. If your appetite for the written word has been truly whetted, then a good tip is to head back west half a mile to immerse yourself in the bookshops of Great Russell Street.

Edmonton Public Library
Stanley A. Milner (Downtown)
Express Check #5

Customer ID: **********3775

Items that you checked out

Title: Origin : a novel
ID: 31221118060214
Due: January-19-18

Title:
 London 2017 : a selection of the best
 restaurants & hotels
ID: 31221116925251
Due: February-02-18

Total items: 2
Account balance: $0.00
January-12-18 3:19 PM
Checked out: 2
Overdue: 0
Hold requests: 1
Ready for pickup: 0

Thank you for visiting the Edmonton
Public Library

www.epl.ca

Anglo

Creative British　　　　　　　　　　　　　　K2

30 St Cross St ✉ ECIN 8UH
☎ 020 7430 1503
www.anglorestaurant.com
⊖ Farringdon

Closed 22 December-17 January,
Saturday lunch, Sunday and
Monday

Menu £45 (dinner) – Carte lunch £35/48　　　　　

As its name suggests, British produce is the mainstay of the menu at this pared-down, personally run restaurant, and these 'home-grown' ingredients are often served in creative rather than conventional ways. Lunch offers a concise à la carte, which gives a preview of what's to come at dinner; the well-paced 7 course tasting menu served in the evening delivers colourful dishes whose appearance is as vibrant as their taste. Cooking is confidently executed, with assured, harmonious flavours. Dishes might include cod with smoked potato and sea fennel or Swaledale lamb with lettuce and spruce, while desserts take recognisable ingredients and serve them in fresh new ways. The chefs bring dishes to the table and are happy to stop and chat.

 # Barbary

World cuisine　　　　　　　　　　　　　　I3

16 Neal's Yard ✉ WC2H 9DP
www.thebarbary.co.uk
⊖ Covent Garden

Closed 25-26 December and
Monday – bookings not accepted

Carte £22/37　　　　　　　　　　　　　　

 The team behind Palomar have opened this sultry, atmospheric restaurant at the entrance to Neal's Yard. It's a tiny place with 24 non-bookable seats squeezed around a horseshoe-shaped, zinc-topped counter – all the cooking takes place here and the chefs are happy to chat as they work. The menu of small sharing plates takes in dishes from the former Barbary Coast. Start with freshly baked naan, Jerusalem bagel and dips before moving onto wholesome, richly flavoured dishes from Land, Sea and Earth. There is grilling over the coals, baking in the clay oven and some raw dishes too, with tahini, harissa and ras el hanout adding depth. Service is keen, as are the prices; impressive given that they don't impose a service charge and water is free.

Barnyard

T r a d i t i o n a l   B r i t i s h   I2

18 Charlotte St ⊠ W1T 2LZ
☎ 020 7580 3842
www.barnyard-london.com
⊖ Goodge Street

Closed 25-26 December
– bookings not accepted

Menu £21 (lunch) – Carte £17/32   ✗

'Dude food' prepared with integrity draws the crowds to this fun little place co-owned by Ollie Dabbous. It ticks all the boxes demanded by your average hipster, from its look which mixes ersatz industrial distress with picket-fence Americana to its appealing menu of dishes divided up by animal. The food arrives all at once on enamel plates, and dishes are full of rustic goodness, whether that's a sausage roll, crispy chicken or simply lard on toast – they may seem simple but there's a care and precision to them one rarely sees in similarly styled restaurants. You won't exactly lose weight eating here but you will certainly leave feeling better about life. Just be prepared to queue, as it seats fewer than 50.

Barrica

S p a n i s h   H2

62 Goodge St ⊠ W1T 4NE
☎ 020 7436 9448
www.barrica.co.uk
⊖ Goodge Street

Closed 25-26 December,
1 January, Sunday and bank
holidays – booking essential

Carte £19/36   ✗

Staff at this lively little tapas bar all appear to be Spanish so perhaps it's national pride that makes them run it with a passion lacking in many of their competitors. They make a concerted effort to look after their diners, of whom there are always many, so it's worth booking ahead unless you're okay squeezing onto a seat at the counter. When it comes to the food, authenticity is high on the agenda and it's hard to avoid temptation. A couple of standouts are lamb chop with romesco sauce, and smoked duck breast with cherry butter; it's worth ordering another savoury dish or one of their Spanish cheeses in place of dessert. They also offer an interesting selection of around 20 sherries and assorted Spanish wines – try one from the blackboard.

Cigala

Spanish

54 Lamb's Conduit St. ⊠ WC1N 3LW
✆ 020 7405 1717
www.cigala.co.uk
⊖ Russell Square

Closed 25-26 December,
1 January, Easter Sunday and
Easter Monday – booking
essential

Menu £24 (weekdays) – Carte £26/39

Cigala may be more restaurant than bar but it was serving authentic Spanish food when all those fashionable little tapas bars were still in short pantalones. The reason for its longevity is that it gives the punters exactly what they want: an extensive menu that regularly changes but also recognises that some dishes must remain perennials, and a lively and convivial atmosphere. The owner personally seeks out producers in Spain and this care is particularly evident in the dried hams, which are a must. Chicken livers in sherry and salt cod fritters are always winners and it's well worth waiting the 30 minutes for a paella. Staff are approachable and it's wise to heed their counsel on what and how much to order.

Bloomsbury • Hatton Garden • Holborn ▲ Plan VI

Drakes Tabanco

Spanish

3 Windmill St ⊠ W1T 2HY
✆ 020 7637 9388
www.drakestabanco.com
⊖ Goodge Street

Closed Sunday and bank holidays

Carte £22/34

Taking advantage of London's newfound fondness for fino is this simple tabanco, courtesy of the people behind nearby Barrica and Copita and named after Sir Francis in honour of the booty of butts he returned home with. Typical of Jerez, these taverns' unique feature is that they serve sherry straight from the barrel using a venencia; order a glass of Rare Old India or Oloroso and you'll wonder why you haven't been drinking sherry for years. The small, Andalusian-inspired tapas menu uses imported produce from Spain alongside British ingredients. Truffled goat's cheese and the pork and oxtail meatballs are musts, as is the board of charcuterie. They even do a tasting menu with a different sherry matched to each course.

Dabbous ❀

39 Whitfield St ✉ W1T 2SF
📞 020 7323 1544
www.dabbous.co.uk
⊖ Goodge Street

Closed 10 days Christmas-
New Year, Easter and Sunday
– booking essential

Menu £28/59

Michelin

The look is stark, dark and ersatz-industrial and, as owner chef
Ollie Dabbous admits, "the only luxurious thing in this place is
the food". Once you've managed to get a table, simply follow the
majority of customers by going for the tasting menu and you'll
be rewarded with seven courses of thrilling culinary magic (at
lunch there's also a short à la carte menu). Visually stunning,
the dishes deliver clean, fresh and distinctive flavours: some
creations come with clever modern twists; others owe more to
classical combinations. However, this is not a kitchen that relies
on trickery or technique to create an effect – there is a sublime
purity to the cooking here, along with a certain restraint too –
and that's what makes the food so easy to eat. There may be a
hard edge to the room but it is not without some charm. The staff
help enormously in this regard, providing service that is evenly
paced, very knowledgeable and refreshingly devoid of arrogance
or conceit. Dabbous remains as busy as ever – and it's very easy
to see why.

First Course	Main Course	Dessert
• Peas with mint.	• Braised turbot with lemon verbena.	• Cherry blossom tea-soaked barley flour sponge with Tahitian vanilla cream.
• Burrata with wild strawberries and fennel pollen.	• Pulled veal breast with white asparagus and summer truffle.	• Blackcurrant leaf ice cream.

Flesh & Buns

A s i a n 13

41 Earlham St ✉ WC2H 9LX
☏ 020 7632 9500
www.fleshandbuns.com
⊖ Leicester Square

Closed 24-25 December
– booking advisable

Menu £19 (lunch and early dinner) – Carte £21/47 ✗

Hot on the heels of the successful ramen shop Bone Daddies comes another hip joint where Japanese and Asian influences are refracted through the prism of New York. This time it's a loud, fun, subterranean spot next to the Donmar, occupying what was previously a micro-brewery. You can expect sashimi, rolls, teriyaki and tempura but star billing, as the slightly unappetising name of the place suggests, quite rightly goes to the hirata bun – the soft little Taiwanese-style steamed pillows of delight that sandwich your choice of meat or fish filling and come with a dipping sauce. Add to the equation communal tables, cocktails, beers and an easy to navigate wine and sake list and you have all the makings of a fun night out with friends.

Great Queen Street

M o d e r n   B r i t i s h J2

32 Great Queen St ✉ WC2B 5AA
☏ 020 7242 0622
www.greatqueenstreetrestaurant.co.uk
⊖ Holborn

Closed Christmas-New Year,
Sunday dinner and bank holidays
– booking essential

Menu £22 (weekday lunch) – Carte £21/38 ✗

This is a great restaurant to choose on a cold winter's night, thanks to its friendly welcome, its bustling atmosphere and its heartwarming food. Its popularity does mean that service can sometimes need a prompt but there is no doubting the staff's enthusiasm for the food they serve. The menu descriptions are unapologetically concise but then dishes come equally unembellished. There's little difference between what constitutes a starter or main course and there's always a daily special or two. Highlights are the shared dishes such as the suet-crusted chicken pie or the seven hour shoulder of lamb, but offal is also done very well. The wine list is thoughtfully put together – and the 'Worker's Lunch' is a steal.

Hakkasan Hanway Place ✿

Chinese 12

8 Hanway Pl. ✉ W1T 1HD
℘ 020 7927 7000
www.hakkasan.com
⊖ Tottenham Court Road

Closed 24-25 December

Menu £38/128 – Carte £32/94

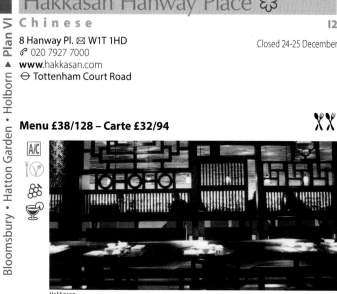

Hakkasan

Over recent years Hakkasans have opened in many cities around the world but it all started here in 2001 in this unexceptional alleyway just off Tottenham Court Road. Thanks to its sensual looks, air of exclusivity and glamorous atmosphere – characteristics now synonymous with the brand – the original Hakkasan wowed London back then and, judging by the crowds, continues to do so today. The restaurant has always managed the art of coping equally well with all types of customers, from large parties out to celebrate to couples on a date, and the well-organised and helpful staff are a fundamental part of that success. Lunchtime dim sum here is a memorable and more relaxed experience; at dinner try the Signature menus which represent better value than the à la carte. Thanks to the brigade of about twenty chefs in the kitchen, the Cantonese specialities are prepared with care and consistency; dishes are exquisitely presented and while there are moments of inventiveness they never come at the expense of flavour.

First Course	Main Course	Dessert
• Dim sum platter.	• Roasted duck with black truffle sauce.	• Jivara bomb.
• Stir-fried wild mushrooms with water chestnut lettuce wrap.	• Spicy prawns with dried chilli and cashews.	• Vanilla-baked yoghurt with pineapple and ginger palmier biscuit.

Honey & Co

World cuisine   **H1**

25a Warren St ✉ **W1T 5LZ**
☏ 020 7388 6175
www.honeyandco.co.uk
⊖ Warren Street

Closed 25-26 December
and Sunday – booking essential

Bloomsbury • Hatton Garden ▲ Holborn ▲ Plan VI

Menu £30 – Carte £25/31   ✗

When Itamar and Sarit decided to open their own place they did so knowing that they didn't have to worry too much about the kitchen – they'd both been head chefs at Ottolenghi restaurants. The philosophy at their sweet little café is to offer the same sort of food and hospitality you'd get if you were guests in their home. The friendly girls certainly provide charming, chatty and tactile service and the cooking is full of freshness and colour. The influences stretch beyond Israel to the wider Middle East; start by sharing some mezze, follow with roasted baby chicken or delicious lamb shawarma. Breads are great, cakes are hard to resist and the prices are commendable – which is another reason why the place is packed most evenings.

Lady Ottoline

Traditional British   **J1**

11a Northington St ✉ **WC1N 2JF**
☏ 020 7831 0008
www.theladyottoline.com
⊖ Chancery Lane.

Closed bank holidays

Carte £26/43

A charming traditional feel and a keen sense of history have always defined this classic Victorian pub – and a change in ownership appears to have had little effect, which is good news for its many regulars. It was named after a member of the Bloomsbury Set, although you can still see its original name, the King's Arms, etched on the windows. The ground floor is where the drinkers gather so head up the steep wooden stairs to their neatly laid out dining room if you want a bit more comfort with your food. The regularly changing menu delivers some robustly flavoured dishes, with choices like chicken liver parfait or Cornish plaice with capers hitting the spot. What the service team lack in acuity, they make up for in politeness.

Kitchen Table at Bubbledogs ✿

Modern cuisine

70 Charlotte St ✉ **W1T 4QG**
✆ 020 7637 7770
www.kitchentablelondon.co.uk
⊖ **Goodge Street**

Closed 1-14 January,
17 August-2 September,
23-27 December, Sunday and Monday
– booking essential – (dinner only)
– (tasting menu only)

Menu £88

A/C

Michelin

Fight your way past the throngs enjoying the curious combination of hotdogs with champagne and head for the curtain – for behind it is where you'll find a horseshoe counter and a look of expectation on the faces of your fellow diners. This is Kitchen Table where chef-owner James Knappett and his small team prepare a no-choice menu of around 12 dishes. Each one is described on the blackboard in a single noun so you have to put your trust in the kitchen. The produce is some of the best you can find and while the cooking has a classical base, the small dishes come with a clever creative edge; they aren't made up of lots of ingredients – instead it is the combinations of flavours and textures that give them depth. With seating for just 19, the atmosphere is very convivial, especially if you're a fully paid up member of the foodie community. The chefs interact with their customers over the counter and offer more comprehensive explanations of each dish; they are helped out by James' wife Sandia, who is charm personified.

First Course	Main Course	Dessert
• Truffle-roasted Jersey Royals with bacon and crème fraîche.	• Cornish lobster with chilli, wild garlic and coral foam.	• Gooseberry and yoghurt parfait with almonds.
• Line-caught Cornish mackerel with green strawberries and oyster leaves.	• Dexter beef with pea and broad bean ragout.	• Dark chocolate cookie crumbs with white chocolate ice cream and caramel.

A pinch of excellence

www.nespresso.com

NESPRESSO
What else?

Mon Plaisir

French

19-21 Monmouth St. ✉ WC2H 9DD
✆ 020 7836 7243
www.monplaisir.co.uk
⊖ Covent Garden

Closed 25-26 December, Easter
Sunday-Monday and Sunday

Menu £16/24 – Carte £32/46 XX

Mon Plaisir couldn't be more French if it wore a beret and whistled La Marseillaise; but because this institution has been around since the 1940s, and under the current ownership since the '70s, it can also give one an unexpected but palpable sense of old London. It's divided into four rooms, all of which have slightly different personalities but share the Gallic theme; even the bar was reportedly salvaged from a Lyonnais brothel. Service may lack some of the exuberance of the past but the serving team do get the job done. All the classics are on offer, from snails to terrines, duck to coq; the set menu represents good value while the à la carte can be a little pricey.

Noble Rot

Traditional British J1

51 Lamb's Conduit St ✉ WC1N 3NB
✆ 020 7242 8963
www.noblerot.co.uk
⊖ Russell Square

Closed 25-26 December and
Sunday – booking advisable

Carte £30/43 X

In 2013 Mark Andrew and Dan Keeling launched a quarterly wine and food magazine for the 21st century oenophile; a couple of years later, this Bloomsbury restaurant and wine bar followed, inheriting the same name. Inside, it's a simple set up with a rustic, somewhat masculine feel; staff are friendly and attentive and customers an interesting mix. Wholesome, unfussy cooking comes with bold, gutsy flavours; Stephen Harris of The Sportsman is a consultant, so expect fish from the Kent coast as well as classics like terrines, rillettes and home-cured meats. The wine list is well-chosen, with strong leanings to France and Spain. Wine and food pairings are a feature; the Rock Oyster Raveneau has quickly established itself as a favourite.

ⓝ The Ninth ✿

Mediterranean cuisine   I2

22 Charlotte St ⊠ W1T 2NB
☎ 020 3019 0880
www.theninthlondon.com
⊖ Goodge Street

Closed Christmas-New Year,
Sunday and bank holidays

Menu £21 (weekday lunch) – Carte £28/47   ✗

A/C

Michelin

Jun Tanaka's career began in the early '90s and this – the ninth restaurant in which he has worked – is also the first he has actually owned. Although situated on foodie Charlotte Street, it's very much a neighbourhood spot, and both the lively downstairs with its counter for walk-ins and the more intimate first floor have a great feel to them. The on-trend menu has sections including 'snacks', 'salads' and 'raw and cured', as well as 'meat' and 'fish'; staff suggest 3 starters, 2 mains and 2 vegetable dishes for two, although their flexible approach means you're equally welcome to come in for a couple of plates and a glass of wine. Skilful cooking uses classical French techniques with a spotlight on the Mediterranean; dishes arrive at a good pace and certainly look the part – but the focus here is firmly on flavour. Vegetables are much more than just an accompaniment, with dishes such as Savoy cabbage with hazelnut pesto or charcoal-roasted celeriac with smoked almonds and wild garlic a real highlight.

First Course

- Smoked duck breast, caramelised chicory and walnuts.
- Flamed mackerel with dill, cucumber and capers.

Main Course

- Charcoal-roasted celeriac with smoked almonds and wild garlic.
- Salted beef cheeks, oxtail consommé, peas and broad beans.

Dessert

- Caramelised lemon tart with fromage frais.
- Tarte Tatin with rosemary ice cream.

Pied à Terre ⁂

34 Charlotte St ⊠ W1T 2NH
℘ 020 7636 1178
www.pied-a-terre.co.uk
⊖ Goodge Street

Closed last week
December-5 January, Saturday
lunch, Sunday and bank holidays
– booking essential

Menu £38/80   𝖃𝖃𝖃

Michelin

Not only has Charlotte Street provided a good illustration of how restaurants have changed the landscape over recent years but it has also witnessed the breakneck speed at which the industry operates. Restaurants have come and gone but for over 25 years David Moore's Pied à Terre has stood apart from the fray, confident in its own abilities and the loyalty of its regulars. One of the reasons for its success has been its subtle reinventions: nothing ever too grandiose – just a little freshening up with some new art or clever lighting to keep the place looking relevant and vibrant. Of course, its longevity is also due to the consistent standard of the cooking. The kitchen offers a plethora of menus that include tasting and vegetarian choices; the food is elegant and refined and doesn't let the modern techniques or more technical components distract or detract from the true flavours. The wine list is divided into two weighty tomes and shows considerable depth and range, including a good selection of bottles for under £30.

First Course	Main Course	Dessert
• Scallop ceviche with cucumber, balsamic and dill.	• Fallow deer with black pearl curry, smoked bacon and beetroot.	• Pineapple with kaffir lime and coriander.
• Norfolk quail with hazelnuts and beetroot.	• Cornish turbot, chanterelles, cauliflower and anchovy.	• Baked vanilla cheesecake with pear, quince and blackberries.

Bloomsbury • Hatton Garden • Holborn ▶ Plan VI

Polpo at Ape & Bird

I t a l i a n   I3

142 Shaftesbury Ave ✉ WC2H 8HJ   Bookings not accepted
☎ 020 7836 3119
www.polpo.co.uk
⊖ Leicester Square

Menu £25 – Carte £12/21

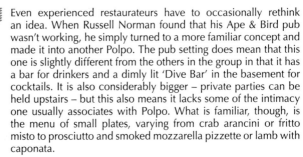

Even experienced restaurateurs have to occasionally rethink an idea. When Russell Norman found that his Ape & Bird pub wasn't working, he simply turned to a more familiar concept and made it into another Polpo. The pub setting does mean that this one is slightly different from the others in the group in that it has a bar for drinkers and a dimly lit 'Dive Bar' in the basement for cocktails. It is also considerably bigger – private parties can be held upstairs – but this also means it lacks some of the intimacy one usually associates with Polpo. What is familiar, though, is the menu of small plates, varying from crab arancini or fritto misto to prosciutto and smoked mozzarella pizzette or lamb with caponata.

Roka

J a p a n e s e   I2

37 Charlotte St ✉ W1T 1RR   Closed 25 December
☎ 020 7580 6464
www.rokarestaurant.com
⊖ Goodge Street

Carte £40/70

Roka has one of those appealingly perceptible pulses that only really busy, well-run restaurants enjoy. It attracts a handsome crowd although they don't just come to glory in their mutual attractiveness but to share food that's original, easy to eat and just as pretty as they are. The kitchen takes the flavours, delicacy and strong presentation standards of Japanese food and adds its own contemporary touches. The menu can appear bewildering but just skip the set menus and order an assortment from the various headings; ensure you have one of the specialities from the on-view Robata grill. Sometimes too many dishes can arrive at once but the serving team are a friendly and capable bunch and they'll ease up on the delivery if you ask.

Salt Yard

M e d i t e r r a n e a n   c u i s i n e   **H2**

54 Goodge St. ✉ **W1T 4NA**
✆ 020 7637 0657
www.saltyard.co.uk
⊖ Goodge Street

Closed 25 and dinner 24 and
31 December, 1 January

Carte £17/28   ✕

The ground floor is the more boisterous and you'll feel like you're in the middle of a fun party; downstairs is better if you don't know your dining companion that well, although it too is full of life. This is all about tapas, although not just about Spanish tapas. One side of the menu has bar snacks, charcuterie and cheese but after ordering some olives or boquerones, turn over and you'll find three headings: Fish, Meat and Vegetable – one plate of each per person should do it. Unusual dishes, like braised gurnard with smoked Jersey Royals, sit alongside more traditional pairings like duck breast with parsnip purée. Prices are excellent; sharing is encouraged and service, young and sincere. Spain and Italy dominate the wine list.

Talli Joe

I n d i a n   **I3**

152-156 Shaftesbury Ave ✉ **WC2H 8HL**
✆ 020 7836 5400
www.tallijoe.com
⊖ Covent Garden

Closed 25-26 December,
1 January and Sunday

Carte £18/28   ✕

Talli means 'tipsy' in Hindi – a fitting name given that this lively place was inspired by India's dive bars. When you enter, it certainly feels more like a bar than a restaurant; cocktails are the thing, so start with a 'Day in Delhi' or a 'Jaipur Fizz' before ordering several of the vibrant, tapas-style small plates. The 'Joe' of its title refers to a fictitious traveller; his journey around India highlighting the regionality of the various dishes, so you'll find creamy curries from the south alongside gutsier offerings from the north. Some dishes, like Aunty Sucorina's Goan pork and offal pickle, are old family favourites of the chef; others, like the devilled quail egg and the Lucknow style nihari on veal bone marrow, have a Western edge.

Bayswater · Maida Vale

There may not appear to be an obvious link between Maida Vale and Italy, but the name of this smart area to the west of central London is derived from a battle fought over two hundred years ago in Southern Italy, and the most appealing visitor attraction in the neighbourhood is the charming canalside **Little Venice.** To stroll around here on a summer's day brings to mind promenading in a more distant European clime; it's hard to believe that the ear-shattering roar of the Westway is just a short walk away. South of this iconic elevated roadway – a snaking route out from Marylebone to the western suburbs – is Bayswater, a busy area of imposing nineteenth century buildings that's the epicentre of London's Middle Eastern community.

During its Victorian heyday, **Bayswater** was a grand and glamorous address for affluent and elegant types who wanted a giant green space (Hyde Park) on their doorstep. The whole area had been laid out in the mid 1800s, when grand squares and cream stuccoed terraces started to fill the acres between Brunel's curvy Paddington station and the park. But during the twentieth century Bayswater's cachet nose-dived, stigmatised as 'the wrong side of the park' by the arrivistes of Knightsbridge and Kensington. Today it's still a backpacker's paradise: home to a bewildering number of tourist hotels, flatshares and B&Bs, converted from the grand houses. But this tells only a fraction of the modern story, because the area has undergone a massive facelift. The hub of this makeover was the **Paddington Basin,** a gigantic reclamation of the old Grand Union Canal basin in the shadow of the rail terminus. From a ramshackle wasteground, it's now a shimmering zone of metal, steel and glass, a phantasmagoria of blue chip HQs, homes, shops and leisure facilities. Even the barges have been turned into permanently moored 'business barges'. Tree-lined towpaths along the perimeter complete the picture of a totally modern waterscape.

Lovers of the old Bayswater can still relish what made it famous in the first place: radiating out from **Lancaster Gate,** away from Hyde Park, is a web of streets with handsome squares and tucked-away mews, and it still retains pockets of close-knit communities, such as Porchester Square, west of Paddington station. Meanwhile, the 'cathedral' of the area, Whiteleys shopping centre in **Queensway**, remains a pivotal landmark, as it has been for more than a century. Just beyond Whiteleys heading away from central London, **Westbourne Grove** is still reassuringly expensive, or at least the bit that heads determinedly towards Notting Hill. But the wind of change has rustled other parts of the neighbourhood: Connaught Street has evolved into a villagey quarter of boutiques, galleries

R. Leaver/Loop Images/Photononstop

and restaurants, while, further west, Craven Hill Gardens is the height of chic.

Little Venice pretty much acts as a dividing line between Bayswater and Maida Vale. Technically, it's the point where the Paddington arm of the Grand Union Canal meets the **Regent's Canal,** but the name, coined by poet Robert Browning who lived close by, has come to encompass the whole area just to the north of the soaring Westway. Narrow boat moorings vie for attention alongside the cafés and pubs that mercifully lack the frantic high street buzz so typical of their kind away from the water's edge. The permanently moored boats were here a long time before those upstarts at Paddington Basin. This is where you can find old-time favourites including a floating art gallery and a puppet theatre barge. A wander round the residential streets of Maida Vale is also very pleasant, dominated by the impressive Edwardian blocks of flats that conjure up a distinctive well-to-do scene.

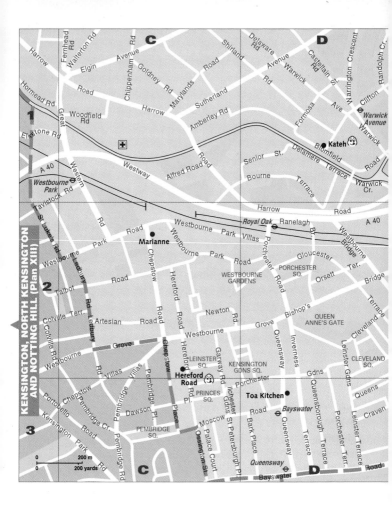

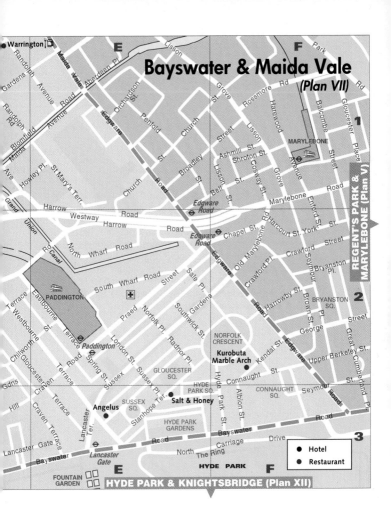

Bayswater & Maida Vale
(Plan VII)

Warrington

Randolph Gardens
Randolph Rd
Blomfield
Maida Ave
Grand Union
Howley Pl.
St Mary's Terr.

Maida Vale
Avenue
Randolph Avenue

Aberdeen Pl.
Orchardson St.
Penfold St.
Church St.
Broadley St.
Lisson Grove
Lisson St.
Bell St.

Edgware Road

Harrow Road
Westway
Harrow Road

North Wharf Road
Union Rd
Canal

South Wharf Road
Street
Sale Pl.
Norfolk Pl.
Radnor Pl.
Southwick St.
Sussex Gardens

PADDINGTON

Eastbourne Terrace
Westbourne Terrace
Chilworth
Gloucester Terrace
Terrace
Craven Terrace
Craven Terrace
Craven Gate

Paddington
London St.
Spring St.
Sussex
Lancaster Ter.
Stanhope Ter.

Lancaster Gate

Bayswater
Lancaster Gate

FOUNTAIN GARDEN

Marylebone Rd
Grove St.
Rossmore Rd
Harewood Ave
Balcombe Street
Gloucester Place
Park Rd

Ashmill St.
Shroton St.
Cosway St.
Lisson Grove

MARYLEBONE

Marylebone Road
Enford St.
York St.

Edgware Road
Chapel St.
Old Marylebone Rd
Harcourt St.
Crawford St.
Seymour Pl.
Crawford Pl.
Bryanston Pl.

Harrowby St.
Brown St.
George Street
BRYANSTON SQ.

Crawford St.
Kendal St.
Upper Berkeley St.
Great Cumberland Pl.

Kurobuta
Marble Arch

Connaught St.
Albion St.
CONNAUGHT SQ.
Seymour St.

NORFOLK CRESCENT

GLOUCESTER SQ.
HYDE PARK SQ.
SUSSEX SQ.
Salt & Honey
Angelus

HYDE PARK GARDENS
Bayswater Road
North Carriage Drive
The Ring

HYDE PARK

REGENT'S PARK & MARYLEBONE (Plan V)

● Hotel
● Restaurant

HYDE PARK & KNIGHTSBRIDGE (Plan XII)

201

Angelus

French   E3

4 Bathurst St ✉ W2 2SD
✆ 020 7402 0083
www.angelusrestaurant.co.uk
⊖ Lancaster Gate

Closed 24-25 December and
1 January

Menu £23 – Carte £40/61   ✗✗

  Angelus has a delightfully warm and inclusive feel and much of
the credit for that goes to its amiable and truly hospitable owner,
Thierry Tomasin – if you're not already one of his regulars, you
soon will be. The restaurant occupies what was formerly the
Archer Tavern and the building dates from the 1850s. It has
been charmingly decorated with art nouveau mirrors and prints
and the bell that his mother would ring to call him in for meals
when he was a boy growing up in the south of France takes
pride of place in the bar. The cooking is French in its base but
English in its ingredients; game will always be a highlight here
but the kitchen is equally adept at lightly grilling some halibut or
whipping up a soufflé.

Good quality cooking
at a great price?
Look out for the Bib
Gourmand ⊛.

Hereford Road

T r a d i t i o n a l   B r i t i s h   **C2**

3 Hereford Rd ⊠ W2 4AB
☎ 020 7727 1144
www.herefordroad.org
⊖ Bayswater

Closed 24 December-3 January
and August bank holiday
– booking essential

Menu £14 (weekday lunch) – Carte £22/32   ✗

Hereford Road is, first and foremost, a local restaurant. Lunch is usually a relaxed affair, with the room brightened by the large domed skylight, while dinner is the livelier feast, where everyone gives the impression that they live near enough to have walked here. The delightful owner-chef Tom Pemberton is often the first person you see, as the open kitchen is by the entrance – this was once a butcher's shop. He is an acolyte of St John and his cooking shares the same principles but not the same prices, so expect seasonal, British ingredients in very tasty dishes devoid of frippery. Offal is handled with aplomb and dishes designed for two, such as the shoulder of lamb or the whole oxtail, are so good you won't actually want to share them.

Kateh

M e d i t e r r a n e a n   c u i s i n e   **D1**

5 Warwick Pl ⊠ W9 2PX
☎ 020 7289 3393
www.katehrestaurant.co.uk
⊖ Warwick Avenue

Closed 25-26 December
– booking essential – (dinner only
and lunch Friday-Sunday)

Carte £21/39   ✗

If you want to join those locals who have already discovered what a little jewel they have here in the form of this buzzy, busy Persian restaurant then you will need to book ahead. Their multinational kitchen produces an appealingly priced menu that offers lots of choice, from small plates to stews and dishes expertly grilled over charcoal. The octopus is delicious; warm sesame-coated flatbreads are moreish; and be sure to finish with an authentic dessert like baklava or 'kolouche' (date and walnut pastries) along with tea made with cardamom. The atmosphere is great and the place is run with spirit, although when it's busy it can suffer from its own success. There's a delightful conservatory at the back.

Kurobuta Marble Arch

Japanese F2

17-20 Kendal St ✉ W2 2AW
℘ 020 3475 4158
www.kurobuta-london.com
⊖ Marble Arch

Closed 25 December

Carte £17/32

Having practiced with a pop-up in Chelsea, the Australian chef-owner hit the ground running when he opened his flagship Japanese restaurant – which was just as well because the crowds soon piled in. It's modelled somewhat on a Japanese izakaya, although it's bigger than anything usually seen in Tokyo. The bar is the best place to sit – start with a cocktail or a beer with a frozen head and then get ordering. The robata grill provides the stickiest BBQ pork belly, which is served in steamed buns; the lamb chops are lip-tinglingly good; the black pepper soft shell crabs fly out of the kitchen; and the yuzu tart is the star of the desserts. The place is a lot of fun and the staff are knowledgeable and helpful.

The symbol 🍇 denotes
a particularly interesting
wine list.

Marianne

French   C2

104a Chepstow Rd ⊠ W2 5QS
☏ 020 3675 7750
www.mariannerestaurant.com
⊖ Westbourne Park

Closed 22 December–
5 January , August bank holiday and
Monday – booking essential – (dinner
only and lunch Friday-Sunday)
– (tasting menu only)

Menu £35/85   ✗✗

Marianne Lumb spent several years travelling the world as a private chef to a host of names from the sunny side of Celebrity Street. She then entered BBC's 'MasterChef: The Professionals' and reached the final. The next step was to open her own restaurant and it's a delightful little place – a panelled corner room that holds just six tables. She has more help in the kitchen now than when she started so, alongside the concise daily lunch menu with a choice of two dishes per course, you'll find a seasonal six course tasting menu. In essence, her food is classically based using sound French principles and, while flavours are pronounced, it also comes with a pleasing lightness of touch; the presentation is impeccable and the desserts stand out.

Salt & Honey

Modern cuisine   E3

28 Sussex Pl ⊠ W2 2TH
☏ 020 7706 7900
www.saltandhoneybistro.com
⊖ Lancaster Gate

Closed 25-26 December,
1 January and Monday
– bookings advisable at dinner

Menu £15 (weekday lunch) – Carte £24/38   ✗

A residential area just north of Hyde Park is the location of the second venture from the owners of Fulham's Manuka Kitchen: this is a cosy spot with a real neighbourhood feel – run with enthusiasm by its hands-on owner. The kitchen creates well-priced, colourful, boldly flavoured dishes using the best British ingredients. You'll find Mediterranean and Middle Eastern flavours on the appealing menu, as well as influences from the chef's homeland, New Zealand – Manuka honey is used in dishes like lemongrass and Manuka honey cured salmon and their famous saffron and Manuka honey crème brûlée. The wine list is short but sweet, with each available by the glass, pichet and bottle. Ask to sit in one of the booths by the entrance.

Toa Kitchen

Chinese   D3

100 Queensway ✉ W2 3RR
☎ 020 7792 9767
www.toakitchen.com
⊖ Bayswater

Closed 25 December

Carte £14/25   ✗✗

Take a pre-prandial stroll along Queensway and you'll be faced with an overwhelming choice of Chinese restaurants, so keep an eye out for Toa Kitchen. At first glance the menu may seem dispiritingly long but search out the "Chef's Specials" and you won't go wrong. These carefully prepared Cantonese specialities, together with the hotpot dishes, are the ones to go for: portions are generous, ingredients good and the flavours authentic. Service is also a cut above average and you'll be well looked after by owner Mr Fung and his team of very capable and friendly ladies. For a more comfortable table, head to the back of the restaurant where the blossom the restaurant gets its name from is attractively displayed.

Is breakfast included? If it is, the cup symbol ☑ appears after the number of rooms.

City of London · Clerkenwell Finsbury · Southwark

Say what you like about London, **The City** is the place where it all started. The Romans developed this small area – this square mile – nearly two thousand years ago, and today it stands as the economic heartbeat of not only the capital, but the country as a whole. Each morning it's besieged with an army of bankers, lawyers and traders, and each evening it's abandoned to an eerie ghost-like fate. Of course, this mass exodus is offset by the two perennial crowd-pullers, **St Paul's** and the **Tower of London**, but these are both on the periphery of the area, away from the frenetic commercial zone within. The casual visitor tends to steer clear of the City, but for those willing to mix it with the daytime swarm of office workers, there are many historical nuggets hidden away, waiting to be mined. You can find here, amongst the skyscrapers, a tempting array of Roman ruins, medieval landmarks and brooding churches designed by Wren and Hawksmoor. One of the best ways of encapsulating everything that's happened here down the centuries is to visit the Museum of London, on London Wall, which tells the story of the city from the very start, and the very start means 300,000 BC.

For those seeking the hip corners of this part of London, the best advice is to head slightly northwest, using the brutalist space of the **Barbican Arts Centre** as your marker. You're now entering **Clerkenwell**. Sliding north/south through here - and ending up at the historic Smithfield Meat Market - is the bustling and buzzy St John Street, home to the original St John restaurant, pioneer of nose-to-tail eating. Further West, Exmouth Market teems with trendy bars and restaurants, popular with those on their way to the perennially excellent dance concerts at Sadler's Wells Theatre. Clerkenwell's revivalist vibe has seen the steady reclamation of old warehouse space: during the Industrial Revolution, the area boomed with the introduction of breweries, print works and the manufacture of clocks and watches. After World War II, decline set in, but these days city professionals and loft-dwellers are drawn to the area's zeitgeist-leading galleries and clubs, not to mention the wonderful floor-to-ceiling delicatessens.

The area was once a religious centre, frequented by monks and nuns; its name derives from the parish clerks who performed Biblical mystery plays around the Clerk's Well set in a nunnery wall. This can be found in **Farringdon Lane** complete with an exhibition explaining all. Close by in St John's Lane is the 16C gatehouse which is home to the Museum of the Order of St John (famous today for its ambulance services), and chock full of fascinating objects related to the Order's medieval history.

Not too long ago, a trip over London Bridge to **Southwark** was for

C. Eymenier / MICHELIN

locals only, its trademark grimness ensuring it was well off the tourist map. These days, visitors treat it as a place of pilgrimage as three of London's modern success stories reside here in the shadow of The Shard. **Tate Modern** has become the city's most visited attraction, a huge former power station that generates a blistering show of modern art from 1900 to the present day, its massive turbine hall a must-see feature in itself. Practically next door but a million miles away architecturally is Shakespeare's **Globe,** a wonderful evocation of medieval showtime. Half a mile east is tourists' favourite, **Borough Market.** Foodies can't resist the organic, feel-good nature of the place, with, its mind-boggling number of stalls selling produce ranging from every kind of fruit and veg to rare-breed meats, oils, preserves, chocolates and breads. And that's just for hors-d'œuvres...

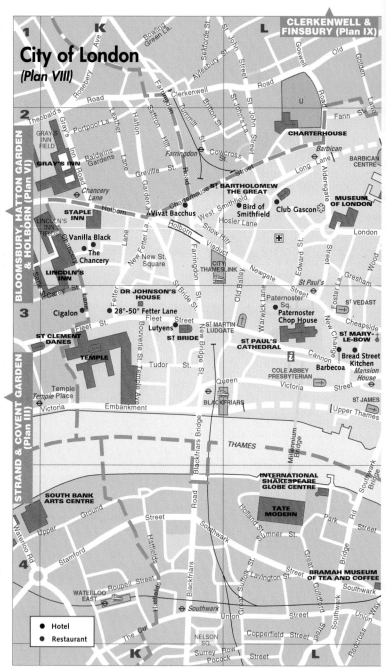

City of London
(Plan VIII)

BLOOMSBURY, HATTON GARDEN & HOLBORN (Plan VI)

STRAND & COVENT GARDEN (Plan III)

Bowling Green La.
Rosebery Ave
Theobald's Rd
GRAY'S INN FIELD
GRAY'S INN
Portpool La.
Baldwins Gardens
Leather Lane
Hatton Garden
Saffron Hill
Clerkenwell Road
Aylesbury St.
Sekforde St.
St John Street
Britton St.
St John's La.
Goswell Road
Old St.
Golden Lane
Fann
U
CHARTERHOUSE
Barbican
Long Lane
Aldersgate St.
BARBICAN CENTRE
MUSEUM OF LONDON

Farringdon Road
Turnmill St.
Cowcross St.
Charterhouse St.
St BARTHOLOMEW THE GREAT
West Smithfield
Bird of Smithfield
Hosier Lane
Club Gascon
London Wall

Greville St.
Chancery Lane
Holborn
STAPLE INN
Vivat Bacchus
Snow Hill
Holborn Viaduct
CITY THAMESLINK
Newgate St.
St Paul's
Foster La.
Gresham St.
St VEDAST

New Fetter La.
New St. Square
Farringdon St.
Old Bailey
Warwick Lane
Paternoster Sq.
Paternoster Chop House
Cheapside
St MARY-LE-BOW

Vanilla Black
The Chancery
LINCOLN'S INN
LINCOLN'S INN FIELDS
Serle St.
Carey St.

Cigalon
Chancery Lane
Fleet St.
DR JOHNSON'S HOUSE
28°-50° Fetter Lane
Fetter Lane
Lutyens
Bouverie St.
St Bride St.
Fleet Street
New Bridge St.
St MARTIN LUDGATE
St BRIDE
St PAUL'S CATHEDRAL
New Change
Bread Street Kitchen
Barbecoa
Mansion House
Cannon St.

St CLEMENT DANES
TEMPLE
Tudor St.
Temple Ave
COLE ABBEY PRESBYTERIAN
Queen Victoria Street
St JAMES

Temple Place
Victoria Embankment
BLACKFRIARS
Upper Thames St.

Blackfriars Bridge
THAMES
Millennium Bridge
Southwark Bridge

SOUTH BANK ARTS CENTRE
Upper Ground
Stamford Street
Hatfields
Blackfriars Road
Southwark St.
Holland St.
Sumner St.
INTERNATIONAL SHAKESPEARE GLOBE CENTRE
TATE MODERN
Park St.
Great Suffolk St.
Southwark Bridge Rd

Waterloo Rd
Roupell Street
WATERLOO EAST
The Cut
Southwark
Lavington St.
Suffolk St.
Union Street
BRAMAH MUSEUM OF TEA AND COFFEE
Guildford St.
Redcross Way

NELSON SQ.
Surrey Row
Pocock Street
Copperfield Street
Union Street
Southwark Bridge Rd

- ● Hotel
- ● Restaurant

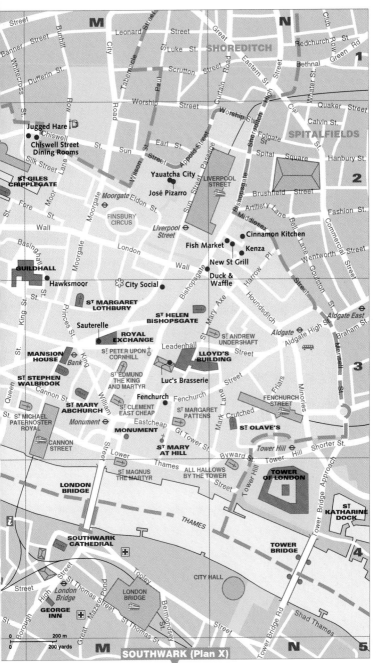

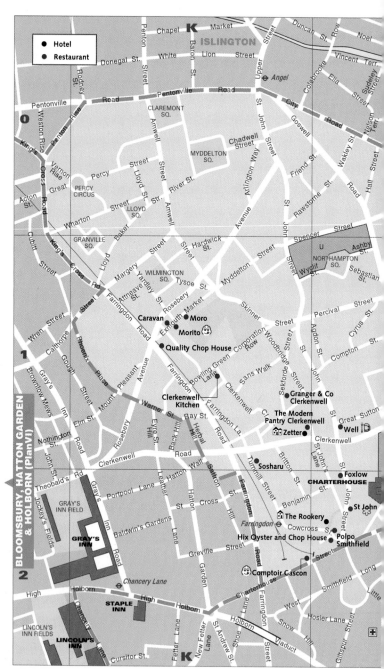

Legend:
- ● Hotel
- ● Restaurant

ISLINGTON

Angel

CLAREMONT SQ.

MYDDELTON SQ.

PERCY CIRCUS

LLOYD SQ.

GRANVILLE SQ.

NORTHAMPTON SQ.

WILMINGTON SQ.

Caravan
Moro
Morito
Quality Chop House

Clerkenwell Kitchen

Granger & Co Clerkenwell
The Modern Pantry Clerkenwell
Zetter
Well

Sosharu

Foxlow
CHARTERHOUSE
St John

The Rookery
Hix Oyster and Chop House
Polpo Smithfield

Comptoir Gascon

GRAY'S INN FIELD
GRAY'S INN
GRAY'S FIELDS

STAPLE INN

LINCOLN'S INN FIELDS
LINCOLN'S INN

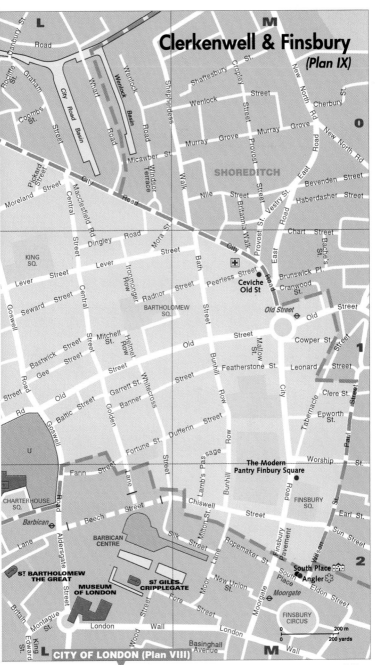

Clerkenwell & Finsbury
(Plan IX)

SHOREDITCH

Ceviche
Old St

Old Street ⊖

The Modern
Pantry Finbury Square

South Place ⌂⌂⌂
Angler ✿

KING
SQ.

BARTHOLOMEW
SQ.

Barbican ⊖

CHARTERHOUSE
SQ.

St BARTHOLOMEW
THE GREAT

MUSEUM
OF LONDON

St GILES
CRIPPLEGATE

BARBICAN
CENTRE

FINSBURY
SQ.

FINSBURY
CIRCUS

200 m

200 yards

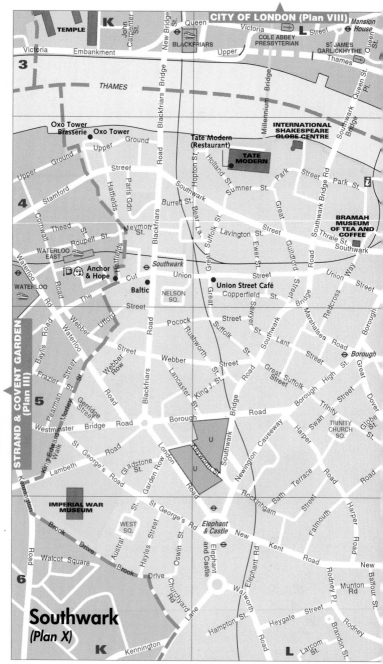

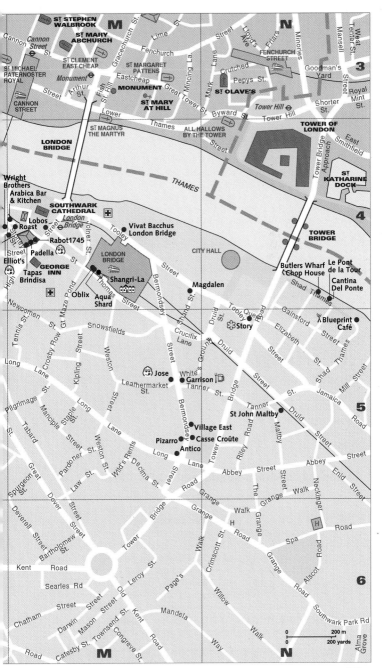

ST STEPHEN WALBROOK **M**

Cannon Street

Cannon St.

ST MARY ABCHURCH

ST CLEMENT EAST CHEAP

ST MICHAEL PATERNOSTER ROYAL

Monument

CANNON STREET

Lime

St

Fenchurch

ST MARGARET PATTENS

Eastcheap

MONUMENT

ST MARY AT HILL

Arthur St.

Lower

Fish St. Hill

ST MAGNUS THE MARTYR

Street

Gracechurch St.

Lloyd's Ave

FENCHURCH STREET

ST OLAVE'S

Pepys St.

Mincing La.

Great Tower St.

Mark Lane

Crutched

Byward St.

ALL HALLOWS BY THE TOWER

Tower Hill

Tower Hill

Street

Minories

Friars

West Tenter St.

Mansel

Goodman's Yard

3

Shorter St.

Royal Mint St.

TOWER OF LONDON

East Smithfield

LONDON BRIDGE

THAMES

Tower Bridge Approach

ST KATHARINE DOCK

4

Wright Brothers

Arabica Bar & Kitchen

SOUTHWARK CATHEDRAL

London Bridge

Lobos

Roast

Rabot1745

Padella

Elliot's

Tapas Brindisa

GEORGE INN

Tooley

Vivat Bacchus London Bridge

CITY HALL

Joiner St.

LONDON BRIDGE

Shangri-La

Oblix

Aqua Shard

Thomas Street

Bermondsey

Street

Street

TOWER BRIDGE

Butlers Wharf Chop House

Magdalen

Tooley

Druid St.

Queen

Shad Thames

Le Pont de la Tour

Cantina Del Ponte

Gainsford

Elizabeth

Shad

Jamaica

Mill Street

Road

Blueprint Café

Street

5

Newcomen

Tennis St.

Crosby Row

Gt Maze Pond

Snowsfields

Weston

Kipling St.

Long

Lane

St.

Story

Druid

Street

Crucifix Lane

Druid St.

Bridge

Pilgrimage

Manciple

Staple St.

Long

Lane

Weston St.

Leathermarket St.

Jose

White

Garrison

Tanner

St.

Bermondsey

Tabard

St.

Pardoner

Law St.

Wild's Rents

Decima St.

St John Maltby

Tanner

Street

Village East

Pizarro

Antico

Casse Croûte

Long

Tower

Lane

Abbey

Street

Riley Road

Maltby

St.

Druid

Street

Abbey

Street

Spurgeon St.

Great Dover Street

Bartholomew St.

Tower

Bridge

Grange

Road

Grange

Walk

The Grange

Grange

Walk

Abbey

Street

Enid Street

Neckinger

6

Kent

Road

Searles Rd

Deverell Street

Spa

Road

H

Road

Crimscott St.

Alscot Road

Southwark Park Rd

Chatham

Street

Darwin

Street

Mason

Street

Catesby St.

Townsend St.

Old Leroy St.

Kent

Road

Congreve St.

Page's

Mandela

Walk

Willow

Way

Grange

Road

Alma Grove

M

N

0   200 m
0   200 yards

215

Anchor & Hope

Modern British

Plan X K4

36 The Cut ⊠ SE1 8LP
☎ 020 7928 9898
www.anchorandhopepub.co.uk
⊖ Southwark.

Closed Christmas-New Year,
Sunday dinner, Monday lunch
and bank holidays – bookings not
accepted

Menu £15 (weekday lunch) – Carte £18/34

The Anchor & Hope is still running at full steam and its popularity shows no sign of abating. It's not hard to see why: combine a menu that changes with each service and is a paragon of seasonality, with cooking that is gutsy, bold and wholesome, and you end up with immeasurably rewarding dishes like suckling kid chops with wild garlic, succulent roast pigeon with lentils or buttermilk pudding with poached rhubarb. The place has a contagiously congenial feel and the friendly staff all pull in the same direction; you may spot a waiter trimming vegetables or a chef delivering dishes to the tables. The no-reservation policy remains, so either get here early or be prepared to wait a while; you can, however, book for Sunday lunch.

Antico

Italian

Plan X M5

214 Bermondsey St ⊠ SE1 3TQ
☎ 020 7407 4682
www.antico-london.co.uk
⊖ London Bridge

Closed 24-26 December, 1 January
and Monday

Menu £17 (lunch and early dinner) – Carte £25/36

At the top end of busy Bermondsey Street – home to numerous pubs, bars and restaurants as well as art galleries, boutiques and markets – is this former antiques warehouse; its exposed brickwork and counter seating typical of the street's rustic-meets-hipster style. Downstairs, cocktail bar 214 Bermondsey offers over 80 gins as well as their own bottled brand of tonic water; back upstairs they serve honest Italian food with the focus firmly on comfort. Start with fluffy focaccia and some plump green olives; homemade pasta dishes like slow-roasted pork shoulder tortelloni are a highlight and desserts like lemon tart, very tasty. The atmosphere is fun, the staff full of smiles and the clientele pleasingly mixed in age and circumstance.

Angler ✿

Seafood

Plan IX M2

South Place Hotel,
3 South Pl ✉ EC2M 2AF
☎ 020 3215 1260
www.anglerrestaurant.com
⊖ Moorgate

Closed 26-30 December, Saturday
lunch and Sunday – booking
advisable

Menu £35 – Carte £42/66

🗙🗙

Angler

It may be built into the eaves of D&D's South Place hotel, but this 7th floor room feels very much like a separate, stand-alone entity. It's a bright and comfortable space and one that feels intimate and elegant; it also comes with its own terrace where, on a warm evening, you'll see the cocktails go flying out. 2016 saw a change at the top when a new head chef arrived in the form of Gary Foulkes, who brought many of his team from The Square with him. As the restaurant's name suggests, fish remains the mainstay of the menu; the majority of it comes from Cornwall and it's immediately clear that its quality is supreme. The kitchen displays a light and delicate touch but there's no compromising on flavour, and colour plays an important role in the visual appeal of the dishes. There's a good value lunch menu available, while dinner is a little more elaborate, with the offer of both an à la carte and a very popular 5 course set menu, which comes with suggested wine pairings.

First Course
- Yellowfin tuna tartare, lime, chilli and avocado.
- Tomatoes with burrata, black olive toast and gazpacho vinaigrette.

Main Course
- Roast fillet of John Dory with langoustines, mushrooms, truffle and pumpkin.
- Cornish turbot with line-caught squid, bonito dashi and coastal herbs.

Dessert
- Chocolate fondant with pistachio ice cream.
- Warm malt tart with malted milk ice cream.

Aqua Shard

Modern cuisine **Plan X M4**

Level 31, The Shard, 31 St Thomas St, ⊠ SE1 9RY

✆ 020 3011 1256

www.aquashard.co.uk

⊖ London Bridge

Closed 25 December

Menu £36 (weekday lunch)/48 – Carte £39/79

The Shard's most accessible restaurant covers all bases by serving breakfast, brunch, lunch, afternoon tea and dinner. You can even come here just for a drink and a gander which is surely preferable to paying for the viewing platform, but be warned – at weekends the queue is at street level and can be dispiritingly long. If you have booked to eat then the express lift will whisk you straight up here to the 31st floor where you should ask to sit on the west side for the better views. The contemporary cooking makes good use of British ingredients and comes with a degree of finesse in both flavour and presentation. The à la carte prices can be a little steep though, so your best bet is to come for lunch and go for the Market Menu.

Arabica Bar & Kitchen

World cuisine **Plan X M4**

3 Rochester Walk, Borough Market ⊠ SE1 9AF

✆ 020 3011 5151

www.arabicabarandkitchen.com

⊖ London Bridge

Closed 25-27 December and Sunday dinner – bookings advisable at dinner

Menu £17/25 – Carte £17/32

Self-taught chef-owner James Walters started selling mezze from a trestle table at Borough Market around 14 years ago so it's no surprise he chose to open his Levantine-inspired restaurant under a railway arch at the side of the market. It's a fun, lively and cavernous place with tightly packed tables and a map on the wall which highlights the countries on which the kitchen's attention is focused: Egypt, Syria, Iraq, Jordan and Lebanon. Order some dips and flatbread from the clay oven while you look at the menu. What stands out is the sheer freshness of the produce and the vivid colours on the plate. This is food to be celebrated and shared, with the charcoal dishes proving particularly succulent and salads pleasingly vibrant.

Baltic

World cuisine

Plan X K4

74 Blackfriars Rd ✉ SE1 8HA
✆ 020 7928 1111
www.balticrestaurant.co.uk
⊖ Southwark

Closed 24-26 December
and Monday lunch – bookings
advisable at dinner

Menu £18 (weekday lunch)/25 – Carte £25/36

With an entrance akin to that of a small bar, this restaurant comes as something of a surprise; carry on past the long cocktail bar and you emerge in a bright, buzzing space with wooden trussed ceilings, skylights and sleek styling. The daily menu is an appealing read and specialises in dishes from various countries out east – Poland, Russia, Bulgaria, and even Siberia. Expect a selection of blinis, assorted dumplings including pierogi and spaetzle, lots of meat dishes such as pork schnitzel and lamb shashlik – and over 70 varieties of vodka, available by the glass or carafe. The cooking is executed with more subtlety than you expect and the largely Polish staff are clearly proud and pleased to be serving food with which they are familiar.

Barbecoa

Meats and grills

Plan VIII L3

20 New Change Passage ✉ EC4M 9AG
✆ 020 3005 8555
www.barbecoa.com
⊖ St Paul's

Closed 25-26 December and
1 January – booking essential

Menu £27 (weekday lunch) – Carte £33/64

Good barbecue is about using prime ingredients and choosing the appropriate cooking method. At Jamie Oliver's Barbecoa the kitchen uses fire pits, smokers, tandoors, grills and ovens to ensure maximum flavour on your plate, whether you've chosen prawns, ribs, pulled pork shoulder or dry-aged British steak. Another thing BBQ needs is a good appetite: ideally you'd have spent the morning chopping down trees although, judging by the clientele and the suit jackets hanging off the backs of the chairs, it seems that working in finance does just as well. Don't ignore the starters, like pig's cheek or beetroot salad, as they're more than a run-up to the main course – and if you manage dessert too then you won't need to eat again for days.

Bird of Smithfield

Traditional British **Plan VIII L2**

26 Smithfield St ✉ EC1A 9LB
✆ 020 7559 5100
www.birdofsmithfield.com
⊖ Farringdon

Closed Christmas, New Year,
Sunday and bank holidays
– booking essential

Menu £18 (lunch and early dinner) – Carte £26/46

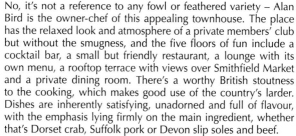

No, it's not a reference to any fowl or feathered variety – Alan Bird is the owner-chef of this appealing townhouse. The place has the relaxed look and atmosphere of a private members' club but without the smugness, and the five floors of fun include a cocktail bar, a small but friendly restaurant, a lounge with its own menu, a rooftop terrace with views over Smithfield Market and a private dining room. There's a worthy British stoutness to the cooking, which makes good use of the country's larder. Dishes are inherently satisfying, unadorned and full of flavour, with the emphasis lying firmly on the main ingredient, whether that's Dorset crab, Suffolk pork or Devon slip soles and beef.

Blueprint Café

Modern cuisine **Plan X N5**

28 Shad Thames, Butlers Wharf ✉ SE1 2YD
✆ 020 7378 7031
www.blueprintcafe.co.uk
⊖ London Bridge

Closed 1 January and
Sunday dinner

Menu £25 (weekday lunch) – Carte £27/47

Retractable floor to ceiling windows and a superb view out over the river to Tower Bridge make this bright white restaurant the go-to choice for a summer lunch, and its classic good looks and welcoming staff contribute to its buzzy, neighbourhood feel. Cooking remains respectful to the original philosophy of founder, Sir Terence Conran: it's light, uncomplicated and easy to eat, making the most of seasonal ingredients and using them in complementary ways. The set menus come with appealing price tags, and Saturday brunch, Sunday roasts, BYO Mondays and the occasional cocktail masterclass all add to the mix. People-watchers can keep an eye on proceedings, safe in the knowledge that they won't be noticed.

Bread Street Kitchen

M o d e r n   c u i s i n e   **Plan VIII L3**

10 Bread St ✉ EC4M 9AJ   Booking advisable
☏ 020 3030 4050
www.breadstreetkitchen.com
⊖ St Paul's

Carte £32/57

Influenced perhaps by the time he has spent in the US in recent years, Bread Street Kitchen is Gordon Ramsay's take on New York loft-style dining. With floor to ceiling windows, a large bar, thumping music, an open kitchen running down one side and enough zinc ducting on the ceiling to kit out a small industrial estate, the space is big, butch and full of buzz. In a further departure from his usual style of operation, the food is quite simple and rustic – think modern bistro dishes with the odd touch of refinement – and there is enough choice to provide something for everyone. The short rib burger is a best seller; the wood oven is used to good effect with dishes like braised pork collar; and the desserts are particularly well done.

The symbol ✿
denotes a particularly
interesting wine list.

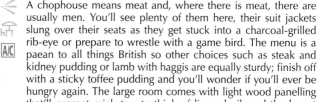

Butlers Wharf Chop House

Traditional British   Plan X N4

36e Shad Thames, Butlers Wharf ⊠ SE1 2YE
☎ 020 7403 3403
www.chophouse-restaurant.co.uk
⊖ London Bridge

Closed 1 January

Carte £25/60   ✗

A chophouse means meat and, where there is meat, there are
usually men. You'll see plenty of them here, their suit jackets
slung over their seats as they get stuck into a charcoal-grilled
rib-eye or prepare to wrestle with a game bird. The menu is a
paean to all things British so other choices such as steak and
kidney pudding or lamb with haggis are equally sturdy; finish off
with a sticky toffee pudding and you'll wonder if you'll ever be
hungry again. The large room comes with light wood panelling
that'll prompt cricketers to think of linseed oil, and the bar at
the entrance offers a simpler and cheaper menu. Come in the
summer for a table on the fantastic terrace – few restaurants can
match the stunning views.

Cantina Del Ponte

Italian   Plan X N4

36c Shad Thames, Butlers Wharf ⊠ SE1 2YE
☎ 020 7403 5403
www.cantina.co.uk
⊖ London Bridge

Closed 25 December

Menu £16/23 – Carte £28/49   ✗

A refurbishment a few years back revitalised this Italian stalwart.
They kept the large mural on one wall and created a pleasantly
relaxing, faux-rustic environment. The menu was also tweaked:
it was out with the pizzas and in with a greater degree of
authenticity. The focus is on appealing and flavoursome dishes
and the set menu represents decent value. There's a good
selection on offer, with the focus very much on recognisable
standards and old favourites; flavours are well-defined and
portions are bigger than expected. The wine list covers all of
Italy and there's ample choice by the glass. The first tables to go
on a summer's day are naturally those on the riverside terrace
under the awning.

Caravan

World cuisine

Plan IX K1

11-13 Exmouth Market ⊠ EC1R 4QD
℘ 020 7833 8115
www.caravanrestaurants.co.uk
⊖ Farringdon

Closed 25,26 and 31 December,
1 January – booking advisable

Carte £26/35

A discernible Antipodean vibe pervades this casual eatery, from the laid-back, easy-going charm of the serving team to the kitchen's confident combining of unusual flavours; even in the excellent flat-whites served by the barista. There's an ersatz industrial feel to the room and a randomness to the decorative touches that belies the seriousness of the ambition. The 100% Arabica beans are roasted daily in the basement, the wine list features an unusual selection of producers and plenty of organic wines, and the owners' travels (hence the name) inform the innovative and inventive cooking. There's something for everyone, from breakfast to small plates to share, or even main courses for two – this really is a caravan of love.

Casse Croûte

French

Plan X M5

109 Bermondsey St ⊠ SE1 3XB
℘ 020 7407 2140
www.cassecroute.co.uk
⊖ London Bridge

Closed Sunday dinner – booking
essential

Carte £28/35

The joys of Bermondsey Street are legion and the variety of restaurants on offer is considerable but if you'd still prefer to feel you're somewhere else then squeeze into this tiny bistro and you'll be instantly transported to rural France. From the fleur de lys decoration and the tiled flooring to the red leather seating and the gingham table cloths, this place is so French that if a film studio had created it they would be accused of perpetuating cultural clichés. The blackboard menu offers just three choices for each course but does evolve during the day, with new dishes added as others run out. The cooking is rustic and authentic and the flavours heartening and wholesome; go the whole way and have the cheese course too.

Ceviche Old St

Peruvian   **Plan IX M1**

2 Baldwin St ⊠ EC1V 9NU
☎ 020 3327 9463
www.cevicheuk.com
⊖ Old Street

Menu £12 (weekday lunch) – Carte £17/32   ✗

A/C This younger sister to the original Ceviche in Soho is housed on
the ground floor of the Grade II listed former Alexandra Trust
Dining Rooms, built in 1898 by tea magnate Sir Thomas Lipton
for the people of East London, who could enjoy a three course
meal for the princely sum of tuppence. These days, the place has
a buzzy brasserie feel and the food is designed for sharing. A
pisco sour is the best way to start proceedings, followed by star
of the show, ceviche. Three small plates per person plus a side
dish is ideal; dishes arrive quickly and are easy to eat, vibrant and
full of flavour. Keep your eyes peeled when nature calls; there is
a constantly changing collection of Peruvian art in the corridor,
all of it for sale.

The Chancery

Modern cuisine   **Plan VIII K2**

9 Cursitor St ⊠ EC4A 1LL
☎ 020 7831 4000
www.thechancery.co.uk
⊖ Chancery Lane

Closed 23 December-4 January,
Saturday lunch, Sunday and bank
holidays

Menu £40/68   ✗✗

A/C The Chancery is an elegant, discreet restaurant that's so close
to the law courts you'll assume your fellow diners are all
barristers, jurors or the recently acquitted. The ground floor,
with its contemporary artwork and smartly laid tables, is slightly
more comfortable than the basement and, despite having to
deal with all those formal types, the service team remain bright
and friendly. The menu is appealingly concise and understated
and most of the dishes have a reassuringly classical backbone,
whether that's the mackerel escabeche or the saddle of rabbit.
The kitchen clearly knows what it is doing – flavours are bold
and sauces are a particular highlight.

Chiswell Street Dining Rooms

M o d e r n   B r i t i s h

Montcalm London City, at the Brewery Hotel
56 Chiswell St ⊠ EC1Y 4SA
☏ 020 7614 0177
www.chiswellstreetdining.com
⊖ Barbican

Closed 25-26 December,
1 January, Saturday and Sunday

Menu £38 – Carte £31/57

The Martin brothers' restaurant in a corner spot at the former Whitbread brewery. It may double as a dining room for the Montcalm Hotel, but the place really comes alive in the evening, thanks in no small part to its lively cocktail bar. There's a pleasing Britishness to the menu and the kitchen makes good use of nearby Billingsgate, with classics like whole Cornish lemon sole, and poached langoustines. Those who prefer more muscular cooking should go for the Hereford snail and smoked bacon pie or Aberdeen Angus rib-eye; and who cannot fail to smile when they see 'Knickerbocker Glory' on a menu? The smartly kitted-out staff cope well and help with the buzzy atmosphere.

Cigalon

F r e n c h

115 Chancery Ln ⊠ WC2A 1PP
☏ 020 7242 8373
www.cigalon.co.uk
⊖ Chancery Lane

Closed Christmas and New Year,
Saturday, Sunday and bank
holidays

Menu £27/35 – Carte £31/37

A huge skylight bathes the room in light while the kitchen pays homage to the food of Provence – this is a restaurant that really comes into its own in the summer. A former auction house for law books, the space is stylishly laid out, with the booths in the centre being the prized seats – ask for No.9 if you want to watch the chefs in action. Along with the traditional dishes such as soupe au pistou, bouillabaisse, salade niçoise and pieds et paquets are popular grilled dishes such as venison, and there's even the occasional detour to Corsica. Equal thought went into the name: it refers to both a 1935 Marcel Pagnol film about a haughty chef and the local name for the summer cicada. There's also a busy bar downstairs in the cellar.

Cinnamon Kitchen

Indian Plan VIII N2

9 Devonshire Sq ✉ EC2M 4YL
☎ 020 7626 5000
www.cinnamon-kitchen.com
⊖ Liverpool Street

Closed Saturday lunch, Sunday
and bank holidays

Menu £20 (lunch and early dinner) – Carte £24/51 ✕✕

Having successfully established Westminster's Cinnamon Club and made it a popular choice with those who run the country, the team behind it opened a second branch here in The City, to appeal to those who own the country. This is all about contemporary Indian dining: the cooking is creative and original, the surroundings light and unobtrusive and the service keen and sprightly. The menu bears little resemblance to the usual Indian fare and includes ingredients like quinoa, red deer and scallops. The arresting presentation doesn't come at the expense of the punchy flavours; the grill section is worth exploring; and enthusiastic amateur cooks should position themselves at the Tandoor Bar to watch all the action.

Clerkenwell Kitchen

Modern cuisine Plan IX K1

27-31 Clerkenwell Cl ✉ EC1R 0AT
☎ 020 7101 9959
www.theclerkenwellkitchen.co.uk
⊖ Farringdon

Closed Christmas-New Year,
Saturday, Sunday and bank
holidays – booking advisable
– (lunch only)

Carte £15/28 ✕

Time spent working in Dorset with Hugh Fearnley-Whittingstall has clearly influenced Emma, the owner of this busy, tucked away eatery: she sources her ingredients from small producers who use traditional methods and is committed to sustainability, recycling and the reduction of food miles. But this is more than just a worthy enterprise – the food is rather good too. Local office workers flock in for breakfast and takeaway sandwiches but it is well worth booking for the appealing daily changing lunch menu. Two of the six main courses will be vegetarian and offer, along with dishes like venison and pancetta pie, plenty of freshness and flavour. Even the juices are seasonal and the tarts, pies and cakes are all made daily.

City Social ⟨⟩

Modern cuisine

Tower 42 (24th floor), 25 Old Broad St ⊠ EC2N
1HQ
✆ 020 7877 7703
www.citysociallondon.com
⊖ Liverpool Street

Closed Sunday
and bank holidays

Carte £43/72

XXX

Michelin

The buzz from the bar is the first thing you notice when you come up in the lift to Jason Atherton's handsome, well-run restaurant on the 24th floor of Tower 42. Dark and moody with a subtle art deco twist, it boasts impressive views of the City's ever-changing skyline – especially if you're sitting at one of the coveted window tables. Large parties should request one of the comfortable circular booths; those wanting to bag themselves a husband or a wife should ask for table 10, the proposal table. The menu is the same at lunch and dinner, but has some flexibility built in. Influences are largely European and dishes like côte de boeuf for two, lobster and chips and black olive potato gnocchi are not only incredibly tasty but also very good value. The kitchen has a deft touch but wisely acknowledges its customer base by making dishes quite robust in flavour and generous in size – this is elegant, refined but satisfying cooking, without the frills and fripperies. The wine list is also noteworthy, with a good mix of styles and prices.

First Course

- Yellowfin tuna tataki with cucumber salad and ponzu dressing.

- Pig's trotter and ham hock with crisp black pudding, apple and Madeira.

Main Course

- Braised Irish short-rib with celery, watercress and red wine sauce.

- Line-caught cod with salt cod brandade, chorizo, baby squid and squid ink sauce.

Dessert

- Chocolate soufflé with orange ice cream.

- Gariguette strawberry parfait with yoghurt sorbet.

City of London • Clerkenwell • Finsbury • Southwark ▶ Plans VIII-X

Club Gascon 🕸

French   **Plan VIII L2**

57 West Smithfield ⊠ EC1A 9DS
☎ 020 7600 6144
www.clubgascon.com
⊖ Barbican

Closed Christmas-New
Year, Monday lunch, Saturday,
Sunday and bank holidays
– booking essential

Menu £35/68 – Carte £37/58

Club Gascon

Those living in Gascony enjoy a diet with the highest fat content in France yet they tend to live longer than their compatriots. Leaving aside the magical powers of Armagnac, this 'Gascony paradox' is surely reason enough to explore further this most indulgent of cuisines. Chef-owner Pascal Aussignac is passionate about all things south-western: get him started on the quality of the produce and he'll talk the hind legs off an âne. Whilst familiar ingredients appear on the menu, the cooking is surprisingly contemporary and often quite original; the ambition may not always be matched by the execution but the dishes will certainly grab your attention. Lunch is a slightly pared down version of the evening menu but the tasting menu remains the benchmark and comes with some intelligent and well-considered wine matches. Service is appropriately and unapologetically Gallic, while marble pillars, panelling and huge floral displays add grandeur to the high-ceilinged room, which was once a Lyons Corner House.

First Course

- Foie gras terrine with caviar and an oceanic crisp.
- Amber tulip flower with quinoa and butter carrots.

Main Course

- Lamb with vermouth sauce, mussels and crisp sweetbreads.
- Glazed black cod with sweet artichokes and crunchy grapes.

Dessert

- Scrambled Brillat-Savarin cheese with truffled honey and pistachio.
- Variations of rhubarb with hibiscus and blood orange rocks.

Comptoir Gascon

French

61-63 Charterhouse St. ✉ EC1M 6HJ
☎ 020 7608 0851
www.comptoirgascon.com
⊖ Farringdon

Closed Christmas-New Year,
Sunday, Monday and bank
holidays – booking essential

Menu £15 (weekday lunch) – Carte £21/34 ✗

 This buzzy restaurant should be subsidised by the French Tourist Board as it does more to illustrate one component of Gascony's famed 'douceur de vivre' – sweetness of life – than any glossy brochure. The wines, breads, foie gras, duck and cheeses all celebrate SW France's reputation for earthy, proper man-food. The menu starts with 'humble beginnings', followed by 'surf and turf'; be sure to order something from the 'best of duck' section, whether as rillettes, confit or in a burger. After these big flavours, it'll come as a relief to see that the desserts are delicate little things. Prices are commendable; even the region's wine comes direct from the producers to avoid the extra mark-up. There's further booty on the surrounding shelves.

Duck & Waffle

Modern cuisine

Heron Tower (40th floor), 110 Bishopsgate
✉ EC2N 4AY
☎ 020 3640 7310
www.duckandwaffle.com
⊖ Liverpool Street

Booking essential

Carte £30/65 ✗✗

 The UK's highest restaurant sits on the 40th floor of the Heron Tower, with the finest view of the Gherkin in the capital. There's an ambitious range of influences on the menu which gives it something of an identity crisis – but this is where the friendly staff step in and offer a little direction. Offal is done well – crispy pig's ears come in a paper bag – and the signature dish of duck confit on a waffle with maple syrup shows they don't take themselves too seriously. It's open 24 hours a day and offers breakfast, lunch and dinner as well as brunch at weekends; those who are stout of heart and thin of artery should sample the foie gras crème brûlée, although they may find themselves sinking faster than the lift on the way out.

Elliot's

Modern cuisine

Plan X M4

12 Stoney St., Borough Market ✉ SE1 9AD
📞 020 7403 7436
www.elliotscafe.com
⊖ London Bridge

Closed Sunday and bank holidays
– booking advisable

Carte £19/31   ✗

This lively, unpretentious café provides a masterclass in keeping things simple. They take top quality ingredients – sourced directly from Borough Market in which the café stands – and marry several of them together to create earthy, uncomplicated dishes that are full of flavour and will leave anyone feeling sated and satisfied. The menu is concise, regularly changing and instantly appealing; try one of their sharing dishes like the slow-cooked lamb shoulder or the 40 day dry-aged Dexter beef; this has become quite a feature, as has the fish from the Sussex day-boats. If you're not sharing, then around four plates per person will suffice; staff are more than happy to guide your choices. Ask for a table at the far end under the skylight.

Fenchurch

Modern cuisine

Plan VIII M3

Level 37, 20 Fenchurch St ✉ EC3M 3BY
📞 0333 772 0020
www.skygarden.london
⊖ Monument

Closed Sunday dinner
– booking advisable

Menu £32 (weekday lunch) – Carte £44/73   ✗✗

It's wise to arrive here at the 'Walkie Talkie' early, not only because you have to go through the faff of airport-style security on the ground floor but also because you'll want to have a wander around the Sky Garden – a vast atrium with some greenery at the top of the building. This is also the time to take in the vista because the restaurant is housed in a glass box within it and actually the views from here aren't great. At least the restaurant understands it has to offer more than a great location, so the welcome is warm, the room is smartly kitted out and the food is prepared with care. The dishes are seasonal and largely British; the flavour combinations are complementary and the ingredients top drawer.

Fish Market

S e a f o o d   **Plan VIII N2**

16b New St ⊠ EC2M 4TR
☎ 020 3503 0790
www.fishmarket-restaurant.co.uk
⊖ Liverpool Street

Closed 25-26 December,
1 January, Sunday dinner
and bank holidays – booking
advisable

Menu £20 – Carte £27/39   ✗

An antidote to the plethora of steakhouses comes in the form of this traditional seafood restaurant, courtesy of the D&D group. Housed within a former warehouse of the East India Company, it has an appealing ersatz industrial look, with cast-iron pillars, rough-hewn walls and limed oak; the chef shucking oysters behind the full-length marble-topped bar adds to the feeling that you've stepped from Liverpool Street straight into St Ives. From its lengthy menu of classics, the kitchen concentrates on delivering familiar flavours – and by using Cornish crab, oysters from Colchester and West Mersea, day-boat plaice, line-caught cod and farmed bass from Greece, it demonstrates it has the appropriate sustainability credentials.

Foxlow

M e a t s   a n d   g r i l l s   **Plan IX L2**

69-73 St John St ⊠ EC1M 4AN
☎ 020 7680 2700
www.foxlow.co.uk
⊖ Farringdon

Closed 24 December-1 January,
Sunday dinner and bank holidays

Menu £18 (weekdays) – Carte £22/41   ✗

When those clever people behind the Hawksmoor chain took over the site of the former North Road restaurant, they decided it would make the ideal spot in which to serve something a little different to the usual offerings found in their various steakhouses. Granted, there are steaks on offer but there are plenty of other choices whose influences come from Italy, Asia and the Middle East – highlights include the 8-hour bacon rib which is smoked overnight, assorted fresh salads and ice cream sundaes in a myriad of flavours. The vibe is fun and lively, especially on the ground floor and the place has a funky look too, with a reclaimed oak floor, glazed bricks from the Tube and chemistry lab tops from a Yorkshire school.

Garrison

Mediterranean cuisine   Plan X M5

99-101 Bermondsey St ✉ SE1 3XB
✆ 020 7089 9355
www.thegarrison.co.uk
⊖ London Bridge.

Closed 25-26 December
– booking essential at dinner

Menu £24/29 – Carte £26/38

You'd be hard pressed to find a more charming pub than the Garrison. With its appealing vintage look, warm atmosphere and delightful staff, it's the perfect antidote to those hard-edged boozers that we've all accidentally found ourselves in at some point. Open from 8am for smoothies and breakfast, it gets busier as the day goes on – and don't bother coming for dinner if you haven't booked. Booth numbers 4 and 5, opposite the open kitchen, are the most popular while number 2 at the back is the cosiest. Daily specials on the blackboard supplement the nicely balanced menu and the cooking is perky and bright, with a subtle Mediterranean slant. Salads are done well and there's a daily steak, while puds are of a more traditional bent.

Granger & Co. Clerkenwell

Modern cuisine   Plan IX K1

50 Sekforde St ✉ EC1R 0HA
✆ 020 7251 9032
www.grangerandco.com
⊖ Farringdon

Closed Sunday dinner

Carte £19/40

By turning to Clerkenwell for his second London restaurant, Aussie food writer and restaurateur Bill Granger showed his knack for picking the right location. This bright and stylish environment proves the ideal backdrop for a menu inspired by his peregrinations around the world. There's something for everyone, with small and big plates, BBQ dishes, pizzas, salads, bowls of rice and grains and, of course, his celebrated breakfasts which include his deliriously creamy scrambled eggs. His best dishes are often those enlivened with the flavours of southeast Asia and are especially appealing after you've spent time exploring the cocktail list. The chummy service contributes considerably to the appealingly laid back atmosphere.

Hawksmoor

Meats and grills   Plan VIII M2

10-12 Basinghall St ✉ EC2V 5BQ
☎ 020 7397 8120
www.thehawksmoor.com
⊖ Bank

Closed 24 December-2 January,
Saturday, Sunday and bank
holidays – booking essential

Menu £28 (lunch and early dinner) – Carte £23/71

 Fast and furious, busy and boisterous, Hawksmoor provides another testosterone filled celebration of the serious business of beef eating – this is about red meat, red wine and red-faced City types in duels to see who can order the biggest steak. It's a handsome room, with its low ceiling, leather seating and wood panelling which was once used in specimen cupboards at the Natural History Museum. The place comes with a great cocktail list and an impressive wine list offering plenty of Mouton Rothschild for the big earners. The Longhorn steaks are nicely aged, particularly the D-Rump, and well-rested before coming to the table. With notice you can order 'meat feasts' which take you on a 7-course 'tour of a cow'.

Hix Oyster and Chop House

Traditional British   Plan IX L2

36-37 Greenhill Rents ✉ EC1M 6BN
☎ 020 7017 1930
www.hixoysterandchophouse.co.uk
⊖ Farringdon

Closed 25-29 December, Saturday
lunch and bank holidays

Menu £10 (weekday lunch) – Carte £20/58

 Utilitarian surroundings, seasonal British ingredients, plenty of offal and prissy-free cooking: this may sound like a description of St John but was in fact Mark Hix's first solo venture and the start of his rapidly expanding restaurant empire. Smithfield Market seems an appropriate location for a restaurant that not only celebrates Britain's culinary heritage with old classics like rabbit brawn, nettle soup and beef and oyster pie but also reminds us of our own natural bounty, from sand eels to asparagus, whiting to laver bread. It's also called an Oyster and Chop House for a reason, with four types of oyster on offer as well as plenty of meat, including Aberdeen beef aged for 28 days and served on the bone.

José 🐾

S p a n i s h

104 Bermondsey St ⊠ SE1 3UB
℘ 020 7403 4902
www.josepizarro.com
⊖ London Bridge

Plan X M5

Closed 24-26 December and
Sunday dinner

Carte £12/28

♿
A/C
🍽

You may be in Bermondsey but, standing inside this tapas bar, you feel you could well be in Barcelona. Standing is what you'll most likely be doing, as it's rather snug, they don't take bookings and like to pack people in – but you won't mind one bit because the atmosphere is so great. Start with a sherry and some of the acorn-fed Iberico ham that hangs above the counter; the food is dictated by the markets but all the classics are here and Pluma Iberica (pork shoulder) is the house speciality. The vibrant dishes are intensely flavoured; five plates per person should be more than enough but it's hard to stop ordering when you see what the person next to you has got. There's a great list of sherries and all wines are available by the glass.

José Pizarro

S p a n i s h

36 Broadgate Circle ⊠ EC2M 1QS
℘ 020 7256 5333
www.josepizarro.com
⊖ Liverpool Street

Plan VIII M2

Closed Sunday

Carte £24/31

☂
♿
A/C
🍽

The Broadgate Circle development was unveiled in 2015 as a new "retail, leisure and food destination". In amongst all the chains is this third operation from José Pizarro who, having called his first 'José' and his second 'Pizarro', has now gone with his full name. Open from breakfast, the place is a good fit for the City as it's flexible and efficiently run. There are tables both inside and out but the counter in front of the open kitchen is the best place to sit. The Spanish menu is an appealing mix of familiar favourites and updated classics; the fish and seafood dishes tend to be the standouts, especially the octopus which is excellent. The exclusively Spanish wine list is well priced, with many wines served by the carafe.

Jugged Hare

Traditional British

42 Chiswell St ⊠ EC1Y 4SA
℘ 020 7614 0134
www.thejuggedhare.com
⊖ Barbican.

Closed 25-26 December
– booking essential

Carte £30/60

The famous 18C recipe created by Hannah Glasse, the UK's first domestic goddess, provided the inspiration for the renaming of this Grade II listed pub, previously known as The King's Head. It's an apt name because committed vegetarians may feel ill at ease – and not just because of the collection of glass cabinets in the bar which showcase the art of taxidermy. The atmospheric and appealingly noisy dining room, which has a large open kitchen running down one side, specialises in stout British dishes, with Denham Estate venison, Yorkshire guinea fowl and Cumbrian Longhorn steaks from the rotisserie and grill being the highlights. If the main course doesn't fill you, puddings like treacle tart or bread and butter pudding will.

Kenza

Lebanese

10 Devonshire Sq. ⊠ EC2M 4YP
℘ 020 7929 5533
www.kenza-restaurant.com
⊖ Liverpool Street

Closed 24-25 December, Saturday
lunch and bank holidays

Menu £30/50 – Carte £29/43

Proving that a party atmosphere and good food are not mutually exclusive, Kenza's Middle Eastern exotica instantly transports you away from the city institutions above. It's not easy to find which adds a frisson of expectation, as does descending the staircase into a room full of Moroccan tiles, beaded lamps, lanterns, silk cushions, mosharabi screens and thumping lounge music. Most of the menu is Lebanese but with Moroccan influences; meze is varied and satisfying and the best main courses are slow-cooked lamb shoulder, chargrilled chicken and marinated swordfish; all meat is Halal. Larger parties need not waste time choosing and can order the 'feasting' menus thus allowing more time to appreciate the skills of the belly dancers.

ⓝ Lobos

S p a n i s h Plan X M4

14 Borough High St ✉ SE1 9QG
☎ 020 7407 5361
www.lobostapas.co.uk
⊖ London Bridge

Closed 25-26 December and
1 January

Carte £14/51

 Dimly lit and decidedly compact, this tapas bar is tucked away under the railway arches near the entrance to Borough Market and has a feel not unlike that of an air raid shelter – complete with Edison light bulbs. Downstairs is for walk-ins and upstairs for bookings; sit here to enjoy the theatre of the open kitchen, with the shouts of the chefs and the sizzle of la plancha. The concise menu offers a range of appetisers alongside traditional tapas like tortilla and croquetas; head for the meat dishes, which are the speciality here, and you can't go wrong – try the leg of slow-roasted Castilian milk-fed lamb or the Iberico pork selection to share. Service comes with a smile, and the wine list covers a good many of the Spanish regions.

Luc's Brasserie

F r e n c h Plan VIII M3

17-22 Leadenhall Mkt ✉ EC3V 1LR
☎ 020 7621 0666
www.lucsbrasserie.com
⊖ Bank

Closed Christmas, New Year, Saturday, Sunday and bank holidays – booking essential – (lunch only and dinner Tuesday-Thursday)

Menu £18 (lunch) – Carte £26/71

An object lesson in understanding your market: Luc's Brasserie regularly serves around 120 people for lunch, many of whom have not just come for the food but because they know they can be in and out within the magical 45 minutes. It's in a great spot looking down over the Victorian splendour of Leadenhall Market and its staff go about their business with impressive efficiency yet still manage to smile and engage with their customers. The menu has all the French favourites you'll ever need, from onion soup to duck rillettes, but many go for the grill section which includes steaks in all sizes and chops aplenty. Needless to say, descending the narrow staircase at the end of the meal requires considerably less resolve than climbing up it.

Lutyens

M o d e r n   c u i s i n e   **Plan VIII K3**

85 Fleet St. ⊠ EC4Y 1AE
✆ 020 7583 8385
www.lutyens-restaurant.com
⊖ Blackfriars

Closed 1 week Christmas-New
Year, Saturday, Sunday and bank
holidays

Menu £25/33 – Carte £30/62   XxX

This impressive building, designed by Sir Edwin Lutyens and previously Reuters' HQ, is now the ideal backdrop to Sir Terence Conran's elegant and understated restaurant. It's a smoothly run operation, with staff dealing promptly and efficiently with the lunchtime full house; dinner is a far more languid affair. The menu closely follows the seasons and is an appealing blend of the classic, like Dover sole, and the more contemporary, such as squid with ink sauce or smoked venison carpaccio. The cooking is crisp and confident, game is handled well and the kitchen avoids any lily-gilding. Over 30 wines are offered by the glass; from the young and exciting to the fine and rare, and in a super range of measures.

Magdalen

M o d e r n   B r i t i s h   **Plan X M4**

152 Tooley St. ⊠ SE1 2TU
✆ 020 7403 1342
www.magdalenrestaurant.co.uk
⊖ London Bridge

Closed Sunday, Saturday lunch
and bank holidays

Menu £17 (lunch) – Carte £29/50   XX

The Magdalen's kitchen is a clever one: super sourcing and direct contact with farmers take care of the ingredients; the cooking demonstrates a solid, unshowy technique and the influences are kept largely from within the British Isles. Shoulder of Middle White pork with fennel and lemon is a highlight and the rabbit leg with broad beans leaves you wondering why this meat isn't sold in every supermarket. French toast with apricots and vanilla ice cream provides a suitably comforting finale. The lunch menu is a steal, the wine list has been thoughtfully put together by someone who knows the menu well and staff are an eager, genial bunch. The restaurant is divided between two floors; it's more fun on the ground floor.

The Modern Pantry Clerkenwell

World cuisine   **Plan IX L2**

47-48 St John's Sq. ✉ EC1V 4JJ
✆ 020 7553 9210
www.themodernpantry.co.uk
⊖ Farringdon

Closed August bank holiday
and 25-26 December – booking
advisable

Carte £26/37

This Georgian building has been everything from a foundry to a carpentry workshop but these days plays host to New Zealander Anna Hansen's fusion restaurant. The smart glass doors lead into a simple, crisp space; there's an upstairs too, split between two rooms, which offers a little more intimacy but lacks the buzz of downstairs. The kitchen's travels are reflected in a menu that has few boundaries. You'll probably need to ask for an explanation of at least one ingredient but the staff are clued up, which is no mean feat since menus change daily as ingredients come in. Despite all that's happening on the plate, flavours are well-judged and complementary. Most dishes also come with thoughtfully suggested wine matches.

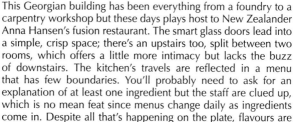

ⓝ The Modern Pantry Finsbury Square

World cuisine   **Plan IX M2**

14 Finsbury Sq ✉ EC2A 1AH
✆ 020 3696 6565
www.themodernpantry.co.uk
⊖ Moorgate

Closed 25 December
and Sunday dinner

Menu £23 (weekday lunch) – Carte £31/47

Anna Hansen's second Modern Pantry is on the ground floor of the imposing, Grade II listed Alphabeta Building. The lively bar counter is the place to come for 'global tapas' like salted liquorice macadamias or pickled garlic, Iranian lime and herb-marinated olives; best when accompanied by a sherry livener. The main part of the operation is the elegant, spacious dining room; there are no prizes for guessing that this was formerly a bank. The extensive menu takes a while to read and digest – Google may have to be your friend when it comes to ingredients like ajowan or wattleseed, or alternatively ask one of the cheery staff. Some of the ingredients may be unusual but every one of them is on the plate for good reason. Puddings are a highlight.

Morito

Spanish **Plan IX K1**

32 Exmouth Mkt ⊠ EC1R 4QE
℘ 020 7278 7007
www.morito.co.uk
⊖ Farringdon

Closed 24 December–
2 January, Sunday dinner and
bank holidays – (bookings not
accepted at dinner)

Carte £14/29 ✗

Morito may not seduce you with its looks but once you start eating you'll find it hard to tear yourself away. This authentic tapas bar comes courtesy of the owners of next door Moro and shares their passion for Moorish cuisine. It's modestly kitted out but endearingly so, with a two-tone formica counter and half a dozen small tables; just turn up and if they haven't got space they'll take your number and you can have a drink in Exmouth Market while you wait. Seven or eight dishes between two should be enough but at these prices you can never overspend. Highlights of the immensely appealing menu include jamon and chicken croquetas and succulent lamb chops with cumin and paprika, all served in authentic earthenware dishes.

Moro

Mediterranean cuisine **Plan IX K1**

34-36 Exmouth Mkt ⊠ EC1R 4QE
℘ 020 7833 8336
www.moro.co.uk
⊖ Farringdon

Closed dinner 24 December–
2 January, Sunday dinner and
bank holidays – booking essential

Carte £31/43 ✗

It's the stuff of youthful dreams – pack up your worldly goods in a camper van, drive through Spain, Portugal, Morocco and the Sahara and then, once back in Blighty, open a restaurant, share your love of Moorish cuisine and never look back. Sam and Sam Clark created something back then that has since been much copied and their peregrinations continue to inform their cooking. The utilitarian look adds a continental feel to the room while the wood-fired oven and chargrill fill the air with wonderful aromas. Freshness is key – don't be surprised to see fish being delivered during service; spicing is subtle and the concise menu changes every three weeks. The wine list is dominated by Spain and has plenty of gems from lesser known regions.

New St Grill

Meats and grills   **Plan VIII N2**

16a New St ⊠ EC2M 4TR
𝒞 020 3503 0785
www.newstreetgrill.com
⊖ Liverpool Street

Closed 25 December-3 January
except dinner 31 December

Menu £27 (lunch and early dinner) – Carte £35/69

The people at D&D, who recognise a trend when they see one, converted this 18th century warehouse to satisfy London's ever increasing appetite for red meat. Out of a building that was once used by the East India Company to store spices, they created an intimate and atmospheric space, with a chic bar attached. The kitchen has a sure hand when it comes to classics like lobster cocktail, Cornish dressed crab and rack of lamb, but beef is the main event here, with steaks cooked on a Josper grill. They use Black Angus and the choice is between grass-fed British beef, aged for 28 days, or corn-fed American beef, aged for 40 days. The wine list is strong on older red Bordeaux and mixes the classic with the more esoteric.

Oblix

Meats and grills   **Plan X M4**

Level 32, The Shard, 31 St Thomas St. ⊠ SE1 9RY
𝒞 020 7268 6700
www.oblixrestaurant.com
⊖ London Bridge

Menu £32 (lunch) – Carte £29/156

Inspired by the bar in Tokyo's Park Hyatt, but with infinitely better views, Oblix occupies the 32nd floor of The Shard and comes from the same stable as Zuma and Roka. Instead of another Japanese restaurant, however, Rainer Becker choose to create a New York grill style operation, where meats and fish from the rotisserie, grill and Josper oven are the stars of the show. Starters are light and easy, from salads to sliced yellowtail, and a NY cheesecake is the only way to end. The designer wisely decided against competing with the far-reaching views; window tables (which are mostly tables for two) are highly prized. An abbreviated version of the menu is available in the adjacent lounge bar – where they also serve brunch at weekends.

Q60

INDULGE YOURSELF

UX3 HN97

INFINITI

EMPOWER THE DRIVE

Oxo Tower

M o d e r n c u i s i n e　　　　　**Plan X K4**

Oxo Tower Wharf (8th floor), Barge House St

✉ SE1 9PH

☎ 020 7803 3888

www.oxotower.co.uk

⊖ Southwark

Closed 25 December

Menu £34 (lunch) – Carte £41/76　　

There can be few brighter restaurants than this one on the 8th floor of the Oxo Tower, thanks to its huge windows and enthusiastic application of white paint. The menu provides a fairly promising read, with dishes made up of ingredients from the luxury end of the spectrum, although the kitchen doesn't always quite deliver the goods. Meanwhile, service is a little more ceremonial than the brasserie next door and all this is reflected in the prices – the final bill can dazzle as much as the surroundings, so at least try to get a table by the window to make it memorable. Lunchtimes are largely invaded by city types from across the river, while at night the restaurant becomes a popular setting for those celebrating special occasions.

Oxo Tower Brasserie

M o d e r n c u i s i n e　　　　　**Plan X K4**

Oxo Tower Wharf (8th floor), Barge House St

✉ SE1 9PH

☎ 020 7803 3888

www.oxotower.co.uk

⊖ Southwark

Closed 25 December

Menu £30 (lunch and early dinner) – Carte £27/49　

The light-filled, glass-encased brasserie on the eighth floor of the iconic Oxo Tower makes much of its riverside location but that's not to say that this is just a spot for a summer's day as the bold, zingy Mediterranean flavours ensure that the cooking is bright and sunny even when it's dull outside. They've moved the bar to the front so that everyone gets a better view these days. Even so, if you've never asked for a window table before, then now is the time to start. Better still, ask for the terrace and face east towards St Paul's for the best views. Staff do their bit by being a responsive bunch and the place really rocks in the evenings. It's much more fun than their restaurant and the prices are friendlier too.

 Padella

I t a l i a n

6 Southwark St, Borough Market ✉ SE1 1TQ
www.padella.co
⊖ London Bridge

Closed 25-26 December, Sunday
dinner and bank holidays
– bookings not accepted

Carte £14/20

A/C   This lively little sister to Trullo isn't difficult to find: just look for the queue. Padella means 'pan' in Italian and the idea behind it is brilliant in its simplicity. This is a restaurant dedicated to pasta, which is hand-rolled in house; sauces and fillings are inspired by the owners' trips to Italy and prices are extremely pleasing to the pocket. Grab a seat at the ground floor counter overlooking the open kitchen; there are a handful of starters on the short, seasonal menu but it's dishes like tagliatelle with smoked eel, cream and Amalfi lemon or papardelle with 8-hour Dexter beef shin ragu that take centre stage. There's a concise but eminently drinkable wine list – and it's hard not to warm to a place that offers free filtered water.

Paternoster Chop House

T r a d i t i o n a l   B r i t i s h

Warwick Ct., Paternoster Sq. ✉ EC4M 7DX
✆ 020 7029 9400
www.paternosterchophouse.co.uk
⊖ St Paul's

Closed 26-30 December,
1 January, lunch Saturday and
dinner Sunday

Menu £20 (lunch and early dinner) – Carte £28/49

   If you could make just one restaurant legally obliged to serve British food then it would probably be the one that lies in the shadow of St Paul's Cathedral, one of Britain's most symbolic landmarks. Fortunately, Paternoster Chop House negates the need for a bye-law by offering classics from all parts of these isles. The first thing you see on the neatly laid-out menu is the comfortingly patriotic sight of a 'Beer of the Day'. Their livestock comes from small farms, their fish from day boats in the southwest and all the old favourites are present and correct: native oysters, cottage pie, potted hough, liver and bacon, and apple crumble. The dining room is large and open; you might have to fight your way through the busy bar.

Pizarro

Mediterranean cuisine   **Plan X M5**

194 Bermondsey St ✉ SE1 3UW
 020 7378 9455
www.josepizarro.com
⊖ Borough

Closed 24-28 December

Menu £35 – Carte £25/45   🍴

 José Pizarro has a refreshingly simple way of naming his establishments: first came José, a bustling little tapas bar, and then Pizarro, a larger, more structured restaurant a few doors down. The good news is that Pizarro now takes bookings so you no longer need to hang around waiting for a window seat or a place at the large communal table; in fact, when you do book it's worth asking for one of the prized semi-circular booths. The atmosphere in the restaurant is great and the food equally enjoyable. The menu offers a selection of small and large plates; dishes such as prawns with piquillo peppers and jamón are as tasty as they are easy on the eye. Larger plates could include hake with artichoke, and pork fillet with almonds.

Le Pont de la Tour

French   **Plan X N4**

36d Shad Thames, Butlers Wharf ✉ SE1 2YE
 020 7403 8403
www.lepontdelatour.co.uk
⊖ London Bridge

Closed 1 January

Menu £20/32 – Carte £34/67   🍴🍴

     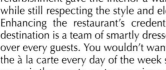 Few London restaurants can boast a more glorious setting than Pont de la Tour, especially on a summer's day when you're sitting on the terrace taking in the breathtaking views of Tower Bridge. To celebrate its 25th anniversary, a sympathetic, top-to-toe refurbishment gave the interior a warmer, more sumptuous feel, while still respecting the style and elegance of the original look. Enhancing the restaurant's credentials as a special-occasion destination is a team of smartly dressed staff who flutter and fuss over every guests. You wouldn't want to encounter the prices on the à la carte every day of the week so the better value Prix Fixe menu is the way to go to experience the French-influenced and appealingly presented dishes.

Polpo Smithfield

Italian   **Plan IX L2**

3 Cowcross St ⊠ EC1M 6DR
✆ 020 7250 0034
www.polpo.co.uk
⊖ Farringdon.

Closed Christmas, New Year and
Sunday dinner

Carte £20/30

If you've been to a Polpo, or even if you've just bought the cookbook, then you'll know what to expect here – refreshingly uncomplicated and inherently satisfying dishes designed for sharing. For his third Venetian-style bacaro, Russell Norman converted a former meat market storage facility and the place has a charming, elegantly battered feel. Head first to the Negroni bar downstairs, with its appealingly wicked atmosphere, and order the eponymous cocktail. Afterwards, you'll find yourself eagerly over-ordering such delights as crisp pizzette or hearty meatballs. The Venetian and North Italian wines come by the glass, carafe and bottle; staff are cool and calm and the atmosphere terrific. Bookings are only taken up to 5.30pm.

Quality Chop House

Traditional British   **Plan IX K1**

92-94 Farringdon Rd ⊠ EC1R 3EA
✆ 020 7278 1452
www.thequalitychophouse.com
⊖ Farringdon

Closed Sunday dinner and bank
holidays – booking advisable

Menu £15 (weekday lunch) – Carte £24/44

This Grade II listed room has been an eating house since 1869 and has an almost Orwellian feel; its etched windows proclaim 'Progressive working class caterer' and 'London's noted cup of tea'. It's in the hands of owners who respect its history and it does a fine job championing gusty British grub: ox tongue, brown crab, Middle White pork, Ayrshire veal and Cornish pollock – they're all here, in refreshingly unadorned dishes. Game is a highlight, as are the steaks from the butcher next door. You're also unlikely to find a better example of a concise wine list – there are gems aplenty, prices are generous and, for something special, check out the Collector's list at the back. The adjoining 'wine bar' has an all-day menu.

Rabot 1745

Modern cuisine

2-4 Bedal St, Borough Mkt ⊠ SE1 9AL
☎ 020 7378 8226
www.rabot1745.com
⊖ London Bridge

Closed 25-30 December,
Sunday and Monday

Carte £26/42 ✗✗

Bored by the ordinary? Looking for something different? Then try Rabot 1745, from the owners of Hotel Chocolat, which celebrates the cocoa bean in all its infinite majesty. Named after their estate in St Lucia and its founding year, the restaurant uses wood from the island to add to the plantation feel of the upstairs room. A light-hearted yet knowledgeable introduction is given at the start of the meal explaining how, in its natural state, the flavour of the bean is bitter with a little spice. These flavours are then used in the classically based cooking, with crushed nibs playing a key role, and the resulting dishes have genuine substance. Naturally enough, the desserts are a highlight – don't miss the trio of chocolate mousses.

Roast

Modern British

The Floral Hall, Borough Mkt ⊠ SE1 1TL
☎ 020 3006 6111
www.roast-restaurant.com
⊖ London Bridge

Closed 25-26 December and
1 January – booking essential

Menu £30/38 – Carte £39/69 ✗✗

These days every restaurant seemingly name-checks its suppliers – but Roast was one of the first and has always been known for promoting British producers, whether they rear pigs or make cider. Mind you, could they do anything else considering their location – bang in the heart of Borough Market? There's a new energy to the kitchen these days and greater care shown in the preparation of the dishes. The highlight is often the 'dish of the day' which could be rare breed suckling pig with apple sauce; prices can be a little high though, as most main courses need side dishes. Service is also more personable and the bar, which hosts live music at night, is becoming a destination in its own right. Ask for a window table on the market side.

St John

26 St John St ✉ EC1M 4AY
☎ 020 7251 0848
www.stjohnrestaurant.com
⊖ Farringdon

Closed Christmas-New
Year, Saturday lunch, Sunday
dinner and bank holidays
– booking essential

Carte £28/49

AC

St John

There's no standing on ceremony here at St John; indeed, very little ceremony at all, and that makes eating here such a joyful experience as one's focus is directed entirely at the food. There's little distraction from the surroundings either, which come in a shade of detention centre white. You can play it safe and go for some crab and then roast beef but this is the place to try new flavours, whether that's cuttlefish or ox tongue. Game is a real favourite and the only gravy will be the blood of the bird – this is natural, 'proper' food. Seasonality is at its core – the menu is rewritten for each service – and nothing sums up the philosophy more than the potatoes and greens: they are always on the menu but the varieties and types change regularly. The waiters wear chef's jackets and spend time in the kitchen so they know what they're talking about and are worth listening to. There are dishes for two as well as magnums of wine for real trenchermen – and be sure to order a dozen warm madeleines to take home.

First Course	Main Course	Dessert
• Roast bone marrow and parsley salad.	• Pheasant and trotter pie.	• Ginger loaf and butterscotch sauce.
• Brown shrimps with white cabbage.	• Turbot with braised chicory.	• Poached apricot with toasted brioche.

St John Maltby

Traditional British

41 Ropewalk, Maltby St ✉ SE1 3PA
☎ 020 7553 9844
www.stjohngroup.uk.com/maltby_street
⊖ London Bridge

Closed Christmas, New Year and
Sunday dinner-Tuesday – booking
advisable – (dinner only and
lunch Friday-Sunday)

Carte £31/35

Those living south of the river no longer have to cross the water to witness just how good British cooking can be, thanks to Fergus Henderson and Trevor Gulliver's place, tucked under a railway arch in deepest Bermondsey. With its austere, industrial-style décor, its scratched chequered floor and its church pews, the utilitarian dining space is far from pretty – and a trip to the bathroom will see you going for a wander down the street. But it's the food that you come for and the food that impresses – tasty, satisfying and as British as John Bull. Start with smoked sprats followed by pigeon; add in some sides and finish off with an Eccles cake or Lancashire cheeses. The earthy, original selection of wines are also available to take away.

Sauterelle

French

The Royal Exchange ✉ EC3V 3LR
☎ 020 7618 2483
www.royalexchange-grandcafe.co.uk
⊖ Bank

Closed Christmas, Easter, Saturday,
Sunday and bank holidays

Menu £25 – Carte £32/44

It can't be easy for this D&D restaurant as it's in the somewhat unenviable position of having to compete with the grandeur of its own setting. It occupies the mezzanine floor of the Royal Exchange overlooking what was once the trading floor and is now the Grand Café. This City landmark was twice destroyed by fire and was rebuilt in 1844, but its layout remains largely true to Sir Thomas Gresham's 1566 original. In this most British of scenes one finds a menu of a largely European persuasion, with a particular fondness for all things French, although the ingredients are largely from within the UK. It's easy to find something appealing and, whilst prices are quite high, the kitchen doesn't skimp on luxury ingredients.

Skylon

M o d e r n   c u i s i n e **Plan III J4**

1 Southbank Centre, Belvedere Rd ⊠ SE1 8XX
℘ 020 7654 7800
www.skylon-restaurant.co.uk
⊖ Waterloo

Closed 25 December

Menu £20/28 – Carte £27/38

The original Skylon was a steel structure built for the Festival of Britain in 1951 to promote better quality design. Its name now lives on as the restaurant within the Royal Festival Hall, which was built just yards from where this 'vertical feature' once stood. The South Bank is now a much appreciated area of London and the restaurant offers wonderful river views. It's a large space, with a busy central cocktail bar, a formally laid out restaurant on one side and a simpler grill-style operation on the other. The latter serves fishcakes, burgers, steaks and the like; the restaurant uses more expensive ingredients and puts a modern spin on classic combinations. Be sure to ask for a window table.

Ⓝ Sosharu

J a p a n e s e **Plan IX K1**

63 Clerkenwell Rd ⊠ EC1M 5RR
℘ 020 3805 2304
www.sosharulondon.com
⊖ Farringdon

Closed bank holidays except
Good Friday and Sunday

Menu £20/30 – Carte £29/52

This is the seventh London restaurant from Jason Atherton and the first serving Japanese food; his right hand man here is chef Alex Craciun, previously of Pollen Street Social, who spent a year in Kyoto in preparation. It's a bustling operation with a long sushi counter; the furniture has been imported from Japan and the style is chic and understated. The menu is extensive but staff will happily guide you through; six small plates with a large rice pot or a 'classic' between two will do nicely – and although prices can be steep, dishes are meant for sharing. Special occasions call for Kisetsu – a private dining room where a set omakase-style menu is served – and special occasion or not, a cocktail in the downstairs bar is a must.

Story

Modern cuisine

199 Tooley St ⊠ SE1 2JX
✆ 020 7183 2117
www.restaurantstory.co.uk
⊖ London Bridge

Closed 2 weeks Christmas-New
Year, Easter, Sunday, Monday
lunch and bank holidays
– booking essential – (tasting
menu only)

Menu £39 (weekday lunch)/100

Michelin

As a teenager, Tom Sellers dreamed of owning his own restaurant – and by the time he was twenty-six, he had achieved his fairytale ending in the shape of Story. What was once a public toilet now resembles a sort of Nordic eco-lodge – all wood, glass and grass; the huge picture window allows light to flood in by day, while by night it's a surprisingly intimate space, with the glassed-in kitchen providing a muted buzz. The Nordic touch is evident not only in the design but also in the food, which comes in a set 6 or 10 course lunch and a 12 course dinner menu; modern techniques and a pleasingly light touch result in food with a back-to-nature feel and strong earthy flavours. A range of imaginative snacks kicks things off thick and fast; idiosyncratic touches like the menu arriving on a Charles Dickens book add to the experience and there's an impressive originality to dishes like the signature bread and dripping. With only 12 tables to serve, staff are refreshingly enthusiastic; getting a seat at one of those tables is another story.

First Course	Main Course	Dessert
• Heritage potato cake with shallots.	• Scallops with ash-roasted cucumber and dill.	• Chocolate and lovage.
• Onion and gin.	• Ravioli of lobster with shellfish velouté.	• Almond and dill.

City of London • Clerkenwell • Finsbury • Southwark ▲ Plans VIII-X

Tapas Brindisa

Spanish   **Plan X M4**

18-20 Southwark St, Borough Market ✉ SE1 1TJ
☎ 020 7357 8880   Bookings not accepted
www.brindisatapaskitchens.com
⊖ London Bridge

Carte £20/32

The owners spent years importing Spanish produce so it was
no surprise that their restaurant on the edge of Borough Market
took off immediately. It not only provided the blueprint for many
of the tapas bars that subsequently sprung up over London but
was also one of the first restaurants not to take bookings – a less
welcome but wholly understandable policy that has become
more widespread. The place has an infectious energy and vitality
and the young staff are as efficient as they are unflappable. Start
with a glass of Fino and crisp parcels of morcilla, then share a
selection of hand-carved Ibérico hams and robust, generously
sized dishes such as Galician-style hake, black rice with squid
and braised ox cheeks.

Tate Modern (Restaurant)

Modern British   **Plan X L4**

Switch House (9th floor), Tate Modern,   Closed 24-26 December – (lunch
Bankside ✉ SE1 9TG   only and dinner Friday-Saturday)
☎ 020 7401 5621
www.tate.org.uk
⊖ Southwark

Carte £27/56

The Tate Modern's striking Herzog and de Meuron designed
Switch House extension, which opened in 2016, is the location
of this contemporary restaurant. Fight your way through the
gallery-goers up to the ninth floor and you'll find yourself in a
light-filled, wood and concrete furnished, faux-industrial space.
Being this high up, you might expect a meal with a view but,
unless you're particularly tall, you won't be able to see much out
of the windows. Focus on the food instead: the seasonal modern
menu champions British ingredients and the kitchen keeps things
relatively light, so lunch need never impinge on plans for post-
prandial art appreciation. Desserts are a highlight and the wine
list interesting and well-priced.

28°-50° Fetter Lane

Modern cuisine

Plan VIII K3

140 Fetter Ln ✉ EC4A 1BT
✆ 020 7242 8877
www.2850.co.uk
⊖ Temple

Closed Saturday,
Sunday and bank holidays

Menu £20 (weekday lunch) – Carte £26/51

A/C
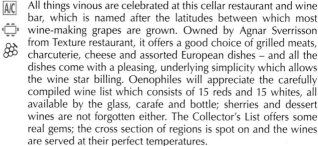

All things vinous are celebrated at this cellar restaurant and wine bar, which is named after the latitudes between which most wine-making grapes are grown. Owned by Agnar Sverrisson from Texture restaurant, it offers a good choice of grilled meats, charcuterie, cheese and assorted European dishes – and all the dishes come with a pleasing, underlying simplicity which allows the wine star billing. Oenophiles will appreciate the carefully compiled wine list which consists of 15 reds and 15 whites, all available by the glass, carafe and bottle; sherries and dessert wines are not forgotten either. The Collector's List offers some real gems; the cross section of regions is spot on and the wines are served at their perfect temperatures.

Union Street Café

Italian

Plan X L4

47-51 Great Suffolk St ✉ SE1 0BS
✆ 020 7592 7977
www.gordonramsayrestaurants.com/union-street-cafe/
⊖ London Bridge

Menu £20 (weekday lunch) – Carte £39/47

&.
A/C

Even the news that David Beckham wasn't actually involved in this Gordon Ramsay restaurant didn't seem to deter all those promiscuous restaurant twitchers from booking tables long before it had even opened his doors. But what began as a Mediterranean restaurant quickly morphed into a fully-fledged Italian one – albeit one that has seemingly spent quite a lot of time in New York. A former warehouse, it ticks all the boxes for that faux industrial look and comes with a basement cocktail bar and excitable diners. The menu, written in a curious lingua franca, stays pretty true to the classics and keeps things simple. Portions are not overly generous though, which means that you may need all four courses to leave feeling satisfied.

Vanilla Black

Vegetarian

17-18 Tooks Ct. ✉ EC4A 1LB
☎ 020 7242 2622
www.vanillablack.co.uk
⊖ Chancery Lane

Closed 2 weeks Christmas and
bank holidays – booking essential

Menu £27/42 ✕✕

One of the stubbornly lingering myths about restaurants in the City is that they mostly cater for red-faced, red-meat eaters in a rush – Vanilla Black proves there's room for every type of restaurant and that includes vegetarian ones. The seriousness with which they run this restaurant is palpable and it's obvious that real thought has gone into the creation of the menu – to such an extent that choosing dishes can be hard as they all sound so appealing. Modern techniques are subtly incorporated; dishes are light and easy to eat and deliver an array of interesting texture and flavour contrasts; and while there are some original combinations they are well judged. The restaurant is warm and comfortable and the service sweet and sincere.

Village East

Modern cuisine

171-173 Bermondsey St ✉ SE1 3UW
☎ 020 7357 6082
www.villageeast.co.uk
⊖ London Bridge

Closed 24-26 December

Carte £27/45 ✕

Village East was one of the first restaurants to open on this trend-setting street. It's sandwiched between two Georgian houses and the bright blue awning and illuminated signs proudly point it out. Counter dining is the focus in the main room, with the tables opposite the kitchen affectionately nicknamed the 'ringside' seats; those celebrating can tuck themselves away in a separate elevated bar. The cocktail list is worth exploring, with names such as 'Nettle Fizz' and 'Orient Express' making an appearance – take some friends along and really get into the party spirit. Cooking mixes contemporary dishes with Mediterranean-inspired plates; the confit turkey leg is a speciality and you'll have to go a long way to find a better burger.

Vivat Bacchus

Meats and grills

Plan VIII K2

47 Farringdon St ✉ EC4A 4LL
☎ 020 7353 2648
www.vivatbacchus.co.uk
⊖ Farringdon

Closed Christmas-New Year,
Sunday and bank holidays

Carte £20/45

Both the name and the Paul Cluver barriques outside offer clues about the make-up of this bustling City spot: it revolves around wine and the owner is South African. From four cellars come a hugely impressive 500 labels and 15,000 bottles, not only paying homage to major players like Château Latour, d'Yquem, Lafite and Romanée Conti, but also featuring South African jewels like Meerlust Rubicon – if you can button-hole owner Gerrie, he'll give you a tour. The restaurant attracts an ebullient City crowd and the menu complements the wine: steaks and charcuterie dominate and the sharing platters are perfect with a glass or three. Ostrich and kangaroo also feature and you can choose your perfectly ripened cheese from the cheese room.

Vivat Bacchus London Bridge

Meats and grills

Plan X M4

4 Hays Ln ✉ SE1 2HB
☎ 020 7234 0891
www.vivatbacchus.co.uk
⊖ London Bridge

Closed Christmas-New Year,
Sunday and bank holidays

Carte £20/45

Here at Vivat Bacchus, wine is regarded as the starting point rather than a supplement. Friends sharing a bottle or two after work make up a healthy part of the business and the menu looks as though it was devised to complement the wine rather than vice versa. As the owners are South African, wines from that country feature heavily, many of which have the necessary muscle for the meat-based menu which includes everything from kangaroo steaks to biltong. Avoid the more ambitious dishes and choose one of the many sharing boards which are largely themed around different countries, perhaps a platter of Italian hams or South African BBQ. It's also worth visiting their cheese room to make your own selection.

Well

M o d e r n   B r i t i s h **Plan IX L1**

180 St John St ✉ EC1V 4JY

Closed 25-26 December

☎ 020 7251 9363

www.downthewell.com

⊖ Farringdon.

Carte £26/41

This well-supported neighbourhood pub may be one of the smallest in the Martin brothers' portfolio but it's also one of the easiest to find thanks to its wide expanse of blue canopy. There's an intimate basement with sofas and bright artwork, but most of the dining takes place on the ground floor, where the windows open wide and the rather wonky tables are shoehorned in. The seasonal menu is a joy to read and whether you choose potted rainbow trout with pickled nectarines or Devonshire kid sausages with creamed polenta, dishes are carefully cooked and not short on flavour. Ingredients are sourced from all over the British Isles: mussels from the Shetland Isles, squid from Cornwall and steak from the artisan butcher round the corner.

Symbols shown in
red 🏠 X×X indicate
particularly charming
establishments.

Wright Brothers

S e a f o o d **Plan X M4**

11 Stoney St., Borough Market ⊠ SE1 9AD
✆ 020 7403 9554
www.thewrightbrothers.co.uk
⊖ London Bridge

Closed bank holidays
– booking advisable

Carte £21/87

A/C If you want to take a breather from the crowds at Borough Market then nip into Wright Brothers, but do it early as it quickly fills. Their motto is 'not just oysters' but then they do excel in them – hardly surprising when you consider that this small place started as an oyster wholesaler. Grab a table and enjoy them raw or cooked, by candlelight, along with the perfect accompaniment – a glass of porter – or else share a bench or the counter and opt for a platter of fruits de mer and a bottle of chilled Muscadet. If the bivalve is not your thing, then there are daily specials such as skate knobs, as well as pies and, for dessert, either chocolate truffles or crème brûlée. An air of contentment reigns.

Yauatcha City

C h i n e s e **Plan VIII M2**

Broadgate Circle ⊠ EC2M 2QS
✆ 020 3817 9880
www.yauatcha.com
⊖ Liverpool Street

Closed 24 December-3 January
and bank holidays

Menu £29 (weekday lunch) – Carte £24/56

For 10 years the only Yauatcha in London was the Soho original but now, after opening branches across India, the Hakkasan Group have created the capital's second. It's a huge operation with seating for around 180 and it takes up half of the newly developed Broadgate Circle. It has a more corporate feel than the original and the circular shape means that some tables leave you feeling you're eating in a corridor, but it does have something Broadwick Street doesn't – a terrace at both ends. You'll find all their dim sum greatest hits on the menu, from venison puffs to scallop shui mai, with desserts from the patisserie downstairs, but the chefs have some work to do to match the high standard, care and precision of the cooking found in Soho.

Chelsea · Earl's Court · Hyde Park · Knightsbridge · South Kensington

Though its days of unbridled hedonism are long gone - and its 'alternative' tag is more closely aligned to property prices than counterculture - there's still a hip feel to **Chelsea.** The place that put the Swinging into London has grown grey, distinguished and rather placid over the years, but tourists still throng to the **King's Road,** albeit to shop at the chain stores which have steadily muscled out SW3's chi-chi boutiques. It's not so easy now to imagine the heady mix of clans that used to sashay along here, from Sixties mods and models to Seventies punks, but for practically a quarter of a century, from the moment in 1955 when Mary Quant opened her trend-setting Bazaar, this was the pavement to parade down.

Chelsea's most cutting-edge destination these days is probably the gallery of modern art that bears the name of Margaret Thatcher's former favourite, Charles Saatchi. Which isn't the only irony, as Saatchi's outlandishly modish exhibits are housed in a one-time military barracks, the Duke of York's headquarters. Nearby, the traffic careers round **Sloane Square,** but it's almost possible to distance yourself from the fumes by sitting amongst the shady bowers in the centre of the square, or watching the world go by from a prime position in one of many cafés. Having said that, *the*

place to get away from it all, and yet still be within striking distance of the King's Road, is the delightful **Physic Garden,** down by the river. Famous for its healing herbs for over 300 years, it's England's second oldest botanic garden.

Mind you, if the size of a green space is more important to you than its medicinal qualities, then you need to head up to **Hyde Park,** the city's biggest. Expansive enough to accommodate trotting horses on Rotten Row, swimmers and rowers in the Serpentine, up-to-the-minute art exhibitions at the Serpentine Gallery, and ranting individualists at Speakers' Corner, the park has also held within its borders thousands of rock fans for concerts by the likes of the Rolling Stones, Simon and Garfunkel and Pink Floyd.

Just across from its southern border stands one of London's most imperious sights, The **Royal Albert Hall,** gateway to the cultural hotspot that is South Kensington. Given its wings after the 1851 Great Exhibition, the area round **Cromwell Road** invested heavily in culture and learning, in the shape of three world famous museums and three heavyweight colleges. But one of its most intriguing museums is little known to visitors, even though it's only a few metres east of the Albert Hall: the Sikorski is, by turns, a moving

C. Eymenier/MICHELIN

and spectacular showpiece for all things Polish.

No one would claim to be moved by the exhibits on show in nearby **Knightsbridge,** but there are certainly spectacular credit card transactions made here. The twin retail shrines of Harvey Nichols and Harrods are the proverbial honey-pots to the tourist bee, where a 'credit crunch' means you've accidentally trodden on your visa. Between them, in **Sloane Street,** the world's most famous retail names line up like an A-lister's who's who. At the western end of Knightsbridge is the rich person's Catholic church of choice, the Brompton Oratory, an unerringly lavish concoction in a baroque Italianate style. Behind it is the enchanting Ennismore

Gardens Mews, a lovely thoroughfare that dovetails rather well with the Oratory.

Further west along Old Brompton Road is **Earl's Court,** an area of grand old houses turned into bedsits and spartan hotels. An oddly bewitching contrast sits side by side here, the old resting alongside the new. The old in this case is Brompton Cemetery, an enchanting wilderness of monuments wherein lie the likes of Samuel Cunard and Emmeline Pankhurst. At its southwest corner, incongruously, sits the new, insomuch as it's the home of a regular influx of newcomers from abroad, who are young, gifted and possessed of vast incomes: the players of Chelsea FC.

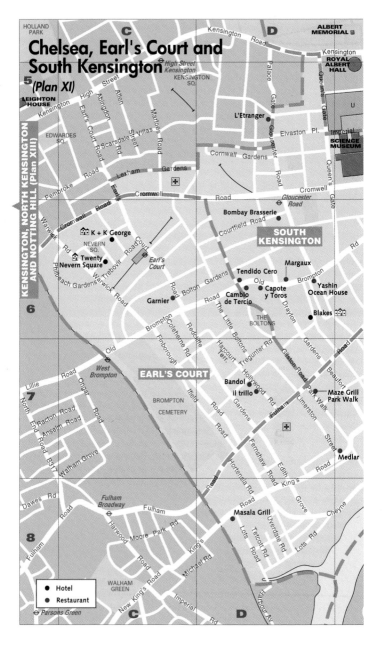

Chelsea, Earl's Court and South Kensington
(Plan XI)

HOLLAND PARK

ALBERT MEMORIAL

Kensington Road

LEIGHTON HOUSE

High Street Kensington

KENSINGTON SQ.

ROYAL ALBERT HALL

Kensington High Street

Abingdon

Allen

Marloes Road

Palace Gate

Queen's Gate

SCIENCE MUSEUM

EDWARDES SQ.

Earl's Court Road

Scarsdale Villas

L'Etranger

Gloucester Road

Elvaston Pl.

Pembroke Road

Lexham Gardens

Cornwall Gardens

Cromwell Road

Cromwell Road

Gloucester Road

Warwick Road

Cromwell Road

Bombay Brasserie

K + K George

Courtfield Road

SOUTH KENSINGTON

NEVERN SQ.

Twenty Nevern Square

Trebovir Road

Earl's Court Road

Earl's Court

Margaux

Philbeach Gardens

Warwick Road

Bolton Gardens

Tendido Cero

Old Brompton Road

Yashin Ocean House

KENSINGTON, NORTH KENSINGTON AND NOTTING HILL (Plan XIII)

Garnier

Coleherne Rd.

Redcliffe

Capote y Toros

Cambio de Tercio

Drayton Gardens

Blakes

Brompton Road

The Little Boltons

THE BOLTONS

Finborough Rd.

Old Brompton Road

West Brompton

Harcourt Terr.

Tregunter Rd.

Gilston Road

Beaufort

EARL'S COURT

Hollywood Rd.

Bandol

il trillo

Maze Grill Park Walk

Lillie Road

Ongar Road

Racton Road

Anselm Road

BROMPTON CEMETERY

Ifield Road

Gardens

Fulham Road

Limerston Street

Park Walk

North End Road B317

Walham Grove

Fernshaw Road

Edith Road

Medlar

Dawes Rd.

Fulham

Fulham Broadway

Fulham Road

Harwood Road

Moore Park Rd.

Hortensia Rd.

King's Road

Masala Grill

Tetcott Rd.

Uverdale Rd.

Grove

Cheyne

WALHAM GREEN

King's Road

Michael Rd.

New King's Road

Lots Road

Harbour Av.

Imperial Rd.

Parsons Green

- ● Hotel
- ● Restaurant

258

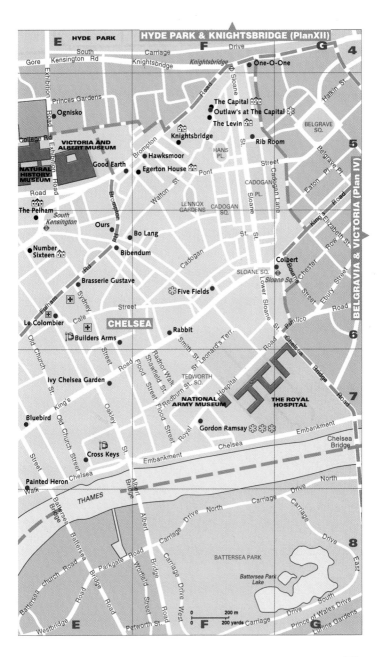

HYDE PARK

South Kensington Rd

Gore

Carriage

Drive

Knightsbridge

Knightsbridge

One-O-One

Halkin St.

Princes Gardens

Ognisko

Exhibition Road

Cottage Rd

VICTORIA AND ALBERT MUSEUM

NATURAL HISTORY MUSEUM

Road

The Pelham

South Kensington

Ours

Number Sixteen

Bibendum

Brasserie Gustave

Le Colombier

Sydney

Cale

Street

CHELSEA

Builders Arms

Ivy Chelsea Garden

King's

Bluebird

Cross Keys

Painted Heron

Chelsea Walk

THAMES

Battersea Bridge

Fish

Old Church

Oakley

Street

Road

Street

Old Church Street

Chelsea

Albert Bridge

Parkgate Road

Wonfield Street

Battersea church Road

Bridge Road

Westbridge

Road

Petworth St.

The Capital

Outlaw's at The Capital

The Levin

Knightsbridge

Hawksmoor

Good Earth

Egerton House

Brompton

Walton St.

Brompton Rd

Bo Lang

Cadogan

Five Fields

Rabbit

Smith St.

St Leonard's Terr.

Radnor Walk

Stawfield St.

Redburn St.

Flood Street

TEDWORTH SQ.

NATIONAL ARMY MUSEUM

Gordon Ramsay

Royal

Chelsea

Embankment

HANS PL.

Pont

Street

LENNOX GARDENS

CADOGAN SQ.

St.

St.

Sloane

CADOGAN PL.

Cadogan Lane

SLOANE SQ.

Sloane Sq.

Lower Sloane

Rib Room

BELGRAVE SQ.

Belgrave Pl.

Eaton Pl.

King's

Elizabeth St.

Row

Colbert

Chester

Ebury

Street

Road

Pimlico

Chelsea

Bridge

Road

THE ROYAL HOSPITAL

Embankment

Chelsea Bridge

North

Carriage

Drive

North

Carriage

Drive

Carriage

Drive

BATTERSEA PARK

Battersea Park Lake

Drive

East

South

Drive

Prince of Wales Drive

Luthine Gardens

Carriage

BELGRAVIA & VICTORIA (Plan IV)

0 — 200 m
0 — 200 yards

E   F   G

259

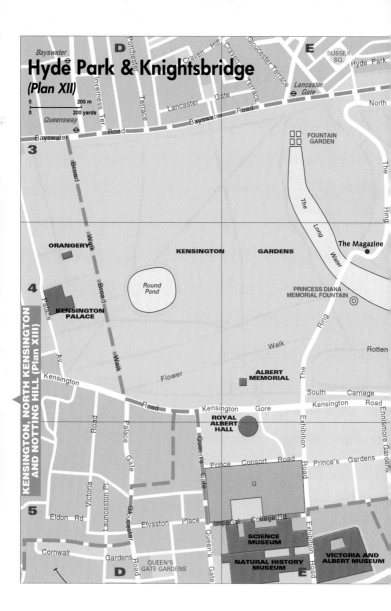

Hyde Park & Knightsbridge
(Plan XII)

0 — 200 m
0 — 200 yards

Bayswater

Queensway

Bayswater

Broad Walk

ORANGERY

KENSINGTON

GARDENS

Round Pond

Palace Walk

KENSINGTON PALACE

Broad Walk

Palace Av.

Kensington

Flower

Walk

Road

Palace Gate

Victoria Road

Launceston Pl.

Eldon Rd

Gloucester Road

Elvaston Place

Cornwall Gardens

QUEEN'S GATE GARDENS

Queen's Gate

Imperial College Rd

Kensington Gore

ROYAL ALBERT HALL

Prince Consort Road

U

Prince's Gardens

Exhibition Road

Exhibition Road

SCIENCE MUSEUM

NATURAL HISTORY MUSEUM

VICTORIA AND ALBERT MUSEUM

Ennismore Gardens

ALBERT MEMORIAL

South Carriage Kensington Road

The Ring

Rotten

Walk

PRINCESS DIANA MEMORIAL FOUNTAIN

Ring

The Long Water

The Magazine

FOUNTAIN GARDEN

Bayswater Road

Lancaster Gate

Lancaster Gate

North

The Ring

Hyde Park

SUSSEX SQ.

Gloucester Terrace

Craven Hill

Craven Terrace

Porchester Terrace

Inverness Ter.

Terrace

Lancaster Gate

Bayswater

D

E

D

E

3

4

5

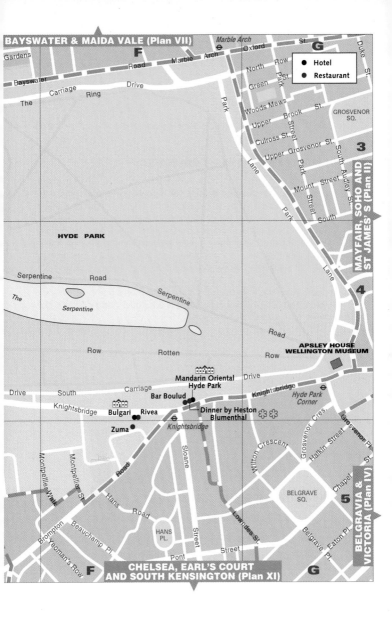

Bandol

Provençal

6 Hollywood Rd ⊠ SW10 9HY
☎ 020 7351 1322
www.barbandol.co.uk
⊖ Earl's Court

Plan XI D7

Closed 24-26 December and
1 January

Menu £20 (weekday lunch) – Carte £29/52

Sister to Margaux in South Kensington, this stylishly dressed restaurant is named after the well-known town and region in South East France. There are seats at the gleaming copper-topped bar but if you're here on a date, head to the more intimate section further back, where hanging brass lamps cast a romantic glow and a 100 year old olive tree brings back memories of sunny days spent on the French Riviera; the best tables are the three to the left with their semi-circular banquettes. Sharing plates take centre stage on the Provençal and Niçoise inspired menu, with dishes like bouillabaisse or fillet of Saint-Pierre being generously sized and full of flavour. Seafood is a highlight and desserts like tarte Tatin pleasingly traditional.

Bar Boulud

French

66 Knightsbridge ⊠ SW1X 7LA
☎ 020 7235 2000
www.mandarinoriental.com/london
⊖ Knightsbridge

Plan XII F4

Menu £19 (weekday lunch) – Carte £26/57

Lyon-born Daniel Boulud built his considerable reputation in New York and these two cities now inform the menu here at his London outpost. Order a plate of excellent charcuterie while you look at the menu; sausages are a highlight and there are plenty of classic French dishes, from fruits de mer to coq au vin, but it's the burgers that steal the show. Designed by Adam Tihany, the restaurant makes the best of its basement location which was previously used by the Mandarin Oriental Hotel as a storeroom. Don't think you'll be in exile if they lead you to a table around the corner: it's a good spot and you'll be facing the open kitchen. Service is fast and furious; prices are sensible and the place is noisy, fashionable and fun.

Bibendum

French   **Plan XI E6**

✉ SW3 6RD
☎ 020 7581 5817
www.bibendum.co.uk
⊖ South Kensington

Closed dinner 24 December,
25-26 December and 1 January

Menu £34 (weekdays) – Carte £27/63

Bibendum is now well into its twenties but very little has changed over those years, which is why it remains a favourite restaurant for so many. The cooking continues to produce the sort of food that Elizabeth David would adore – it's French with a British point of view. The set lunch menu is joined by a small à la carte selection; evening menus are handwritten; and the roast chicken with tarragon for two remains a perennial presence. Side dishes can bump the final bill up but the food is easy to eat and satisfying - and you've always got the oyster bar downstairs. The striking character of Michelin's former HQ, dating from 1911, is perhaps best appreciated at lunch when the sun lights up the glass Bibendum, aka the Michelin Man.

Bluebird

Modern British   **Plan XI E7**

350 King's Rd. ✉ SW3 5UU
☎ 020 7559 1000
www.bluebird-restaurant.co.uk
⊖ South Kensington

Menu £20 (lunch and early dinner) – Carte £27/87

Bluebird isn't just for a night out – as well as a restaurant, this former garage also hosts a foodstore, wine cellar, bakery, café and courtyard so there's enough here for a day out too. It's worth coming in a group and at peak times because a restaurant this size needs to be virtually full to generate an atmosphere. Order cocktails at the table as the menu is extensive and simply reading through it takes time. There are global influences, British classics, steaks, salads, a plat du jour and assorted shellfish – this is one of those places where you can have a burger or a whole turbot. With side orders, your bill can escalate quite sharply but the restaurant's buffed and bronzed clientele don't seem to mind.

Bo Lang

C h i n e s e **Plan XI E6**

100 Draycott Ave ✉ **SW3 3AD**
☎ 020 7823 7887
www.bolangrestaurant.com
⊖ South Kensington

Menu £22 (weekday lunch) – Carte £25/48

It's all about dim sum at this diminutive Hakkasan wannabe and they get a lot of things right: the kitchen has a deft touch; the cocktails are very good; the service is polite; the look is cool and the lighting moody. While there are more substantially sized 'main courses' on the menu you're better off sticking with the dim sum, particularly the traditional steamed items, and sharing with friends to mitigate the effects of some fairly ambitious pricing. What doesn't quite work are those dishes made up of more unusual flavour combinations, the small tables, which are not particularly conducive to this style of eating, and the intrusively loud music which, in such a small space, hints at a lack of nerve on someone's part.

Bombay Brasserie

I n d i a n **Plan XI D6**

Courtfield Rd. ✉ **SW7 4QH**
☎ 020 7370 4040
www.bombayb.co.uk
⊖ Gloucester Road

Closed 25 December – bookings advisable at dinner

Menu £25 (weekday lunch) – Carte £34/47

One of the reasons why The Bombay Brasserie has been going strong since 1982 is that it always seems to have just finished – or to be just about to start – a programme of redecoration to keep it looking fresh. Plushness abounds, from the murals and huge chandeliers of the large main room to the show kitchen of the conservatory and the very smart bar. The staff look the part in their burgundy waistcoats and offer efficient and professional service. The menu isn't forgotten either and these days they've replaced the predictable with the more creative, while at the same time respecting traditional philosophies; influences are a combination of Bori, Parsi, Maharashtrian and Goan cuisine. The weekend buffet remains as hugely popular as ever.

Brasserie Gustave

4 Sydney St ✉ SW3 6PP
℘ 020 7352 1712
www.brasserie-gustave.com
⊖ South Kensington

Closed 24-30 December

Menu £20/28 – Carte £32/69

 Barely a week goes by in London these days without a restaurant with a brand new 'concept' opening. Brasserie Gustave has taken the opposite stance and proves that when 'traditional' food is done well, especially French food, it really hits the spot. All the classics are here, from onion soup and snails to boeuf Bourguignon and rum baba, and all are prepared in a way that would make Escoffier proud – nothing is reimagined, reworked or deconstructed; it is simply cooked as it should be cooked and you leave feeling immeasurably satisfied. The restaurant itself is a facsimile of a classic brasserie, with studded leather seating and art deco-style posters and has been sensibly located in London's 'French quarter'.

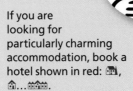

If you are looking for particularly charming accommodation, book a hotel shown in red: ⌂, ⌂...🏠.

Chelsea • South Kensington • Earl's Court • Hyde Park • Knightsbridge ▶ Plans XI-XII

Builders Arms
Builders Arms

Traditional British

Plan XI E6

13 Britten St ⊠ SW3 3TY
☎ 020 7349 9040
www.geronimo-inns.co.uk
⊖ South Kensington.

Bookings not accepted

Carte £23/42

A/C The Builders Arms is very much like a packed village local – the only difference being that, in this instance, the village is Chelsea and the villagers are all young and prosperous. The inside delivers on the promise of the smart exterior but don't expect it to be quiet as drinkers are welcomed just as much as diners. In fact, bookings are only taken for larger parties but just tell the staff that you're here to eat and they'll sort you out. The cooking reveals the effort that has gone into the sourcing of some decent ingredients; the rib of beef for two is a perennial favourite. Dishes are robust and satisfying and are not without some flair in presentation. Wine is also taken seriously and their list has been thoughtfully put together.

Cambio de Tercio

Spanish

Plan XI D6

163 Old Brompton Rd. ⊠ SW5 0LJ
☎ 020 7244 8970
www.cambiodetercio.co.uk
⊖ Gloucester Road

Closed 2 weeks December and 2 weeks August

Menu £45/55 – Carte £30/66 s

A/C

Never standing still is the key to the longevity of this Spanish restaurant – something the passionate and excitable staff take quite literally as they're forever bobbing between tables, engaging with their customers and generally adding to the energy in the room. Their recommendations are also worth following, especially on the wine list – which proves there is so much more to Spanish wines than rioja – and the sherry list, which is one of the best in town. The menu is a mix of the modern and the traditional – and it's best to mix the dishes up. Don't miss the El Bulli inspired Spanish omelette, or classics like roast suckling pig, and save room for the 'London Underground' dessert – you'll never look at your Oyster Card in the same way again.

Capote y Toros

S p a n i s h

157 Old Brompton Road ⊠ SW5 0LJ
☎ 020 7373 0567
www.cambiodetercio.co.uk
⊖ Gloucester Road

Closed 2 weeks Christmas,
Sunday and Monday – (dinner
only)

Menu £30 – Carte £20/51

From the owners of not-quite-next-door Cambio de Tercio comes the compact and vividly coloured Capote y Toros which celebrates sherry, tapas and ham. Named after the matador's cape and his foe, there are enough bullfighting references to satisfy enthusiasts of Hemingway proportions, including a large wall of photos. However, it is sherry that takes centre stage and there's a huge variety and choice on offer. Those as yet unmoved by this most underappreciated of wines should start by trying 5 varieties in a 'flight'. Meanwhile, the menu revolves around about 25 dishes; try 3 per person - the Iberico ham and the octopus are excellent. Bookings are now taken but you have a limited time at the table. A guitarist plays in the evenings.

Colbert

F r e n c h

50-52 Sloane Sq ⊠ SW1W 8AX
☎ 020 7730 2804
www.colbertchelsea.com
⊖ Sloane Square

Closed 25 December
– booking advisable

Carte £23/54

With its posters, chessboard tiles and red leather seats, Colbert bears more than a passing resemblance to a Parisian pavement café and there can't be a better spot for one than here on Sloane Square, next to the Royal Court. This is the old Oriel café and it was transformed by seasoned restaurateurs Chris Corbin and Jeremy King. It's an all-day, every day operation and the menu lists all the French classics; you can pop in for a croque monsieur, linger over a steak Diane or come for breakfast at any time of day. The best dishes are the simpler ones and if you haven't booked, try the bar. Despite the somewhat dispiriting sight of an anachronistic cover charge, this place feels set to become part of the local fabric for some time.

Le Colombier

F r e n c h   **Plan XI E6**

145 Dovehouse St. ✉ SW3 6LB
✆ 020 7351 1155
www.le-colombier-restaurant.co.uk
⊖ South Kensington

Menu £20 (lunch) – Carte £34/61

 Le Colombier is as warm and welcoming as it is honest and reliable, and thereby offers proof that being a good neighbourhood restaurant takes more than just being in a good neighbourhood. French influences abound, from the accents of the staff and the menu content to the inordinate amount of double cheek kissing that occurs – most of the customers appear to know one another or feel they should like to know one another. In summer, when the full-length windows fold back, the terrace is the place to sit although the underfloor heating ensures the place is equally welcoming in winter. Oysters, game in season, veal in various forms and regional cheeses are the highlights, as are the classic desserts from crêpe Suzette to crème brûlée.

Cross Keys

M o d e r n   c u i s i n e   **Plan XI E7**

1 Lawrence St ✉ SW3 5NB   Closed 24 December dinner and
✆ 020 7351 0686   25 December
www.thecrosskeyschelsea.co.uk
⊖ Sloane Square.

Carte £29/44

A/C Chelsea's oldest pub, dating from 1708, was in danger of being converted into a house but a well-organised campaign persuaded the council to see sense and refuse permission – and in 2015 this delightful neighbourhood pub triumphantly reopened, much to the joy of those fortunate enough to live in this neck of the woods. It's now operated by the team who run the Brown Cow and they've made a great job of updating the place while respecting its past. The style of cooking is largely contemporary, with Asian influences being especially prevalent, although there is a section marked 'traditional dishes' for those who prefer classic pub fare. Service comes from well-meaning chaps who appear to be known to most of the customers.

Dinner by Heston Blumenthal

Traditional British

Mandarin Oriental Hyde Park Hotel,
66 Knightsbridge, ✉ SW1X 7LA
☎ 020 7201 3833
www.dinnerbyheston.com
⊖ Knightsbridge

Closed 17-31 October

Chelsea • South Kensington • Earl's Court • Hyde Park • Knightsbridge ▶ Plans XI-XII

Menu £40 (weekday lunch) – Carte £58/121

✕✕✕

Mandarin Oriental Hyde Park

For a country with a less than stellar reputation for the quality of its food, we sometimes need reminding about the glories of our own culinary heritage. So hats off then to Heston Blumenthal because his mischievously named restaurant at the Mandarin Oriental Hyde Park should stir feelings of pride in all of us regarding our native cuisine. Don't come expecting 'molecular' alchemy; the menu reads like a record of historic kitchen triumphs, with the date of origin attached to each dish and a fashionably terse list of its parts – on the reverse you can read more. A kitchen brigade of 45 works with calm efficiency, meticulous attention to detail and intelligence to produce food that looks deceptively 'simple' but tastes sublime. The large, light room has quirky touches, like wall sconces shaped as jelly moulds, but the main focus is on the open kitchen, with its oversized watch mechanics powering the spit to roast the pineapple that goes with the Tipsy Cake (c.1810).

First Course	Main Course	Dessert
• Mandarin, chicken liver parfait and grilled bread (c.1500).	• Roast Iberico pork chop with spelt, ham hock and sauce Robert (c.1820).	• Tipsy cake with spit-roast pineapple (c.1810).
• Savoury porridge with frogs' legs, girolles, garlic, parsley and fennel (c.1660).	• Roast turbot with mussel & seaweed ketchup, salmon roe and sea rosemary (c.1830).	• Chocolate bar with passion fruit jam and ginger ice cream (c.1730).

L'Etranger

C r e a t i v e Plan XI D5

36 Gloucester Rd. ⊠ SW7 4QT Booking essential
☏ 020 7584 1118
www.etranger.co.uk
⊖ Gloucester Road

Menu £25 (weekdays)/45 – Carte £29/61

Messing around with classic French cooking is considered sacrilegious in certain parts of France but L'Etranger has escaped the tyranny of tradition by locating itself in South Kensington, London's own little Gallic ward. It offers an eclectic mix of French dishes that are heavily influenced by Japan, so a veal chop will come with wasabi sauce and salmon is poached in sake. Not every dish has a Nipponese constituent but it certainly makes for an original experience. The room is dark and moody and better suited to evenings, while service is a little more formal than it need be. The clientele is a mix of well-heeled locals and homesick French and Japanese émigrés, who also appreciate the depth and breadth of the impressive wine list.

Garnier

F r e n c h Plan XI C6

314 Earl's Court Rd ⊠ SW5 9QB Closed Monday and Tuesday
☏ 020 7370 4536
www.garnier-restaurant-london.co.uk
⊖ Earl's Court

Menu £18/22 – Carte £34/55

Earl's Court has never been overburdened by decent restaurants so local residents must have considered getting out the bunting when the experienced Garnier brothers decided to open a brasserie on their doorstep. Sandwiched by nondescript shops, it has an authentic, traditional Gallic feel, thanks to a wall of mirrors and rows of simply dressed tables. But the decoration is not the point – it's all about the comforting food here. London was once full of French restaurants but these days finding escargots, pigeon rôti and crêpes Suzette all on the same menu is not so easy, and the extensive menu of reassuring classics is such a good read, you'll find it hard to choose. The wine list has good representation from Burgundy and Bordeaux.

Five Fields ✿

M o d e r n c u i s i n e   **Plan XI F6**

8-9 Blacklands Terr ⊠ SW3 2SP
✆ 020 7838 1082
www.fivefieldsrestaurant.com
⊖ Sloane Square

Closed Christmas-mid January,
first 2 weeks August,
Saturday-Sunday and bank
holidays – booking essential
– (dinner only)

Menu £60   ✗✗✗

&♿ &A/C &📷 &❀

Five Fields

Its name comes from that given to the neighbourhood by the
18C cartographer John Rocque, and over the years this charming
Chelsea restaurant has certainly built up a loyal local following.
It is a formally run yet intimate place, with a discreet atmosphere
and a warm, comfortable feel. The room is luxuriously decorated
in crisp creams and the smart, suited staff who work it are
professional and engaging. The chef-owner – blessed with the
great name of Taylor Bonnyman – has worked in some illustrious
kitchens around the world and his cooking is very much in a
modern style. His dishes are skilfully conceived, quite elaborate
constructions; attractively presented and packed with flavour.
Produce is top-notch and includes the occasional Asian
ingredient, and many of the herbs and vegetables come from
the restaurant's own kitchen garden in East Sussex. Alongside
the classic burgundies and bordeaux, the extensive wine list
also offers some more esoteric bottles from Eastern Europe and
the Middle East. The tasting menu allows you to enjoy some
interesting wine pairings.

First Course	Main Course	Dessert
• Veal sweetbread with carrot, apple and tamarind.	• Herdwick mutton with green olive, anchovy and baby gem.	• Ginger, rhubarb and vanilla.
• Green pea, smoked eel, hazelnut and scallop tartare.	• John Dory with sweetcorn, courgettes and jamón.	• Strawberry mousse and meringue with white chocolate ice cream.

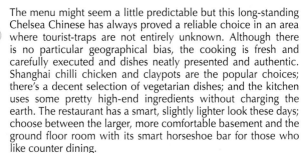

Good Earth

C h i n e s e **Plan XI E5**

233 Brompton Rd. ⊠ SW3 2EP
☎ 020 7584 3658
www.goodearthgroup.co.uk
⊖ Knightsbridge

Closed 23-31 December

Carte £26/51 ✗✗

The menu might seem a little predictable but this long-standing Chelsea Chinese has always proved a reliable choice in an area where tourist-traps are not entirely unknown. Although there is no particular geographical bias, the cooking is fresh and carefully executed and dishes neatly presented and authentic. Shanghai chilli chicken and claypots are the popular choices; there's a decent selection of vegetarian dishes; and the kitchen uses some pretty high-end ingredients without charging the earth. The restaurant has a smart, slightly lighter look these days; choose between the larger, more comfortable basement and the ground floor room with its smart horseshoe bar for those who like counter dining.

Hawksmoor

M e a t s   a n d   g r i l l s **Plan XI F5**

3 Yeoman's Row ⊠ SW3 2AL
☎ 020 7590 9290
www.thehawksmoor.com
⊖ South Kensington

Closed 24-26 December and
1 January

Menu £28 (weekday lunch) – Carte £26/94 ✗✗

The Hawksmoor people turned to the more rarefied surroundings of Knightsbridge for their fifth London restaurant and this meant a few subtle tweaks to their formula. Steak is obviously still the star of the show and the choice of 70% of customers, but the menu here also offers a decent selection of fish and seafood dishes which prove particularly popular at lunchtime. The customers in these parts are a sophisticated bunch – you're more likely to see negronis being ordered than shots – and they don't seem put off by the basement surroundings. To counter this, the restaurant comes with a degree of art deco elegance and the staff are a confident and engaging bunch who spend time getting to know their customers.

Chelsea • South Kensington • Earl's Court • Hyde Park • Knightsbridge ▶ Plans XI-XII

Gordon Ramsay ⍟⍟⍟

French

68-69 Royal Hospital Rd. ⊠ SW3 4HP
℘ 020 7352 4441
www.gordonramsayrestaurants.com
⊖ Sloane Square

Closed 21-28 December,
Saturday and Sunday
– booking essential

Menu £65/110

XXXX

A/C
🍴🖤
🍇

Gordon Ramsay

Gordon Ramsay may have the highest media profile of any Chef, as well as many restaurants throughout the world, but this restaurant, tucked away in a corner of Chelsea, is the undoubted flagship of his company – and the seriousness with which he protects its reputation is palpable. Calmness rules the elegant room, thanks largely to the way it is run by Jean-Claude – the manager who has been here since the day it opened. The service from his team is very attentive, polished and professional, but it also comes with personality and this puts everyone at ease, especially those on their first visit. The main reason everyone is here is for the food however, which is as good as ever. The style of cooking manages to bridge both classical and modern schools and is executed with enormous confidence and considerable poise. The attention to detail is exemplary and the component parts of each dish marry perfectly – and it is this balance, coupled with an extraordinary lightness of touch, that makes them so effortlessly easy to enjoy.

First Course	Main Course	Dessert
• Ravioli of lobster with langoustine, salmon, oxalis and wood sorrel.	• Dover sole with razor clams, young peas and lemon beurre noisette.	• Lemonade parfait with honey, bergamot and sheep's milk yoghurt.
• Sautéed foie gras and veal sweetbreads with carrots, almonds and cabernet sauvignon.	• Braised, roast and confit Herdwick lamb, with spring vegetable navarin.	• Chocolate bar with toasted milk mousse and tonka bean ice cream.

il trillo

I t a l i a n **Plan XI D7**

4 Hollywood Rd ✉ SW10 9HY
☎ 020 3602 1759
www.iltrillo.net
⊖ Earl's Court

Closed 10 days August and
1 week Christmas – (dinner only
and lunch Saturday-Sunday)

Carte £33/55 ✗✗

The Bertuccelli family have been making wine and running a restaurant in the Tuscan Hills for over 30 years. Two of the brothers are now in London, running this smart neighbourhood restaurant which showcases the produce and wine from their region. A third brother, who's an architect, designed the room and nearly everything was brought over from Italy, from the marble to the tables and chairs. Most of the ingredients are shipped over weekly too, either from their own farm or suppliers they've known for years. The cooking is gutsy and the breads and homemade pasta stand out, as does the signature dish of stuffed onions cooked in Vermentino. The courtyard has been transformed into a pleasant decked garden, complete with lemon trees.

ⓝ Ivy Chelsea Garden

T r a d i t i o n a l B r i t i s h **Plan XI E7**

197 King's Rd ✉ SW3 5ED
☎ 020 3301 0300
www.theivychelseagarden.com
⊖ South Kensington

Booking essential

Carte £26/68 ✗✗

This Ivy spin-off is set right in the heart of Chelsea and its appeal is clear to see: the interior is cosy and sophisticated, the atmosphere distinctly animated, and the clientele strikingly glamorous. Stop off at the zinc-topped cocktail bar for a Sloane Ranger or an Ivy Garden Royale; the liveliest seats are up here, so for a more intimate table, head down to the Orangery or out into the garden. The menu covers all bases: from breakfast through to lunch, afternoon tea and dinner; there's brunch at weekends and even a 'light and healthy' section on the menu for supermodel appetites. Plump for classics like the fish cakes, the chicken Milanese or the rack of lamb – and be aware that bread, sides and sauces will push up your final bill.

The Magazine

Modern cuisine

Plan XII E4

Serpentine Sackler Gallery, West Carriage Dr,
Kensington Gardens ⊠ W2 2AR
☎ 020 7298 7552
www.magazine-restaurant.co.uk
⊖ Lancaster Gate

Closed Monday – (lunch only)

Menu £24 – Carte £26/40

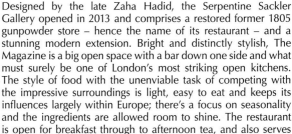

Designed by the late Zaha Hadid, the Serpentine Sackler Gallery opened in 2013 and comprises a restored former 1805 gunpowder store – hence the name of its restaurant – and a stunning modern extension. Bright and distinctly stylish, The Magazine is a big open space with a bar down one side and what must surely be one of London's most striking open kitchens. The style of food with the unenviable task of competing with the impressive surroundings is light, easy to eat and keeps its influences largely within Europe; there's a focus on seasonality and the ingredients are allowed room to shine. The restaurant is open for breakfast through to afternoon tea, and also serves brunch at weekends.

Margaux

Mediterranean cuisine

Plan XI D6

152 Old Brompton Rd ⊠ SW5 0BE
☎ 020 7373 5753
www.barmargaux.co.uk
⊖ Gloucester Road

Closed 24-26 December and
1 January

Menu £15 (weekday lunch) – Carte £30/52

Spain and Italy are the primary culinary influences at this appealing modern bistro and a glance at the menu would suggest there's nothing here to scare les chevaux. You can expect classics aplenty made using good quality, Mediterranean ingredients like porcini risotto or veal chop but, on closer inspection, there is also clear evidence of some boundary-pushing with dishes such as duck leg confit with cocoa and blackberry, and Iberico pork with fennel and pineapple. The wine list by the glass and carafe provides a good choice of varietals from quality producers along with plenty of gems from top growers. While the kitchen's influences are largely European, the ersatz industrial look of the place is far more Downtown Manhattan.

Masala Grill

I n d i a n   **Plan XI D8**

535 King's Rd ✉ SW10 0SZ   (dinner only and Sunday lunch)
✆ 020 7351 7788
www.masalagrill.co
⊖ Fulham Broadway

Carte £24/39

 When Chutney Mary's owners announced her move to St James's shortly after she'd celebrated her 25th birthday, her many local fans must have felt bereft. Fortunately, in her place, they've installed another Indian restaurant which they should like just as much. This time the menu is a little less expensive and offers an assortment of cooking styles, ranging from home-cooking and the ubiquitous street food to more sophisticated fare. Main courses are the highlight, whether a grilled dish like the succulent lamb chops, or a curry such as prawn Malabar with its rich and creamy sauce. The room still has its conservatory and is awash with colour and vitality. Service is also as caring and enthusiastic as it always was.

Maze Grill Park Walk

M e a t s   a n d   g r i l l s   **Plan XI D7**

11 Park Walk ✉ SW10 0AJ
✆ 020 7255 9299
www.gordonramsayrestaurants.com/maze-grill-
park-walk
⊖ South Kensington

Carte £24/80

 When Gordon Ramsay snapped up the lease here at Park Walk it came as no great surprise – this was the site of Aubergine, the restaurant where it all started for him back in the mid '90s. As Maze Grill it now follows the example set by the Mayfair original and specialises in steaks. The meats are dry-aged in-house and the selection includes native and rare breeds, along with grain-fed US and Japanese breeds. Having a basement kitchen ruled out a Josper so instead they use a big beast called a Montague grill which gets the job done by charbroiling the meat at 400°C. The restaurant is comfortable and well-organised, with a large bar the focal point of the room. There's another Maze Grill close by in Royal Hospital Road.

Medlar

Modern cuisine

Plan XI E7

438 King's Rd ✉ SW10 0LJ
✆ 020 7349 1900
www.medlarrestaurant.co.uk
⊖ South Kensington

Closed 24-26 December and
1 January

Menu £28/46

Medlar is an established landmark at this end of Chelsea and the two young owners have shown that being alumni of Chez Bruce proves to be a pretty good blueprint for your own place. The two restaurants share a warm and welcoming atmosphere and a feeling of being a genuine neighbourhood spot – you sense that a majority of the customers on any given night all know one another. The young service team here in Chelsea get the tone right too: they do their job but are also willing to engage with their customers. The menu is nicely balanced and the ingredients are clearly good; preparation is done with obvious care and dishes deliver distinct flavours in relatively classic combinations.

Ognisko

Polish

Plan XI E5

55 Prince's Gate, Exhibition Rd ✉ SW7 2PN
✆ 020 7589 0101
www.ogniskorestaurant.co.uk
⊖ South Kensington

Closed 24-26 December and
1 January

Menu £22 (lunch and early dinner) – Carte £27/37

Ognisko Polskie Club was founded in 1940 and became an important cultural centre for the Polish community in exile after the war. It is housed in the magnificent surroundings of an impressive 1870s townhouse and now, thanks to experienced restaurateur Jan Woroniecki, its restaurant is open to the public. Head first to the bar for a quick sharpener provided by home-flavoured vodka, then plunge straight into the unapologetically traditional menu, which celebrates cooking that is without pretence and truly from the heart. The dumplings are good and available as starters or mains; the roast duck is popular and the Krupnik or Bigos just perfect for a winter's day. On a summer's day ask for a table on the terrace overlooking Prince's Gardens.

Chelsea • South Kensington • Earl's Court • Hyde Park • Knightsbridge ▶ Plans XI-XII

One-O-One

Seafood **Plan XI F4**

Park Tower Knightsbridge Hotel, 101
Knightsbridge ✉ SW1X 7RN
☎ 020 7290 7101
www.oneoonerestaurant.com
⊖ Knightsbridge

Menu £20 (lunch and early dinner) – Carte £43/106

A/C Walking past the Park Tower Knightsbridge hotel, one of London's less majestic buildings, you'd never know there was a restaurant behind those heavy net curtains, and a rather good one to boot. Granted, the room size and shape can mean an animated atmosphere remains elusive – but the food is good and that food is mostly fish. There are tasting menus alongside an appealing à la carte so there is something for everyone and all occasions, whether that means sharing a whole turbot or just enjoying a bowl of bouillabaisse. Much of the produce comes from Brittany and Norway; the latter gives us the King crab legs which are the stars of the show. The kitchen is also unafraid of adding a little playfulness to its classical base.

Ours

Modern cuisine **Plan XI E6**

264 Brompton Rd ✉ SW3 2AS
☎ 020 7100 2200
www.restaurant-ours.com
⊖ South Kensington

Closed 24-28 December
booking advisable

Menu £45/55 – Carte £30/69 XX

 For the French diaspora who have made this area of London their own, the name means 'bear', but it's actually meant to signify 'What's ours is yours'; a phrase highlighted in neon on the wall above the bar. Green banquettes, trees and a living plant wall of 1,200 flower pots give the place a back-to-nature feel. Its immense size means it can lack atmosphere at lunch so come in the evening for a livelier vibe, when the fairy lights twinkle and the mezzanine level bar-lounge fills up with fun-seekers. The modern menu offers seasonal, ingredient-led dishes with a fresh, light style. Portions are not large, so sides are needed which can push prices up. There's also a distinct lack of carbs – which no doubt appeals to the local fashionistas.

Outlaw's at The Capital

The Capital Hotel,
22-24 Basil St. ⊠ SW3 1AT
✆ 020 7591 1202
www.capitalhotel.co.uk
⊖ Knightsbridge

Closed Sunday and Easter
Monday – booking essential

Menu £29/55   ✗✗

Michelin

Nathan Outlaw's elegant yet informal restaurant is the perfect fit for this longstanding, personally run hotel; its understated style putting the emphasis not on the room itself, but on the highly accomplished cooking and the exceptional wine list. The seasonal menus are all about sustainable seafood, with fresh fish shipped up from Cornwall on a daily basis, and while the 5 course tasting menu shows off the kitchen's abilities, the excellent value lunch menu makes the perfect pit-stop after shopping at nearby Harrods. The modern, delicately flavoured cooking is ingredient-led with the spotlight firmly on the freshness of the fish – and the wine list is a wonderfully balanced tome of vinous delights and includes the refreshing and herbaceous Levin Sauvignon Blanc from the owner's estate in the Loire. The room is good-looking, with the main feature being views into the kitchen through the large picture window. Service is relaxed yet attentive and the restaurant's many regulars are testament to the diligence of the staff.

First Course	Main Course	Dessert
• Cured monkfish with fennel, parsley and lemon.	• Hake with mussels, cider and clotted cream sauce.	• Passion fruit tart and sorbet with white chocolate and pistachio.
• Quail with hazelnut, apple and kohlrabi.	• Lemon sole with seaweed butter, potato terrine and leeks.	• Vanilla ice cream sandwich with pear & ginger beer sorbet.

Chelsea • South Kensington • Earl's Court • Hyde Park • Knightsbridge ▶ Plans XI-XII

Painted Heron

I n d i a n   **Plan XI E7**

112 Cheyne Walk ✉ SW10 0DJ
☎ 020 7351 5232
www.thepaintedheron.com
⊖ Fulham Broadway

Closed lunch 1 January

Menu £15 (lunch) – Carte £26/42

Ever fancied a Cohiba after your curry? Proof that The Painted Heron is not your typical Indian restaurant – this is Cheyne Walk after all – comes in the form of a smart, heated cigar terrace with a retractable roof for those who like a post-prandial puff. The restaurant itself is conscientiously run, stylishly kitted out and cleverly designed so that it always feels more intimate than its size would suggest. But what really sets it apart is the food: the influences come from across all parts of India but instead of the ubiquitous classics, the kitchen concentrates on seasonality. Dishes are quite elaborate in their construction and game is a speciality. The tasting menu offers the best overview of the kitchen's ability.

Rabbit

M o d e r n   B r i t i s h   **Plan XI F6**

172 King's Rd ✉ SW3 4UP
☎ 020 3750 0172
www.rabbit-restaurant.com
⊖ Sloane Square

Closed 22 December-2 January

Menu £14 (weekday lunch)/37 – Carte £22/31

Following the success of The Shed, the Gladwin brothers turned to Chelsea for their second restaurant and took over the site occupied since the 1950s by Choys Chinese. The playful, rustic look, complete with tractor seats and corrugated iron panelling, works well in this locale as does the service which is youthful and full of easy-going charm. The menu shares the same concept as The Shed – small plates of earthy, robustly flavoured dishes using produce from their farm – but there are some differences too: Chelsea residents are, apparently, slightly less enthusiastic about sharing than their Notting Hill cousins but are keener on game which is appropriate considering the name. As you'd expect, the rabbit dishes really are the standouts.

Rib Room

M e a t s   a n d   g r i l l s   **Plan XI F5**

Jumeirah Carlton Tower Hotel,
✉ SW1X 9PY
✆ 020 7858 7250
www.theribroom.co.uk
⊖ Knightsbridge

Menu £28 (weekday lunch) – Carte £50/120

The Rib Room is something of a London institution and a restaurant designed for those who didn't get where they are today by wasting time looking at prices. The menu would delight the most traditional of British trenchermen: one can start with smoked salmon or half a dozen Angel oysters then move on to Dover sole, a steak or, more appropriately, rib of Aberdeen Angus. The kitchen does things properly and wisely avoids trying to be too clever. The last designer successfully managed to add a little elegance to the room while also maintaining the overriding sense of masculinity that's often associated with this style of dining. The bar is an integral part of the set up and lends the place a pleasant buzz.

Rivea

M e d i t e r r a n e a n   c u i s i n e   **Plan XII F4**

Bulgari Hotel,
171 Knightsbridge ✉ SW7 1DW
✆ 020 7151 1025
www.rivealondon.com
⊖ Knightsbridge

Menu £26 (lunch) – Carte £39/49

In the basement, beneath the Bulgari Hotel's sleek bar, is the not-quite-so-sunny sister to the 'Rivea' restaurant in St Tropez; an elegantly appointed room where blues and whites make reference to warmer climes. Unfussy cooking also focuses on the French – and Italian – Riviera, offering an interesting range of small plates which are vibrant in both colour and flavour. Four or five dishes per person should suffice and sharing is the way to go for those who just can't quite decide. Alongside the must-try pasta dishes you'll find the likes of roasted duck with tender turnips and beetroots, and sea bass with violin courgettes and flowers. These are accompanied by an eclectic wine list which showcases varietals purely from the Med.

Tendido Cero

S p a n i s h

Plan XI D6

174 Old Brompton Rd. ⊠ SW5 0LJ
☎ 020 7370 3685
www.cambiodetercio.co.uk
⊖ Gloucester Road

Closed 2 weeks
Christmas-New Year

Menu £35 (dinner) – Carte £21/51

It's all about the vibe here at Abel Lusa's tapas bar, just across the road from his Cambio de Tercio restaurant. Oil lamps throw shadows across the excited faces of Kensington's pretty young things as they pass around plates of Iberico ham, Padron peppers, Galician octopus and patatas bravas. On warm summer evenings tables tumble out onto the pavement as temperatures rise in the cramped and frantic open kitchen. The interior is awash with bold colours and the staff work with reassuring efficiency – they're used to being busy as dishes arrive at a steady pace. Bread is sneakily added to the bill but the green olives and Marcona almonds come gratis. The wine list proves there's more to Spain than Rioja – don't miss the range of Vega Sicilia.

An important
business lunch or
dinner with friends?
The symbol ✣ indicates
restaurants with private
rooms.

Yashin Ocean House

J a p a n e s e **Plan XI D6**

117-119 Old Brompton Rd ✉ SW7 3RN
✆ 020 7373 3990
www.yashinocean.com
⊖ Gloucester Road

Closed Christmas

Carte £20/86

XX

It seems you can't open a restaurant these days without it having a 'concept'. The USP of this modern Japanese restaurant – sister to Yashin in Kensington – is 'head to tail' eating, although, as there's nothing here for carnivores, perhaps 'fin to scale' would be more accurate. The stylish interior includes large cabinets of dry-aged fish to get you in the mood for this style of eating, which is actually pretty commonplace in Japan. Take a seat at the counter or grab a table opposite the curiously incongruous full-sized horse lampstand and get cracking with a few small dishes like mackerel bone and fish skin for a joyous umami hit. Some dishes work better than others so stick with the specialities, like the whole dry-aged sea bream.

Zuma

J a p a n e s e **Plan XII F5**

5 Raphael St ✉ SW7 1DL
✆ 020 7584 1010
www.zumarestaurant.com
⊖ Knightsbridge

Closed 25 December
– booking essential

Carte £30/80

XX

Zuma may have become a global brand, with branches stretching from Istanbul to Hong Kong, but this is the original and it's still giving its fashionable band of fans – which includes a high quotient of celebrities and enough footballers to make up a whole team – exactly what they want. Glamorous surroundings with an open kitchen, a great cocktail bar, intelligent service and easy-to-share modern Japanese food mean that the large, stylish space is rarely less than bursting, especially at night. The menu covers all bases but instead of sushi, sashimi or tempura your best bet is to head straight for the delicately presented, modern constructions as well as those dishes cooked on the robata grill, which range from beef to sea bass.

Kensington · North Kensington · Notting Hill

It was the choking air of 17C London that helped put **Kensington** on the map: the little village lying to the west of the city became the favoured retreat of the asthmatic King William III who had Sir Christopher Wren build **Kensington Palace** for him. Where the king leads, the titled follow, and the area soon became a fashionable location for the rich. For over 300 years, it's had no problem holding onto its cachet, though a stroll down Kensington High Street is these days a more egalitarian odyssey than some more upmarket residents might approve of.

The shops here mix the everyday with the flamboyant, but for a real taste of the exotic you have to take the lift to the top of the Art Deco Barkers building and arrive at the Kensington Roof Gardens, which are open to all as long as they're not in use for a corporate bash. The gardens are now over seventy-five years old, yet still remain a 'charming secret'. Those who do make it up to the sixth floor discover a delightful woodland garden and gurgling stream, complete with pools, bridges and trees. There are flamingos, too, adding a dash of vibrant colour.

Back down on earth, Kensington boasts another hidden attraction in **Leighton House** on its western boundaries. The Victorian redbrick façade looks a bit forbidding as you make your approach, but step inside and things take a dramatic turn, courtesy of the extraordinary Arab Hall, with its oriental mosaics and tinkling fountain creating a scene like something from *The Arabian Knights.* Elsewhere in the building, the Pre-Raphaelite paintings of Lord Leighton, Burne-Jones and Alma-Tadema are much to the fore. Mind you, famous names have always had a hankering for W8, with a particular preponderance to dally in enchanting **Kensington Square,** where there are almost as many blue plaques as buildings upon which to secure them. William Thackeray, John Stuart Mill and Edward Burne-Jones were all residents.

One of the London's most enjoyable green retreats is **Holland Park,** just north of the High Street. It boasts the 400 year-old Holland House, which is a fashionable focal point for summer-time al fresco theatre and opera. Holland Walk runs along the eastern fringe of the park, and provides a lovely sojourn down to the shops; at the Kyoto Garden, koi carp reach hungrily for the surface of their pool, while elsewhere peacocks strut around as if they own the place.

Another world beckons just north of here – the seedy-cum-glitzy environs of **Notting Hill.** The main drag itself, Notting Hill Gate, is little more than a one-dimensional thoroughfare, but to its south are charming cottages with pastel shades in leafy streets, while to the north the appealing **Pembridge**

B. Gardel/hemis.fr

Road evolves into the boutiques of Westbourne Grove. Most people heading in this direction are making for the legendary Portobello Road market – particularly on Saturdays, which are manic. The market stretches on for more than a mile, with a chameleon-like ability to change colour and character on the way: there are antiques at the Notting Hill end, followed further up by food stalls, and then designer and vintage clothes as you reach the Westway. Those who don't fancy the madding crowds of the market can nip into the Electric Cinema and watch a movie in supreme comfort: it boasts two-seater sofas and leather armchairs. Nearby there are another two film-houses putting the hip into the Hill – the Gate, and the Coronet, widely recognised as one of London's most charming 'locals'.

Hidden in a mews just north of **Westbourne Grove** is a fascinating destination: the Museum of Brands, Packaging and Advertising, which does pretty much what it says on the label. It's both nostalgic and evocative, featuring thousands of items like childhood toys, teenage magazines… and HP sauce bottles.

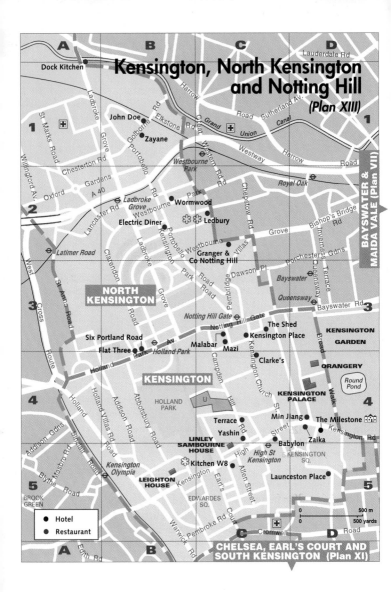

Kensington, North Kensington and Notting Hill
(Plan XIII)

A B C D

Lauderdale Rd

Dock Kitchen

Harrow Road
Sutherland Av.

Grand
Union Canal

Westway Harrow Road

St. Marks Road
Ladbroke Grove

John Doe
Golborne Rd Elkstone Rd

Zayane

Chesterton Rd

Oxford Gardens
Wilsford Av. A 40 Lancaster Road

Westbourne Park

Royal Oak

Ladbroke Grove
Westbourne

Wormwood

Portobello Rd Park Rd

Electric Diner

Ledbury

Chepstow Rd

Grove

Bishop's Bridge Rd

Inverness Terrace

Porchester Gdns

Clarendon Road

Latimer Road

Ladbroke Grove
Kensington Park Road
Portobello Road
Westbourne Grove

Granger &
Co Notting Hill

Pembridge Villas
Dawson Pl.

Bayswater

Queensway

Queensway Bayswater Rd

**NORTH
KENSINGTON**

West Cross Route
St. Ann's Road

Notting Hill Gate

Notting Hill Gate

The Shed

**KENSINGTON
GARDEN**

Six Portland Road

Malabar Mazi

Kensington Place

Flat Three
Holland Park Av. Holland Park

Clarke's

ORANGERY

Round
Pond

Holland

Campden Hill

Kensington Church St.

**KENSINGTON
PALACE**

Kensington Walk

Holland Villas Rd
Addison Road
Abbotsbury Road

KENSINGTON

**HOLLAND
PARK**

U

Terrace Rd
Yashin

Min Jiang
Babylon

Zaika

The Milestone

Kensington Rd

Addison Gdns

Masbro Road

Blythe Road

Kensington Olympia

**LINLEY
SAMBOURNE
HOUSE**

Kitchen W8

High St
Kensington
High Street
Allen Street

**KENSINGTON
SQ.**

**LEIGHTON
HOUSE**

Kensington

Earl's Court Rd

Launceston Place

**BROOK
GREEN**

Shepherd's Bush Rd

**EDWARDES
SQ.**

Warwick Road Pembroke Rd

0 500 m
0 500 yards

● Hotel
● Restaurant

Earls Ct Rd

Cromwell Road

**CHELSEA, EARL'S COURT AND
SOUTH KENSINGTON (Plan XI)**

**BAYSWATER &
MAIDA VALE (Plan VII)**

A B C D

Babylon

M o d e r n   c u i s i n e   **C4**

The Roof Gardens, 99 Kensington High St
(entrance on Derry St) ⊠ W8 5SA
☏ 020 7368 3993
www.roofgardens.virgin.com
⊖ High Street Kensington

Closed 24-30 December,
1-2 January and Sunday dinner

Menu £28 (lunch) – Carte £42/58   XX

Take the lift on Derry Street up to the 7th floor and you'll find
yourself staring down at trees, shrubs and possibly even a
flamingo in an amazing 1½ acre rooftop garden. The restaurant's
terrace must surely be one of the city's best spots for a cocktail
and a view, with the easterly skyline visible through the oak
and fruit trees. However, be aware that private parties often
have exclusive access. The food can't always compete with this
bucolic scene and presentation can sometimes be at the expense
of flavour but the menu does offer plenty of choice. Dishes are
not too heavy, which is a plus for later as dinner at weekends
entitles you to discounted access to The Club. You could also
consider coming on a Tuesday as that's jazz night.

Clarke's

M o d e r n   c u i s i n e   **C4**

124 Kensington Church St ⊠ W8 4BH
☏ 020 7221 9225
www.sallyclarke.com
⊖ Notting Hill Gate

Closed 2 weeks August,
Christmas-New Year,
Sunday and bank holidays
– booking advisable

Menu £27/39 – Carte £41/55   XX

Over thirty years on and Sally Clarke has lost none of her passion
for her Kensington kitchen. To celebrate this milestone, she
made a few changes to her restaurant, converting downstairs
into a private dining room and transforming the space previously
occupied by her shop – which is now across the road – into
the Bar Room, which is open all day for breakfast, coffee,
light lunches and teas. What hasn't changed is her unwavering
insistence on using the freshest of ingredients. From the excellent
breads to the hand-rolled truffles, there is a clear understanding
of the less-is-more principle and clear confidence in the cooking
– just some of the many reasons why this restaurant has instilled
such unwavering loyalty from so many for so long.

Dock Kitchen

Mediterranean cuisine A0/1

Portobello Dock, 342-344 Ladbroke Grove
✉ W10 5BU
☎ 020 8962 1610
www.dockkitchen.co.uk
⊖ Ladbroke Grove

Closed Christmas, Sunday dinner
and bank holidays

Carte £23/38

 What started as a pop-up restaurant became a permanent feature in this former Victorian goods yard and the space is shared with designer Tom Dixon, some of whose furniture and lighting is showcased here. The open kitchen dominates one end of the room where steel girders and exposed brick add to the industrial aesthetic. The similarities to Moro, River Café and Petersham Nurseries are palpable, not just in the refreshing lack of ceremony and the fashionable crowds that flock here, but also in the cooking, where quality ingredients are a given and natural flavours speak for themselves. The chef's peregrinations also inform his cooking; look out for his themed set menus which could be Sardinian one week, Moroccan the next.

Electric Diner

Meats and grills B2

191 Portobello Rd ✉ W11 2ED
☎ 020 7908 9696
www.electricdiner.com
⊖ Ladbroke Grove

Closed 30-31 August and
25 December

Carte £17/34

 Any cinema that's over 100 years old deserves to be shown respect, so treat your visit to the Electric Cinema as a special occasion and start, or finish, with a meal next door at the Electric Diner. It's a loud, fun and brash all-day operation with a simple but all-encompassing menu that changes daily. The long counter, red leather booths and low ceiling certainly create the mood and look of the classic American diner – even the music comes from a reel-to-reel. Au Cheval diner in Chicago has supplied most of the influences so be prepared for big portions that are heavy on flavour. The room fills with smoke from the grill; the steak and pork chops could easily feed two and the lemon meringue pie is of Desperate Dan dimensions.

Flat Three

C r e a t i v e   B3/4

120-122 Holland Park Ave ✉ W11 4UA
☏ 020 7792 8987
www.flatthree.london
⊖ Holland Park

Closed
26 December-6 January, 15-
26 August, Sunday and Monday
– (dinner only and lunch Friday-
Saturday)

Menu £33 (early dinner) – Carte £31/77

 A restaurant blending the cuisines of Scandinavia, Korea and Japan needs planning and indeed, it was while living.at Flat 3 that the owner first had the idea. It was also where she developed the menu and honed the cooking, along with the chef, by hosting supper clubs. Only an obsessive foodie with an encyclopaedic mind will recognise all the ingredients and while some dishes are more style over substance, there are others that do work well such as those involving the wood-fired oven. They make their own soy and miso, press their own juices and, needless to say, serve more foraged ingredients than you'll find in Ray Mears' pocket. Presentation is minimalist – rather like the basement room – and there's a menu specifically for vegetarians.

Granger and Co. Notting Hill

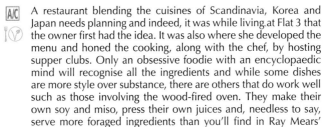

M o d e r n   c u i s i n e   C2

175 Westbourne Grove ✉ W11 2SB
☏ 020 7229 9111
www.grangerandco.com
⊖ Bayswater

Closed August bank holiday
weekend and 25-26 December
– bookings not accepted

Carte £23/43

 Having relocated from the sun of Sydney to the cool of Notting Hill, Bill Granger decided to open a local restaurant. He brought with him that disarmingly charming 'matey' service that only Australians can do, along with his breakfast sweetcorn fritters and ricotta hotcakes, and a zesty menu that features everything from pasta to pork chops. At dinner a BBQ section is added along with a daily fish dish, while various puds replace the cakes offered during the day. The room is bright and open, prices are reasonable and the Asian accents lend many of the dishes an easy-to-eat quality, which makes you feel healthier than when you arrived and allows you to forget that you probably had to queue for a table.

Kensington Place

S e a f o o d   C3

201-209 Kensington Church St. ⊠ W8 7LX
℘ 020 7727 3184
www.kensingtonplace-restaurant.co.uk
⊖ Notting Hill Gate

Closed Sunday dinner,
Monday lunch and bank holidays

Menu £20 (lunch and early dinner) – Carte £28/47

2017 marks the 30th birthday of this iconic brasserie, which was at the vanguard of a new wave of restaurants at the time when London's dining scene changed forever. While its glory years may be behind it, it remains relevant in this more competitive age by being well run and authentic. Its owners – the D&D group – have wisely resisted the urge to change its appearance too much, save for a little freshening up here and there. Fish is the focus of the fairly priced menu which mixes classics like prawn cocktail and fish pie with more modern dishes such as cod with a seaweed dressing. The selection of the day's fish from the market is often the best choice, which you can have grilled or roasted.

Launceston Place

M o d e r n   c u i s i n e   D5

1a Launceston Pl ⊠ W8 5RL
℘ 020 7937 6912
www.launcestonplace-restaurant.co.uk
⊖ Gloucester Road

Closed 25-30 December,
1 January, Tuesday lunch and
Monday – bookings advisable
at dinner

Menu £30/55

There are few restaurants that engender a greater sense of customer loyalty and proprietorial pride than Launceston Place. Its pretty façade has made it one of the more recognisable restaurants in Kensington and, when you eat here, you get a real sense of neighbourhood, albeit one that few of us can afford to live in. These days it's looked after by the D&D group and they've hired a confident front of house team; they in turn try to ensure that their relatively formal style of service doesn't impinge too much on their customers' enjoyment. A new French chef arrived in 2016 and with him came a style of cooking that wasn't afraid of trying new things, although his dishes are all underpinned by a classical training.

Kitchen W8 ✿

M o d e r n   c u i s i n e   **C5**

11-13 Abingdon Rd ✉ W8 6AH
✆ 020 7937 0120
www.kitchenw8.com
⊖ High Street Kensington

Closed 24-26 December
and bank holidays

Menu £25 (lunch and early dinner) – Carte £35/53

A/C

Michelin

Kitchen W8 is the sort of restaurant every neighbourhood should have because it succeeds on so many levels. Whether you're here for a special occasion on a Saturday night or a quick bite for lunch during the week, the staff will get the tone of the service just right and the food will be meticulously prepared yet very easy to eat. The restaurant is a joint venture between experienced restaurateurs Rebecca Mascarenhas and Philip Howard and their influence is clear to see. Head Chef Mark Kempson puts as much care into the great value lunch and early evening menu as he does the main à la carte; all are produce driven and his confident cooking delivers great flavours and subtle degrees of originality so that the dishes have both personality and depth. The restaurant may not be quite as informal as the name suggests but it is certainly free of pomp or pomposity. On Sunday the restaurant entices even more locals in by making it a corkage free night which encourages them to open up their own cellars.

First Course	Main Course	Dessert
• Salad of veal with charred asparagus, peas and truffle pesto.	• Fillet of Cornish turbot with St Austell Bay mussels, mousserons, onions and parsley.	• Passion fruit cream with cured pineapple, lime and mango.
• Brittany artichokes with truffle, egg yolk, hazelnut and parmesan.	• Rack & shoulder of lamb with pink firs and charred gem.	• Chocolate pavé with cherries, buckwheat and vanilla.

Ledbury ✿✿

C2

127 Ledbury Rd. ✉ W11 2AQ
✆ 020 7792 9090
www.theledbury.com
⊖ Notting Hill Gate

Closed 25-26 December,
August bank holiday and lunch
Monday-Tuesday

Menu £50/95   ✗✗✗

Michelin

Brett Graham is a chef who understands his ingredients. His deep-rooted knowledge of husbandry and his close working relationship with his suppliers are revealed through his menus and reflected on the plate. The quality of the produce really shines through and the kitchen's ability and deft touch means that the strikingly original flavour combinations will linger long in the memory. Lovers of game have much to savour in the season and it is not unknown for Brett to head off up to Norfolk after service to shoot some venison. The wine list offers good value at all levels, is strong across the regions and includes a great selection by the glass. The Ledbury has always had to work hard to attract lunchtime business so the fixed price lunch menu represents excellent value and often includes some unexpectedly luxurious ingredients, like Red Ruby beef or hand-dived scallops. At weekends, only a tasting menu is offered for dinner. Whenever you come, you'll find this a smart yet unshowy restaurant with a satisfying hum and smooth, engaging service.

First Course

- White beetroot baked in clay with English caviar and smoked & dried eel.

- Artichokes with Muscat grapes, walnuts and grated foie gras.

Main Course

- Berkshire muntjac with smoked bone marrow, quince and vegetables.

- Cornish turbot with salsify, oyster cream and brown bread.

Dessert

- Brown sugar tart with stem ginger ice cream.

- Poached rhubarb with olive oil shortbread.

Malabar

Indian   C3

27 Uxbridge St. ✉ **W8 7TQ**
📞 020 7727 8800
www.malabar-restaurant.co.uk
⊖ Notting Hill Gate

Closed 1 week Christmas
– (dinner only and lunch
Saturday-Sunday)

Carte £15/39 s

 One of the reasons why Malabar has been going strong since 1983 is that it has kept on top of its appearance, as, it seems, do most of its Notting Hill customers. These days the front has a sleek, understated look; the interior is a fashionable grey; and the staff do their bit by dressing in black. What doesn't change is the quality of the food, from the breads to the piping hot thalis. The favourites remain but the seafood section has been beefed up with the addition of a monkfish curry and a whole gilt-head bream; and just because the tandoori dishes sit beside the starters on the menu, don't assume they come in starter sizes. The excellent value Sunday buffet lunch, when children under 12 eat for free, still packs them in.

Mazi

Greek   C2

12-14 Hillgate St ✉ **W8 7SR**
📞 020 7229 3794
www.mazi.co.uk
⊖ Notting Hill Gate

Closed 24-26 December and
1-2 January

Menu £13 (weekday lunch) – Carte £28/54

Apart from one or possibly two exceptions, Greek restaurants in the capital have been less than inspiring over the years – but that may start to change thanks to Mazi, which means 'together'. The kitchen seeks inspiration from traditional recipes then adds contemporary twists to create vibrant, colourful and fresh tasting dishes. It's all about sharing here, with cold dishes such as tarama with lemon confit served in glass jars; bigger, more robust dishes include braised saddle of lamb with its shoulder, and rabbit ragout with pasta. The wine list is exclusively Greek and much of the imported produce is available to buy. The simple room is bright and fresh and there are few more charming spots than the garden terrace at the back.

Min Jiang

Chinese D4

Royal Garden Hotel,
2-24 Kensington High St (10th Floor) ✉ W8 4PT
✆ 020 7361 1988
www.minjiang.co.uk
⊖ High Street Kensington

Menu £40/80 – Carte £30/98

It's got great views of Kensington Palace and Gardens (ask for tables 11 or 16) but because of its own good looks and its collection of vases influenced by the Ming Dynasty, this stylish Chinese restaurant on the 10th floor of the Royal Garden hotel can more than hold its own. The speciality is wood-fired Beijing duck in two servings - order it in advance; its glistening meat is carved at the table and one then has the difficult task of choosing one of the four options offered for the second serving. The cuisine covers all provinces, although Cantonese and Sichuanese are the most dominant. Signature dishes include sea bass with shredded chicken, sautéed Gong Bao chicken and spicy pork belly with leeks.

The Shed

Modern British C3

122 Palace Gardens Terr ✉ W8 4RT
✆ 020 7229 4024
www.theshed-restaurant.com
⊖ Notting Hill Gate

Closed Monday lunch and Sunday

Carte £18/30

Names add to expectations, so if you call your place the Grand Palace it really doesn't give you anywhere to hide. The Gladwin brothers behind The Shed instead opted for understatement and it works a treat. This is the old Ark restaurant and is obviously more than just a shed, even though it comes with a healthy dose of the outdoors. There are farming tools, upturned barrels for tables and even an old tractor engine, all adding to its higgledy-piggledy charm. One brother cooks, one manages, and the third runs the farm in West Sussex from where much of the produce comes. The cooking is appropriately British, earthy and satisfying, with the small plates divided into 'slow' or 'fast': a reference to the cooking process.

Six Portland Road

F r e n c h **B3**

6 Portland Rd ✉ **W11 4LA**
☎ 020 7229 3130
www.sixportlandroad.com
⊖ Holland Park

Closed Christmas-New Year, last
2 weeks August, Monday and
Sunday dinner

Carte £27/56 🍴

A/C If North Kensington is your hood, then this is a neighbour who'll soon become a firm friend. A cosy, intimate place, it's owned by Oli Barker, who brought his head chef along with him when he left Terroirs in the Strand. He personally welcomes his regulars – of which there are many – and has found a relaxed and friendly team of servers who clearly know their stuff. The seasonal menu changes frequently and has a strong French accent; dishes are reassuringly recognisable, skilfully constructed and very tasty. Start with half a dozen of County Waterford's best oysters or a robust pork and pistachio terrine; a satisfying main of turbot comes with broad beans, mousserons and beurre blanc, while griottines add a kick to a silky chocolate mousse.

Wormwood

M e d i t e r r a n e a n   c u i s i n e **B2**

16 All Saints Rd ✉ **W11 1HH**
☎ 020 7854 1808
www.wormwoodnottinghill.com
⊖ Westbourne Park

Closed 28 August-
3 September 24-28 December,
1-2 January, Monday lunch and
Sunday

Carte £26/39 🍴

 The look is New England with a Moorish edge and it's named after the primary herb in absinthe rather than the nearby clink; throw in North African dominated Mediterranean food with a creative, modern edge and you have a Notting Hill restaurant doing something a little different. The owner-chef hails from Algeria and his flavours are adventurous and at times original – particularly on the dinner menu when his ambition is allowed full reign. You're encouraged to share, but it's best to stick to your own small plates (four each is about right). The young team are super friendly and much thought has also gone into the drinks list: 80% of wines are organic and the cocktail list is enticing and original in equal measure.

Yashin

Japanese C4

1a Argyll Rd. ✉ W8 7DB
℘ 020 7938 1536
www.yashinsushi.com
⊖ High Street Kensington

Closed 24-25 and 31 December,
1 January – booking essential

Carte £38/89 ✗✗

Two experienced sushi chefs joined forces to create this contemporary restaurant with its crisp, appealing black and white theme. Their worthy ambition to wean diners off fermented soya bean is reflected in their grammatically challenging but charmingly equitable slogan: "without soy sauce… but if you want to". There are three omakase choices offering 8, 11 or 15 pieces of sushi selected by the chefs and served together. The quality of the fish is clear and originality comes in the form of minuscule garnishes adorning each piece and the odd bit of searing. Service is knowledgeable and endearing but be sure to ask for a counter seat, as one of the joys of sushi comes from watching the chefs' dextrous knife skills and their deft handling of the fish.

Zaika

Indian D4

1 Kensington High St. ✉ W8 5NP
℘ 020 7795 6533
www.zaikaofkensington.com
⊖ High Street Kensington

Closed 25-26 December, 1 January
and Monday lunch

Menu £22 (lunch) – Carte £28/67 ✗✗

After a short-lived and rather curious venture into modern European cooking, the Tamarind Collection wisely returned their Kensington outpost to what it did best and re-opened it as Zaika. The cooking focuses on the North of India and the influences of Mughal and Nawabi, so you can expect rich, satisfying and fragrantly spiced dishes that include tandoor-cooked kebabs and succulent Gosht Dum biryani. With its wood-panelled walls and ornate ceiling, it comes as no surprise that this softly-lit room was once a bank, but the sepia prints now add a hint of colonialism and the cocktail bar lends a touch of modernity. Factor in the friendly and attentive service and you have a restaurant that should never have gone away.

 Zayane

Moroccan B1

91 Golborne Rd ⊠ W10 5NL
℘ 020 8960 1137
www.zayanerestaurant.com
⊖ Westbourne Park

Carte £27/36 ✗

AC This intimate neighbourhood restaurant is a delight for the senses: the scent of exotic spiced candles hits you as you walk in, modern African music pumps from the speakers, hanging lamps cast an atmospheric glow and colourful crockery and a framed national dress provide a visual treat. And then there's the food: the Moroccan cooking comes with modern techniques and authentic flavours; Casablanca-born owner Meryem tastes each dish personally and the chef adjusts them accordingly. Start with warm bread and fresh, zingy olives; starters might include pan-fried scallops chermoula with chickpeas or a smoked octopus salad; main courses could be a full-flavoured poussin tangine or, the fast-becoming-a-cult-dish, Morrocan-spiced short rib of beef.

On a budget?
Take advantage
of lunchtime prices.

Kensington • North Kensington • Notting Hill ▶ **Plan XIII**

Greater London

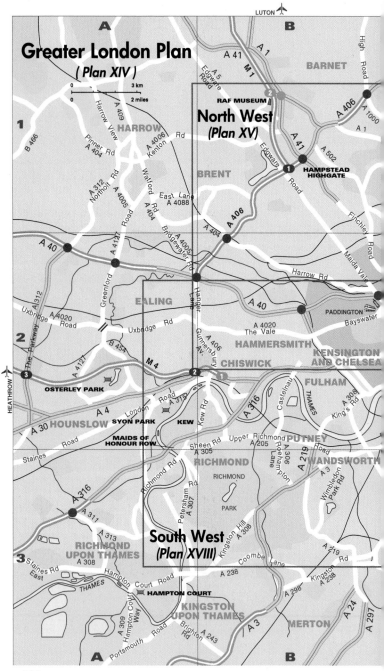

Greater London Plan
(Plan XIV)

LUTON

BARNET

RAF MUSEUM

North West
(Plan XV)

HARROW

BRENT

HAMPSTEAD
HIGHGATE

EALING

PADDINGTON
Bayswater

HAMMERSMITH

CHISWICK

KENSINGTON
AND CHELSEA

FULHAM

OSTERLEY PARK

HEATHROW

HOUNSLOW   SYON PARK   KEW

MAIDS OF
HONOUR ROW

PUTNEY

WANDSWORTH

RICHMOND

RICHMOND

PARK

South West
(Plan XVIII)

RICHMOND
UPON THAMES

THAMES

HAMPTON COURT

KINGSTON
UPON THAMES

MERTON

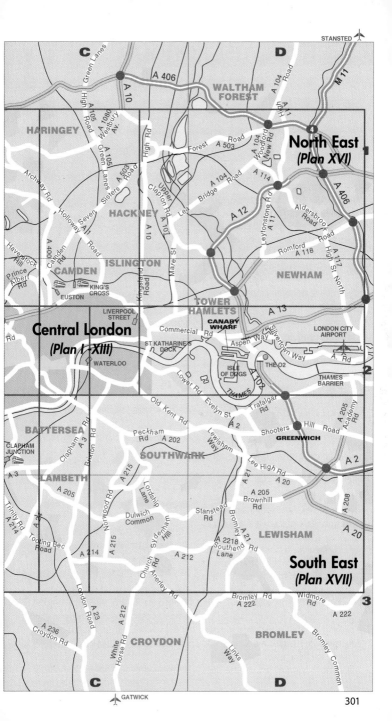

North-West London

Heading north from London Zoo and Regent's Park, the green baton is passed to two of the city's most popular and well-known locations: Hampstead Heath and Highgate Wood. In close proximity, they offer a favoured pair of lungs to travellers emerging from the murky depths of the Northern Line. Two centuries ago, they would have been just another part of the area's undeveloped high ground and pastureland, but since the building boom of the nineteenth century, both have become prized assets in this part of the metropolis.

People came to seek shelter in **Hampstead** in times of plague, and it's retained its bucolic air to this day. Famous names have always enjoyed its charms: Constable and Keats rested their brush and pen here, while the sculptors Henry Moore and Barbara Hepworth were residents in more recent times. Many are drawn to such delightful places as Church Row, which boasts a lovely Georgian Terrace. You know you're up high because the thoroughfares bear names like Holly Mount and Mount Vernon. The Heath is full of rolling woodlands and meadows; it's a great place for rambling, particularly to the crest of **Parliament Hill** and its superb city views. There are three bathing ponds here, one mixed, and one each for male and female swimmers, while up on the Heath's northern fringes, **Kenwood House,** along with its famous al fresco summer concerts, also boasts great art by the likes of Vermeer and Rembrandt. And

besides all that, there's an ivy tunnel leading to a terrace with idyllic pond views.

Highgate Wood is an ancient woodland and conservation area, containing a leafy walk that meanders enchantingly along a former railway line to **Crouch End,** home to a band of thespians. Down the road at Highgate Cemetery, the likes of Karl Marx, George Eliot, Christina Rossetti and Michael Faraday rest in a great entanglement of breathtaking Victorian overdecoration. The cemetery is still in use – recent notables to be buried here include Douglas Adams and Malcolm McLaren.

Next door you'll find **Waterlow Park,** another fine green space, which, apart from its super views, also includes decorative ponds on three levels. Lauderdale House is here, too, a 16C pile which is now an arts centre; more famously, Charles II handed over its keys to Nell Gwynn for her to use as her North London residence. Head back south from here, and **Primrose Hill** continues the theme of glorious green space: its surrounding terraces are populated by media darlings, while its vertiginous mass is another to boast a famously enviable vista.

Of a different hue altogether is **Camden Town** with its buzzy edge, courtesy of a renowned indie music scene, goths, punks, and six earthy markets selling everything from tat to exotica. Charles Dickens grew up here, and he was none too complimentary; the area

J.-M. Charles/age fotostock

still relishes its seamy underside. A scenic route out is the **Regent's Canal,** which cuts its way through the market and ambles to the east and west of the city. Up the road, the legendary Roundhouse re-opened its arty front doors in 2006, expanding further the wide range of Camden's alt scene.

One of the music world's most legendary destinations, the **Abbey Road** studios, is also in this area and, yes, it's possible to join other tourists making their way over that zebra crossing. Not far away, in Maresfield Gardens, stands a very different kind of attraction. The Freud Museum is one of the very few buildings in London to have two blue plaques. It was home to Sigmund during the last year of his life and it's where he lived with his daughter Anna (her plaque commemorates her work in child psychiatry). Inside, there's a fabulous library and his working desk. But the pivotal part of the whole house is in another corner of the study – the psychiatrist's couch!

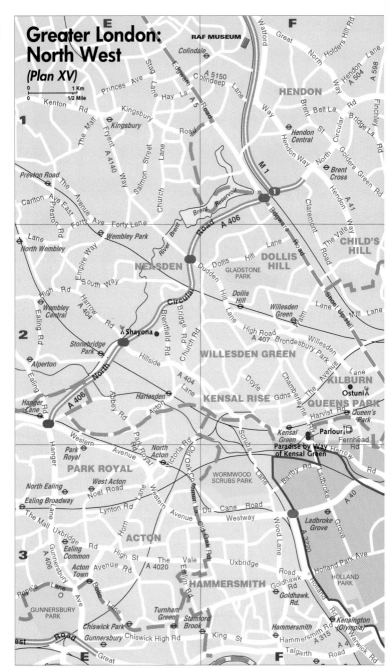

Greater London:
North West
(Plan XV)

0 ———— 1 Km
0 ———— 1/2 Mile

RAF MUSEUM

Colindale

A 5150
Colindeep Lane

HENDON

Hendon Central

Brent Cross

Watford Way

M 1

North Circular Rd

Golders Green Rd

Finchley
A 504
A 598

Hendon Way

Claremont Road

The Vale

CHILD'S HILL

Princes Ave

Stag Lane

Hay La.
Edgware Rd
A 5

Kenton Rd

The Mall

Kingsbury

Kingsbury Road

Fryent
A 4140 Way

Salmon Street

Church Lane

Preston Road

Carlton Ave East
A Preston Rd
The Avenue

North Wembley

Forty Ave
Forty Lane

Wembley Park

Empire Way

South Way

Brent Reservoir

River Brent

Edgware Road

A 406

Dollis Hill Lane

DOLLIS HILL

NEASDEN

Dudden Hill Lane

GLADSTONE PARK

Dollis Hill

Willesden Green

Shoot Up Hill

Mill Lane

High Rd

Harrow Rd
A 404

Wembley Central

Ealing Rd

Brentfield Rd

2

Stonebridge Park

Λ **Shayona**

North Circular

Bridge Rd

Church Rd

Hillside

A 404 Lane

High Road
A 407

Brondesbury Park

WILLESDEN GREEN

Chamberlayne

The Avenue

Willesden Lane

KILBURN

Ostuni Λ

QUEENS PARK

Alperton

Ealing Rd

Hanger Lane

Abbey Rd

Harlesden

Acton Lane

Doyle

Gdns

KENSAL RISE

Harvist Rd

Queen's Park

Parlour ⌂

Kensal Green

Fernhead Rd

Paradise by Way of Kensal Green

A 406

Western

Park Royal

Avenue

North Acton

Park Royal Rd

PARK ROYAL

Victoria Rd

Old Oak Common Lane

Scrubs Lane

Barlby Rd

Ladbroke Rd

A 40

North Ealing

West Acton

Noel Road

Lynton Rd

Western Avenue

Horn Lane

Hanger Lane

Western

WORMWOOD SCRUBS PARK

Du Cane Road

Westway

Wood Lane

A 3220

Ladbroke Grove

Ealing Broadway

The Mall

Uxbridge Rd

ACTON

Ealing Common

Acton Town

High St

Avenue Rd

The Vale
A 4020

Emlyn Rd

Uxbridge Road

Holland Park Ave

HOLLAND PARK

3

Gunnersbury
A 406

Popes Lane

Bollo Lane

GUNNERSBURY PARK

Chiswick Park

Gunnersbury

Turnham Green

Stamford Brook

Chiswick High Rd

HAMMERSMITH

Goldhawk Rd

Goldhawk Rd.

King St

Hammersmith

Hammersmith Rd
A 315

Kensington (Olympia)

Holland Rd

Warwick Rd

East

Road

Great

Talgarth Road

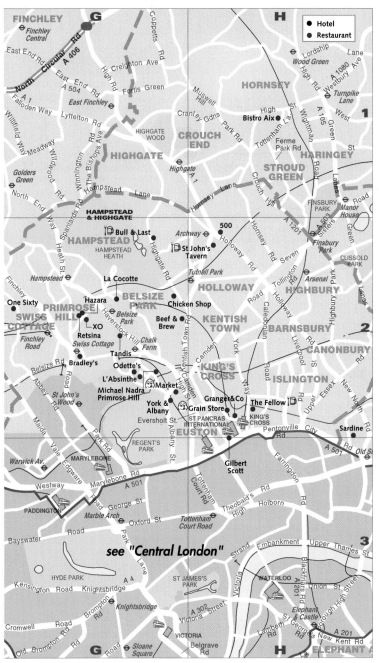

FINCHLEY G H

● Hotel
● Restaurant

Finchley Central

East End Rd
North Circular Rd A 406

Coppetts Rd

Creighton Ave

East End Rd
A 504
A 1 Falloden Way

East Finchley

High Rd

Fortis Green

HORNSEY

Wood Green

Lordship Lane
High Rd
A 1080 Westbury Av.
Turnpike Lane

Lyttelton Rd

Muswell Hill

Cranley Gdns

Park Rd
A 105 Green
West

Wightman Rd
Tottenham La

Golders Green

Wilfield Way Meadway

Willifield Way

Winnington Rd
The Bishops Ave

North End Way

Heath Dr
Spaniards Rd

HIGHGATE
WOOD

CROUCH
END

High

Bistro Aix ●

HARINGEY

Ferme Park Rd

St

HIGHGATE

Hampstead Lane

Highgate ◉
A 1

STROUD
GREEN

Crouch Hill

FINSBURY
PARK

Manor House

HAMPSTEAD
& HIGHGATE

Hornsey Lane

Finsbury Park

Road

A 503 Seven Sisters

CLISSOLD
PARK

Hampstead St

Hampstead Heath

🏨 **Bull & Last** ●

HAMPSTEAD

HAMPSTEAD
HEATH

Highgate Rd

Archway ◉

🏨 St John's Tavern ●

500 ●

Holloway Rd

Hornsey Rd

A 503

A 1201

Green Lanes

Arsenal ◉

HIGHBURY

Finchley Rd

La Cocotte ●

Hampstead ◉

Tutnell Park ◉

HOLLOWAY

Tollington Rd

Caledonian Rd

Highbury Fields

Hampstead St

One Sixty ●

Hazara ●

**BELSIZE
PARK**

Chicken Shop ●

KENTISH
TOWN

Road

Liverpool Rd

Upper St

Essex Rd

North Rd

PRIMROSE
HILL

**SWISS
COTTAGE**

Belsize Park

Haverstock Hill

Beef &
Brew ●

York Way

BARNSBURY

CANONBURY

Finchley Road

Retsina ●

● XO

Swiss Cottage

Chalk
Farm ◉

Camden

**KING'S
CROSS**

ISLINGTON

Bradley's ●

Belsize Rd

Tandis ●

Kentish Town Rd

Camden High St

Abbey Road

St John's Wood

Odette's ●

L'Absinthe ●

🏨 Market ●

Michael Nadra
Primrose Hill ●

York &
Albany ●

Grain Store ●

Granger&Co ●

**KING'S
CROSS**

The Fellow ● 🏨

Upper St

City Rd

Sardine ●

Old St

A 501

Maida Vale

Park Rd

REGENT'S
PARK

Albany St.

Eversholt St.

ST PANCRAS
INTERNATIONAL

EUSTON 🚉

Pentonville Rd

Warwick Av.

MARYLEBONE

Marylebone Rd
A 501

Gilbert
Scott ●

Tottenham Court Rd

Theobald's Rd

Farringdon Rd

High Holborn

Westway

George St

PADDINGTON

Marble Arch

Oxford St

Tottenham
Court Road

Bayswater

Road

Park Lane

see "Central London"

Strand

Embankment

Upper Thames St

Blackfriars Rd A 201

HYDE PARK

A 4

ST JAMES'S
PARK

WATERLOO

Union St

Borough High Street

Kensington Road Knightsbridge

ST JAMES'S
PARK

Victoria Embankment

Elephant
& Castle

Brompton Rd

Knightsbridge

A 302

St George's Rd

New Kent Rd
A 201

Cromwell Road

Old Brompton Rd

Road

Sloane Square

VICTORIA

Belgrave Rd

Victoria Street

Lambeth Rd

ELEPHANT A

G H

500

Italian   H2

Archway   Closed 2 weeks summer
782 Holloway Rd ⊠ **N19 3JH**   and 2 weeks Christmas-New Year
☎ 020 7272 3406   – booking essential – (dinner only
www.500restaurant.co.uk   and lunch Friday-Sunday)
⊖ Archway

Carte £22/31

 It's named after the cute little Fiat and that couldn't be more appropriate because here is a restaurant which is small, fun, well-priced and ideal for London. The owner is an ebullient fellow who takes an active role in the service, as does the chef who likes to see the look of satisfaction on his customers' faces. Their shared passion is evident in the cooking: homemade breads and pastas are very good; the fluffy gnocchi with sausage ragu delivers a kick; the tender veal chop is a winner, and the rabbit is the house special. The menu, which has occasional Sardinian leanings, changes regularly and the sheet of daily specials includes great little snacks to have with a drink. Black and white photos of old Holloway are the only incongruity.

St John's Tavern

Modern cuisine   H2

Archway   Closed 25-26 December,
91 Junction Rd ⊠ **N19 5QU**   1 January and Monday lunch
☎ 020 7272 1587   – booking advisable
www.stjohnstavern.com
⊖ Archway.

Carte £18/36

 A Junction Road landmark, St John's Tavern has been providing sustenance to the good people of Islington since the 1860s – generally in the form of beer. Tapas is a rather more modern addition – these days served in the front bar – so choose from such delights as plaice goujons, globe artichoke, patatas bravas and jamon croquetas. For a more structured meal, head to the vast and hugely appealing rear dining room with its art and lithographs. The well-crafted dishes are mainly British with a nod to the Med, and could include pig's head terrine with piccalilli, octopus risotto or pork belly with quince aioli. Add in friendly service and a great selection of artisan beers and you'll see why this is still very much a favourite with the locals.

Hazara

Indian   G2

Belsize Park

44 Belsize Ln ✉ NW3 5AR
✆ 020 7423 1147
www.hazararestaurant.com
⊖ Belsize Park

Closed 25-26 December and
1 January – (dinner only and
lunch Saturday-Sunday)

Carte £19/33

He trained as a lawyer and spent eight years as a teacher but Tajinder, the owner, realised a long held ambition when he opened his own restaurant. He named it after his grandfather and staffed it with conscientious waiting staff and chefs who trained with the Taj Group and had experience of cooking specialities from all regions of India. The extensive menu does offer a few old classics but the more adventurous diner will be faced with an appealing choice, including dishes which make good use of game in season; fish dishes are also particularly good and Tajinder goes personally to Smithfield and Billingsgate to ensure the quality of the produce. The brighter, modern ground floor is the better place to sit.

Retsina

Greek   G2

Belsize Park

48-50 Belsize Ln ✉ NW3 5AR
✆ 020 7431 5855
www.retsina.squarespace.com
⊖ Belsize Park

Closed 25-26 December,
1 January, Monday lunch and
bank holidays

Carte £24/34

As private equity companies and international conglomerates continue on the path to world domination, there's something very reassuring about finding a restaurant that's still family-owned and part of the neighbourhood. It's quite a simple-looking place – bright, airy and enlivened with some modern artwork. Regulars across all age groups are literally welcomed with open arms and, with a little wishful thinking and a touch of imagination, one could almost be eating with the locals on a Greek island. The menu has all the Greek classics, from dolmathes to spanakopita, kleftico to moussaka but, bearing in mind they have a proper charcoal grill in the kitchen, the kebabs, cutlets and souvla are worthy choices.

Tandis

Belsize Park   Closed 25 December

73 Haverstock Hill ✉ NW3 4SL
✆ 020 7586 8079
www.tandisrestaurant.com
⊖ Chalk Farm

Carte £16/26

The appeal of Tandis and its enticing Persian and Middle Eastern cooking stretches way beyond the Iranian diaspora – plenty of locals were also seduced as soon as they tasted the traditional flat bread baked in a clay oven and the Masto Khiyar. Start with the complex flavours of Kashke Badem, then move on to an invigorating khoresh stew, such as lamb and split peas, or try a succulent kabab; vegetarians are also well catered for. Newcomers shouldn't be afraid to ask for a little guidance; dishes are substantial and sharing is the key – and make sure you finish with the refreshing Persian sorbet with rosewater. A very successful takeaway service doesn't seem to affect the efficiency with which it is run.

XO

Belsize Park   Closed 25-26 December
                                                  and 1 January

29 Belsize Ln ✉ NW3 5AS
✆ 020 7433 0888
www.rickerrestaurants.com/xo
⊖ Belsize Park

Menu £10 (lunch) – Carte £22/51

Who knew Belsize Park was so trendy? Apart from estate agents, obviously. This branch of Will Ricker's small chain of glossy pan-Asian restaurants may not be quite as frenetic as the others but it still attracts plenty of shiny happy people, many of whom are holding hands. It follows the same theme as the others: a busy front bar that serves decent cocktails, behind which is the slick, uncluttered restaurant in shades of lime. The menu trawls through most of Asia; start with some warm edamame while reading through it. Highlights include the ever-popular crispy squid and the tender and tasty Indonesian lamb rendang curry. Sharing is the key, especially as those who come in large parties get the booths.

Market

Modern British   G2

43 Parkway ⊠ NW1 7PN
📞 020 7267 9700
www.marketrestaurant.co.uk
⊖ Camden Town

Closed 25 December-2 January,
Sunday dinner and bank holidays
– booking essential

Menu £12 (weekday lunch)/18 – Carte £28/35

The name is spot on because this is all about market fresh produce, seasonality and cooking that is refreshingly matter of fact, with big, bold flavours and John Bull Britishness. Dishes come as advertised, with no pointless ornamentation, and you can expect to find the likes of brawn, ox tongue fritters and devilled kidneys alongside stews and shepherd's pie in winter, followed by proper puddings, not desserts. Be sure to have lamb or beef dripping on toast as a pre-starter – it'll leave you licking your lips for the next few hours. The exposed brick walls, zinc-topped tables and old school chairs work very well and the atmosphere is fun without ever becoming too excitable. The terrific prices entice plenty of passers-by.

York & Albany

Modern cuisine   G2

127-129 Parkway ⊠ NW1 7PS
📞 020 7592 1227
www.gordonramsayrestaurants.com/york-and-albany
⊖ Camden Town

Menu £21 (weekday lunch) – Carte £30/49

This 1820s John Nash coaching inn is a handsome fellow. Rescued by Gordon Ramsay a few years back after lying almost derelict, its reputation now brings customers from all parts of northwest London. It's a moot point, though, whether it still qualifies as an inn or is more of a restaurant these days; granted, you can drop in for a drink at the bar but then that's after you've been welcomed by a hostess at the door. The food certainly veers more towards a restaurant style: instead of burgers and pasta, there are seared scallops with celeriac or red leg partridge with barley, although you can get quite robust dishes like ox cheeks and steaks. The bright, apron-wearing staff provide confident, breezy service and there are bedrooms available.

Shayona

Indian   **E2**
Church End   Closed 19-20 October
54-62 Meadow Garth ⊠ NW10 8HD   and 25 December
☎ 020 8965 3365
www.shayonarestaurants.com
⊖ Stonebridge Park

Menu £10 (weekday lunch) – Carte £13/20

Shayona sits in the shadow of Neasden's remarkable Shri Swaminarayan Mandir and is actually owned by the temple. In contrast to the splendour of this Hindu gem, the restaurant is housed within a building that looks, from the outside, a little like a supermarket and indeed somewhat resembles one on the inside too – but head past the sweet counter and you'll find yourself in a comfortable and vibrantly decorated room. The fresh, balanced cooking here is sattvic, which means it is vegetarian and 'pure' and so avoids certain foods like onion or garlic. The large and varied menu covers all parts of India and includes curries from the north, dosas from the south and street snacks from Mumbai. There is no alcohol available so choose a refreshing lassi instead.

Bistro Aix

French   **H1**
Crouch End   Closed 24, 26 December and
54 Topsfield Par, Tottenham Ln ⊠ N8 8PT   1 January – (dinner only and
☎ 020 8340 6346   lunch Saturday-Sunday)
www.bistroaix.co.uk
⊖ Crouch Hill

Menu £18 – Carte £25/49

Bistro Aix has enough local followers that it doesn't need to entice passers-by, which is just as well as there aren't usually too many boulevardiers wandering Tottenham Lane in search of duck confit. It's easy to see why Crouch Enders have taken this bistro to their hearts: the French food is unfussy and dependable, the surroundings are rustic and relaxed, the wine list is competitively priced and the atmosphere, welcoming. The menu offers bags of choice, with around 20 starters and just as many main courses, and the kitchen does the classics, like snails, onion soup, rabbit with mustard, and tarte Tatin, particularly well. There is the added attraction of a very appealingly priced set menu Tuesday to Thursday and Sunday evenings.

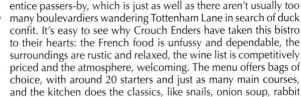

Bull & Last

T r a d i t i o n a l   B r i t i s h   **G2**

Dartmouth Park   Closed 23-25 December
                                                  – booking essential
168 Highgate Rd ✉ **NW5 1QS**
✆ 020 7267 3641
www.thebullandlast.co.uk
⊖ **Tufnell Park.**

Carte £25/44

 This Victorian corner pub is well loved by the locals and it's easy to see why. It's full of character and life – and the food is gloriously robust and wholesome. Stay on the ground floor as it has more character than upstairs; if you haven't booked, it's worth trying your luck anyway as they keep the odd table back – mind you, with enticing bar snacks like ham and corn croquettes and buttermilk chicken wings, you may simply find happiness at the bar ordering these with a pint. The daily menu can sometimes change between services, depending on what ingredients come in. The kitchen knows its way around an animal – the charcuterie boards and terrines are very good, and game in season is not to be missed. They do a pretty good breakfast too.

Paradise by way of Kensal Green

M o d e r n   B r i t i s h   **F2**

Kensal Green   (dinner only and lunch Saturday
                                                        and Sunday)
19 Kilburn Ln ✉ **W10 4AE**
✆ 020 8969 0098
www.theparadise.co.uk
⊖ **Kensal Green.**

Carte £26/45

AC Calling 'Paradise' a pub hardly does it justice – this is a veritable fun palace. Named after a line from a GK Chesterton poem, this gloriously bohemian place is spread over three floors and means different things to different people: some come along for comedy nights and cocktails or party nights and DJs; others pop in for drinks in the Reading room or snacks in the bar; many come to eat in the restaurant; and you can even get married here. The food is a reassuring mix of British favourites and European themed dishes, all made using good ingredients from trusted suppliers and prepared with obvious care. The surroundings are wonderfully quirky and idiosyncratic, the staff are contagiously enthusiastic and the vibe, effortlessly cool.

Parlour

Modern British   F2

Kensal Green

5 Regent St ✉ NW10 5LG
✆ 020 8969 2184
www.parlourkensal.com
⊖ Kensal Green

Closed 1 week August, 10 days
Christmas-New Year and Monday

Menu £15 (weekday lunch) – Carte £20/40

It may not quite be a pub but nor is it a restaurant so let's focus more on what Parlour actually is – a fun, warmly run and slightly quirky neighbourhood hangout. Open from breakfast until late, it has one room dominated by a large bar and the other, with an appealingly higgledy-piggledy look, set up for eating. They do a decent cocktail and a great range of beers and the menu is a wonderfully unabashed mix of tradition, originality and reinvention. Approaching legendary status is their cow pie which even Dan, however Desperate, would struggle to finish. The vegetable 'ravioli' is a cleverly thought-out construction and the marshmallow Wagon Wheel something for the children. On warm nights ask for one of the cabanas in the garden.

Beef & Brew

Meats and grills   G2

Kentish Town

323 Kentish Town Rd ✉ NW5 2TJ
✆ 020 7998 1511
www.beef-and-brew.co.uk
⊖ Kentish Town

Closed Monday lunch – bookings
advisable at dinner

Carte £18/27

A/C
The name really tells you all you need to know. The steaks here tend to be less familiar cuts, like onglet or flat iron, which keep the prices down, and the beers are from small artisan brewers, the nearest of which is Camden Brewery just down the road. The simple, pared-down look makes it appear not unlike a butcher's shop, where the only decorative feature is an image of a cow displaying the various cuts. Kick off with the lip-smacking brisket jam nuggets, which have become something of a signature, and then have a steak or something in a bun like the intensely-flavoured beef cheek. Beer is not just offered to drink – it can also feature in the cheese, the ice cream or as a porter sauce for the Brewer's Mess dessert.

Discover Restaurants You Love

Bookatable by Michelin is Europe's leading restaurant reservations website: helping millions of diners make bookings at restaurants they love. Discover **gastro pubs** and **high street favourites**, **Michelin star restaurants** and hot-off-the-press deals, and make free, instantly confirmed bookings.

www.bookatable.co.uk

A service of

MICHELIN

Chicken Shop

M e a t s   a n d   g r i l l s   **G2**

Kentish Town

79 Highgate Rd ⊠ NW5 1TL
📞 020 3310 2020
www.chickenshop.com
⊖ Kentish Town

Bookings not accepted – (dinner
only and lunch Saturday-Sunday)

Carte £16/21   ✗

The concept is so simple, you'll leave wondering why you didn't
think of it yourself. There's no menu, just chicken – marinated,
steamed and then finished over wood and charcoal. You simply
order a quarter, half or whole bird, choose a side from crinkle-
cut chips, proper coleslaw, sweetcorn or salad and it's quickly
delivered on enamel plates. The chicken is great: the skin is crisp
and the meat beneath it moist and succulent. Pudding is just as
straightforward: a brownie or a slice of cheesecake or apple pie.
It all happens in a noisy, mildly chaotic basement but it's great
fun and good value – look out for the hessian bag on the front
door or you'll never find it. Queuing is a certainty unless you
arrive ridiculously early.

Fellow

M o d e r n   c u i s i n e   **H2**

King's Cross St Pancras

24 York Way ⊠ N1 9AA
📞 020 7833 4395
www.thefellow.co.uk
⊖ King's Cross St Pancras.

Closed 25-27 December

Carte £24/37

This clever Fellow established itself well before the regeneration
of King's Cross finished so was all ready for the influx of new
customers. Don't be fooled by its rather anonymous façade – this
is a pub 'de nos jours', complete with a slick cocktail bar and a
kitchen with worthy ingredient-sourcing credentials. Most of the
action takes place on the ground floor which looks a little dark
and moody but the atmosphere is brightened considerably by
the staff who make a genuine effort to look after their customers.
A relatively small kitchen means they keep the menu lean and
clean and influences remain largely within Europe. Fish from the
Cornish day boats is often a highlight; cheeses are British and
puds are well worth a flutter.

Gilbert Scott

T r a d i t i o n a l   B r i t i s h H2/3

King's Cross St Pancras

St Pancras Renaissance Hotel, Euston Rd
✉ NW1 2AR ☎ 020 7278 3888
www.thegilbertscott.co.uk
⊖ King's Cross St Pancras

Menu £21 (lunch) – Carte £28/61

 Britain's less than stellar reputation for the quality of its food won't change until more people come and see what's cooking in our kitchens, so snaring those tourists as soon as they step off the Eurostar is no bad thing. Run under the aegis of Marcus Wareing and named after the architect who designed this Gothic masterpiece of a hotel in 1873, the restaurant has the splendour of a Grand Salon but the buzz of a busy brasserie. More significantly, the kitchen celebrates our culinary heritage by trumpeting both our native produce and regional specialities. In amongst the Eccles cakes, Manchester tart, Cullen skink and Glamorgan sausages are also dishes like 'soles in coffins' and 'Tweed kettle' that prove someone's done their research.

Grain Store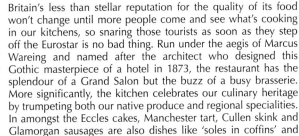

M o d e r n   c u i s i n e H2

King's Cross St Pancras

Granary Sq, 1-3 Stable St ✉ N1C 4AB
☎ 020 7324 4466
www.grainstore.com
⊖ King's Cross St Pancras

Closed 24-25 December,
1 January and Sunday dinner

Carte £15/35

 The redevelopment of King's Cross may not yet be finished, but already train travellers and locals have a wealth of eating places close by. Grain Store is a big, buzzing 'canteen' from Bruno Loubet and the people behind the Zetter hotel, so you know it's going to be run properly. However, don't come expecting the same style of cooking – here it's about bringing together Bruno's experiences from around the world. On offer is an exciting array of eclectic, well-priced dishes that show thought, imagination and intelligence; they're packed with interesting tastes and textures, and vegetables often take the principle role. Sustainability and seasonality are more than mere buzz words here and the large kitchen rightly takes centre stage.

Granger & Co. King's Cross

Modern cuisine

H2

King's Cross St Pancras

Closed 25-26 December

Stanley Building, 7 Pancras Sq. ⊠ N1C 4AG

☏ 020 3058 2567

www.grangerandco.com

⊖ King's Cross St Pancras

Carte £22/30

𝄪

This is the third London outpost for Australian chef Bill Granger, and – as with the others – you know as soon as you walk through the door that you're in for a good time. The welcome is warm enough to bring some Aussie sunshine to the dullest of British days, and the buzz of happy customers is all around. Yes, you may need to wait, but that just gives you the opportunity to indulge in a couple of ripper cocktails. The menu is a clever mix of small plates, barbecue dishes, and bowls and grains, with plenty of South East Asian flavours for good measure. Dishes like prawn and bok choi pot-stickers and parmesan-crumbed chicken schnitzel are vibrant, fresh and uplifting – and the wine list is one of the most fairly priced in town.

L'Absinthe

French

G2

Primrose Hill

Closed 1 week Christmas and
Monday dinner

40 Chalcot Rd ⊠ NW1 8LS

☏ 020 7483 4848

www.labsinthe.co.uk

⊖ Chalk Farm

Menu £10 (weekday lunch) – Carte £22/38

𝄪

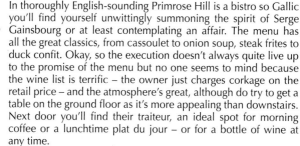

In thoroughly English-sounding Primrose Hill is a bistro so Gallic you'll find yourself unwittingly summoning the spirit of Serge Gainsbourg or at least contemplating an affair. The menu has all the great classics, from cassoulet to onion soup, steak frites to duck confit. Okay, so the execution doesn't always quite live up to the promise of the menu but no one seems to mind because the wine list is terrific – the owner just charges corkage on the retail price – and the atmosphere's great, although do try to get a table on the ground floor as it's more appealing than downstairs. Next door you'll find their traiteur, an ideal spot for morning coffee or a lunchtime plat du jour – or for a bottle of wine at any time.

Michael Nadra Primrose Hill

Modern cuisine G2

Primrose Hill

42 Gloucester Ave ✉ NW1 8JD

Closed 24-28 December
and 1 January

☏ 020 7722 2800

www.restaurant-michaelnadra.co.uk/primrose

⊖ Camden Town

Menu £27/38

When you have a successful restaurant in Chiswick, opening a second branch in Primrose Hill would suggest that not only have you recognised similarities between the two neighbourhoods but also that you know a pretty decent shortcut to get you across town. Michael Nadra took over the old Sardo Canale premises in 2012; it's a modern space which comes with lots of glass, judicious lighting, a pleasant terrace and comfortable bar which offers a selection of over 20 martinis. His menu closely resembles the one in Chiswick, which means that flavours from the Mediterranean feature widely but he's not averse to introducing the occasional Asian accent and his cooking shows a careful hand when balancing flavours.

Odette's

Modern cuisine G2

Primrose Hill

130 Regent's Park Rd. ✉ NW1 8XL

Closed 25 December-7 January
and Monday except December

☏ 020 7586 8569

www.odettesprimrosehill.com

⊖ Chalk Farm

Menu £22 (weekday lunch) – Carte £31/48

It's amazing what a window can do: they installed a big one at the front of the restaurant and it opened the whole place up and made it feel far more welcoming. Locals used to regard Odette's as being a little bit standoffish but service is now a lot chattier and the atmosphere more relaxed, which in turn makes it feel more a part of the community. The cooking is also a little less complicated than it was and is all the better for it, although there is still depth to the dishes. Flavours are robust and braised dishes a highlight; the owner clearly has a passion for his Welsh roots. The lunch and early evening menus are a steal and change every fortnight; there are also tasting and vegetarian menus alongside the à la carte.

Ostuni

I t a l i a n   **F2**

Queens Park   Closed 25 December

43-45 Lonsdale Rd ⊠ NW6 6RA
℡ 020 7624 8035
www.ostuniristorante.co.uk
⊖ Queen's Park

Carte £16/40

 The cuisine of Puglia, the red hot heel in Italy's boot, is celebrated
at Ostuni – which now also has a sister in Highgate. Start with
 olives or taralli, then order the creamy burrata or mackerel before
heading to the orecchiette – the region's ear-shaped pasta made
from durum wheat. For the main course, carnivores should look
no further than the sausages or bombette (cheese encased in
pork) from the charcoal oven, or the ox cheek which comes with
another speciality – fava bean purée. Even dessert celebrates all
things Pugliese: the panna cotta is topped with a sweet reduction
of Primitivo. The room has an appealing, rustic look and a large
terrace; seats at the bar and at the counter of the open kitchen
are kept for locals who haven't booked.

Bradley's

M o d e r n   c u i s i n e   **G2**

Swiss Cottage   Closed Sunday dinner

25 Winchester Rd. ⊠ NW3 3NR
℡ 020 7722 3457
www.bradleysnw3.co.uk
⊖ Swiss Cottage

Menu £28 – Carte £33/43

 For over 20 years Simon Bradley's well-liked restaurant has been
a stalwart of the Swiss Cottage dining scene. His loyal followers
are always guaranteed a warm welcome and ticket holders to
Hampstead Theatre won't find a more convenient spot for a
bite before curtain up. The room has a fairly contemporary feel,
with the tables at the large window always in demand, along
with the two cosy booths. The array of menus on offer can be
a little bewildering but always includes a competitively priced
set menu and an extensive à la carte. Many head for the tried-
and-tested classics like Mediterranean fish soup or veal Holstein,
while others prefer the more ambitious dishes like foie gras with
onion confit.

One Sixty

North American   **G2**

West Hampstead

291 West End Ln. ✉ NW6 1RD
☎ 020 7794 9786
www.one-sixty.co.uk
⊖ West Hampstead

Closed 25-30 December – (dinner
only and lunch Saturday-Sunday)

Carte £25/38   ✗

The battle for supremacy between independents and chains
in West Hampstead has intensified in recent years. In 2014,
reinforcements for those fighting high street homogenisation
arrived in the form of One Sixty, a lively local bar and restaurant
based on an American smokehouse. It's a loud, buzzy, stripped
back sort of place, with the kind of food you eat with your fingers.
The pork ribs, ox cheek and lamb are smoked in-house for 8
hours to a temperature of 160°F – hence the name – and food
comes in enamel bowls; the dry-aged burger is also proving very
popular. Extras like mac & cheese and corn on the cob can be
ordered on the side and there's an impressive choice of over 50
craft beers from around the world – the ideal accompaniment.

If you are
looking for
particularly charming
accommodation, book a
hotel shown in red: ,
🏠...🏛️.

North-East London

If northwest London is renowned for its leafy acres, then the area to its immediate east has a more urban, brick-built appeal. Which has meant, over the last decade or so, a wholesale rebranding exercise for some of its traditionally shady localities. A generation ago it would have been beyond the remit of even the most inventive estate agent to sell the charms of Islington, Hackney or Bethnal Green. But then along came Damien Hirst, Tracey Emin et al, and before you could say 'cow in formaldehyde' the area's cachet had rocketed.

Shoreditch and **Hoxton** are the pivotal points of the region's hip makeover. Their cobbled brick streets and shabby industrial remnants were like heavenly manna to the artists and designers who started to colonise the old warehouses thirty years ago. A fashionable crowd soon followed in their footsteps, and nowadays the area around **Hoxton Square** positively teems with clubs, bars and galleries. Must-sees include Rivington Place, a terrific gallery that highlights visual arts from around the world, Deluxe (digital installations) and Hales (contemporary art). Before the area was ever trendy, there was the Geffrye Museum. A short stroll up Hoxton's **Kingsland Road,** it's a jewel of a place, set in elegant 18C almshouses, and depicting English middle-class interiors from 1600 to the present day. Right behind it is St. Mary's Secret Garden, a little oasis that manages to include much diversity including a separate woodland and herb area, all in less than an acre. At the southern end of the area, in Folgate Street, Dennis Severs' House is an original Huguenot home that recreates 18 and 19C life in an original way – cooking smells linger, hearth and candles burn, giving you the impression the owners have only just left the place. Upstairs the beds remain unmade: did a certain local artist pick up any ideas here?

When the Regent's Canal was built in the early 19C, **Islington's** fortunes nose-dived, for it was accompanied by the arrival of slums and over-crowding. But the once-idyllic village managed to hold onto its Georgian squares and handsome Victorian terraces through the rough times, and when these were gentrified a few years ago, the area ushered in a revival. **Camden Passage** has long been famed for its quirky antique emporiums, while the slinky Business Design Centre is a flagship of the modern Islington. Cultural icons established themselves around the Upper Street area and these have gone from strength to strength. The **Almeida** Theatre has a habit of hitting the production jackpot with its history of world premieres, while the King's Head has earned itself a reputation for raucous scene-stealing; set up in the seventies, it's also London's very first theatre-pub. Nearby, the Screen on the Green boasts a wonderful old-fashioned neon billboard.

Even in the 'bad old days', Islington drew in famous names, and

C. Eymenier / MICHELIN

at Regency smart **Canonbury Square** are the one-time homes of Evelyn Waugh (no.17A) and George Orwell (no.27). These days it houses the Estorick Collection of Modern Italian Art; come here to see fine futuristic paintings in a Georgian villa. To put the history of the area in a proper context, head to St. John Street, south of the City Road, where the Islington Museum tells the story of a colourful and multi-layered past.

Further up the A10, you come to **Dalston,** a bit like the Islington of old but with the buzzy Ridley Road market and a vibrant all-night scene including the blistering Vortex Jazz Club just off Kingsland Road. A little further north is **Stoke Newington,** referred to, a bit un-kindly, as the poor man's Islington. Its pride and joy is Church Street, which not only features some eye-catching boutiques, but also lays claim to Abney Park Cemetery, an enchanting old place with a wildlife-rich nature reserve.

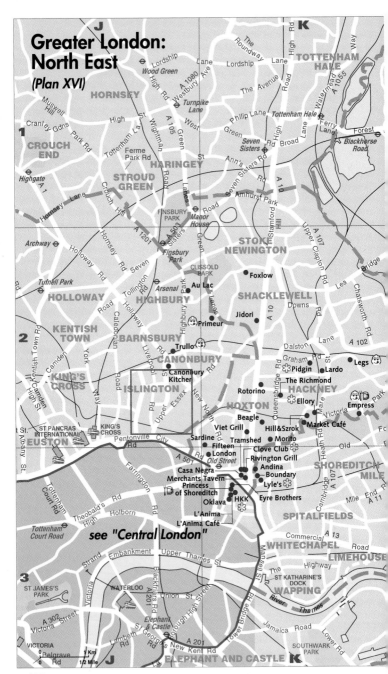

Greater London:
North East
(Plan XVI)

HORNSEY

Lordship
Wood Green

The Roundway
Lane

High

Way

**TOTTENHAM
HALE**

Lordship

Lane

The Avenue

A 1055

Waterhead

Muswell
Hill

High
St

A 1080 Westbury Ave

Turnpike
Lane

Phillip Lane

Tottenham Hale

Ferry
Lane

Forest

**CROUCH
END**

Cranley Gdns

Park Rd

Tottenham La

West

A 105

Green

Ferme Park Rd

Wightman

St

HARINGEY

Seven
Sisters

Ann's Rd

Broad
Lane

**Blackhorse
Road**

Highgate

A 1

Hornsey

Lane

**STROUD
GREEN**

Crouch Hill

Road

Lanes

Seven Sisters Rd

A 10

Amhurst Park

Archway

Holloway

Hornsey

Rd

Seven

A 1201

A 503 Sisters

**FINSBURY
PARK**

**Manor
House**

Green

Stamford

**STOKE
NEWINGTON**

A 107 Upper Clapton Rd

Bridge

Tufnell Park

HOLLOWAY

Tollington
Rd

Holloway

Road

Finsbury
Park

**CLISSOLD
PARK**

Arsenal

Highbury

Park

Lanes

• Foxlow

Lea

Chatsworth Rd

HIGHBURY

Au Lac

Downs

SHACKLEWELL

A 10

**KENTISH
TOWN**

Caledonian

Holloway

Road

• Jidori

A 102

Camden

York

Liverpool

Rd

BARNSBURY

• Primeur

Trullo ✿

CANONBURY

Dalston

Lane

**KING'S
CROSS**

Camden
High St.

Way

ISLINGTON

**Canonbury
Kitcher**

Upper

St

Essex

New North

Rd

Graham

Rd

• Pidgin

• Lardo

Legs •

HACKNEY

Rotorino

• Ellory

Mare

Victoria

Empress

HOXTON

Queensbridge

Rd

Beagle

**St. PANCRAS
INTERNATIONAL**

EUSTON

**KING'S
CROSS**

Pentonville

Rd

City

Viet Grill

Hill&Szrok

Market Café

St. Albany

St.

Sardine

Tramshed

• Morito

Heath

Rd

Old

Farringdon

A 501

Fifteen

**• London
Old Street**

Clove Club ✿

SHOREDITCH

Theobald's

Rd

High

Holborn

Casa Negra

Rivington Grill

Andina

Boundary

Cambridge

A 107

MILE

Merchants Tavern

**Princess
of Shoreditch**

Lyle's ✿

Mile End

Rd

A 11

**Tottenham
Court Road**

Oklava

HKK

Eyre Brothers

L'Anima

SPITALFIELDS

L'Anima Café

see "Central London"

Commercial

A 13

Road

WHITECHAPEL

LIMEHOUSE

Strand

Embankment

Upper Thames St

The

Highway

**ST KATHARINE'S
DOCK**

WAPPING

**ST JAMES'S
PARK**

WATERLOO

Victoria

Blackfriars Rd

Union St

Borough High Street

Tower Bridge

Rd

River

Thames

Jamaica Road

Lower Rd

VICTORIA

A 302

Victoria

Street

**Elephant
& Castle**

Lambeth
Rd

St. Georges

New Kent Rd

A 201

**SOUTHWARK
PARK**

Belgrave
Rd

0   1 Km
0   1/2 Mile

ELEPHANT AND CASTLE

J

K

322

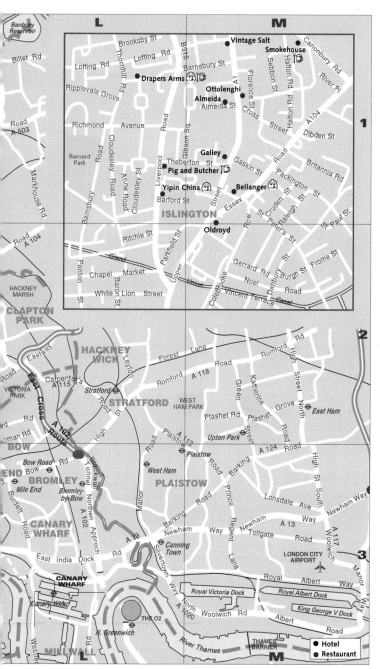

Canonbury Kitchen

Italian   J2

Canonbury

19 Canonbury Ln ⊠ N1 2AS
℘ 020 7226 9791
www.canonburykitchen.com
⊖ Highbury & Islington

Closed Sunday dinner – (dinner only and lunch Saturday-Sunday)

Menu £12 – Carte £26/36   🍴

Inserting the word 'kitchen' into the name of one's restaurant is becoming more and more common as it instantly evokes images of simple food and unpretentious dining. That certainly applies to Canonbury Kitchen, which comes with an appropriately light, fresh look, thanks to its exposed brick walls, high ceiling and painted floorboards. With seating for just forty it also feels like the very epitome of a neighbourhood restaurant. Owner Max and his team provide gently reassuring service and the kitchen – on-view at the far end – sensibly keeps things simple. That includes an ever-popular fritto misto made with cuttlefish and octopus, pan-fried hake with herbs, and a lemon tiramisu with limoncello replacing the marsala.

Primeur

Modern cuisine   K2

Canonbury

116 Petherton Rd ⊠ N5 2RT
℘ 020 7226 5271
www.primeurn5.co.uk
⊖ Canonbury

Closed Christmas, Monday, dinner Sunday and lunch Tuesday-Thursday

Carte £20/31   🍴

A relaxed restaurant where locals can pop in for a few small plates of unfussy seasonal food, with no standing on ceremony: this was the vision held by its owners and one that has certainly been fulfilled in the creation of this neighbourhood restaurant. The 'Barnes Motors' sign tells you that this used to be a garage and its huge concertina doors fold back to reveal an equally quirky interior with counter seating around the edges and a large communal table. The blackboard is chalked up daily with a dozen or so dishes; these are matched with wines which are all available by the glass. Plates are small and designed for sharing; understated but packed with flavour – simplicity is the key here, allowing the quality ingredients to really shine.

Smokehouse

Modern cuisine

North-East ▶ Plan XVI

M1

Canonbury

63-69 Canonbury Rd ✉ N1 2DG
✆ 020 7354 1144
www.smokehouseislington.co.uk
⊖ Highbury & Islington.

Closed 24-26 December
– booking advisable – (dinner
only and lunch Saturday-Sunday)

Carte £28/34

If, to you, barbecuing means a burnt chicken leg, warm wine and a wet garden then a visit to Smokehouse will set you straight. You can smell the oak chips in the smoker as you approach this warm, modern pub, which was previously called The House. Meat is the mainstay of the very appealing menu – the peppered ox cheeks have understandably become a firm favourite – but whilst the flavours are undeniably gutsy, the smoking and barbecuing manages to add a little something to the ingredients without ever overpowering them. With portion sizes to appease Desperate Dan, only the committed may make it to dessert but chocolate lovers should try the Friday pie. The pub is enthusiastically run and staff are eager to recommend dishes.

Trullo

Italian

J2

Canonbury

300-302 St Paul's Rd ✉ N1 2LH
✆ 020 7226 2733
www.trullorestaurant.com
⊖ Highbury & Islington

Closed Christmas-New Year and
Sunday dinner
– booking essential

Carte £22/38

It's named after the conical-shaped buildings of southern Italy used primarily by farm workers for meeting and eating: a most appropriate moniker for a restaurant always full of noisily contented diners. While the ground floor has kept its well-worn, homely feel, the basement has an all-American look, with exposed brick, industrial ducting and red banquettes – the three booths being the most sought-after seats in the house. Its style may be reminiscent of a U.S. diner, but the food stays resolutely Italian: expect rustic, well-priced dishes bursting with flavour, including meats and fish cooked on the charcoal grill and great pasta, hand-rolled fresh before each service. Young, enthusiastic and cheery staff deliver dishes with aplomb.

Jidori

J a p a n e s e K2

Dalston

89 Kingsland High St ✉ E2 8BP
✆ 020 7686 5634
www.jidori.co.uk
⊖ Dalston Kingsland

Closed 25-26 December,
1 January and Sunday – bookings
not accepted – (dinner only and
lunch Wednesday-Friday)

Carte £17/28   ✗

This sweet neighbourhood restaurant models itself on traditional Japanese yakitori-ya: small, unadorned places serving succulent skewers of grilled chicken. The first section of the menu offers small plates such as sesame and chilli marinated cucumber or a spicy curry scotch egg to spike the tastebuds; the second, the yakitori, features different parts of the chicken – wing with shiso and grilled lemon; thigh with spring onion or perhaps the parson's nose. The charming staff recommend two plates from each section; there are two yakitori skewers per plate and these are cooked quickly on the charcoal-fired Kama-Asa Shoten grill to give a charred exterior to the juicy meat. There's a good selection of cocktails, sake and craft beers too.

The Richmond

S e a f o o d K2

Dalston

316 Queensbridge Rd ✉ E8 3NH
✆ 020 7241 1638
www.therichmondhackney.com
⊖ Dalston Junction

Closed 25-26 December
– booking essential

Carte £21/35   ✗

Running a restaurant in Borough Market, as Brett Redman does with Elliot's, means there's no hiding place when it comes to ingredients. He's now opened his second operation here in Dalston and has bought with him that passion for insisting on only the freshest and the best produce. This was once a pub but where the bar was is now a counter where you're likely to see someone shucking oysters, because it's seafood and in particular raw seafood that lies at the core of the menu. Little is required, apart from a home-baked muffin, to embellish crab when it's as fresh as this; the same can be said for the octopus and mussels that feature in the Nduja spiced stew. There are a few non-fishy dishes for non-believers.

Rotorino

Italian

Dalston

434 Kingsland Rd ⊠ **E8 4AA**
℘ 020 7249 9081
www.rotorino.com
⊖ Dalston Junction

Closed 23 December-2 January
– (dinner only and Sunday lunch)

Menu £19 (early dinner) – Carte £22/36   ⅄

Some restaurants you just warm to straight away – and this stylish yet down to earth Italian on Kingsland Road is one of them. There's lots of texture to the decoration, which includes bare brick and plaster, wood and some wonderful tiles. The long table you notice when you walk in is for those who've failed to book; those who do like to plan ahead should ask for one of the prized booths at the back. Wherever you sit, the staff will make you feel welcome and will impress you with their knowledge of the menu. The kitchen's efforts go into offering fresh tasting and great value Southern Italian specialities, such as a delightful caponata, beautifully light gnudi, delicious Sasso chicken – and possibly the cheapest hanger steak in town.

If you are looking for particularly charming accommodation, book a hotel shown in red: 🏠,
🏠...🏯.

 Legs

Modern British   K2

Hackney   Closed Sunday-Tuesday
120 Morning Ln ⊠ E9 6LH   – (dinner only)
☏ 020 3441 8765
www.legsrestaurant.com
⊖ Hackney Central

Carte £25/35   ✗

This urban, no-frills bistro has been brought to life by Magnus Reid, an Australian-born former tattoo artist. Reid spends time ensuring that the quality of his produce is top-notch, and his food is bursting with freshness and flavour. He also shows equal respect for his customers and you get the feeling that the friendly staff here really enjoy what they do. Lunch offers some interesting sandwiches – perhaps suckling pig with chilli jam roll – while dinner means a daily changing selection of about 10 vibrant small plates for sharing. Time has evidently also been spent on the wine list, which focuses on organic wines from small producers; 'Legs' refers to the residual wine left on a glass – an indicator of its sugar and alcohol content.

Au Lac

Vietnamese   J2

Highbury   Closed 24-26 December,
82 Highbury Park ⊠ N5 2XE   1-2 January and 1 week early
☏ 020 7704 9187   August – (dinner only and lunch
www.aulac.co.uk   Thursday-Friday)
⊖ Arsenal

Carte £12/24   ✗

It's unlikely to ever attract passers-by on looks alone but fortunately enough people know about this long-standing Vietnamese restaurant, run by two brothers, to ensure that its phone rings red hot most nights. The comforts inside may also be fairly unremarkable but that just allows everyone to focus their attention on the lengthy menu, to which new dishes are added regularly. The pho noodle soup is a favourite but along with the traditional dishes there are plenty of more contemporary creations, all exhibiting the same freshness and lively flavours. The prices are kept honest, especially as the generous portion sizes mean that you don't have to order too many dishes to feel satisfied. They also do a roaring trade in takeaways.

Beagle

T r a d i t i o n a l   B r i t i s h   **K2**

Hoxton   Closed Sunday dinner

397-400 Geffrye St ✉ **E2 8HZ**
✆ 020 7613 2967
www.beaglelondon.co.uk
⊖ Hoxton

Menu £19 (weekday lunch) – Carte £21/36

 Occupying three converted railway arches, and named after the
steam train that ran on the line above, Beagle is a big, bustling
operation. One arch is used as a bar; one as the dining room;
and the third is a kitchen and private dining room. Lots of brick,
reclaimed materials and clever lighting add to the atmosphere
and the terrace, overlooking The Geffrye, is a good spot to enjoy
one of their cocktails. The British menu changes twice a day
and its contents are largely determined by whatever seasonal
produce arrives at the kitchen door – the descriptions are
derivatively terse. There are occasional Italian touches, like a
braised beef shin pappardelle, and blackboards announce the
dishes for two, such as whole steamed sea bass.

Fifteen London

M o d e r n   B r i t i s h   **K3**

Hoxton   Closed 25-26 December and
                                                          1 January – booking essential
15 Westland Pl ✉ **N1 7LP**
✆ 020 3375 1515
www.fifteen.net
⊖ Old Street

Carte £24/50

 Fifteen was created fifteen years ago to provide training and
development in the hospitality industry for youngsters who've
faced difficulties in their lives, and you get the impression that
the keen, chatty staff are very happy to be working here. The
focus is on seasonal British food with some Italian influences;
the cooking certainly has personality and the wood-fired oven
is used to good effect, delivering some great flavours. The same
menu is offered in both the ground floor restaurant with its open
kitchen, and the livelier, noisier cellar below, while the bar is a
great place to come for a cocktail and a catch-up. Fifteen may
not come cheap but it's a very worthy cause; you'll leave lighter
in pocket but with a heartwarming glow.

Morito

S p a n i s h   **K2**

Hoxton

195 Hackney Rd ✉ E2 8JL
✆ 020 7613 0754
www.moritohackneyroad.co.uk
⊖ Hoxton

*Closed Christmas, Monday lunch
and bank holidays*

Carte £25/40

Sam and Sam Clark have branched out with their third restaurant – a second Morito – this time bringing their brand of Moorish cuisine to the vibrant East London dining scene. The Hackney Road offshoot has all the utilitarianism of its older sister but much more space; a horseshoe bar takes centre stage and there are several counters, including one in the window. The menu features small plates under the headings para picar, vegetables, fish, meat and dulce and dishes draw their influences not only from Spain, but also from North Africa and the Eastern Mediterranean, including chef Marianna's homeland, Crete. Choose around 3 dishes each – these will come when they're ready, which can make for a mixed up meal but adds to the fun of this lively spot.

Sardine

F r e n c h   **J2**

Hoxton

Parasol Art Gallery, 15 Micawber St ✉ N1 7TB
✆ 020 7490 0144
www.sardine.london
⊖ Old Street

*Closed Christmas-New Year
and Monday*

Carte £28/35

It's named for the food, which focuses on Southern Europe; particularly France, but it could equally be a reference to how you feel squeezed into this compact space. It's set within the Parasol Art Gallery and has a communal table at the heart of proceedings; counter seats are available at the kitchen and the bar and staff move between tables with the grace of ballerinas. Chef-owner Alex Jackson's cooking comes from the heart; this is food he loves and respects, and dishes like soupe au pistou; red mullet, pastis, courgettes and mussels en papillote, and apricot galette are rustic, unfussy and incredibly tasty. Stand-outs include the lamb à la ficelle: leg of lamb tied on a string and cooked over an open fire.

Almeida

Modern British M1

Islington

30 Almeida St. ⊠ N1 1AD

✆ 020 7354 4777

www.almeida-restaurant.com

⊖ Angel

Closed 26 December, 1 January, Sunday dinner and Monday lunch

Menu £19 (lunch and early dinner) – Carte £30/67 ✗✗

Islington and Upper Street are barely recognisable from when Almeida first opened its doors. Okay, so the continued success of the Almeida Theatre opposite means this D&D restaurant is propitiously placed to benefit twice nightly from its audience but increased local competition means that, like all good restaurants, it still has to undergo a little reinvention now and then. The menu's influences are largely European and now there's more innovation and less of a traditional French approach to the cooking: dishes are clean and unfussy and their main components and flavours are given the space to shine. The room itself is comfortable and grown up and the staff provide smooth and assured service.

ⓝ Bellanger

French M1

Islington

9 Islington Grn ⊠ N1 2XH

✆ 020 7226 2555

www.bellanger.co.uk

⊖ Angel

Closed 25 December – bookings advisable at dinner

Carte £21/43 ✗✗

Corbin and King evidently have another success on their hands; this time in the form of an all-day brasserie, modelled on those opened in Paris by the Alsatians at the turn of the century. No stone has been left unturned in the desire to recreate the sumptuous style of an authentic grand café and the long, high ceilinged room features wood panelling, spacious booths and a bar with counter seating – even the toilets have been given the star treatment! Regional French and particularly Alsatian-inspired fare is served from breakfast until late and there's some good value to be had with dishes like the celeriac remoulade or sausages with braised lentils – as well as sharing dishes like coq au Riesling for up to four to share.

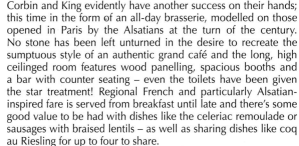

Drapers Arms

Modern British   **L1**

Islington

44 Barnsbury St ✉ N1 1ER
✆ 020 7619 0348
www.thedrapersarms.com
⊖ Highbury & Islington.

Closed 25-26 December
– bookings advisable at dinner

Carte £23/32

Good food, decent prices and an easy-going atmosphere are all
on offer at this busy Islington pub, whose shabby chic interior
contrasts with its handsome Georgian façade. It understands
that celebrating British cuisine means more than just putting a
few old favourites on the menu – it's about making intelligent
use of indigenous ingredients and introducing them to a wider
audience. Dishes are gutsy and affordable and offal is a highlight,
yet the kitchen can also demonstrate a light touch when needed.
The wine list is well thought out and dominated by the Old
World, with a well-priced selection by the glass and carafe. The
bar snacks are the size of a generous starter and are well worth
exploring.

Galley

Seafood   **M1**

Islington

105-106 Upper St ✉ N1 1QN
✆ 020 3670 0740
www.galleylondon.co.uk
⊖ Highbury & Islington

Closed 25 December and
1 January

Menu £18/28 – Carte £30/57

Chef-owner Marcel spent many years working at Randall and
Aubin, before joining forces with his sister Oriona to create this
refreshingly different fish restaurant (she's in charge of interior
design and has created a smart, colourful space with the feel of
a brasserie). There's a bar at the front and a few prized booths,
but the best seats in the house are those at the counter of the
galley kitchen, where you can chat to the chefs and watch their
craft close-up. This is a place that's serious about seafood; its all-
day menu led by what fish is available, fresh from the day-boats.
Small plates might mean galley fish stew; large plates, lobster
pappardelle; oysters are always a good bet, and the hot or cold
seafood platters are great to share.

Oldroyd

M o d e r n   B r i t i s h   M1

Islington   Closed 25-26 December

344 Upper St ⌂ N1 0PD
☏ 020 8617 9010
www.oldroydlondon.com
⊖ Angel

Menu £15 (weekday lunch) – Carte £21/32   ✗

This is one of those places where you leave feeling satisfied by both the food that you've eaten and the size of the bill you've just paid. The eponymous Oldroyd is Tom, who left his role with the Polpo group to open this little bistro in what was previously a deli. It's all about small plates, with one main ingredient always taking centre stage. The ingredients are largely British, influences are from within Europe and the dishes are very easy to eat – five plates between two should be enough. The meatballs are always popular, the mackerel is great and the zucchini fries are worth the price of admission alone. The place is open all day every day, which seems to be the only way to cope with the huge demand for seats.

Ottolenghi

M e d i t e r r a n e a n   c u i s i n e   M1

Islington   Closed 25-26 December, and
287 Upper St. ⌂ N1 2TZ   dinner Sunday and bank holidays
☏ 020 7288 1454   – booking essential
www.ottolenghi.co.uk
⊖ Highbury & Islington

Carte £23/45   ✗

It's common for customers to bump into each other in the entrance to Ottolenghi, so drawn are their eyes to the fresh, vibrantly coloured salads and the how-can-one-possibly-choose cakes on display. Two communal tables form the centrepiece of this coolly decorated restaurant, and a seat at one of these makes you feel you could be sitting in a friend's kitchen. Yotam Ottolenghi has done more travelling than Gulliver and the frequently changing menu reflects this. Different sections list dishes from the counter and the kitchen; three each is a good amount – although you'll probably find yourself ordering more once you've tasted your first mouthful! Don't worry about saving room for pudding, as you can always buy a few treats to take home with you.

Pig and Butcher

Traditional British L1

Islington

80 Liverpool Rd ✉ N1 0QD
☎ 020 7226 8304
www.thepigandbutcher.co.uk
⊖ Angel.

Closed 25-27 December
– booking advisable – (dinner
only and lunch Friday-Sunday)

Carte £28/44

This corner pub dates from the mid-19C, when cattle drovers taking their livestock to Smithfield Market would stop for a swift one. Now sympathetically restored, it enjoys the same ownership as the Princess of Shoreditch as well as Islington and Chiswick's 'Smokehouse's. The busy bar offers an impressive number of bottled beers, while the dining room is secreted behind shelves of bric-a-brac. There's a strong British element to the menu and not just because they use words like 'Beeton' and 'Mrs'. Meat comes straight from the farm and is butchered and smoked in-house; fish comes from day boats off the south coast. Roasts take centre stage on Sundays; "just like your mother's" they claim, which presumably means something different to us all.

Vintage Salt

Fish and chips M1

Islington

189 Upper St ✉ N1 1RQ
☎ 020 3227 0979
www.vintagesalt.co.uk
⊖ Highbury & Islington

Closed 25-27 December and
lunch Monday-Friday – booking
essential at dinner

Carte £16/33 ✗

Having worked for Caprice Holdings, the owner knows a thing or two about successful restaurants. For his first solo project, he unexpectedly opened this fish and chip shop, although the fact that you can order cocktails and have brunch at weekends tells you this is not your run-of-the-mill chippy. It comes with an appealing post-war feel with booths and counters. The menu, on brown paper, is also different. Starters are hearty affairs – the Isle of Man crab on toast is almost a main course in itself. Butties are fun for a quick snack and puds are the real deal, with Knickerbocker Glory in summer and fruit cobbler in winter – but most punters are here simply for the Camden Hells battered fish. Takeaway and delivery options spread the fun further.

Yipin China

Chinese   **L1**

Islington   Closed 25 December

70-72 Liverpool Rd ⊠ N1 0QD
𝒞 020 7354 3388
www.yipinchina.co.uk
⊖ Angel

Carte £19/42   🍴

A/C   The menu at this modest little spot features Hunanese, Cantonese
and Sichuanese specialities, but it is the spicy, chilli-based dishes
from Hunan province – which use techniques like smoking and
curing – that really stand out. Dry-wok dishes are a speciality
here, as are the spicy pig's intestines and offal slices. Chairman
Mao red-braised pork (he came from Hunan) is a fragrant, glossy
stew, and the sea bass, which comes with an enormous number
of salted chillies, is exhilaratingly fresh and flavoursome. The
room, with its pink and cream colour scheme, is unlikely to win
any design awards but the prices are more than fair. The staff may
seem a little shy at first but they will help with recommendations
if prompted.

Hill & Szrok

Meats and grills   **K2**

London Fields   Closed 23 December-3 January

60 Broadway Market ⊠ E8 4QJ   – bookings not accepted
𝒞 020 7254 8805   – (dinner only and Sunday lunch)
www.hillandszrok.co.uk
⊖ Bethnal Green

Carte £17/34   🍴

   Butcher's shop by day; unpretentious, meat-focused restaurant
by night: Hill & Szrok is the ultimate carnivore's dream. At the
end of the working day, most of the meat is cleared away, and
the central marble-topped counter becomes a communal table,
with seats round the edge of the room adding space for a few
more diners. The staff are friendly, the atmosphere is buzzing,
but bookings aren't taken, so you may have to queue up. The
daily menu offers around 3 starters – perhaps pan-fried chicken
livers or a plate of cured ham – but it's the main courses which
really excite, particularly the top quality steaks, which are aged
for a minimum of 60 days. If you're here with friends, go for the
chateaubriand. They also have an outpost in Hoxton.

◎ Ellory ❀

Modern British   **K2**

London Fields

Netil House, 1 Westgate St ✉ E8 3RL

✆ 020 3095 9455

www.ellorylondon.com

⊖ London Fields

Closed 23 December-3 January,
Sunday dinner and Monday
– (dinner only and lunch Friday-
Sunday)

Carte £27/36   ✗

Michelin

Given its unadorned surroundings and its no-frills menu, the depth of the dishes served at this East London restaurant comes as something of a surprise. The wonderful sourdough sets the tone, while the simply described, modern dishes that follow – perhaps raw mackerel, orange and horseradish or spring chicken, chicory and anchovy – are not only originally conceived and beautiful to look at but also perfectly balanced and rich in flavour. Located on the ground floor of Netil House – a warehouse turned creative commune – Ellory is a collaboration between chef Matthew Young and sommelier Jack Lewens. Hackney's bright young things have clearly taken to the unpretentious, stripped back place – all skimmed concrete and bare lightbulbs – and the short à la carte makes it just as easy to pop in for a snack and a glass of wine at the bar as to come here for a full-on meal. As you might expect with a sommelier at the helm, the wine list makes for an interesting read, with an appealing selection by the glass.

First Course

• White asparagus, seaweed and trout roe.

• Smoked eel broth, peas and egg yolk.

Main Course

• Turbot with lardo and artichoke.

• Lamb neck, anchovy and green beans.

Dessert

• Rhubarb with cow's curd ice cream and tarragon.

• Chocolate mousse and cherry sorbet.

Lardo

Italian **K2**

London Fields Closed 21 December-2 January

197-205 Richmond Rd ✉ E8 3NJ

℘ 020 8985 2683

www.lardo.co.uk

⊖ Hackney Central

Carte £15/34

Evidence of Hackney's nascent gentrification comes in the form of this delightful Italian eatery. It's housed within the striking 1930s Arthaus building, and though it may boast the ubiquitous faux industrial look, there's no artifice when it comes to the cooking. As hinted by the name, they cure their own meats so the daily changing menu of small plates may include fennel pollen salami or lardy loin. The well-priced dishes really hit the spot – try a creamy burrata, white bean bruschetta, or sweet and sour sardines and be sure to leave room for the torta del giorno. The gas-fired oven – which resembles a giant glitter ball – does sterling work in the open kitchen and pizzas, including those of the gluten free variety, are another major draw.

Market Cafe

Mediterranean cuisine **K2**

London Fields Closed 25 December

2 Broadway Mkt ✉ E8 4QG

℘ 020 7249 9070

www.market-cafe.co.uk

⊖ Bethnal Green

Carte £16/34

Forget data studies and economic analysis – an area's gentrification can be largely gauged by the arrival of two things: delis and restaurants. Broadway Market's steady advance towards middle class hipdom was given a nudge by the opening of Market Cafe, a former pub beside the canal. Research was clearly done because it ticks all the zeitgeist boxes, from the Formica table tops to the salvaged chairs, the pierced-and-inked young staff to the terse menu descriptions. There's a distinct Italian accent to many of the dishes, with homemade pastas a feature. The kitchen uses the local market for its meat, bread and coffee, the cooking is fresh and generous and the prices fair – especially the 'workers lunch'. Weekend brunches are very popular.

North-East ▶ **Plan XVI**

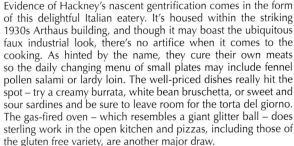

Pidgin ❀

Modern British   K2

London Fields

52 Wilton Way ✉ E8 1BG
✆ 020 7254 8311
www.pidginlondon.com
⊖ Hackney Central

Closed Monday –
booking essential – (dinner only
and lunch Saturday and Sunday)
– (tasting menu only)

Menu £37   ✗

Michelin

If simplicity is the ultimate in sophistication, then this sweet little place tucked away in a residential area of Hackney, is as sophisticated as they come; the only adornments here being a few dried branches and some shelves of wine. Owners James and Sam previously ran a North London supper club and see Pidgin as a natural progression; there are only eleven closely packed tables and they provide a personable welcome to their customers, many of whom are regulars. The décor may be understated but this puts the focus firmly where it belongs – on the food: the no-choice four course menu changes weekly, as do the cocktails and the equally concise but ever-so-interesting wine list, with each bottle designed to match the dishes and also available by the glass. The kitchen has considerable skill and shows its confidence through its restraint; the modern British cooking is easy on the eye, thoughtfully conceived and full of flavour – and all at prices that leave you feeling like you really got your money's worth.

First Course	Main Course	Dessert
• Fried chicken with caviar, buttermilk and walnut.	• Cauliflower, juniper, pine and brown butter.	• Jasmine rice ice cream with apricot and elderflower.
• Sea urchin with squid ink and dashi.	• Lamb with pearl barley, broad beans, grilled lettuce and wild leaves.	• Rhubarb with yoghurt sorbet and smoked ginger biscuit.

Andina

Peruvian   **K3**

Shoreditch   Booking essential

1 Redchurch St ✉ E2 7DJ
☎ 020 7920 6499
www.andinalondon.com
⊖ Shoreditch High Street

Menu £9 (lunch) – Carte £17/33   ✗

Andina may be smaller and slightly more chaotic that its sister Ceviche, but this picantería with its Peruvian specialities and live music is proving equally popular. The friendly staff are keen to share their knowledge and offer sound advice – and if you come for lunch you're rewarded with a steal of a menu. Start off with some crunchy corn or Cancha; then head for the ceviche – there are usually around six types to choose from and they pack a punch. The skewers are also popular and the salads are excellent; veggies and vegans will also find they have plenty of choice. If you can muster enough friends, the Music Room at the back is a great place for a private dinner surrounded by an interesting collection of LPs.

L'Anima

Italian   **K3**

Shoreditch   Closed 25-26 December, Saturday
                                    lunch, Sunday and bank holidays
1 Snowden St, Broadgate West ✉ EC2A 2DQ   – booking essential
☎ 020 7422 7000
www.lanima.co.uk
⊖ Liverpool Street

Menu £35/40 – Carte £35/72   ✗✗✗

You know you've got a successful restaurant on your hands when the live music in the bar is barely audible above the noise being made by your contented diners. With its limestone walls, impeccably laid tables, white leather chairs and clever lighting, L'Anima is an extremely handsome restaurant, and one that looks as though it should be located somewhere slightly more glamorous than the edge of The City. The kitchen team hail from all parts of Italy and their à la carte menu offers a mix of the classic and the more unusual – look out for the lesser known varieties of pasta or an occasional Moorish influence; there's also a good value midweek menu. It's worth asking for a window table or one on the raised section at the back.

L'Anima Café

Italian K3

Shoreditch

Closed Saturday lunch and
Sunday

10 Appold St ✉ EC2A 2AP
☎ 020 7422 7080
www.lanimacafe.co.uk
⊖ Liverpool Street

Carte £22/40

The name succeeds in conveying the fact that this is a baby
sister to L'Anima around the corner, but calling it a 'café' does
it something of an injustice because it is so much more than
that. This is a big, bright restaurant with a fashionable bar that
pulls in the after-work crowd and a busy deli for those wanting
something to cook at home; there are even DJs on Thursday and
Friday nights to help celebrate the end of the working week. The
pizzas are popular and done well, although look closely at that
large pizza oven and you'll see it's gas-fired; the rest of the menu
has its roots in southern Italy and includes a decent selection
of well-made pasta dishes; the prices are fair and the cooking,
straightforward and tasty.

Boundary

French K3

Shoreditch

Closed Sunday dinner

2-4 Boundary St ✉ E2 7DD
☎ 020 7729 1051
www.theboundary.co.uk
⊖ Shoreditch High Street

Menu £29 (dinner) – Carte £29/67

When the management team took over his restaurant group, many
thought Sir Terence Conran's days of opening restaurants were
over. Not a bit of it, because he was soon back with a bang with
Boundary. As is his way, he took an interesting building, in this
case a large warehouse and former printworks, and turned it into
a veritable house of fun. From the top, you have a Mediterranean
restaurant on the roof; Albion is a ground floor 'caff' alongside a
shop and bakery, and Boundary is the French-inspired 'main'
restaurant below. The room is stylish, good-looking and works
well, while the kitchen serves up reassuringly familiar cross-
Channel treats, including fruits de mer. The fourth part of the
equation are the comfy, individually designed bedrooms.

Clove Club ❄

Modern cuisine K3

Shoreditch

380 Old St ⊠ EC1V 9LT
☎ 020 7729 6496
www.thecloveclub.com
⊖ Old Street

Closed 2 weeks Christmas-
New Year, August bank
holiday, Monday lunch and
Sunday – bookings advisable at
dinner – (tasting menu only)

Menu £65/95 – Carte lunch £37/56 ✗

Clove Club

'Crowdfunded' into existence by a trio of young chefs who made
their names in pop-ups, the Clove Club has once more pulled
off a maverick manoeuvre with the introduction of its online
prepay booking system. Said chefs perform centre stage in the
smart, blue-tiled kitchen of the Grade II listed Shoreditch Town
Hall, whose sparse dining room has been softened slightly by
the introduction of window blinds and foliage; sit here rather
than in the adjacent bar so you don't miss out on the buzz.
Cooking has a Scandic touch, with only a set menu of 5 or 9
courses offered – this is a kitchen fanatical about sourcing top
notch British produce so expect scallops from Orkney, mackerel
from Cornwall and veal from Dorset. The meal starts with a few
canapés which set the tone: there is originality, verve and flair
but flavours are always expertly judged and complementary,
with fish and seafood dishes a highlight. Wonderfully simple-
looking dishes often have a deceptive depth to them, with full-on
flavours extracted from the humblest of produce.

First Course

- Raw Orkney
  scallop, hazelnut,
  clementine and
  Périgord truffle.

- Montgomery
  cheddar tart and
  crystal malt.

Main Course

- Dry-aged Challans
  duck in three
  servings.

- Yorkshire suckling
  pig with south
  Indian spices.

Dessert

- Warm blood orange,
  sheep's milk yoghurt
  mousse and fennel
  granité.

- 'Grain, grains, grains'.

Eyre Brothers

S p a n i s h K3

Shoreditch

70 Leonard St ✉ EC2A 4QX
☎ 020 7613 5346
www.eyrebrothers.co.uk
⊖ Old Street

Closed
24 December-4 January, Sunday
dinner and bank holidays

Carte £25/45

Thanks to their pioneering pub, The Eagle, the Eyre name will be forever linked to the rise of the gastropub, but this sleek and confidently run 100-seater shows that they know how to do restaurants as well. The menu celebrates all things Iberian and draws on memories of their upbringing in Mozambique. Tiger prawns piri-piri has been on since day 1; the 'Cinco Jotas' ham is deliciously sweet and the meats are all cooked over lumpwood charcoal, which adds a wonderful aroma to proceedings. If you're in a larger party, pre-order paella or a whole suckling pig. The wine list is Iberian too, with Riojas for every pocket and a great selection of Madeira and Jerez. Everyone leaves feeling satisfied, even if you've just popped in for tapas at the bar.

Merchants Tavern

T r a d i t i o n a l   B r i t i s h K3

Shoreditch

36 Charlotte Rd ✉ EC2A 3PG
☎ 020 7060 5335
www.merchantstavern.co.uk
⊖ Old Street

Closed 25-26 December and
1 January

Menu £18 (lunch) – Carte £31/53

It sounds like a pub, looks like one and even feels like one, but once you're settled in you'll soon realise there's more to this place than you initially thought. The 'pub' part – a Victorian warehouse – morphs into a big restaurant with an open kitchen and some very appealing booths beneath a skylight, which are the prized seats. Neil Borthwick and his partner Angela Hartnett are part-owners, along with the founders of Canteen, and the cooking is based on the simple yet sublime pleasures of seasonal British cooking. The kitchen has the confidence to stick to recognisable combinations in order to deliver flavours that are reassuringly familiar and satisfying, like trotters on toast, roast chicken with sweetcorn or gingerbread with caramel sauce.

HKK 🏵

Chinese　　　　　　　　　　　　　　　　　　　**K3**

Shoreditch　　　　　　　　　　Closed 25 December and Sunday

88 Worship St ✉ EC2A 2BE
✆ 020 3535 1888
www.hkklondon.com
⊖ Liverpool Street

Menu £35/88 – Carte lunch £28/65　　　　　　　　　　XX

HKK

Cantonese has always been considered the finest of the Chinese cuisines and here at HKK it is given an extra degree of refinement. The kitchen examines the seasonal ingredients available, considers what is being served in China and then designs a dish around them. The result is intriguing and original, with flavours that are sharp and well-defined and combinations that are well-judged. A perennial highlight is the duck: roasted to order in a cherry wood fired oven, it is expertly carved and served in three different ways. The presentation of all of the dishes is sublime and they also come with well-chosen wine pairings. The room is understated, elegant and graceful, and the service smooth, assured and unobtrusive. As time is money in this part of town, the lunch menu has been designed with consideration towards those who have to return to work – to really experience what HKK is all about, come for dinner when you're presented with their well-balanced 8 course menu, which evolves on a monthly basis.

First Course	Main Course	Dessert
• HKK chicken and truffle soup.	• Cherry wood roast Peking duck.	• Green apple parfait with cardamom cake and crispy apple noodle.
• Grilled dumpling with black truffle vinegar.	• Slow-cooked veal with brown jasmine rice, black bean and goji berry.	• Lemon peel brûlée with smoked apricot.

343

Lyle's ❀

Modern British

Shoreditch

Tea Building, 56 Shoreditch High St ✉ E1 6JJ

✆ 020 3011 5911

www.lyleslondon.com

⊖ Shoreditch High Street

Closed Sunday and bank holidays
– (set menu only at dinner)

Menu £49 (dinner) – Carte lunch £26/36   ✗

ⒶⒸ

Michelin

The building was once owned by Lipton, the tea people, and the pared-down, ersatz industrial look is bang on trend. With its tiles and concrete floor, the space may be more about functionality than comfort but help is at hand from the open kitchen which is very much part of the room and adds colour and animation. Warmth and personality also come from the young service team, who share the passion of the kitchen, offer great advice and really know their menu. One glance at that menu tells immediately of the influence of Fergus Henderson – and sure enough, the young chef-owner previously ran the kitchen at St John Bread and Wine. Where this operation differs is that only a set menu is offered at dinner – although for lunch you can choose an array of dishes in smaller sizes – and in the occasional use of modern cooking techniques. Where they converge is in the use of superb seasonal British ingredients which result in flavours that are clean, natural, unadulterated and a joy to experience.

First Course	Main Course	Dessert
• Gloucester Old Spot, chicory and apple mustard.	• Dover sole with rape greens and whey butter.	• Concorde pear with oats.
• Peas and Ticklemore.	• Lamb's offal with radishes and treacle.	• Caramel espresso with espresso meringue.

Oklava

T u r k i s h

Shoreditch

74 Luke St ✉ EC2A 4PY
☎ 020 7729 3032
www.oklava.co.uk
⊖ Old Street

K3

Closed Sunday dinner and bank
holidays – booking essential

Carte £24/38   ✗

With its concrete floor and its grey iron girders; its open kitchen and its counter dining, there's not much to distinguish this restaurant from many others in the area. Apart from the food, that is. An oklava is a traditional Turkish rolling pin used to make pastries and pides, both of which appear on the menu; for the chef is a Turkish Cypriot and cooks her interpretations of classic dishes from these countries. 3 or 4 of the well-priced small plates constitute a satisfying meal – the most popular are those cooked in the stone oven, like the filled flatbreads, or over the flaming charcoal grill, like the crispy lamb's breast with yoghurt. Sociable staff are happy to explain dishes or to recommend wines from the small, exclusively Turkish list.

Princess of Shoreditch

T r a d i t i o n a l   B r i t i s h

Shoreditch

76-78 Paul St ✉ EC2A 4NE
☎ 020 7729 9270
www.theprincessofshoreditch.com
⊖ Old Street

K3

Closed 24-26 December
– booking essential

Carte £27/38

Apparently there has been a pub on this corner site since 1742 but it is doubtful many of the previous incarnations were as busy or as pleasant as the Princess is today. The owners have always been very hands-on and their welcoming attitude has rubbed off on their friendly staff; the pub comes with an appealing buzz and, to cap it all off, the prices are more than fair. It's set over two floors and the same menu is served throughout – although you can book upstairs. The menu changes daily, and sometimes between services; the food appears quite simple but the best dishes are those that come with a satisfying rustic edge, whether that's the buttery goose rillettes, the chicken pie with terrific mash or the tender pulled pork.

Rivington Grill

Traditional British K3

Shoreditch Closed 25-26 December

28-30 Rivington St ✉ EC2A 3DZ
☏ 020 7729 7053
www.rivingtonshoreditch.co.uk
⊖ Old Street

Carte £21/41

 The fact that this converted warehouse is surrounded by design studios, galleries and printing premises means that it's popular with the artistically inclined – it also shows artwork, including a Tracey Emin neon "Life without you, never". It is close to The City, so head left when you enter as larger groups tend to occupy the tables on the right. The seasonal British menu will fill you with patriotic fervour: oysters are a speciality and pies, chops and faggots are listed alongside Welsh rarebit, fish and chips and roast chicken. There are plenty of bottles under £30 on the drinks list and over 100 gins to choose from too, with a different gin promoted every week – perfect for a quick stiffener on your way home from work.

Tramshed

Meats and grills K3

Shoreditch Closed 25 December

32 Rivington St ✉ EC2A 3LX
☏ 020 7749 0478
www.chickenandsteak.co.uk
⊖ Old Street

Carte £18/66

 A Grade II listed warehouse, built in 1905 to house the generators for the trams, provides the backdrop to Mark Hix's impressive brasserie which is best enjoyed, like most things in life, in the company of friends. The striking piece of work by Damien Hirst of a tank containing a Hereford cow and a cockerel in formaldehyde is not just an impressive feature in the cavernous room, but also a clue as to what's on the menu. The Swainson House Farm chickens and the various cuts of Glenarm beef are accurately cooked and delicious; sides are good too and there are regularly changing starters and puds. The best seats are the booths around the wall. Service is alert and capable and they cope well with the numbers.

Viet Grill

V i e t n a m e s e   K2
Shoreditch   Booking essential

58 Kingsland Rd ✉ E2 8DP
☎ 020 7739 6686
www.vietgrill.co.uk
⊖ Hoxton

Carte £20/35   ✗

As Vietnamese restaurants are proving so popular around here maybe it's time this part of Hackney was twinned with Hanoi. The reason Viet Grill attracts so many customers is not down to its bright neon lighting, but because it is owned by the same team behind Cây Tre, which means that the service is charming and helpful and the food is fresh and authentic. From the slurpable pho noodle soups to Devon crab (most ingredients are sourced within the UK) and La Vong monkfish for two, you'll find dishes packed with flavour and vibrancy; meats grilled on the robata also stand out. Those who don't plan ahead can take advantage of their takeaway menu; those who do can order one of their 'feast' menus, which require 48 hours' notice.

Empress 😳

M e d i t e r r a n e a n   c u i s i n e   K2
South Hackney   Closed 25-26 December and
Monday lunch except bank
130 Lauriston Rd, Victoria Park ✉ E9 7LH   holidays
☎ 020 8533 5123
www.empresse9.co.uk
⊖ Homerton.

Carte £25/33   🍴🍺

This 1850s pub used to be known as the Empress of India but was changed after people came expecting chicken tikka – information which will dishearten history teachers everywhere. Queen Victoria was then demoted to Empress E9, and eventually ended up as plain Empress. Food is at the centre of what they do here, although don't be surprised to see locals sprawled on the sofas enjoying a drink, as this is a neighbourhood pub at heart. The menu is short, simple and pleasingly seasonal, with dishes like smoked eel, blood orange and mustard leaf salad or crispy polenta, burrata, chilli and wild garlic pesto demonstrating that this is a kitchen with confidence and intelligence. Prices are kept in check and Sunday lunch is a very languid affair.

ⓝ The Woodford

Modern British

South Woodford

Closed Monday and Tuesday

159 High Rd ✉ **E18 2PA**
📞 020 8504 5952
www.thewoodford-e18.com
⊖ South Woodford

Menu £24 (weekday lunch) – Carte £36/64

 With a glitzy cocktail bar the perfect spot for an aperitif, and the first floor Churchill Lounge a fitting backdrop for a post-prandial, piano-accompanied tipple, this restaurant is the sort of place where you'll want to make a night of it. The former PM is thus honoured because Woodford was once his constituency; quite whether he'd approve of this former nightclub's lavish décor is debatable, although he would almost certainly approve of the wine list, with its strong champagne selection and the inclusion of his favourite, Pol Roger. Like the décor, the cooking is eye-catching and modern with the odd playful note; dishes demonstrate chef Ben Murphy's understanding of classical French techniques and desserts are a highlight.

Foxlow

Traditional British

Stoke Newington

K2

Closed 24 December-1 January

71-73 Church St ✉ **N16 OAS**
📞 020 7481 6377
www.foxlow.co.uk
⊖ Canonbury

Menu £18 (weekdays) – Carte £25/42

 Foxlow is the less bellicose brand from the people behind the Hawksmoor steakhouses. Instead of being all about men and meat, this restaurant is more concerned with fitting into the neighbourhood and appealing to local families. They offer a kids' menu and an environment that's friendly and welcoming; but they also realise that many diners, including presumably a few of the parents, are even more grateful for – and possibly in need of – a decent cocktail list. The menu is safe and appealing – it could include some roast salmon with fennel or ricotta dumplings but it would be churlish to avoid the meat, especially as they share the same suppliers as Hawksmoor, and the 55-day matured rump steak with skin-on fries is hard to beat.

Provender

F r e n c h

Wanstead

17 High St ⊠ E11 2AA
☎ 020 8530 3050
www.provenderlondon.co.uk
⊖ Snaresbrook

Menu £13 (weekdays) – Carte £20/46 ✗

Wanstead High Street may not necessarily be the first place one would expect to find great French bourgeois cooking but the locals must be mightily glad that Max Renzland decided to pitch up in their arrondissement. Max's reputation for creating terrific French restaurants was forged in the suburbs, albeit at the opposite end of town, and Provender has his stamp all over it. That means you can expect authentic and satisfying food; plenty of choice; and prices, for the menus and the exclusively French wine list, that are very competitive. The fish is good here, as are the charcuterie boards, and there are dishes to share and even a separate menu for 'les enfants'. It's no wonder the split-level room hums with the sound of contentment.

An important business lunch or dinner with friends? The symbol ✿ indicates restaurants with private rooms.

South-East London

Once considered not only the wrong side of the tracks, but also most definitely the wrong side of the river, London's southeastern chunk has thrived in recent times courtesy of the Docklands Effect. As the gleaming glass peninsula of **Canary Wharf** (ironically, just north of the Thames) sprouted a personality of its own – with bars, restaurants, slinky bridges and an enviable view, not to mention moneyed residents actually putting down roots – the city's bottom right hand zone began to achieve destination status on a par with other parts of London. You only have to stroll around the glossy and quite vast **Limehouse Basin** – a slick marina that was once a hard-grafting East End dock – to really see what's happened here.

Not that the area hasn't always boasted some true gems in the capital's treasure chest. **Greenwich,** with fabulous views across the water to the docklands from its delightfully sloping park, has long been a favourite of kings and queens: Henry VIII and Elizabeth I resided here. The village itself bustles along with its market and plush picturehouse, but most visitors make their way to the stand-out attractions, of which there are many. The **Royal Observatory** and the Meridian Line draw star-gazers and hemisphere striders in equal number, while the palatial Old Royal Naval College is a star turn for lovers of Wren, who designed it as London's answer to Versailles. On the northern edge of Greenwich Park, the **National Maritime Museum** has three floors of sea-faring wonders; down by the pier, the real thing exists in the shape of the **Cutty Sark**. Up on the peninsula, the O2 Arena's distinctive shape has become an unmistakable landmark, but if you fancy a contrast to all things watery, the Fan Museum on Crooms Hill has more hand-held fans (over 3,000 of them) than anywhere else on earth. Strolling south from Greenwich park you reach **Blackheath,** an alluring suburban village, whose most striking feature is the towering All Saints' Church, standing proud away from the chic shops and restaurants.

Of slightly less spectacular charms, but a real crowd-pleaser nevertheless, is **Dulwich Village,** hidden deeper in the southeastern enclaves. It's a leafy oasis in this part of the world, with a delightful park that boasts at its western end, next to the original buildings of the old public school, the Dulwich Picture Gallery. This was designed in 1811, and its pedigree is evident in works by the likes of Rembrandt, Rubens, Van Dyck and Canaletto. Half an hour's walk away across the park is the brilliant Horniman Museum, full of natural history and world culture delights – as well as a massive aquarium that seems to take up much of southeast London.

GREENWICH MARKET

ERECTED· MDCCCXXXI·

C. Eymenier / MICHELIN

A bit further east along the South Circular, there's the unexpected gem of Eltham Palace, originally the childhood home of Henry VIII with a magnificent (and still visible) Great Hall. What makes it unique is the adjacent Art Deco mansion built for millionaires in the 1930s in Ocean Liner style. It's the closest you'll ever get to a setting fit for hog roast and champagne. Heading back towards London, a lifestyle of bubbly and banquets has never really been **Peckham**'s thing, but it boasts a couple of corkers in the shape of the South London Gallery with its zeitgeist-setting art shows, and the Peckham Library, a giant inverted 'L' that looks like a lot of fun to go into.

Back in the luxury flat-lands of the **Docklands, Wapping** has become an interesting port of call, its new-build architecture mixing in with a still Dickensian feel, in the shape of glowering Victorian warehouses and Wapping New Stairs, where the bodies of pirates were hanged from a gibbet until seven tides had showered their limp bodies. You can catch a fascinating history of the whole area in the nearby Museum Of London Docklands.

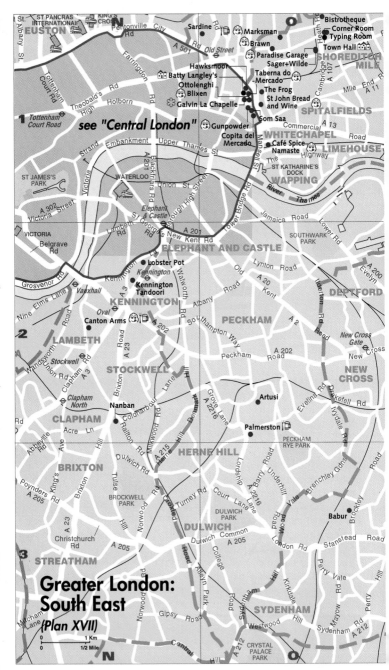

Greater London:
South East
(Plan XVII)

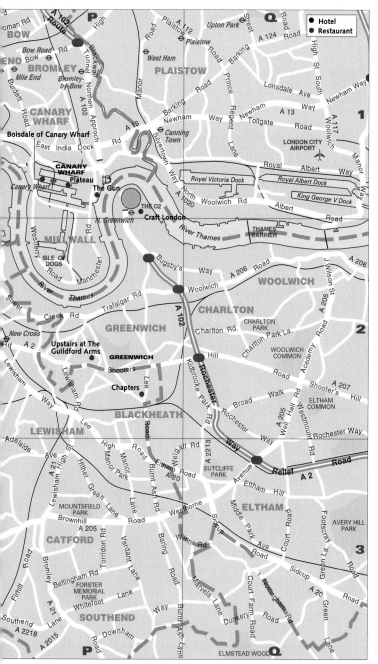

Bistrotheque

French 01

Bethnal Green
23-27 Wadeson St ⊠ E2 9DR
📞 020 8983 7900
www.bistrotheque.com
⊖ Bethnal Green

Closed 24-26 December
– booking advisable – (dinner
only and lunch Saturday-Sunday)

Menu £23 (early dinner) – Carte £23/55

When a restaurant has an exterior as irredeemably bleak as this, it can only mean one thing: it's going to be painfully cool inside. Converted from an old sweatshop, the owners purposely left the exterior bereft of any sign of gastronomic life – just head past the anguished graffiti and take the stairs in the courtyard up to the 1st floor. Here you'll find a warmly run, wonderfully bustling industrial-looking space, with beams and girders, ducting and concrete. It's all great fun, especially as the restaurant rubs shoulders with a bar and cabaret. The menu is predominantly French bistro in style with some British classics thrown in. A good value set menu is offered early and late in the evening and weekend brunch comes with live music.

Brawn

Modern cuisine 01

Bethnal Green
49 Columbia Rd. ⊠ E2 7RG
📞 020 7729 5692
www.brawn.co
⊖ Bethnal Green

Closed Christmas-New Year,
Sunday dinner, Monday lunch and
bank holidays

Carte £23/33

Found in a Victorian former furniture warehouse, away from the West End, this terrific neighbourhood restaurant is simply kitted out, with wooden tables and white brick walls hung with local artists' work. The name really captures the essence of the cooking perfectly: it is rustic and muscular, follows a nose-to-tail ethos and makes particularly good use of pig. Order about four dishes per person such as prosciutto or rillettes; mussels or prawns; something raw like Tuscan beef; and something slow-cooked like duck confit. It's all immeasurably satisfying and the polite young staff appear genuinely proud of the menu and happily proffer advice. The interesting wine list has an emphasis on natural and organic wines.

Corner Room

Creative   01

Bethnal Green   Bookings advisable at dinner

Town Hall Hotel, Patriot Sq ⊠ E2 9NF

✆ 020 7871 0461

www.cornerroom.co.uk

⊖ Bethnal Green

Menu £23/45 – Carte £20/29   ✗

Hidden away above the Typing Room in the old town hall is a warm and intimate space called Corner Room – and it's somewhere that is just a little bit different. The narrow room features wood panelling juxtaposed with bright white tiles and a backdrop of ornate and antique hanging light fittings for an extra bit of whimsy. From a small menu, the kitchen uses all sorts of modern techniques to produce dishes that are assured and very effective – there is originality here but also an avoidance of any needless elaboration; flavours are distinct and you feel you're getting a real taste of nature. The core ingredient of each dish is British, be it Longhorn beef or Tamworth pork.

Marksman

Traditional British   01

Bethnal Green   Closed 25 December, 1 January,

254 Hackney Rd ⊠ E2 7SJ   Sunday dinner and Monday

✆ 020 7739 7393

www.marksmanpublichouse.com

⊖ Hoxton.

Carte £19/35

With its quirky, brown-tiled façade, the Marksman has long been a local landmark. Inside, it's a place of two halves: the wood-panelled bar retains the cosy, unaffected feel of a traditional boozer, while the first floor dining room is far more modern. There's a roof terrace for alfresco dining and the friendly atmosphere really adds to the pub's appeal. Owners Tom Harris and Jon Rotheram are St John alumni and their considerable experience is evident in the food. The simply cooked, seasonal dishes are wonderfully fresh, perfectly balanced and full of flavour – we're talking proper British cooking with the likes of devilled mussels on toast, skate with shrimps and turnip tops, or pheasant and trotter pie for two.

ⓝ Paradise Garage

Traditional British   01

Bethnal Green

Arch 254, Paradise Row ⊠ E2 9LE

✆ 020 7613 1502

www.paradise254.com

⊖ Bethnal Green

Closed 2 weeks Christmas-New
Year, Sunday dinner, Monday and
lunch Tuesday

Menu £25 (weekday lunch) – Carte £25/36   ✗

This north-of-the-river sister to Clapham's Manor and Dairy is set under the railway arches in lively Bethnal Green and shares a menu format with its older siblings. When they're open, the oversized folding doors give the feeling you're dining alfresco, but there's counter dining too for those who like to watch chefs doing their thing. The constantly evolving collection of small plates are British at heart and, refreshingly, arrive in the sequence you ordered them. An excellent rustic sourdough paired with whisky-smoked butter kicks things off nicely and dishes like a wonderful scorched venison tartare are artfully presented and come with compelling contrasts in temperature, texture and flavour. The set 4 course midweek lunch menu is a steal.

ⓝ Sager + Wilde

Mediterranean cuisine   01

Bethnal Green

250 Paradise Row ⊠ E2 9LE

✆ 020 7613 0479

www.sagerandwilde.com

⊖ Bethnal Green

Closed Monday and Tuesday
– (dinner only and
lunch Friday-Sunday)

Menu £38   ✗

There's a friendly neighbourhood buzz to this rustic restaurant, set under a railway arch in busy Bethnal Green, and the regular rumble of trains overhead only adds to its appeal. It started life as a wine bar, like its Hackney sister, and some people do just pop in for a glass of wine or a cocktail, but it's worth staying to eat, even if just to enjoy bar nibbles like pickled Tokyo turnip or salt baked celeriac. Tasty, well-priced, creative dishes have a Mediterranean heart and an eye-catching modern style, with some interesting – and sometimes challenging – combinations of ingredients, like baked artichoke with caramelised yoghurt or langoustine with millet and rice porridge. The wine list is thoughtfully chosen and mark-ups, modest.

Typing Room

Modern cuisine   **O1**

Bethnal GreenTown Hall Hotel,

Patriot Sq ✉ E2 9NF

☎ 020 7871 0461

www.typingroom.com

⊖ Bethnal Green

Closed Sunday dinner
and Monday

Menu £24/75   **XX**

The first thing you notice is the colony of chefs beavering away in the open kitchen – this remains the focal point of the room, which was once home to the erstwhile town hall's typing pool. There is a simpler menu available at lunchtime but most diners are here to enjoy the 5 or 7 course menus, as well as the thoughtful wine pairings that accompany them. Heavily influenced by new Nordic cuisine, the kitchen adopts plenty of techniques, like fermenting and smoking, to create dishes that are earthy, elaborate and feature lots of contrasting textures. The snacks that kick things off are excellent, as is the IPA sourdough bread. The tone and style of the clued-up service suits the place perfectly.

Chapters

Modern cuisine   **P2**

Blackheath

43-45 Montpelier Vale ✉ SE3 0TJ

☎ 020 8333 2666

www.chaptersblackheath.com

Closed 2-3 January

Menu £18 (weekdays) – Carte £23/33   **XX**

Flexibility has been the key to Chapters' success. This classic brasserie seems to know just what the locals want and they reward it by coming in their droves. It's open for breakfast and brunch at weekends; it has a great value menu Monday to Thursday, and their à la carte has something for everyone. Specialities from the Josper grill are a highlight, especially the double Barnsley chop, though there are also steaks from Cumbria, Omaha and Limousin for meat-eating enthusiasts. Add in main courses with a Mediterranean slant; blackboard specials; a kids' menu; and a good size wine list with plenty by the glass or pichet, and you can see why it seems as though all of Blackheath is in the room. Ask for the ground floor, rather than the basement.

Boisdale of Canary Wharf

Traditional British

Canary Wharf

Cabot Pl ⊠ E14 4QT

Closed bank holidays
– booking advisable

𝒞 020 7715 5818

www.boisdale.co.uk

⊖ Canary Wharf

Carte £29/80

✗✗

This is two operations under one roof. Get out of the lift on the 1st floor for the art deco inspired Oyster Bar - a richly decorated, tartan room centred around a marble topped bar; here it's about relaxed dining, with an impressive selection of crustacea along with burgers and steaks. It also has a lovely terrace overlooking Cabot Square and a walk-in humidor with an impressive selection of Cuban cigars. Climb out, instead, on the 2nd floor and three things hit you: the fabulous bay window, a stage and a remarkable wall of whiskies. Things here are grander and more comfortable and there's live jazz for which a charge is made. In amongst the caviar, top quality steaks and assorted dishes of Scottish persuasion is the more moderately priced Great British Menu.

Take note of the classification:
you should not expect
the same level of service
in a ✗ or 🏠 as in a ✗✗✗✗
or 🏠🏠🏠🏠.

Plateau

Canary Wharf

Canada Place (4th floor), Canada Square ✉ E14 5ER

☏ 020 7715 7100

www.plateau-restaurant.co.uk

⊖ Canary Wharf

Menu £25 (weekdays) – Carte £31/61

Closed 25 -26 December, 1-2 January and Sunday

Plateau is geared to a largely business clientele and seems to deal confidently with their demands. It is also a restaurant that surprises you with its aspect – with the sun reflecting off the surrounding glass buildings, you could be forgiven for thinking you're in Wall Street rather than Canary Wharf. The large room comes with its own retro 1960s look, with white plastic chairs and steel ball lighting, and the bar offers an impressive cocktail list for those here to celebrate or commiserate. There are two choices for food: the Grill is the place for steaks cooked on the Josper grill while the restaurant is a smarter affair offering an array of recognisable, if at times slightly over ambitious, French-inspired dishes.

Palmerston

East Dulwich

91 Lordship Ln ✉ SE22 8EP

☏ 020 8693 1629

www.thepalmerston.co.uk

⊖ East Dulwich (Rail).

Closed 25-26 December and 1 January

Menu £15 (weekday lunch) – Carte £28/55

The Palmerston has long realised that success for any pub lies in being at the heart of the local community. Since its last makeover, this Victorian pub has been popular with families – just look at all those highchairs – and local artists' work decorates the walls. It has a comfortable, lived-in feel, along with a snug, wood-panelled rear dining room with an original and quite beautiful mosaic floor. The menu is as reassuring as the service and the cooking has a satisfying, gutsy edge. There's plenty of choice, from chowders and soups to well-judged fish but it's the meat dishes that stand out, like the mature steaks or lamb chops – and if they have grouse on the menu, then forsake all others and get in quick.

Babur

I n d i a n   O3

Forest Hill   Closed 26 December

119 Brockley Rise ✉ SE23 1JP
✆ 020 8291 2400
www.babur.info
⊖ Honor Oak Park

Menu £31/37 – Carte £27/36   ✗✗

A/C It's not just its good looks and innovative cooking that set Babur
apart – this long-standing Indian restaurant is also run with
great passion and enthusiasm. Regular customers are invited to
tastings and can even have an input on the quarterly changing
menus – and the make-up of each dish is fully explained when
dishes are presented at the table. The south and north-west of
India feature most predominantly on the menu but there are
also Western-influenced dishes available, like crab claws with
asparagus and saffron. Seafood is certainly a highlight, so look
out for the periods of the year when the separate 'Treasures of
the Sea' menu appears. You'll find suggested wine pairings for
each dish, along with some inventive cocktails.

Craft London

M o d e r n   B r i t i s h   P1

Greenwich   Closed Christmas-New Year,
                                        Sunday and Monday – (dinner
Peninsula Sq ✉ SE10 0SQ   only and Saturday lunch)
✆ 020 8465 5910
www.craft-london.co.uk
⊖ North Greenwich

Menu £35/55 – Carte £31/49   ✗

& On the doorstep of the O2 arena is a building bursting with
activity and full of the seductive smell of roasting and charred
A/C wood. Chef Stevie Parle, in conjunction with long-time
collaborator and designer Tom Dixon, has created a striking
space which includes a coffee shop serving light snacks on the
ground floor, a cocktail bar upstairs with views and a terrace,
and a restaurant championing the most British of produce. They
do their own curing of meats, roasting of coffee, and their own
pickling and smoking; they grow their own herbs; and even
get their honey from bees in the nearby grounds. The food is
modern, interesting and a little different – try the well-judged
smoked eel with layers of flavour or the juicy pork loin.

Upstairs at The Guildford Arms

Modern British   **P2**

Greenwich

55 Guildford Grove ⊠ SE10 8JY
📞 020 8691 6293
www.theguildfordarms.co.uk
⊖ Greenwich (DLR)

Closed 25-26 December
and Sunday-Tuesday
– (dinner only)

Carte £29/33   ✗

The Guildford Arms is a handsome corner pub dating from 1808: downstairs does a roaring trade in steaks, salads and snacks; but upstairs, in a small, more formal room, a different kitchen headed by Simon Wills is creating accomplished dishes which showcase the finest produce that his home county, Kent, has to offer. The concise à la carte – there's also a 5 course tasting menu – has headings like 'Garden of England' and 'From the Farm' and understated dish descriptions list Romney Marsh lamb, Mallards Farm rhubarb and Brockley cheese among their top class ingredients. Dishes are skilfully executed, with well-defined flavours; portions are equivalent to a generous starter, so 3 or 4 will more than satisfy. Attentive service adds to the experience.

Kennington Tandoori

Indian   **N2**

Kennington

313 Kennington Rd ⊠ SE11 4QE
📞 020 7735 9247
www.kenningtontandoori.com
⊖ Kennington

Closed 25-26 December
– booking advisable

Menu £33 – Carte £20/35   ✗✗

 One of the best things about this contemporary looking Indian restaurant is that even on your first visit you get the impression you'll be remembered the next time you turn up. Kowsar Hoque runs it with enormous pride and this filters through to the staff who display great care and enthusiasm. As a result, the place is usually home to quite a number of regulars on any given evening, be they MPs, cricket fans or locals, and many of them no longer bother reading a menu and just order their 'usual'. For newcomers, the menu is quite a long affair but it's worth taking a look at the loose page of seasonal specialities which also doubles as a set menu. The curries have depth and the side dishes and breads are prepared with equal care.

Lobster Pot

French N2

Kennington

3 Kennington Ln. ✉ SE11 4RG
☎ 020 7582 5556
www.lobsterpotrestaurant.co.uk
⊖ Kennington

Closed 25 December-2 January,
Sunday and Monday

Carte £41/85 ✗

Ignore the fairly shabby exterior, dive straight in and you'll think you've stumbled onto a French film set. Fish tanks, portholes, the cries of seagulls and the hoots of ferries… the place has the lot and it's hard to avoid getting caught up in the exuberance of it all. It's no surprise that it's also all about fish. The chef-owner, from Vannes in Brittany, goes to Billingsgate each morning and he knows what he's doing: his menu is classical and appetising, with fruits de mer, plenty of oysters, a lobster section and daily specials on the blackboard. Be sure to make room for the crêpes, which are great. It's not cheap but it is an experience. Underlining the family nature of the business, the son has opened a brasserie next door.

Artusi

Italian O2

Peckham

161 Bellenden Rd ✉ SE15 4DH
☎ 020 3302 8200
www.artusi.co.uk
⊖ Peckham Rye

Closed 2 weeks Christmas and
bank holidays – booking essential
at dinner

Carte £19/35 ✗

Whether the 'Bellenden Village' moniker for this part of Peckham will ever catch on is a moot point; what is sure is that places like Artusi are a clear indication of a neighbourhood on the move. This Italian restaurant is named after Pellegrino Artusi who wrote a seminal work, "The Science of Cooking and the Art of Fine Dining", in 1891. The seasonal blackboard menu is quite short which helps keep costs and prices down and there's something very honest about the cooking. It is clear the kitchen has respect for the ingredients, with dishes a blend of the traditional and the modern; pasta, gelato and bread are all made in-house. Service is knowledgeable and keen, and if you're with a few friends ask for the long table by the pass.

Blixen

Mediterranean cuisine   O1

Spitalfields   Closed Sunday dinner

65a Brushfield St ✉ E1 6AA
✆ 020 7101 0093
www.blixen.co.uk
⊖ Liverpool Street

Menu £24 – Carte £16/37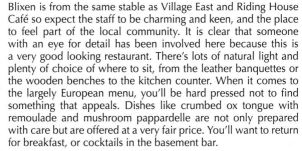

Blixen is from the same stable as Village East and Riding House Café so expect the staff to be charming and keen, and the place to feel part of the local community. It is clear that someone with an eye for detail has been involved here because this is a very good looking restaurant. There's lots of natural light and plenty of choice of where to sit, from the leather banquettes or the wooden benches to the kitchen counter. When it comes to the largely European menu, you'll be hard pressed not to find something that appeals. Dishes like crumbed ox tongue with remoulade and mushroom pappardelle are not only prepared with care but are offered at a very fair price. You'll want to return for breakfast, or cocktails in the basement bar.

Copita del Mercado

Spanish   O1

Spitalfields   Closed Christmas-New Year,
                                                     Easter and Sunday

60 Wentworth St ✉ E1 7AL
✆ 020 7426 0218
www.copitadelmercado.com
⊖ Aldgate East

Carte £17/51

Petticoat Lane is the mercado in question and is where the owners have done their best to disguise the 'fitted out unit' feel with tiles, an open-kitchen and a copper-topped bar. The restaurant is a little more comfortable that its sister in Soho and here you can also book. The menu, too, differs by offering a little more in the way of originality; you can get the croquettes or anchovies but it's worth trying the grilled octopus with arrocina beans and sobrasada, or squash with truffled hispy cabbage and duck egg yolk. The daily specialities on the blackboard, such as chicken with salsify and hazelnuts, are also worth exploring. Along with the sherries and the Spanish wines is a good selection of gins, which are something of a speciality.

Galvin La Chapelle ⭐⭐

Spitalfields

Closed dinner 25-26 December
and 1 January

35 Spital Sq ✉ E1 6DY
✆ 020 7299 0400
www.galvinrestaurants.com
⊖ Liverpool Street

Menu £29 (lunch and early dinner) – Carte £48/67 ✕✕✕

Galvin La Chapelle

These days, it is rare to walk into a restaurant in London and be taken aback with the grandeur and sheer scale of a room. However, this venture from the Galvin Brothers, who have already proved themselves expert restaurateurs, is one that will dazzle the most jaded of diner. The Victorian splendour of St Botolph's Hall, with its vaulted ceiling, arched windows and marble pillars, lends itself effortlessly to its role as a glamorous restaurant. There are tables in booths, in the wings or in the middle of the action and those who like some comfort with their food will not be disappointed. It is also a fitting backdrop to the cooking, which is, in essence, bourgeois French but with a sophisticated edge, which means it is immensely satisfying. There are no unnecessary fripperies, just three courses of reassuringly familiar combinations with the emphasis on bold, clear flavours. Add in a service team who are a well-drilled, well-versed outfit and you have somewhere that will be part of the restaurant landscape for years to come.

First Course	Main Course	Dessert
• Home-cured Shetland salmon with fennel, avocado and ruby grapefruit.	• Tagine of Bresse pigeon with couscous and harissa sauce.	• Tarte Tatin with crème Normande.
• Roast quail with asparagus, Montgomery cheddar fondue and hazelnuts.	• Cornish red mullet with caponata and sage & olive beignets.	• Peanut butter mousse with banana & thyme sorbet.

Gunpowder

Indian   O1

Spitalfields   Closed Sunday
                                          – bookings not accepted
11 White's Row ✉ E1 7NF
✆ 020 7426 0542
www.gunpowderlondon.com
⊖ Liverpool Street

Carte £20/30   ✗

 This Indian restaurant has exploded onto the Spitalfields food
scene with a bang; a loud buzzy place with just ten, tightly
packed tables serving vibrant small plates from across the Indian
regions. Arrive within ten minutes of opening or you will have to
wait; they take your number and text you when a table becomes
available, so you're free to enjoy a drink elsewhere. The name
is a reference to the chef's daily-made spice mix and his menu
takes its influence from old family recipes. Dishes like spicy
venison doughnut and sigri-grilled mustard broccoli are worth
trying, while standouts include deep-fried soft shell crab and the
crispy pork ribs with layer upon layer of flavour. 3 dishes are
sufficient – and give pud a miss.

Hawksmoor

Meats and grills   O1

Spitalfields   Closed 24-26 December
                                              and Sunday dinner
157a Commercial St ✉ E1 6BJ   – booking essential
✆ 020 7426 4850
www.thehawksmoor.com
⊖ Shoreditch High Street

Menu £25 (weekdays)/28 – Carte £23/60   ✗

A/C Hawksmoor was a 17C architect and a student of Sir Christopher
 Wren so you could expect this steakhouse to be found in a building
of note rather than in this modern edifice of little aesthetic value.
Inside is equally unremarkable but no matter because this place
is all about beef and, more specifically, British beef which has
been hung for 35 days. It comes from Longhorn cattle raised by
the Ginger Pig Co in the heart of the North Yorkshire Moors and
the quality and depth of flavour is exceptional. Just choose your
preferred weight – go for 400g if you're hungry. Starters and puds
don't come close in quality but again, no matter, because when
you've got some fantastic red meat in front of you, all you need
is a mate and a bottle of red wine.

Ottolenghi

Mediterranean cuisine   **O1**

Spitalfields

50 Artillery Ln ⊠ **E1 7LJ**
✆ 020 7247 1999
www.ottolenghi.co.uk
⊖ Liverpool Street

Closed dinner 24-27 and
31 December, 2 January, 2 and
30 May and Sunday dinner
– booking essential

Carte £26/67

 The development of the Ottolenghi 'brand' continues apace with
 this hugely popular spot a stone's throw from Spitalfield Market.
It's something of a cross between the original shop in Upper
Street where it all started and Nopi, their restaurant in Soho. The
bright white look of the room works well in reminding you that
this is food that's all about freshness. Largely Mediterranean, the
dishes are as flavoursome as they are colourful, show respect
for the ingredients and benefit from simple cooking techniques
– starters come from the display counter and are cold. Sharing
is the norm as everything comes on small plates – you can even
share a table if you want. For dessert, you might just want to buy
one of their vast meringues to take home.

St John Bread and Wine

Traditional British   **O1**

Spitalfields

94-96 Commercial St ⊠ **E1 6LZ**
✆ 020 7251 0848
www.stjohnbreadandwine.com
⊖ Liverpool Street

Closed 25-26 December and
1 January

Carte £26/40

 Less famous but by no means less loved than its sibling, this
English version of a classic comptoir is the sort of place we would
all like to have at the end of our road. Breakfast is served every
day and includes a wonderful rare breed bacon sandwich, while
the main menu changes twice a day and depends on what's in
season. Dishes are starter-sized and perfect for sharing, and the
Britishness of their ingredients and their promotion of forgotten
recipes will enthuse everyone, not just culinary genealogists.
There's plenty of man-food like roast pig spleen or 'raw Angus'
on the menu, but also lighter dishes such as plaice with samphire
or roast tomato with goat's curd and mint. For dessert, the Eccles
cakes are a must.

Som Saa

T h a i 01

Spitalfields

43a Commerical St ✉ E1 6BD

☏ 020 7324 7790

www.somsaa.com

⊖ Aldgate East

Closed Christmas and dinner
Sunday – bookings advisable at
dinner

Carte £25/29 ✕

What began as a pop-up became a permanent fixture in 2016; the result of a collaboration between two chefs who first met at former Belgravia restaurant, Nahm, back in the noughties. It has a rustic, industrial look and as lively an atmosphere as its precedent pop-up; there are a few bookable booths and tables but most are communal and kept for walk-ins. Dishes from the north of Thailand and its borders are a feature, but their desire to showcase the diversity of Thai cuisine means that you'll find lesser known dishes from all over the country on the menu. Signature dishes include Burmese-style pork curry and whole deep-fried sea bass with roasted rice. 4 or 5 dishes between two are recommended – and don't forget to try a cocktail or two!

Taberna do Mercado

P o r t u g u e s e 01

Spitalfields

Old Spitalfields Market, 107b Commercial St
✉ E1 6BG

☏ 020 7375 0649

www.tabernamercado.co.uk

⊖ Liverpool Street

Closed Christmas and
Sunday dinner – (Bookings not
accepted at dinner)

Menu £15 – Carte £16/32 ✕

Despite – or perhaps because of – the simplicity of Nuno Mendes' second restaurant, this modest little place in Old Spitalfields serving small plates of Portuguese classics has fast become a destination restaurant in itself. Grab a seat on the terrace (which is actually still inside the market hall): here, you can enjoy ethereal scents from the open kitchen and build up an appetite watching the chargrilling of the breads. The menu lists charcuterie and cheese as well as traditional offerings, but look closer and you'll see staples elevated to a higher level: alheira, Bísaro pork and prawn rissois all deliver wonderful flavours, as does the Abade de Priscos – and the specials are just that. The wine, staff and crockery are all Portuguese too.

The Frog

Modern cuisine

O1

Spitalfields

Closed Sunday dinner and
Monday – booking essential

2 Ely's Yard, Old Truman Brewery, Hanbury St.
⊠ E1 6QR
✆ 020 3813 9832
www.thefrogrestaurant.com
⊖ Shoreditch

Carte £24/36

Ambitious young chef Adam Caxton is making a splash with his restaurant, set in the old Truman brewery; a space full of indy shops, cafés and bars. As is de rigueur for any E1 eatery worth its salt, the décor comes in a nice shade of neutral; the floor is an expanse of concrete and the kitchen is well and truly open. Small plates are listed under sections entitled 'snacks', 'garden', 'sea', 'land', 'cheese' and 'desserts', with 3 or 4 per person about right. Dishes are modern, creative and quite intricate, with vibrant flavour and texture combinations; some – like the nitro salmon, peas and wasabi; the bread with chicken butter; and the cheese, doughnut and truffle – incorporate playful elements. Craft beers and cocktails add to the fun.

Canton Arms

Traditional British

N2

Stockwell

Closed Christmas-New Year,
Monday lunch, Sunday dinner
and bank holidays – bookings not
accepted

⊠ SW8 1XP
✆ 020 7582 8710
www.cantonarms.com
⊖ Stockwell.

Carte £19/35

 Its appreciative audience proves that the demand for fresh, honest, seasonal food is not just limited to smart squares in Chelsea or Islington. The oval-shaped bar dominates the room; the front half busy with drinkers and the back laid up for diners, although it's all very relaxed and you can eat where you want. The kitchen's experience in places like the Anchor & Hope and Great Queen Street is obvious on their menu which features rustic, earthy British food, of the sort that suits this environment so well. Lunch could be a kipper or tripe and chips; even a reinvented toasted sandwich. Dinner sees a short, no-nonsense menu offering perhaps braised venison or grilled haddock, with daily specials like steak and kidney pie for two.

South-East ▶ Plan XVII

Pharmacy 2

Modern British   **Plan IV J6**

Vauxhall

Newport Street Gallery, Newport St ✉ SE11
6AJ

☎ 020 3141 9333

www.pharmacyrestaurant.com

⊖ Vauxhall

Closed Christmas,
Sunday dinner and Monday

Carte £27/55

The name will induce nods of recognition from those who remember their '90s restaurants: Pharmacy was the place to be for a while, yet was never destined to last. In 2016 Damien Hirst revived the name for the restaurant on the first floor of his Newport Street Gallery, where you'll find much of his work. Like hearing a decent cover version of a much-loved song, the medicinally-themed decoration is at once new yet familiar, although this time everything just seems a little more vivid. When it came to the food, he paired up with Mark Hix, so there is a distinct seasonal feel to the menu. Brunch is an all-day affair and the best dishes are the more British sounding ones. The mini-sized desserts allow you to try two.

Cafe Spice Namaste

Indian   **O1**

Whitechapel

16 Prescot St. ✉ E1 8AZ

☎ 020 7488 9242

www.cafespice.co.uk

⊖ Tower Hill

Closed Saturday lunch,
Sunday and bank holidays

Menu £35 (weekdays) – Carte £25/40

Cyrus Todiwala has built up quite a following since opening in this former Victorian magistrate's court back in 1995. In that time he's also cooked for the Queen, grown a little empire and collected an OBE – not bad for someone who only planned on staying in the UK for 5 years. The menu here is extensive and appealing and makes good use of seasonal British ingredients. The Parsee and tandoor dishes are specialities; there are dishes to share; and vegetables get their own special menu. There may be no artificial colouring in the food but they certainly went to town on the room which is awash with bright yellows and blues – even the jaunty waistcoats of the staff catch your eye. Cyrus' wife Pervin oversees the service and she rarely misses a thing.

South-West London

Meandering like a silver snake, **The Thames** coils serenely through south-west London, adding definition to the area's much-heralded middle-class enclaves and leafy suburbs. It's the focal point to the annual **university boat race** from **Putney** to **Mortlake,** and it serves as the giant glass pond attractively backing countless bank-side pubs. This area has long been regarded as the cosy bourgeois side of town, though within its postcode prowls the lively and eclectic **Brixton,** whose buzzing street markets and lauded music venues add an urban lustre and vibrant edge.

In most people's minds, though, south-west London finds its true colours in the beautiful terrace view from the top of **Richmond Hill,** as the river bends majestically through the meadows below. Or in the smart **Wimbledon Village,** its independent boutiques ranged prettily along its own hill, with the open spaces of the Common for a back garden. Or, again, in the Italianate architecture that makes **Chiswick House** and grounds a little corner of the Mediterranean close to the Great West Road.

Green space is almost as prolific in this zone as the streets of Victorian and Edwardian villas. **Richmond Park** is the largest royal park in the whole of London and teems with kite flyers, cyclists and deer – though not necessarily in that order. From here, round a southerly bend in the river, delightful grounds surround **Ham House,** which celebrated its 400th birthday in 2010, although

not so excessively as during the seventeenth century when it was home to Restoration court life. Head slightly north to **Kew Gardens** whose world famous 300 acres can be viewed from above – the treetop walkway, takes you 60 feet up to offer some breath-taking views. Just across the river from here is another from the historical hit-list: **Syon Park,** which boasts water meadows still grazed by cattle, giving it a distinctly rural aspect. Syon House is considered one of architect Robert Adam's finest works; it certainly appealed to Queen Victoria, who spent much of her young life here. Up the road in bourgeoning Brentford, two unique museums bring in hordes of the curious: the Musical Museum includes a huge Wurlitzer theatre organ (get lucky and watch it being played), while almost next door, the London Museum of Water & Steam shows off all things steamy on a grand scale, including massive beam engines which pumped London's water for over a century.

Hammersmith may be known for its bustling Broadway and flyover, but five minutes' walk from here is the Upper Mall, which has iconic riverside pubs and Kelmscott House, the last home of artistic visionary William Morris: down in the basement and coach house are impressive memorabilia related to his life plus changing exhibitions of designs and drawings. From here, it's just a quick jaunt across **Hammersmith Bridge** and down the arrow-straight Castelnau to the

D. Chapuis / MICHELIN

Wetland Centre in Barnes, which for nearly two decades has lured wildlife to within screeching distance of the West End. **Barnes** has always revelled in its village-like identity – it juts up like an isolated peninsula into the Thames and boasts yummy boutiques and well-known restaurants. The Bulls Head pub in Lonsdale Road has featured some of the best jazz in London for over half a century.

In a more easterly direction, the urbanised areas of **Clapham** and **Battersea** have re-established themselves as desirable places to live over the last decade. **Clapham Common** is considered prime southwest London turf, to the extent that its summer music festivals are highly prized. It's ringed by good pubs and restaurants, too. Battersea used to be famous for its funfair, but now the peace pagoda in the park lends it a more serene light. And if you're after serenity on a hot day, then a cool dip in the wondrous **Tooting** Lido is just the thing.

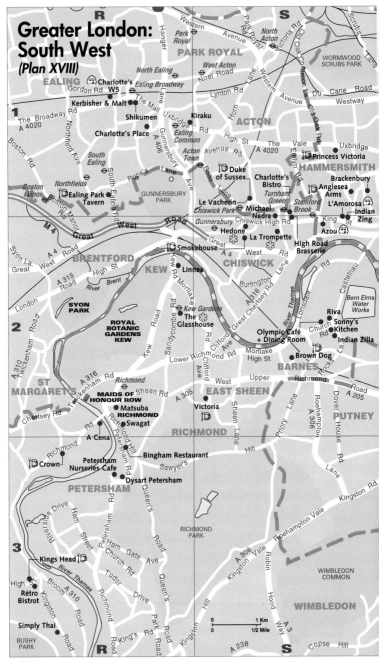

Greater London: South West
(Plan XVIII)

R

Western Avenue
Park Royal
North Acton
Scrubs
WORMWOOD SCRUBS PARK

PARK ROYAL

S

Victoria Rd
Oak Common Lane
Old Oak Rd
Du Cane Road
Westway

EALING
North Ealing
West Acton
Noel Road
Charlotte's W5
Ealing Broadway
Gordon Rd
The Mall
Kerbisher & Malt
1
The Broadway A 4020
Northfield Ave
Boston Rd
Shikumen
Charlotte's Place
Uxbridge Rd
Kiraku
Ealing Common
ACTON
High St
Lynton Road
Western Avenue
Horn Lane
Hanger Lane
Gunnersbury Ave
A 406
Uxbridge Rd
Vale
Emlyn Rd
HAMMERSMITH
Uxbridge
Princess Victoria
Brackenbury

South Ealing
Northfields
Boston Manor
Northfield Ave
South Ealing Rd
Ealing Park Tavern
Popes Lane
Acton Town
Bollo Lane
Duke of Sussex
Charlotte's Bistro
Le Vacherin
Chiswick Park
Turnham Green
Michael Nadra
Stamford Brook
Anglesea Arms
L'Amorosa
Indian Zing
King St
Azou

Boston Manor
M 4
A 4
Great West Road
GUNNERSBURY PARK
Gunnersbury
Chiswick High Rd
Hedone
La Trompette
High Road Brasserie
CHISWICK
Great West Road
A 4
Castelnau

BRENTFORD
KEW
High St
River Brent
A 315 Road
London Road
A 4 Great West Road
Syon La.
Smokehouse
Linnea
Kew Rd
Mortlake Rd
Burlington Lane
A 316 Great Chertsey Rd
Lonsdale Rd
River Thames
Bern Elms Water Works

SYON PARK
ROYAL BOTANIC GARDENS KEW
Sandycombe Rd
Kew Gardens
The Glasshouse
Clifford Ave
Clifford Rd
Lower Richmond Rd
Mortlake High St
Olympic Café + Dining Room
Church Rd
Brown Dog
Riva
Sonny's Kitchen
Indian Zilla
Rocks Lane
BARNES

2
A 310 Twickenham Road
ST MARGARET'S
A 316 Twickenham Rd
Richmond
Sheen Rd
MAIDS OF HONOUR ROW
Matsuba
RICHMOND
Swagat
Richmond Hill
Petersham Rd
A 305
West Sheen Rd
EAST SHEEN
Victoria
Sheen Lane
Upper Richmond Road A 205
Priory Lane
Roehampton Lane A 306
Dover House Rd
PUTNEY

Chertsey Rd
A Cena
RICHMOND
Richmond Rd
Bingham Restaurant
Sawyer's Hill
Crown
Petersham Nurseries Cafe
Dysart Petersham
PETERSHAM
Queen's Road
Ham Gate Ave
RICHMOND PARK
Kingston Rd
Kingston Vale
Roehampton Vale

3
River Drive
Ham Street
Kings Head
Petersham Rd
Church Rd
River Thames
Broom A 310 Road
Tudor Drive
Richmond Road
Queen's Road
King's Road
A 308 Kingston Vale
Robin Hood Lane
WIMBLEDON COMMON
A 3

Rétro Bistrot
High St
Kingston Road
Simply Thai
BUSHY PARK
King's Road
A 238
WIMBLEDON
Hood Way A 3
Copse Hill

R
0   1 Km
0   1/2 Mile
S

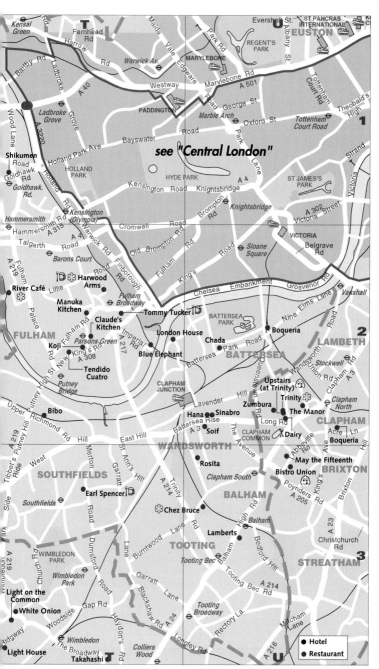

see *"Central London"*

● Hotel
● Restaurant

Duke of Sussex

Mediterranean cuisine   S1

Acton Green

75 South Par ✉ W4 5LF
☎ 020 8742 8801
www.realpubs.co.uk
⊖ Chiswick Park.

Carte £23/35

The Duke of Sussex may seem like a typical London pub, even from the front bar, but step through into the dining room and you'll find yourself in what was once a variety theatre from the time when this was a classic gin palace, complete with proscenium arch, glass ceiling and chandeliers. If that wasn't unusual enough, you could then find yourself eating cured meats or fabada, as the menu has a strong Spanish influence. Traditionalists can still get their steak pies and treacle tart but it's worth being more adventurous and trying the sardines, the paella and the crema Catalana. This is a fun, enthusiastically run and bustling pub and the kitchen's enthusiasm is palpable. On Mondays it's BYO; Sunday is quiz night.

Le Vacherin

French   S1

Acton Green   Closed Monday lunch

76-77 South Par ✉ W4 5LF
☎ 020 8742 2121
www.levacherin.com
⊖ Chiswick Park

Menu £28 – Carte £29/53

Le Vacherin calls itself a bistro but, with its brown leather banquette seating, mirrors and belle époque prints, it feels more like a brasserie, and quite a smart one at that. The most important element of the operation is the appealing menu of French classics which rarely changes, largely because they don't need to but also because the regulars wouldn't allow it. The checklist includes oeufs en cocotte, escargots, confit of duck and crème brûlée. Beef is something of a speciality, whether that's the côte de boeuf, the rib-eye or the chateaubriand. Portions are sensible, flavours distinct and ingredients good. The only thing missing in terms of authenticity are some insouciant French staff and a little Piaf playing in the background.

Lamberts

T r a d i t i o n a l   B r i t i s h   U3

Balham

Closed 25-27 December,
Sunday dinner and Monday

2 Station Par, Balham High Rd. ⊠ SW12 9AZ
☏ 020 8675 2233
www.lambertsrestaurant.com
⊖ Balham

Carte £27/36   ✗

 Mr Lambert and his eponymous restaurant have succeeded by offering the locals exactly what they want: relaxed surroundings, hospitable service and tasty, seasonal food. The menu is updated each month and small suppliers have been sought out. The cooking is quite British in style and has a satisfying wholesomeness to it; Sunday's ribs of Galloway beef or legs of salt marsh lamb are hugely popular. Equal thought and passion have gone into the commendably priced wine list, which includes some favourites offered in 300ml decanters. Other nice touches include filtered water delivered gratis and velvety truffles brought with the coffee. The owner's enthusiasm has rubbed off on his team, for whom nothing is too much trouble.

Brown Dog

M o d e r n   B r i t i s h   S2

Barnes

Closed 25 December

28 Cross St ⊠ SW13 0AP
☏ 020 8392 2200
www.thebrowndog.co.uk
⊖ Barnes Bridge (Rail).

Carte £23/42

To the untrained eye, this dog can look a little forlorn, but then, if you live on one of the many residential streets adjoining it, what your local looks like from the outside is not going to be your primary concern. Mind you, this is a pub which needn't bother looking too attractive because it's concealed within a maze of terraced houses and passing trade is rare. Inside, the lived-in look gives the place a relaxed and homely feel, especially as it's accompanied by easy-going service executed with a smile. The balanced menu offers a decent range of traditional fare like venison pie or haddock fishcake, all done 'properly'; the dishes are flavoursome and the kitchen uses some lesser cuts like bavette to keep the prices down.

Indian Zilla

Indian S2

Barnes
2-3 Rocks Ln. ⊠ SW13 0DB
☎ 020 8878 3989
www.indianzilla.co.uk

Closed 25 December
– (dinner only and Sunday lunch)

Carte £20/43

Judging by the crowds, Barnes' locals are clearly delighted that their district was chosen as the third location for this bourgeoning little group, following on from the success of Indian Zing and Indian Zest. The bright restaurant has a lovely buzz to it and the young, eager-to-please service team are very attentive. The new-wave Indian cooking is surprisingly light yet full of flavour, with many of the dishes using organic ingredients. Whilst a few old favourites are offered, it is the more delicate options that really stand out, such as lobster Balchao and specialities from the owner's home province of Maharashtra, like vegetable Bhanavla. The breads are super as is the lemon and ginger rice, and be sure to end with the Tandoori figs.

Olympic Café + Dining Room

Modern British S2

Barnes
117-123 Church Rd ⊠ SW13 9HL
☎ 020 8912 5161
www.olympiccinema.co.uk

Closed 25 December – bookings
advisable at dinner

Carte £22/57

This is not just a casual restaurant but a place of pilgrimage, for this is a building with a unique history. Built in 1906, it became one of the greatest recording studios on the planet; its halcyon days were in the late '60s and '70s when artists like the Rolling Stones, The Beatles, Jimi Hendrix and Led Zeppelin recorded seminal albums here. There's sadly nothing in this all-day brasserie-style operation to reflect this illustrious past but it does come with a cinema and a private members club. Instead of "Goat's Head Soup" there's an appealing selection of British-inspired comfort food which includes everything from a steak and stilton sandwich to roast cod with reassuringly creamy mash. It's good value and run with quiet efficiency.

Riva

Italian   S2

Barnes

169 Church Rd. ⊠ SW13 9HR

✆ 020 8748 0434

Closed 2 weeks August, Easter,
Christmas-New Year, bank
holidays and Saturday lunch

Carte £33/52   ✗

 Customer loyalty is the sine qua non of any successful restaurant; those seeking guidance on how to build it should get down to Barnes and learn from Andrea Riva. His secret is to shower so much attention on his regulars that all other diners sit imagining the day when they will be treated in the same way – when he will tell them what he's going to cook especially for them. That could be some milk-fed lamb, game, suckling pig or risotto; all expertly rendered using tip-top, seasonal ingredients. While you wait for graduation, you'll be served by a friendly young female team and still get to enjoy some gutsy, flavoursome food. Andrea is also a keen wine collector so if you can talk oenology it could improve your chances of joining the club.

Sonny's Kitchen

Mediterranean cuisine   S2

Barnes

94 Church Rd ⊠ SW13 0DQ

✆ 020 8748 0393

www.sonnyskitchen.co.uk

Closed 25-26 December,
1 January and bank holiday
Mondays

Menu £20 (weekday lunch) – Carte £26/38   ✗

 This longstanding and much-loved neighbourhood favourite is co-owned by industry heavyweights Rebecca Mascarenhas and Philip Howard, who are both Barnes residents. The place has a bright, relaxed feel, with a slight Scandinavian edge; there's a bar and deli at the front and a striking collection of art on the walls from Rebecca's private collection. The menu is appealingly all-encompassing and the kitchen takes good ingredients, treats them with respect and keeps dishes simple and easy to eat. Bread and desserts are highlights and portions surprisingly generous – which is just as well as prices can be steep. Weekends here are especially popular, due to the brunches, roasts and Sunday night BYO, for which no corkage is charged.

Boqueria

S p a n i s h   U2

Battersea   Closed 25 December

278 Queenstown Rd ⊠ **SW8 4LT**
☎ 020 7498 8247
www.boqueriatapas.com
⊖ Clapham Junction

Carte £12/20

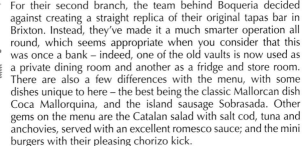

For their second branch, the team behind Boqueria decided against creating a straight replica of their original tapas bar in Brixton. Instead, they've made it a much smarter operation all round, which seems appropriate when you consider that this was once a bank – indeed, one of the old vaults is now used as a private dining room and another as a fridge and store room. There are also a few differences with the menu, with some dishes unique to here – the best being the classic Mallorcan dish Coca Mallorquina, and the island sausage Sobrasada. Other gems on the menu are the Catalan salad with salt cod, tuna and anchovies, served with an excellent romesco sauce; and the mini burgers with their pleasing chorizo kick.

Chada

T h a i   U2

Battersea   Closed Sunday and bank holidays
                                                                        – (dinner only)

208-210 Battersea Park Rd. ⊠ **SW11 4ND**
☎ 020 7622 2209
www.chadathai.com
⊖ Clapham Junction

Carte £18/37

Chada opened in Battersea Park Road back in 1986 and has remained a much loved local Thai restaurant ever since. Its longevity is due in no small part to the owner, who runs it with considerable charm and who is always checking to see that her guests have everything they need. The extensive menu has been revamped a little and includes a selection of 'small eats' which represent a version of street food, albeit with a degree of refinement. Worth ordering, along with the classic soups and salads, are the steamed dumplings and the signature dish of crisp pork belly with red curry and ginger. The restaurant has also had a little touch-up and is bright and fresh and decorated with eye-catching Thai art and artefacts.

Hana

Korean   **U2**

Battersea   Closed 24-26 December

60 Battersea Rise ✉ SW11 1EG
📞 020 7228 2496
www.facebook.com/londonhana
🚇 Clapham Junction

Carte £16/26

Most of the decent local restaurants are up at the Common end, so it's nice to see a few places opening further down the hill. The young owners of this sweet, warmly run little Korean restaurant are also benefitting from the growing popularity of Korean food in the capital. The cooking style may have been slightly westernised but the dishes still have plenty of vibrancy and freshness, and the aromas fill the air. Yang Yeum chicken and the Pa Jeon seafood pancake are popular starters; the bibimbap mixed rice dishes burst with flavour; they have their own take on the classic Bossam dish; and seafood cooked on the barbeque is particularly good. You can also try Korean teas, beers, wine and soju.

London House

Modern British   **T2**

Battersea

7-9 Battersea Sq, Battersea Village ✉ SW11 3RA
📞 020 7592 8545
www.gordonramsayrestaurants.com/london-house
🚇 Clapham Junction

Menu £20 (weekday lunch) – Carte £32/44

Neighbourhood restaurants are not a concept generally associated with Gordon Ramsay but with London House he veered from his norm – a fact for which the locals must be truly grateful. It was always a relaxed kind of place but they've listened to their customers and now it's even more so – and all the better for it. The converted 18C coal store is a place of two halves: there's a lively bar where you can watch the sport or catch up with friends over cocktails and snacks, while the restaurant is set over several smart rooms – and there's also a lovely courtyard garden at the back. The seasonal menu is based around the classics and hearty steaks from the grill; some modern touches are added to the dishes and the component ingredients marry well.

Rosita

Mediterranean cuisine U3

Battersea

124 Northcote Rd ✉ SW11 6QU

✆ 020 7998 9093

www.rositasherry.net

⊖ Clapham Junction

Closed 25-26 December and
lunch 1 January

Carte £11/23

The owner's aunt provided the name for this fun sherry and tapas bar. Brightly painted ceramic tiles and brass lanterns lend a subtle Moorish look to the room and cheery service adds to the buzzy atmosphere. Plate sizes vary from the diminutive to the generous – the latter being the more flavoursome and expensive dishes involving meats and seafood cooked on the Josper grill. The best course of action is to ask for advice as the staff are great at guiding you through ordering – and they are also keen to know you're enjoying yourself. The other aim of the place is to showcase the versatility of sherry: there's plenty of choice by the glass as well as suggested pairings with certain dishes.

Sinabro

Modern cuisine U2

Battersea

28 Battersea Rd ✉ SW11 1EE

✆ 020 3302 3120

www.sinabro.co.uk

⊖ Clapham Junction

Closed 2 weeks mid-August,
25 December,1 January,
Sunday and Monday

Menu £13 (weekday lunch) – Carte £29/44

 'Sinabro' is Korean for 'slowly but surely without noticing', and is a fitting name for Yoann Chevet's restaurant, which has established itself as part of the local dining scene. The main room feels almost kitchen-like, courtesy of a wall of stainless steel; grab a seat at the wooden counter – made by Yoann's father – then sit back and watch the show. Menus evolve constantly and give just a hint of what is to come, with descriptions such as 'salmon, pomegranate, spinach' or 'duck, polenta, peach'. Confidently prepared dishes allow quality ingredients to speak for themselves; they rely largely on classic French flavours but are modern in style. Brunch is served on Saturdays and the Tuesday-Friday lunch 'plat du jour' is particularly good value.

Soif

French U2

Battersea

27 Battersea Rise ⊠ SW11 1HG
℘ 020 7223 1112
www.soif.co
⊖ Clapham Junction

Closed Christmas and New
Year, Sunday dinner, Monday
lunch and bank holidays
– booking essential at dinner

Carte £29/42 ✗

Wholesome food, an appealingly louche look and a thoughtfully
compiled wine list; fair prices, a great atmosphere and delightfully
natural service: there's a lot to love about this busy bistro-cum-
wine-bar. Cooking is French but with regular excursions across
the border into Italy, so you might find moules marinières next
to burrata in the 'small plates' section and duck rillettes as well
as salame under 'charcuterie'. It comes as no surprise to find that
drinks are given equal billing with the food chez Soif – in fact this
restaurant doubles as a wine shop: the predominantly French list
includes plenty of 'natural' wines from artisan winemakers and
there are 20 wines to choose from at shop prices on what are
known as Happy Mondays.

Boqueria

Spanish U2

Brixton

192 Acre Ln. ⊠ SW2 5UL
℘ 020 7733 4408
www.boqueriatapas.com
⊖ Clapham North

Closed 25 December – (dinner
only and lunch Saturday-Sunday)

Carte £11/19 ✗

Named after – and inspired by – Barcelona's famous food
market, this contemporary tapas bar is a welcome addition to
the neighbourhood and has quickly established a local fan-base.
The menu doubles as a place mat and is a mix of recognisable
classics and more adventurous offerings; it is also supplemented
by specials on the blackboard. As everyone involved appears
to hail from Andalucía, it makes sense to kick off with a glass
of sherry. The Ibérico hams are in excellent order, the lamb
medallions are full of flavour and be sure to save room for a
particularly good crema Catalana. It's worth sitting at the counter
as the main dining area at the back lacks a little personality. Their
café next door serves coffee and churros.

Nanban

J a p a n e s e   **N2**

Brixton   Closed Monday lunch

426 Coldharbour Ln ✉ **SW9 8LF**

☎ 020 7346 0098

www.nanban.co.uk

⊖ Brixton

Carte £13/25

A/C   Back in 2011, American Tim Anderson was crowned the youngest winner of BBC's MasterChef. Several years and several pop-ups later, he is now the proud owner of this ramen-bar-cum-izakaya, tucked away at the back of Brixton Market. A concrete floor and plain walls give the place an industrial feel, while cookery books and a great display of sake and shochu add colour (there's also a rather nice collection of Japanese craft beers). The intoxicating smell of chicken stock jolts the olfactory receptors into action; staff are happy to make recommendations but be aware that dishes arrive in no particular order unless you specifically ask. Food is fresh and full of flavour; the spicy, super-crispy chicken karaage will have you coming back for more.

Charlotte's Bistro

M o d e r n c u i s i n e   **S1**

Chiswick   Booking advisable

6 Turnham Green Terr ✉ **W4 1QP**

☎ 020 8742 3590

www.charlottes.co.uk

⊖ Turnham Green

Carte £25/38

A/C   Unlike some desirable London neighbourhoods, Chiswick has always had plenty of restaurants, so locals never feel the need to venture too far from home for dinner. This little sister to nearby Ealing's Charlotte's Place provides them with another pleasantly unpretentious option. A large bar takes up most of the front section and then it's a few steps up to the bright dining room with a glass roof. The menu changes regularly and has a European accent, with dishes such as crab and celeriac tian, cod brandade, pan-fried halloumi, rolled leg of lamb and fishcakes. There's also a nice little cheese menu. Wines are listed by character and include bottles from some small producers. Service and prices are equally friendly.

Hedone

Modern cuisine

Chiswick

301-303 Chiswick High Rd ✉ W4 4HH
✆ 020 8747 0377
www.hedonerestaurant.com
⊖ Chiswick Park

Closed 2 weeks summer, 2 weeks
Christmas-New Year, Sunday
and Monday – booking essential
– (dinner only and lunch Friday-
Saturday) – (surprise menu only)

Menu £45/125

Michelin

Mikael Jonsson's restaurant continues to flourish but this former lawyer and food blogger turned chef is not one for complacency, so it also continues to evolve. A reduction in the number of diners served has meant changes to the seating arrangements; this in turn means better views of the open kitchen and a feeling that the chefs are cooking just for you at your table. Surprise menus of either 7 or 10 courses come with wine pairings; the content of these menus is governed by what ingredients are in their prime, and it is this passion for seeking out the best seasonal produce – be it suckling pig or salt marsh lamb – which underpins the superlative cooking. Watching the chefs at work, one can see the attention to detail involved and the respect with which the ingredients are treated. This results in refined, immeasurably satisfying dishes where the combinations of flavours ooze personality. Fish plays a key role, seasoning is judicious, and the sourdough is some of the finest you'll find in the city.

First Course	Main Course	Dessert
• Warm Devon crab with velvet crab consommé, hazelnut mayonnaise and Granny Smith apple.	• Squab pigeon with chard, olive and coffee-powdered carrots, pigeon jus.	• Vanilla millefeuille with aged balsamic vinegar.
• Scallop with dashi and amontillado foam.	• Steamed John Dory with violet artichoke.	• Tarte Tatin with verbena ice cream and passion fruit caramel.

High Road Brasserie

French S2

Chiswick Booking essential

High Road House Hotel,
162 Chiswick High Rd. ✉ W4 1PR
☏ 020 8742 7474
www.highroadhouse.co.uk
⊖ Turnham Green

Carte £20/36

 It's usually so busy you'll have trouble getting in the door –
quite literally, sometimes, as the entrance is often crowded with
evening drinkers or lunchtime pushchairs. This modern take on a
brasserie certainly has the look, with its mirrors, panelling and
art deco lighting; turn right for the more comfy seating. Staff
are used to being busy and get the job done, although without
much time for pleasantries. What is surprising is that, despite
the volume of customers, the kitchen is able to deliver a good
standard of accurately cooked classics including steak frites,
duck confit, grilled lobster or whole sea bass, along with salads
and sandwiches. The bill can rise quickly as sides are required,
but there's a good value daytime menu.

Michael Nadra

Modern cuisine S1/2

Chiswick Closed 24-27 December,
6-8 Elliott Rd ✉ W4 1PE 1 January and Sunday dinner
☏ 020 8742 0766
www.restaurant-michaelnadra.co.uk
⊖ Turnham Green

Menu £27/38

 Half way down a residential street in Chiswick sits this intimate
little restaurant which has always proved a very good fit for the
area. The cooking is bright, contemporary and at times quite
elaborate; the influences are kept largely within Europe and
the quality of the ingredients is good. The chef-owner, who
must spend hours on the North Circular travelling between this
restaurant and his other one in Primrose Hill, understands the
importance of getting the pricing right – his six course tasting
menu is not only a good way to experience the kitchen's skill
and ambition but is also sensibly priced, especially when
accompanied by the chosen wines. Tables are set quite close
together which adds to the warm neighbourhood feel of the
place.

Smokehouse

T r a d i t i o n a l   B r i t i s h   S2

Chiswick   Closed Monday-Thursday lunch

12 Sutton Ln North ✉ **W4 4LD**
✆ 020 3819 6066
www.smokehousechiswick.co.uk
⊖ Chiswick Park.

Carte £28/34

The success of the first Smokehouse in Canonbury meant a
second was inevitable, although the owners were sensible enough
to avoid making a carbon copy. The menu at this sizeable pub,
which has a lovely rear garden, still centres around barbeque but
it's not quite as 'in your face' as Islington – residents of Chiswick
are perhaps a little more demure. The Belted Galloway burgers
with pulled pork fly out of the kitchen but the winning dish is the
short rib Bourguignon with creamy mash. The kitchen frequently
cook a whole beast, like a Gloucester Old Spot and then make
terrines and potted meats, hams and charcuterie. There are
lighter dishes on offer and, if you make it to dessert, they do a
mean rum and raisin rice pudding.

Bistro Union

M o d e r n   B r i t i s h   U3

Clapham Common   Closed 24-27 December
                                                    – booking advisable

40 Abbeville Rd ✉ **SW4 9NG**
✆ 020 7042 6400
www.bistrounion.co.uk
⊖ Clapham South

Menu £26 (weekday dinner) – Carte £22/40

One look at the menu and it's pretty clear that this sister to
Trinity understands what it is you need to do if you want to
be considered a proper neighbourhood restaurant: it does
brunch every day, can do a light lunch, has an all-day children's
menu and offers an appealing set dinner on a Sunday night to
encourage everyone out of their houses for one last weekend
hurrah. The main menu itself is also flexible, so you can drop in
for some Cornish mussels or order roast chicken for two. If you
are pushing the boat out, it's worth eschewing the starters in
favour of the 'snacks' which could include anchovy toast or crisp
sweetbreads. The appeal of the place is further enhanced by its
warm atmosphere and eager, sweet-natured staff.

La Trompette ✿

Chiswick

5-7 Devonshire Rd ⊠ W4 2EU
☎ 020 8747 1836
www.latrompette.co.uk
⊖ Turnham Green

Closed 24-26 December and
1 January – booking essential

Menu £30 (lunch and early dinner)/50

Michelin

One of the reasons for the success of La Trompette is that it has always looked after its customers: when the shop next door was bought and the restaurant expanded, the owners didn't add more tables, they merely used the extra room to add more space between the existing ones. The very pleasant service team also ensure that customers keep returning – they manage the feat of making service seem effortless and the diners do their bit by creating a warm, congenial atmosphere. These days there is a greater distinction between the lunch and dinner menus. Lunch is all about great value; dishes are quite simple but just as skilfully prepared and the kitchen uses lesser known cuts and fewer luxury ingredients. At dinner the mackerel is replaced by turbot and the cooking is a tad more ambitious, but it's never over-elaborate. Another reason for La Trompette's continued success is that, despite the very accomplished cooking, it never gives the impression that it would rather be in Mayfair – it suits Chiswick and the locals clearly like having it.

First Course	Main Course	Dessert
• Raw scallops with pickled cucumber, kohlrabi and English wasabi.	• Shoulder of suckling pig, creamed potato, white sprouting broccoli, chilli and garlic.	• Rhubarb crumble soufflé with rhubarb ripple ice cream.
• French quail with black pudding, watercress, turnip and hazelnuts.	• Organic chicken with girolles, spinach and roasting juices.	• Crème fraîche tart with clementine sorbet.

Dairy

Creative British   U2

Clapham Common

15 The Pavement ✉ SW4 0HY
℘ 020 7622 4165
www.the-dairy.co.uk
⊖ Clapham Common

Closed Christmas, Sunday dinner,
Monday and Tuesday lunch
– booking essential at dinner

Menu £25 (weekday lunch) – Carte £22/28   ✗

London's markets supplied much of the furniture and crockery, and the higgledy-piggledy look of this fun, lively restaurant adds to its charm. What one doesn't expect to find in this environment is food that is so innovative. The chef-owner's cooking is informed by his travels and his experience gleaned in some famous kitchens. His menu is driven by the ingredients – they grow their own herbs and some fruit and veg on the rooftop, and have three beehives – and all the modern techniques such as pickling and fermenting are there. The food is earthy, original and very labour intensive, but it's also easy to eat – the set menu, with some unusual drinks pairings, is the best option. It's also worth trying the pintxos bar next door.

The Manor

Creative British   U2

Clapham Common

148 Clapham Manor St ✉ SW4 6BX
℘ 020 7720 4662
www.themanorclapham.co.uk
⊖ Clapham Common

Closed 21-27 December,
1 January, Sunday dinner, Tuesday
lunch and Monday

Menu £25 (weekday lunch) – Carte £20/30   ✗

Those who like the Dairy down the road will like The Manor – not only do they share the same ownership but they also share the same menu format and style of cuisine. It is slightly bigger here and, with its distressed looks and informal yet informed service from a delightful young team, it perfectly captures the zeitgeist. The cooking is heavily influenced by modern Scandic kitchens and first timers should go for the tasting menu. The dishes show plenty of innovation, and all the modern techniques – from smoking and charring to pickling and fermenting – are used to good effect. The dishes are not just artfully presented but are surprisingly robust in flavour and the contrast in textures is one aspect that's particularly memorable.

May the Fifteenth

Clapham Common

47 Abbeville Rd ✉ **SW4 9JX**
✆ 020 8772 1110
www.abbevillekitchen.com
⊖ Clapham South

Closed 24-26 and 31 December
and 1 January – bookings
advisable at dinner – (dinner only
and lunch Friday-Sunday)

Menu £20 (weekday lunch) – Carte £23/38 ✗

It might have seemed like an odd decision to change the name when everyone knew this neighbourhood bistro as Abbeville Kitchen, but when the head chef took over he wanted to make it his own and so named it after the day he signed the forms. Gone too is the Gallic feel to the place – a lick of paint inside and out now makes you feel you're in Brighton rather than Brittany. At least the food hasn't changed – it remains gutsy and wholesome and the daily changing menu offers the option of ordering small tasting plates or a more traditional three-courser. The choice is varied – it's not often you see empanadas and Swaledale lamb on the same menu – and the prices are fair. The charcuterie boards stand out, as do dishes for two like roast chicken.

Upstairs (at Trinity)

Clapham Common

4 The Polygon ✉ **SW4 0JG**
✆ 020 7622 1199
www.trinityrestaurant.co.uk
⊖ Clapham Common

Closed 24-30 December,
1-2 January, Sunday and Monday
– (dinner only)

Carte £20/36 ✗

When Adam Byatt gave his Trinity restaurant its most recent makeover he also created a separate operation upstairs. It has a more relaxed feel than downstairs, with the open-plan kitchen being the focus of the room. The food is all about sharing – about five dishes between two should be enough but as everything sounds so appealing and the prices are so reasonable, you'll be tempted to over-order. The seasonal British ingredients are used to good effect to create visually appealing dishes; they come with a Mediterranean bias and certainly deliver on flavour – be sure to end with the salted caramel tart. Wine plays a big part with the 'by the glass' selection showcasing some lesser-known names and producers.

Trinity 🕄

Modern cuisine

U2

Clapham Common

Closed 24-30 December and
1-2 January

4 The Polygon ⊠ SW4 0JG
✆ 020 7622 1199
www.trinityrestaurant.co.uk
⊖ Clapham Common

Menu £30 (weekday lunch) – Carte £37/52

Michelin

Clapham Old Town has hosted Trinity for a decade but the cooking now is the best it has ever been. It's as if the kitchen has relaxed a little and trusted more in its talent, because the cooking is less elaborate that it was previously and is so much the better for it. There are no extraneous elements or unnecessary decorative flourishes on the plate – the focus remains firmly on the primary ingredient, whether that's a perfectly cooked piece of sea bass or a succulent Iberico pork chop. This confidence extends to the desserts too – even those averse to sharing should consider ordering the tarte Tatin with prune and Armagnac ice cream for two. Service is warm and confident and the last refurbishment of the restaurant left it looking brighter and more contemporary in style, with windows into the kitchen and out onto the small terrace. As this is a true neighbourhood restaurant away from the West End, you won't be chucked off your table as soon as you swallow your last mouthful.

First Course	Main Course	Dessert
• Crispy pig's trotters, sauce gribiche and crackling. • Ravioli of crab with crab soup and ginger.	• Fillet of sea bass with roast onions, fennel, shrimps and basil. • Pot-roast pigeon with salt-baked celeriac and madeira.	• Salted caramel custard tart. • Yorkshire rhubarb and custard.

Zumbura

Indian U2

Clapham Common

36a Old Town ⊠ SW4 0LB
📞 020 7720 7902
www.zumbura.com
⊖ Clapham Common

Closed 25 December and
1 January – (dinner only)

Carte £13/28

Going from running a furniture business to opening a restaurant may seem a curious career path but it seems to be working for the three friends behind Zumbura. It's no surprise they've got the look right – the narrow room is nicely lit, comes in contemporary colours and boasts some clever little touches. Perhaps more surprising is that they've got the food right too. One of the owners grew up in northern India and the cooking is inspired by the food he ate at home. You'll need to be quite expansive in your ordering as it's all about small plates, which you'll find fresh tasting, subtly spiced and surprisingly light. If you haven't booked, there's usually room at the 5 metre bar, which was fashioned out of single piece of oak.

Charlotte's Place

Modern cuisine R1

Ealing

16 St Matthew's Rd ⊠ W5 3JT
📞 020 8567 7541
www.charlottes.co.uk
⊖ Ealing Common

Closed 26 December and
1 January

Menu £20/42

It's been a sweet shop, a transport café and a private club but it really found its niche as an honest and warmly run local restaurant. The ground floor offers views over the Common so is more popular at lunch; downstairs is ideal for couples who only have eyes for each other. The à la carte offers ample choice and the cooking is largely British, with smoked fish, traditional Sunday lunches and homely puddings done well; there are also one or two Mediterranean influences and the beef onglet enjoys a constant presence. There is a small cover charge but it does pay for bread and unlimited amounts of filtered water, rather than being an accountant's wheeze for squeezing more money out of the customers.

Charlotte's W5

Modern cuisine

Ealing

Dickens Yard, Longfield Ave ✉ W5 2BF

☎ 020 3771 8722

www.charlottes.co.uk

⊖ Ealing Broadway

Carte £24/34

This bright, buzzy restaurant occupies a previously derelict stable block and opened in 2016 to coincide with the large development of new apartments which surrounds it. It's all about flexibility – you can pop in for brunch, a drink, a snack or a full meal and it stays open all day. It also manages that rare trick of being just as suited to couples on dates as it is to family gatherings. The other clever aspect is the modern European menu: every dish is available in a choice of three sizes to make sharing easier, whatever your number. Similarly, every bottle of wine is also offered by the glass or carafe. Add in a great bar list, a charming service team and sensible prices – and there's little wonder it's proving so popular.

Kerbisher & Malt

Fish and chips

Ealing

53 New Broadway ✉ W5 5AH

☎ 020 8840 4418

www.kerbisher.co.uk

⊖ Ealing Broadway

Carte approx. £16

There may have been a revolution in British cooking over the last two decades, but for many people, especially tourists, fish and chips will always be our national dish. Restaurants have been doing decent versions for years but Kerbisher & Malt represents a new wave of ethical fish and chip shops that are raising this classic dish to new heights. The fish here is fresh, sustainably sourced and cooked to order in rapeseed oil (which is then turned into biofuel); chips are made from British spuds and are fried separately; and all packaging is biodegradable. Choose your fish and a side order of thick 'Yorkshire caviar' or pickled onion rings, along with a pot of great tartare sauce. There's another branch in Hammersmith.

Kiraku

Japanese R1

Ealing

Closed Christmas-New Year
and Monday

8 Station Par, Uxbridge Rd. ✉ W5 3LD
☎ 020 8992 2848
www.kiraku.co.uk
⊖ Ealing Common

Carte £13/38

Ayumi and Erica became so frustrated with the lack of a decent local Japanese restaurant that they decided to open one themselves; and now it is not just the bourgeoning Japanese community who flock to this cute little place. It's modestly styled and brightly lit, but service is very charming. Look out for the daily changing dishes on the blackboard. Zensai, or starters, include the popular Agedashi dofu; these can then be followed by assorted skewers, noodles and rice dishes. Fish is purchased daily and their sushi now displays a more modern touch; Bara Chirashi is the house speciality. Be sure to end with matcha ice cream or green tea sponge cake. The restaurant's name means 'relax and enjoy' and it's hard not to.

Shikumen

Chinese R1

Ealing

26-42 Bond St ✉ W5 5AA
☎ 020 8567 2770
www.shikumen.co.uk
⊖ Ealing Broadway

Carte £18/28

Unlike the branch in Shepherd's Bush, this Shikumen specialises exclusively in dim sum – at both lunch and dinner. The menu offers around 50 choices: you can either choose from the various sections or just go for one of the nicely balanced set menus. The star of the show is the roast pork cheung fun, although the seafood congee is also worth ordering; the rice pots, like sea bass with tofu, ensure that you won't leave hungry. Everyone should try traditional Cantonese Afternoon tea at least once and here you'll find a good selection of teas to go with the dim sum and the sweet treats. The restaurant isn't quite as big as its sister but it too is located within a corporate-minded hotel and decorated in a dark and sultry style.

Victoria

M o d e r n   B r i t i s h S2

East Sheen

10 West Temple Sheen ✉ SW14 7RT
✆ 020 8876 4238
www.thevictoria.net
⊖ Mortlake (Rail).

Carte £26/44

Chef-owner Paul Merrett is something of a food hero in these parts: he gives cookery classes at the school next door and the ethos of his pub is, first and foremost, to serve the local community. It has a pleasant lived-in feel, with the nooks and crannies of the bars usually busy with loungers and drinkers; if you're here to eat you're better off heading for the conservatory, which overlooks their terrace. The appealing menu offers a good range of dishes and comes with a distinct Mediterranean slant, with Middle Eastern influences never far away. You can start with chickpea and basil hummus, then move on to chargrilled lemon chicken or falafel or, if you prefer something simpler, there's a well-priced selection of burgers available.

Blue Elephant

T h a i T2

Fulham

The Boulevard, Imperial Wharf ✉ SW6 2UB
✆ 020 7751 3111
www.blueelephant.com
⊖ Imperial Wharf

Closed 25-26 December,
1 January and Monday
– booking advisable – (dinner
only and Sunday lunch)

Carte £34/51

The Blue Elephant was a Fulham Road landmark for so long that everyone was taken by surprise when it packed its trunk and relocated. Fortunately for its followers, it didn't wander too far and these swankier premises within the large development that is Imperial Wharf have given it a new lease of life. Spread over two floors, the decoration is as exotic as one would expect – except that instead of the koi ponds you have the Thames outside, along with two terrific terraces; even the golden dragon made the journey from the old address and can now be found in a different guise at the bar. The appealing menu traverses Thailand and in amongst the classic dishes are a few more contemporary offerings; the curries here are always worth ordering.

Claude's Kitchen

Modern cuisine T2

Fulham

51 Parsons Green Ln ⊠ SW6 4JA

✆ 020 7371 8517

www.amusebouchelondon.com

⊖ Parsons Green.

Closed Sunday – booking essential – (dinner only)

Carte £27/38 ✕

The eponymous Claude has created two little operations within one converted Victorian pub. On the ground floor is 'Amuse Bouche', a champagne bar where the bubbles are sold at competitive prices, along with assorted boards of cheese or cured meats. Upstairs is a small and intimate dining room where you'll find a concise but nicely balanced à la carte menu which changes every Tuesday. Everything is homemade here, including the terrific bread, and the food is colourful and fresh, although Claude does have the occasional urge to drop in one or two challenging flavour combinations. Come before 7pm and the menu is available at a reduced - great value - price. Do try the delicious pomme 'Daniele' as a side - and leave room for pudding too!

The sun's out? Enjoy eating outside on the terrace: 🖽.

Harwood Arms 🌼

Modern British   T2

Fulham

Walham Grove ✉ SW6 1QP   Closed 24-27 December, 1 January
☎ 020 7386 1847   and Monday lunch except bank
www.harwoodarms.com   holidays – booking essential
⊖ Fulham Broadway.

Menu £36 (weekday lunch)/43

Harwood Arms

It may be a very handsome pub in a smart postcode and have all its tables laid up for dining but there's nothing stuck-up or snooty about this place – in fact, the only thing that's superior is the cooking. It's British to its core, with its reassuringly concise, daily changing menu resolutely governed by our country's own seasonal produce. Cornish fish, Herdwick lamb, Cumbrian chicken and Wiltshire pork can all feature and game is a real strength of the kitchen whether it's rabbit, grouse or Hampshire Muntjac. Dishes have real depth and flavours are bold and satisfying. Service is smooth and assured and comes courtesy of a young yet experienced team and the well-chosen wine list offers a particularly good choice of mature claret. If you're sitting beneath the skylight then look up and you'll spot the rooftop vegetable and herb 'garden'. As this is still a pub, you can just pop in for a drink at the bar but if you do then be sure to order some of the great bar snacks like game rissoles or a venison scotch egg.

First Course	Main Course	Dessert
• Wye Valley asparagus on toast with Cornish crab, watercress and pressed egg.	• Haunch of Berkshire fallow deer with wild garlic, beetroot and smoked bone marrow.	• Vanilla custard tart with date and sticky toffee ice cream.
• Whipped chicken livers with crispy chicken skin, balsamic onions and thyme Hobnobs.	• Cornish monkfish tail with white bean broth, tomato and basil.	• Honey mousse with buttermilk, apricot and bee pollen.

Koji

J a p a n e s e T2

Fulham

Closed 24-26 December and
Monday

58 New King's Rd ⊠ SW6 4LS

☏ 020 7731 2520

www.koji.restaurant

⊖ Parsons Green

Carte £31/54

You don't run a London restaurant for 30 years without getting to know your market. In 2014, owner Mark Barnett retired his Mao Tai Chinese restaurant and in its place opened his own version of an izakaya which, in this case, looks like a wine bar serving Japanese food. The front section is all bar, with a large list of cocktails and wines; at the back is a sushi counter and dining area with lots of natural light and a contemporary look. The menu mixes the classic and the more modern, with plenty of obvious influences from Nobu. Purists shouldn't get too hung up on authenticity – especially when they see the word 'tapas' on the menu – and instead should order some of the popular tempura and dishes from the robata grill.

Manuka Kitchen

M o d e r n   c u i s i n e T2

Fulham

Closed 25-26 December,
Sunday dinner and Monday lunch

510 Fulham Rd ⊠ SW6 5NJ

☏ 020 7736 7588

www.manukakitchen.com

⊖ Fulham Broadway

Carte £23/35

A chef and an ex hotel manager chanced upon this former Italian restaurant and thought it the perfect spot for a venture of their own. Using only their own funds, they subsequently created this simply furnished little place, which they run with great enthusiasm. Their aim is to provide wholesome food at keen prices without compromising on the quality of the ingredients. Tyler, the chef, is from New Zealand, as is Manuka honey which is purported to have magical powers. His menu is appealing in its variety and dishes come with plenty of punch; the crispy squid is proving a very popular choice, as is the bolognese which uses Wagyu beef. Honey does also make an occasional appearance – perhaps with the cheese or in a crème brûlée.

Tendido Cuatro

Spanish

Fulham

Closed 2 weeks Christmas

108-110 New Kings Rd ⊠ SW6 4LY
📞 020 7371 5147
www.cambiodetercio.co.uk
⊖ Parsons Green

Menu £30 (lunch and early dinner) – Carte £21/44 ✗

A/C

Any resemblance to their other restaurant in Old Brompton Road is entirely intentional: here too the front panels burst open in summer to reveal a warm interior where vivid colours are used with wild abandon. The main difference is that, along with tapas, the speciality is the Valencian classic, paella. Using bomba rice, the choice varies from seafood to quail and chorizo; vegetarian to cuttlefish ink. They are designed for two but that assumes a more than eager appetite, especially if you've had a couple of small dishes as a run-up. The tapas is nicely varied, from refreshing baby anchovies to crisp pig's ears. Service is spirited and the room comes alive later in the evening as the locals return from work and wander over.

The symbol ✆
guarantees a peaceful
night's sleep.

Tommy Tucker

T2

Traditional British

Fulham

Closed 25 December

22 Waterford Rd ✉ **SW6 2DR**
✆ 020 7736 1023
www.thetommytucker.com
⊖ Fulham Broadway.

Carte £19/35

Locals will remember this as The Pelican, a relatively quiet pub that would get overwhelmed whenever Chelsea were playing at home. The people behind Claude's Kitchen in nearby Parsons Green then gave it a head-to-toe revamp and the TT, as they call it, is now the sort of place everyone would want on their street. The black façade doesn't really give the right impression because inside it's bright and open-plan – the nicest part is the 'music room' with its sheet music wallpaper. The menu is unstructured and divided under headings of 'meat', 'fish' and 'fruit and veg', with asterisks marking the dishes available as starters. The food is rustic, earthy and satisfying and the service is thoughtful and sincere.

L'Amorosa

Italian

Hammersmith

278 King St ✉ **W6 0SP**
✆ 020 8563 0300
www.lamorosa.co.uk
⊖ Ravenscourt Park

S1

Closed 1 week August, 1 week Christmas, Sunday dinner, Monday and bank holidays

Menu £16 (weekday lunch) – Carte £25/36

Andy Needham's name and reputation were established when he was head chef at Zafferano. He now has his own place and his considerable experience is clear to see. This is the sort of relaxed Italian restaurant we'd all like to have at the end of our street. The cooking provides a lesson in sincerity and the importance of trusting in the quality of the ingredients; the homemade pasta is always a delight and the regulars, of whom they are many already, will no doubt never allow the tiramisu to be removed from the menu. The restaurant is bright and sunny, with the best seats being those on the raised floor at the back; service is well-meaning; prices are more than fair; and the atmosphere is relaxed and unhurried.

Anglesea Arms

M o d e r n   B r i t i s h   **S1**

Hammersmith   Closed 24-26 December

35 Wingate Rd ⊠ W6 0UR
✆ 020 8749 1291
www.angleseaarmspub.co.uk
⊖ Ravenscourt Park

Carte £22/34

 The Anglesea Arms was one of the daddies of the gastropub movement, and for several decades has given those who live nearby an excuse never to venture too far for dinner; with its warm, laid-back atmosphere, friendly young staff – and food that's a cut above your usual pub fodder. The nicely seasonal menu gives the impression that it's written by a Brit who occasionally holidays on the Med – there are some suitably robust dishes but the kitchen is also capable of displaying a pleasing lightness of touch. Plates are never overly crowded with ingredients and modern versions of old-school desserts like rice pudding and apple crumble certainly hit the spot. The pub also offers a regularly changing selection of regional real ales.

Azou

N o r t h   A f r i c a n   **S2**

Hammersmith   Closed 1 January and
375 King St ⊠ W6 9NJ   25 December – booking essential
✆ 020 8563 7266   – (dinner only)
www.azou.co.uk
⊖ Stamford Brook

Carte £20/38   ✗

A/C   You'll probably walk past the first time and not notice this unassuming little place but, once visited, you won't walk past again. Inside is all silks, lanterns and rugs but it is also very personally run; the owner will often pop out from his kitchen to offer guidance – and his advice is well worth listening to. The cooking skips across North African countries – order some Algerian olives while you choose from the wide choice of main courses. Understandably, most of the regulars come here for a tajine, especially the Constantine with its tender lamb and triple-steamed couscous. Highlights to start include the terrific baba ganoush with homemade bread and fresh briouat. It's the perfect food to share as the dishes come in large portions.

Brackenbury

M e d i t e r r a n e a n   c u i s i n e   S1

Hammersmith

129 - 131 Brackenbury Rd ✉ W6 OBQ
✆ 020 8741 4928
www.brackenburyrestaurant.co.uk
⊖ Ravenscourt Park

Closed Christmas, New Year,
Easter, August bank holiday,
Sunday and Monday

Menu £16 (weekday lunch) – Carte £27/42

 It was a sad day for many when The Brackenbury ran out of steam a few years ago. Many thought that would be it, but in 2014 the doors reopened, the much-loved name reappeared and the lucky locals raised a loud cheer. It always was the quintessential neighbourhood spot and that hasn't changed – the cosy, hassle-free atmosphere is what you remember here rather than the decoration or the well-intentioned service. Food-wise, the kitchen looks to Italy, then France and then the Med for inspiration and doesn't waste time on presentation; the dishes feel instinctive and the flavours marry well – and the short wine list is nicely balanced and priced. Competition may be a little stiffer these days but there's always room for The Brackenbury.

Indian Zing

I n d i a n   S1

Hammersmith

236 King St. ✉ W6 0RF
✆ 020 8748 5959
www.indianzing.co.uk
⊖ Ravenscourt Park

Menu £12/15 – Carte £20/43

 The menu tells you all you need to know: this is not your typical high street Indian restaurant. Chef-owner Manoj Vasaikar seeks inspiration from across the country and his cooking cleverly balances the traditional with the more contemporary. Evident care goes into the preparation of the fragrant dishes, which deliver many layers of flavours – lamb dishes are particularly good, as are the various breads. However, you'll see many customers giving the menu no more than a cursory glance – that's because they're regulars who know what they want before they get here, and is the reason why Karwari fish curry, lamb rogan josh and the thalis can never be taken off the menu. Service is courteous and unhurried and the room judiciously lit.

River Café ✿

I t a l i a n   T2

Hammersmith

Thames Wharf, Rainville Rd ✉ W6 9HA
✆ 020 7386 4200
www.rivercafe.co.uk
⊖ Barons Court

Closed Christmas-New Year,
Sunday dinner and bank holidays
– booking essential

Carte £60/82   ✕✕

River Cafe

They should run a shuttle service from local catering colleges to the River Café so that the students can learn the secret of good cooking: good ingredients. There's a vigour and honesty to the kitchen and, with the chefs all on view as they go about their work, there seems to be more of a relationship here between cook and customer than is found in most restaurants. The big wood-fired oven really catches the eye and the restaurant seems to attract a wonderfully mixed bunch of customers, united in their appreciation of what makes a restaurant tick. That includes charming service: on looks alone, the team can rival those in glossier and glitzier restaurants but they break ranks here by actually smiling and caring about their customers. The menu is still written twice a day and head chef Sian Wyn Owen brings an added sparkle to the cooking. Things taste just the way you want them to taste. Ordering a pasta dish ought to be made compulsory and the Chocolate Nemesis dessert should be a recognised treatment for depression.

First Course	Main Course	Dessert
• Chargrilled squid with red chilli and rocket.	• Wood-roasted veal chop with salsa verde and slow-cooked peas.	• Chocolate Nemesis.
• English asparagus with anchovy butter and parmesan.	• Scottish scallops with zucchini fritti, chilli and mint.	• Almond tart with strawberries.

The Glasshouse ✾

Modern cuisine R2

Kew

14 Station Par. ✉ TW9 3PZ
✆ 020 8940 6777
www.glasshouserestaurant.co.uk
⊖ Kew Gardens

Closed 24-26 December and
1 January

Menu £30 (weekday lunch)/50

A/C
🍇

The Glasshouse

The Glasshouse is the very model of a modern neighbourhood restaurant. It sits in the heart of lovely, villagey Kew, always seems to be busy and is known for the quality and reliability of its cooking. The food is confident yet unshowy – much like the locals themselves, who are the restaurant's biggest fans – and comes with distinct Mediterranean flavours along with the occasional Asian hint. The kitchen is also using more Welsh ingredients these days, especially beef and lamb, as the chef is from north Wales. The wine list is well worth closer examination as it offers an interesting range by the glass and a particularly good selection of grower champagnes. The floor to ceiling windows create a feeling of space which cleverly distracts you from realising that actually the place is quite cramped – just don't let the staff sit you in the middle of the room as you'll feel surrounded by diners and staff rushing by. Service is eager and youthful.

First Course

- Duck breast with foie gras parfait, balsamic and beetroot.

- Egg yolk ravioli with pancetta, sunflower seeds, rocket and basil pesto.

Main Course

- Loin of lamb with braised shoulder, boulangère potatoes and pea & wild garlic emulsion.

- Wild halibut with brown shrimps, black rice and fennel purée.

Dessert

- Warm custard brioche with roasted apples and tarte Tatin ice cream.

- Passion fruit meringue with coconut ice cream and caramelised mango.

Linnea

Modern British R2

Kew

Closed Christmas, Sunday dinner
and Monday

12 Kew Grn. ✉ TW9 3BH
✆ 020 8940 5696
www.linneakew.co.uk
⊖ Kew Gardens

Menu £20/28 ✗✗

A/C Horticulturists will not be surprised to learn that the chef-owner of this attractive neighbourhood restaurant is from Sweden, as Linnea is his country's national flower. It's also a rather apt name for a restaurant overlooking the Green and so close to Kew Gardens. The room, designed by Jonas's wife Elia, has a pared-down yet elegant look and a Scandic feel, with candlelight casting a warm glow at night. The monthly changing menu offers a range of modern, unfussy, classically influenced dishes with the Scandinavian techniques of pickling, curing and air-drying in evidence; go for any dish that includes mushrooms or berries. Flavours are clear and fresh and presentation is as pretty as the flower. Linnea is a restaurant that deserves to blossom.

Bibo

Italian T2

Putney

Closed 25-26 December, Monday
lunch and bank holidays

146 Upper Richmond Rd ✉ SW15 2SW
✆ 020 8780 0592
www.biborestaurant.com
⊖ East Putney

Menu £17/23 – Carte £26/36

Few restaurateurs are as adept as Rebecca Mascarenhas in creating great neighbourhood restaurants and, with Bibo, she A/C hit the bullseye once again. This fun Italian restaurant has all the right component parts, from an appealing environment and clued-up service to food that's well-priced and effortlessly easy to enjoy. It also ticks the accessibility box as it's somewhere you can just pop into for a drink and a plate of great nibbles. The same appealing menu is served at lunch and dinner, the British and imported Italian produce is top notch and dishes are refreshingly uncomplicated yet full of flavour. The Latin name means 'to drink', so it's no surprise that the wholly Italian wine list is also worth exploring.

405

Bingham Restaurant

Modern cuisine R3

Richmond Closed Sunday dinner

Bingham Hotel,
61-63 Petersham Rd. ✉ **TW10 6UT**
☎ 020 8940 0902
www.thebingham.co.uk
⊖ Richmond
Carte £25/55

Its riverside location has always made The Bingham hotel a popular choice for a wedding but it is also known for having a very good restaurant. Start with a drink in the cocktail bar or on the balcony terrace overlooking the garden and river before heading into the comfortable dining room. The menus offer plenty of choice, with an à la carte and a market menu, but the incurably indecisive need not panic because they can go for the mystery menu and leave it all to the kitchen. The food is a blend of the modern and the classical and, pleasingly, more thought has been given to the flavours than to the embellishments. The service team, rather like the clientele, are younger than expected – which also adds to the atmosphere.

Dysart Petersham

Modern cuisine R3

Richmond Closed Sunday dinner and
Monday – booking advisable

135 Petersham Rd ✉ **TW10 7AA**
☎ 020 8940 8005
www.thedysartpetersham.co.uk

Menu £28 (weekdays) – Carte £37/50

Overlooking Richmond Park and built in the early 1900s as part of the Arts and Crafts movement, the Dysart is named after the family who once lived in Ham House. The owners decided to run it as a restaurant rather than a pub and have created a bright and fresh space that successfully blends its period features with more contemporary design elements. Service comes with a formality that seems somewhat at odds with this environment yet the formula clearly pleases the locals. The menu is also a blend of styles – the young chef uses top-notch ingredients and his cooking comes with a classical base to which he adds subtle Asian tones to create quite refined, delicately flavoured dishes. Look out for the occasional music recital evening.

Matsuba

J a p a n e s e

Richmond

10 Red Lion St ✉ TW9 1RW

✆ 020 8605 3513

www.matsuba-restaurant.com

⊖ Richmond

R2

Closed 25-26 December,
1 January and Sunday

Menu £39 – Carte £22/42

Matsuba is a small, family-run place that is so understated it's easy to miss – look out for the softly lit sign above the narrow façade. The interior is equally compact and low-key, with just a dozen or so tables, along with a small counter at the back with room for four more. In fact the biggest thing in the room is the menu, which offers a comprehensive tour through most recognisable points in Japanese cooking. The owners are Korean so you can also expect to see bulgogi, the Korean barbecue dish of marinated meat that comes on a sizzling plate. All the food is fresh and the ingredients are good; lunch sees some very good value set menus. The service is well-meaning and it's hard not to come away thinking kind thoughts.

Petersham Nurseries Café

M o d e r n   c u i s i n e

Richmond

Church Ln (off Petersham Rd) ✉ TW10 7AG

✆ 020 8940 5230

www.petershamnurseries.com

R3

Closed 24-27 December and
Monday – booking essential
– (lunch only)

Carte £28/52

On a summer's day there can be few more delightful spots for lunch than the Café at Petersham Nurseries. Buy into the whole Sunday-supplement charm of the place and you'll find that, whether you're on the terrace or inside the greenhouse with its wobbly tables and soil floor, the hustle and hassle of modern life seem a world away. The cooking is a perfect match for this rural retreat: it uses the freshest of seasonal produce in unfussy and flavoursome dishes. Nothing – apart from the daily sorbet – is frozen here and fridges are nigh on empty at the end of each day. Many herbs and leaves come from their own gardens and dishes, like shoulder of lamb with cime di rapa and anchovies, come with a subtle Italian accent.

Swagat

I n d i a n R2

Richmond

86 Hill Rise ✉ TW10 6UB
✆ 020 8940 7557
www.swagatindiancuisine.co.uk
⊖ Richmond

Closed 25 December – booking
essential – (dinner only)

Menu £30 – Carte £20/35

 This likeable little Indian restaurant is run by two friends; they met while training with Oberoi hotels in India before coming to London to work in some of the capital's best Indian restaurants. One partner organises the warm, well-meaning service, while the other ensures his kitchen delivers authentic and satisfying cooking, some of which comes with north Indian influences. Dishes display a pleasing degree of lightness and subtlety so the first taste is always that of the prime ingredient rather than the spice; there's a health dividend to some of the dishes, such as sea bass with chilli and ginger; and vegetarians have plenty of choice. Add in complimentary poppadoms and chutneys and you can see why it's a hit with the locals.

Princess Victoria

T r a d i t i o n a l   B r i t i s h S1

Shepherd's Bush

217 Uxbridge Rd ✉ W12 9DH
✆ 020 8749 5886
www.princessvictoria.co.uk
⊖ Shepherd's Bush.

Closed 24-27 December

Menu £13 (weekday lunch) – Carte £23/47

 London has a wealth of fine Victorian gin palaces but few are as grand as the Princess Victoria. From the friezes to the etched glass, the portraits to the parquet floor, the last restoration created a terrific pub. Mind you, that's not all that impresses: there's a superb, wide-ranging wine list, with carafes and glasses providing flexibility; enticing bar snacks ranging from quail eggs to salt cod croquettes; a great menu that could include roasted skate wing or homemade pork and herb sausages; and, most importantly, cooking that's executed with no little skill. Those with proclivities for all things porcine will find much to savour – charcuterie is a passion here and the board may well include pig's cheeks and rillettes.

Shikumen

Chinese

T1

Shepherd's Bush

Closed Christmas

58 Shepherd's Bush Grn ✉ W12 8QE
☎ 020 8749 9978
www.shikumen.co.uk
⊖ Shepherd's Bush

Carte £22/48

One glance at the menu of this sleek-looking Cantonese restaurant and any spirits dashed by the terminal blandness of this end of Shepherd's Bush will be instantly uplifted. It offers an appealing selection of authentic dishes and makes good use of top quality ingredients like Scottish lobster and beef. The standout is the Peking duck, which needs 45 minutes' notice at busy times, and which comes in two servings: the first with pancakes; the second with rice or noodles. It's well worth coming at lunch for the handmade dim sum and that includes their Xiao Long Bao which boasts an impressive 15 pleats. The name of the restaurant translates as 'stone gate' and refers to a style of house which blends Chinese and Western styles. There's a sister branch in Ealing.

Ealing Park Tavern

Modern British

R1

South Ealing

222 South Ealing Rd ✉ W5 4RL
☎ 020 8758 1879
www.ealingparktavern.com
⊖ South Ealing

Menu £19 (lunch and early dinner) – Carte £33/57

 This west London landmark, an impressive Arts and Crafts property dating from 1886, has been reborn and brought right up-to-date thanks to a splendid refurbishment from the Martin Brothers. With a panelled bar complete with stuffed animals, a bright, cavernous dining room, a suntrap terrace and the 'Long Arm Brewing Co.' at the back of the pub providing three bespoke ales (try the American IPA-OK), this is the sort of place we'd all like to live near. Service is charming and friendly and the cooking is robust yet comes with a refined edge, whether that's the freshest fish from Billingsgate, Yorkshire game in season, the chop or pie of the day, or the delightful old school puds. For larger groups, 'Feasting' menus can be arranged.

Earl Spencer

M e d i t e r r a n e a n   c u i s i n e   **T3**

Southfields   Closed lunch Monday-Thursday

260-262 Merton Rd ✉ **SW18 5JL**
✆ 020 8870 9244
www.theearlspencer.com
⊖ Southfields.

Carte £24/35

The owner worked at this Edwardian pub over a decade ago
and so jumped at the chance of actually buying it himself – he
felt he had "unfinished business" here. It's a handsome pub,
standing a baseline lob away from the All England Tennis Club
and its small terrace overlooks a showroom of the finest 4-wheel
thoroughbreds. Inside is bright and welcoming, with many of the
original features and fittings restored, but it's the cooking that
really sets it apart. The experienced brigade are strict apostles of
seasonality – the menu can sometimes change twice a day – and
everything is homemade. The one entry in the debit column is
that you have to keep going up to the bar to order everything.

King's Head

M o d e r n   c u i s i n e   **R3**

Teddington

123 High St ✉ **TW11 8HG**
✆ 020 3166 2900
www.whitebrasserie.com
⊖ Teddington (Rail).

Menu £10 (weekday lunch) – Carte £23/40

Britain has its pubs and France its brasseries; The King's Head
does its bit for the entente cordiale by combining both. Raymond
Blanc's team has given this Victorian pub a tidy makeover and,
although there might not be much character left, they have
created a suitably warm environment. The brasserie at the back
is run by a pleasant, enthusiastic team and the menus offer
all comers plenty of choice. Classic brasserie dishes such as
Toulouse sausages and beef stroganoff come with a satisfyingly
rustic edge, while the dual-nationality element is maintained
through the inclusion of a ploughman's board alongside the
charcuterie. Steaks from the charcoal grill are popular and
families are lured in by the decent kiddies menu.

Rétro Bistrot

French   R3

Teddington   Closed Sunday dinner and
114-116 High St ✉ TW11 8JB   Monday
☎ 020 8977 2239
www.retrobistrot.co.uk
⊖ Teddington (Rail)

Menu £11/23 – Carte £28/55

 Gallic charm is in abundance at this classic bistro deluxe. The
ebullient owner, Vincent, offers 'un accueil chaleureux' and the
service team display great commitment to the cause as cheeks
are kissed and cries of "bon appétit" ring out. The mix of bold
wallpaper, exposed brick walls, comfy banquettes and art for
sale creates a very genial environment; sit in the right hand room,
which is lighter and more airy thanks to the large windows. The
French kitchen know their blanquette from their beurre noisette
and offer all the French classics, from onion soup and pork
terrine to coq au vin or Chateaubriand for two. Desserts like
Mirabelle plum soufflé are a highlight and the set menu is big on
flavour and excellent value for money.

Simply Thai

Thai   R3

Teddington   Closed 25-26 December
196 Kingston Rd. ✉ TW11 9JD   – (dinner only)
☎ 020 8943 9747
www.simplythai-restaurant.co.uk
⊖ Hampton Wick (Rail)

Carte £21/31

Over the years, this simple Thai restaurant in the heart of
suburbia has built up a loyal clientele. They describe the cooking
as 'a healthy approach to eating' and there's a bewildering
array of dishes to choose from; if you're struggling to decide,
pick one of Patria's signature dishes. What the cooking lacks in
authenticity (it's adjusted for Western tastes), it makes up for in
its commendable use of British ingredients. You might find cod
dumplings in green curry sauce or rack of lamb marinated with
Thai spices. The budget conscious should come on a Sunday
for the street food selection, while the dipping sauces, made in
house, are good any day of the week. Service is friendly but
don't be surprised if things slow down as the place fills up.

A Cena

Italian   R2

Twickenham

418 Richmond Rd. ⊠ TW1 2EB

☎ 020 8288 0108

www.acena.co.uk

⊖ Richmond

Closed 2 weeks August,
Sunday dinner, Monday lunch and
bank holidays

Menu £10 (weekday lunch) – Carte £21/40

A/C The constantly evolving menu at this bigger-than-you-first-think
Italian restaurant, just over Richmond Bridge, covers all parts
of the country, although you can expect more of a nod to the
north in the colder months when dishes become a little heartier.
The cooking is fresh and tasty; pasta is most certainly a highlight
and desserts, although limited in choice, are usually done well
too. The front section of the restaurant can feel a little cramped
and it's at the back where it all seems to be happening. The
owners are not actually Italian but his mother is and she clearly
exerted quite an influence because his passion and enthusiasm
are obvious. They also own a nearby foodstore and butcher's.

Crown

Traditional British   R3

Twickenham   Closed 26 December

174 Richmond Rd, St Margarets ⊠ TW1 2NH

☎ 020 8892 5896

www.crowntwickenham.co.uk

⊖ St Margarets (Rail).

Carte £21/40

Much to the delight of St Margarets residents, this fine-looking
Georgian pub has been revived and revitalised. Setting the scene
are an old lantern hanging above the entrance and a mosaic
floor inlaid with the pub's name, while inside it feels relaxed
and stylish, with parquet floors, feature fireplaces and bright
colours; sit in the airy, elegant rear restaurant, with its high
vaulted ceiling and garden view. There's something for everyone
on the global menus, from sharing boards and classic pub dishes
to Mediterranean-influenced fish stew or Asian-inspired Tom
Yum Thai prawns and squid. Portions are ample and cooking
fresh, tasty and reliable. Service is enthusiastic and the pretty
beer garden is popular with drinkers and diners alike.

Chez Bruce ✿

French

Wandsworth

2 Bellevue Rd ✉ SW17 7EG
✆ 020 8672 0114
www.chezbruce.co.uk
⊖ Tooting Bec

Closed 24-26 December and
1 January – booking essential

Menu £30/50

✗✗

Chez Bruce

Chez Bruce has had a successful formula for many years and epitomises all that is wonderful about neighbourhood restaurants, even having to extend into the adjacent deli a few years back in order to satisfy the demand for a table. What keeps customers keen is its flavoursome and uncomplicated food, its sensible prices; the sprightly service from a charming team and the buzzing yet easy-going atmosphere. Matthew Christmas is the head man in the kitchen, having worked closely with owner Bruce Poole for many years. His cooking provides an object lesson in the importance of flavours and balance: dishes are assured, the plate is never too crowded and natural flavours are to the fore. The base is largely classical French but comes with Mediterranean tones, so expect to find words like parfait, pastilla, brandade and confit on the menu, which lists around seven dishes per course. The wine list is a work of art; the cheese trolley is always worth exploring and coffee comes with shortbread at lunch and terrific palmiers at dinner.

First Course	Main Course	Dessert
• Fishcake with moules marinière, poached egg and sprouting broccoli.	• Rump of veal with leek & bacon sausage, gnocchi, wild garlic and thyme.	• Cherry jelly with chocolate mousse and pistachio madeleine.
• Foie gras and chicken liver parfait with toasted brioche.	• Roast cod with olive oil mash, Provençal tomato and gremolata.	• Apricot and pistachio sablé Breton with apricot kernel ice cream.

Light House

Mediterranean cuisine   **T3**

Wimbledon

75-77 Ridgway ✉ SW19 4ST

℘ 020 8944 6338

www.lighthousewimbledon.com

⊖ Wimbledon

Closed 25-26 December,
1 January and Sunday dinner

Menu £16/25 – Carte £27/41   ✗

♿
A/C
A neighbourhood favourite, the Light House offers Mediterranean cooking in smart, comfortable surroundings, with a light and spacious feel. While they do offer the occasional Thai dish, it is in Italy where the majority of the menu and the kitchen's strengths lie, with a roll-call of favourites that include tagliatelle, gnocchi, saltimbocca and panna cotta. The food is wholesome and confident, with plenty of bold flavours; puddings are a highlight and prices at lunch and in the early evening are attractive, which ensures that it is often very busy. The result is that the young team can sometimes struggle to keep up, but they remain admirably calm and cheery. As this was once a shop selling lights and fittings, it is fittingly well lit.

Light on the Common

Traditional British   **T3**

Wimbledon

48 High St ✉ SW19 5AX

℘ 020 8946 3031

www.lightwimbledon.co.uk

⊖ Wimbledon

Closed 25 December
and Sunday dinner

Menu £23 (weekday dinner) – Carte £24/40   ✗

One of the signs of success for a neighbourhood restaurant is when it's used by regulars throughout the day; this sister to Light House is a case in point, with locals popping in for a coffee or a snack as often as booking a table for a three course meal. Things kick off at breakfast with an extensive menu offering everything from bircher muesli or pancakes to salt beef hash or a full English. Lunch sees an equally wide choice, with starters, salads and sandwiches available alongside dishes like fish pie or a rare breed burger; dinner broadens things further, and the set dinner menu, available Monday–Thursday, offers great value for money. Add in friendly staff and a bright, modern backdrop and you can see why it's a hit.

Takahashi

Japanese T3

Wimbledon

228 Merton Rd ⊠ SW19 1EQ
✆ 020 8540 3041
www.takahashi-restaurant.co.uk
⊖ South Wimbledon

Closed Monday and Tuesday
– booking essential – (dinner only
and lunch Saturday-Sunday)

South-West ▶ Plan XVIII

Menu £22/37 – Carte £19/60 ✗

A/C

Eponymous chef-owner Nobuhisa Takahashi spent 14 years at Nobu in Tokyo, London and Capetown and his experience is plain to see in dishes like black cod miso and salmon carpaccio with yuzu salsa. This sweet, unadorned spot is far from a Nobu facsimile, however, and the judicious use of Mediterranean ingredients and its 'tapas' menu sections show that this is a broad-minded kitchen with a creative bent. Dishes offer up pure, delicate flavours; the sushi and sashimi are a must, as are signature dishes Portobello mushroom ajillo and crispy pork belly with aubergine miso. Taka's charming wife Yuko runs the service with a very personal touch. If you are not sure what to order then ask her advice – or go for one of the two tasting menus.

 # White Onion

Modern cuisine T3

Wimbledon

67 High St ⊠ SW19 5EE
✆ 020 8947 8278
www.thewhiteonion.co.uk
⊖ Wimbledon

Closed first 2 weeks August,
25 December-5 January, Monday,
lunch Tuesday-Wednesday and
Sunday dinner

Menu £20 (lunch) – Carte £29/48 ✗

♿ A/C

The relaxed atmosphere that exists within the deep blue walls of this bistro deluxe makes it incredibly easy to feel at home here – this is the sort of restaurant every high street could do with having. There's a handsome marble-topped bar at the entrance, modern artwork hanging on the walls and a young serving team who are attentive and professional without undue pomp. Everything from the bread to the ice cream is homemade and the flavoursome French cooking has a classical base and clever modern touches. Don't miss the terrine of ox cheek and ham hock or the monkfish rolled in crispy potatoes. The set lunch menu offers great value for money and the wine list is carefully chosen, with a terrific selection by the glass and carafe.

Where to **stay**

▶ These 50 recommended hotels are extracted from the Great Britain & Ireland 2017 guide, where you'll find a larger choice of hotels selected by our team of inspectors.

Artist Residence

H6

52 Cambridge St ✉ SW1V 4QQ
✆ 020 7931 8946
www.artistresidencelondon.co.uk
⊖ Victoria

10 rm – †£190/230 ††£210/450, ☕ £10

A/C

Artist Residence

Victoria and Pimlico have always been something of a wilderness when it comes to good restaurants. They may not be entirely bereft but considering the diverse population who work and live in these areas, they should offer much more choice and variety. This looks set to change in the next few years with a plethora of openings planned and once the areas become better known and more fun, there will hopefully be a knock-on effect with the arrival of more interesting local accommodation on offer. One hotel that got in early is this converted pub in a street of attractive Regency houses. It's a handsome place whose very name is a clue that it offers something a little different. There are certainly enough quirky little design touches, like reclaimed furniture, old Bakelite phones, mini Smeg fridges and Pop Art for you to feel you're a world away from one of those bland, corporate-owned monoliths. Transport links make it a good base from which to explore London and the staff are a helpful, pleasant bunch.

Batty Langley's

12 Folgate St ⊠ E1 6BX
☏ 020 7377 4390
www.battylangleys.com
⊖ Liverpool Street

29 rm – ♦£195/280 ♦♦£280/1,000,⌑ £12 – 1 suite

Batty Langley's

It looks like an 18C townhouse – and indeed one did once stand on this site – but in fact all has been rebuilt, even the façade. Those who know the owners' other properties, Hazlitt's and The Rookery, will be aware of the astonishing care and attention they undertake to ensure the period details are just so, and this hotel is no exception. It's named after an early 18C writer of handbooks on gardens and architecture and the hotel's impressive reception area with its antique furniture sets the tone. There is no restaurant – breakfast is served in the bedrooms – but there are three small, intimate guest areas – the Library, Parlour and the Tapestry Room, with the latter leading out onto a delightful courtyard terrace. The bedrooms are even more impressive: each one is named and individually themed; there are clever touches and appealing little quirks, with fireplaces, antiques and flowing drapes adding to the period charm. The bathrooms are equally delightful and not just for students of antique plumbing apparatus.

The Beaumont

G3

Brown Hart Gdns ⊠ W1K 6TF
☎ 020 7499 1001
www.thebeaumont.com
⊖ Bond Street
✶ **Colony Grill Room** *(See restaurant listing)*

73 rm☲ – **♦£435/585 ♦♦£435/585 – 10 suites**

The Beaumont

Chris Corbin and Jeremy King don't just excel at restaurants; their first hotel, The Beaumont, quickly established itself as one of London's most stylish addresses. It occupies a 1926 former garage which serviced the cars belonging to customers of nearby Selfridges. To create the striking look inside, they created a fictional character called Jimmy Beaumont, who had supposedly come over from New York to create an art deco hotel. In anyone else's hands this pre-war look could have been mere parody or pastiche but such is the style and attention to detail here that it works magnificently. From the chestnut panelling in the lobby to the lavish marble bathrooms, the hotel exudes understated luxury. The art deco theme continues with the undeniably masculine bedrooms – although there are many on the smaller side. The most exclusive is the ROOM which was created by Antony Gormley and is entombed within the vast, cubistic steel figure that emerges from the façade. Just come for cocktails in the American bar or oysters in the Colony Grill Room and you'll soon see what all the fuss is about.

Berkeley

Wilton Pl ⊠ SW1X 7RL
𝒞 020 7235 6000
www.the-berkeley.co.uk
⊖ Knightsbridge
⚞ **Marcus** *(See restaurant listing)*

210 rm – ♦£540/750 ♦♦£600/870,⊇ £32 – 28 suites

The Berkeley

This discreet, comfortable hotel is perhaps best known for Marcus Wareing's luxury restaurant; it also hosts the wonderful Blue Bar – a cocktail bar which is as cool as its name suggests – and the Collins Room whose target audience is obvious when you consider that tea is called "Prêt-à-Portea" and the biscuits look like mini handbags. By using a number of different designers, bedrooms have been given both personality and a sense of individualism; the most recent have softer, calmer colours and a lighter, more contemporary feel, while the classic rooms feel richer thanks to their deeper, more intense colours. All the rooms are immaculately kept and several of the suites have their own balcony; if you want a quiet room then ask for one overlooking the church. The most unique area of the hotel must be the 7th floor, with its rooftop pool, treatment rooms and personal training services to satisfy the most slavishly health-conscious traveller. Staff levels are high and the standard of service is second to none.

Blakes

33 Rowland Gdns ⊠ SW7 3PF
℘ 020 7370 6701
www.blakeshotels.com
⊖ Gloucester Road

45 rm – †£220/270 ††£330/600,⊊ £16 – 8 suites

Blakes

Created by Anouska Hempel in the early '80s, this black-painted townhouse was one of London's original, design-led 'boutique' hotels. It was exuberantly decorated then and remains so now; it has had considerable funds invested in its upgrade and upkeep and represents the perfect antidote to the plethora of generic corporate hotels that seemingly pop up overnight. The lavish decoration, the dramatic four-poster beds and the rich fabrics remind you that staying in a hotel can be a thrilling, erotic and sensual experience – this isn't the sort of hotel for those who get excited by the sight of a trouser-press and a miniature kettle. That being said, the mod cons are all here, but they're camouflaged and concealed. For the ultimate in glamour, go for one of the Signature Suites like the opulent Cardinal Suite: an atmospheric love palace decorated in deep shades of red and gold. On the ground floor you'll find a spacious restaurant serving modern Mediterranean dishes – and there is also a charming courtyard at the back, perfect for hiding out.

Brown's

33 Albemarle St ✉ W1S 4BP
✆ 020 7493 6020
www.roccofortehotels.com
⊖ Green Park
☆ **Hix Mayfair** *(See restaurant listing)*

117 rm – ♦£420/905 ♦♦£420/950, ⌑ **£35** – **28 suites**

Brown's

The Union Flag flutters outside many a London hotel but few can boast of being such a bastion of Britishness as Brown's. The hotel was opened by James Brown, Lord Byron's butler, in 1837 and its illustrious history really sets it apart: it was here, for example, where Alexander Graham Bell first demonstrated his telephone and The Kipling Suite is just one of many named after a former guest. Now under the stewardship of the Rocco Forte group, the hotel manages to marry British tradition with modern comforts and expectations. Afternoon tea in its wood panelled drawing room is perhaps its most famous feature – the selling point, apart from the pianist, is that your waiter replenishes everything without any extra charge. The Donovan Bar is another of the hotel's great strengths, with its striking collection of black and white photos both by, and of, the great photographer. Bedrooms have an appealing, uncluttered feel and the restaurant, Hix Mayfair, is a fairly formal affair with comfort food and British classics to the fore.

Bulgari

171 Knightsbridge ⊠ SW7 1DW
☎ 020 7151 1010
www.bulgarihotels.com/london
⊖ Knightsbridge
⚘ **Rivea** *(See restaurant listing)*

85 rm – †£560/790 ††£560/790,⚏ £34 – 23 suites

Bulgari

Having wowed them in Milan, Bulgari waited until they'd found the perfect location before creating this London jewel. This is a hotel that shouts style, with silver its underlying theme in homage to the brand's silversmith origins. Actually, it is so cool, so impeccably tailored, it wouldn't possibly be caught shouting anything. The dark lobby, with its camouflaged staff, sets the tone of restrained elegance and leads into the sleek bar. From there it is down a sweeping staircase to the Alain Ducasse restaurant, where the Italian and French small plates are bursting with colour and freshness. The hotel is on 15 floors but six of those are underground and used for a state-of-the-art spa, a ballroom and a terrific cinema. The bedrooms are stunning and all about sensual curves, polished mahogany, silks and black marble; the bathrooms are worth the price of admission alone and there are some delightful touches, such as minibars hidden within upright trunks. Unlike other fashion-led hotels, there is real substance behind the style here and an emphasis on comfort.

Café Royal

68 Regent St ✉ W1B 4DY
☎ 020 7406 3333
www.hotelcaferoyal.com
⊖ Piccadilly Circus

160 rm – †£330/500 ††£330/600,☕ £32 – 16 suites

Café Royal

No history of London's social scene through the last 150 years would be complete without a chapter or two dedicated to Café Royal – this famous landmark has hosted everyone from royalty to rascals. Its metamorphosis into a hotel came about with the acquisition of the two adjoining buildings and, while the entrance is on Air St, you really need to walk in on Regent Street to experience the grandeur and feel the history. The wining and dining options are many and varied and include Ten Room, a brasserie with an appealing menu of favourites; the Oscar Wilde Bar, a fine rococo room which was once the iconic Grill Room but now hosts afternoon tea and evening cabaret, and the Domino Room, their smart first floor restaurant with a contemporary menu and its own kitchen. The bedrooms mix the classic with the modern and are beautiful, elegant, understated and all about comfort. The top rooms come with butler service and membership of the Café Royal Club, but all rooms boast an impressive level of service.

The Capital

Chelsea ▲ Plan XI

F5

22-24 Basil St. ⊠ SW3 1AT
✆ 020 7589 5171
www.capitalhotel.co.uk
⊖ Knightsbridge
🕱 **Outlaw's at The Capital** *(See restaurant listing)*

49 rm – †£250/355 ††£295/550,⬭ £17 – 1 suite

The Capital

The Capital is one of London's most enduringly discreet and comfortable hotels and is thoroughly British in its feel. It is owned by David Levin, who opened it in 1971, and it is this continuity which has led to the number of head chefs it has had in over 45 years remaining in single figures. The restaurant is as elegant as ever, with a menu filled with classic British dishes and an extensive wine list that includes selections from the Levins' own winery in the Loire. Bedrooms remain classically chic and the contemporary embellishments are restrained and in keeping with the general atmosphere. Each floor is slightly different and uses designs from the likes of Mulberry, Ralph Lauren and Nina Campbell. What has always raised The Capital to greater heights than similarly styled hotels has been the depth and detail of the service. No one can walk through the small lobby without being greeted and the concierge is old-school in the best sense of the word and can arrange anything for anyone.

15 Charlotte St ✉ W1T 1RJ
☎ 020 7806 2000
www.charlottestreethotel.co.uk
⊖ Goodge Street

52 rm – †£225/470 ††£225/470,☲ £15 – 4 suites

Firmdale

Expect the lobby and bar to be full of men with man-bags and horn-rimmed specs, for Charlotte Street is the hotel of choice for those in the advertising industry. But even if you've never pitched, promoted or placed a product and are just after a stylish, contemporary hotel in a street thronged with bars and restaurants then get on the mailing list here. Oscar is the busy bar and restaurant that spills out onto the street in summer; its sunny, contemporary European menu and vivid mural brighten it in winter. Film Club is on Sunday evening: dinner followed by a film in the downstairs screening room. Those after some quiet can nab one of the sofas in the Drawing Room or Library. The bedrooms are, as with all hotels in the Firmdale group, exceptionally well looked after. Every year, three or four are fully refurbished and one thing you'll never see is a bit of dodgy grouting or a scuff mark. They are all decorated in an English style but there is nothing chintzy or twee about them. Bathrooms are equally immaculate and the baths face little flat screen TVs.

Chiltern Firehouse

1 Chiltern St ✉ W1U 7PA
☎ 020 7073 7676
www.chilternfirehouse.com
⊖ Baker Street
⚘ **Chiltern Firehouse** *(See restaurant listing)*

26 rm – ♦£495/1,020 ♦♦£495/1,020,☟ £25 – 16 suites

⚘
⚔
⬍
♿
A/C

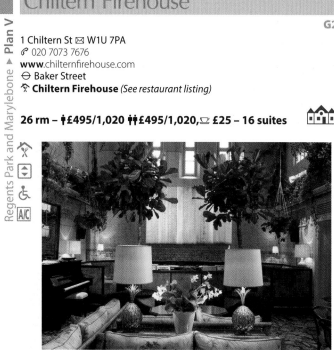

Chiltern Firehouse

Anyone familiar with André Balazs' portfolio of properties will know that where he goes, the celebrity world follows. From Chateau Marmont in Hollywood to The Mercer in New York, his group of hotels are so effortlessly cool that they exist beyond the mere vicissitudes of fashion. For his grand London entrance, he took a Gothic Victorian fire station in Marylebone and sympathetically restored and extended it. Compared with the frenzy that is the Chiltern Firehouse restaurant, this is a veritable sanctuary of calm and tranquility. From the snug sitting room to the handsome cocktail bar, the style is accompanied by an easy elegance and the real joy of the place is that it hardly feels like a hotel at all. The 26 rooms are a striking mix of modern and art deco forms, in a mix of colours and styles – there is no uniformity to be found anywhere in this building. Even the staff are chosen for the care they will give, rather than for the experience they have garnered.

Claridge's

Brook St ✉ W1K 4HR
☎ 020 7629 8860
www.claridges.co.uk
⊖ Bond Street
☆ **Fera at Claridge's** (See restaurant listing)

197 rm – ♦£480/1,140 ♦♦£480/1,140,⌍ £34 – 62 suites

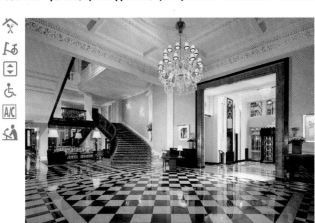

Claridge's

Claridge's has a long and very illustrious history dating back to
1812 and this iconic and very British hotel has been a favourite
of the royal family over generations. The hotel has kept its
place at the top table of London addresses by recognising that
reputations are forged because of the quality of the service rather
than mere longevity or striking architecture. That being said,
no modern, purpose-built hotel could afford the extravagance
of having such wide corridors, such ornate decoration or such
sumptuous bedrooms. The hotel is known for its striking art
deco design features, which are kept suitably fresh and buffed.
Despite its glittery past, Claridge's has never been in danger
of becoming a museum piece: the David Collins designed bar
attracts a fairly youthful crowd while the Fumois has a glamorous
and more intimate feel; The Foyer, with its eye-catching light
sculpture, proves that afternoon tea need not be a stuffy or
quaint affair; and Fera, the restaurant under the aegis of chef
Simon Rogan, has proved an excellent fit.

Connaught

G3

Carlos Pl. ✉ W1K 2AL
☏ 020 7499 7070
www.the-connaught.co.uk
⊖ Bond Street
♗ **Hélène Darroze at The Connaught** *(See restaurant listing)*

121 rm – †£540/990 ††£630/1,110 – 25 suites

The Connaught

The restored, refurbished and rejuvenated Connaught still retains a sense of effortless serenity and exclusivity – but has now been discovered by a new generation. These sprightlier guests should take the stairs up to their room, that way they'll see the largest mahogany staircase in the country. The bedrooms are now more contemporary in style; they have wooden floors, leather worked into the soft furnishings and come with larger marble bathrooms; some overlook a small oriental garden, others peer down on mews houses. All rooms have full butler service and use linen specially woven in Milan and toiletries from Daylesford. The Coburg Bar honours the hotel's original name and its seats are so deep it's a wonder anyone ever leaves. In contrast, the Connaught Bar attracts a more youthful clientele. Hélène Darroze oversees the restaurant with her refined French cooking and Espelette is an all-day venue just off the lobby that offers a weekly changing list of classic French and British dishes. If you need anything, just ask one of the hotel's 300 members of staff.

Covent Garden

I3

Bloomsbury ▶ **Plan VI**

10 Monmouth St ⊠ WC2H 9HB
✆ 020 7806 1000
www.firmdalehotels.com
⊖ Covent Garden

59 rm – †£230/300 ††£300/370, ☕ £20

Firmdale

The Covent Garden Hotel has always been hugely popular with
those of a theatrical bent, whether cast or audience member, not
least because of its central location, a mere saunter away from
the majority of playhouses and productions. The hotel was once
a French hospital – the words 'Nouvel hopital et dispensaire
francais' are still etched into the brickwork – but the style is
essentially British. Mannequins, soft fabrics and antique furniture
are juxtaposed with crisp lines and contemporary colours to
create a very stylish and comfortable environment. The first floor
residents only wood-panelled sitting room is a delight and so
is occasionally used by a visiting grandee for a backdrop to an
interview; the presence of an honesty bar adds further to the
appeal. The Screening Room holds weekend dinner-and-a-
film nights, while Brasserie Max feels much more like a proper
restaurant than a mere addendum; its menu is appealingly
accessible and afternoon tea is a popular event.

Dorchester

G4

Mayfair ▶ Plan II

Park Ln ✉ W1K 1QA
℘ 020 7629 8888
www.dorchestercollection.com
⊖ Hyde Park Corner
↑ **Alain Ducasse at The Dorchester and The Grill and China Tang**
(See restaurant listing)

250 rm – ♦£325/925 ♦♦£355/995,⊆ £35 – 51 suites

The Dorchester

A byword for luxury and elegance since it opened in the 1930s, The Dorchester is one of the capital's iconic properties, with constant reinvestment ensuring that this grandest of hotels remains one of London's finest. The Promenade takes centre stage and is the first port of call for many; the ever-popular afternoon tea can be enjoyed in its gilded surroundings or on the balcony overlooking the lobby. If you're here to dine you have the choice of three restaurants: the re-launched Grill is for all things British; the luxuriously adorned Alain Ducasse restaurant, with its exceptional cuisine, waves Le Tricolore, while downstairs China Tang celebrates the cuisine of the Orient. Bedrooms are elegant and eminently comfortable, with marble-decked bathrooms and all the facilities one would expect from a top class hotel. The six signature suites are the ultimate in luxury and the park-facing bedrooms must be some of the most sought after real estate in the capital. But comfort is nothing without service – and standards here remain impeccable.

Dukes

35 St James's Pl. ✉ SW1A 1NY
📞 020 7491 4840
www.dukeshotel.com
⊖ Green Park

90 rm – ♦£346/440 ♦♦£400/490,☕ £24 – 6 suites

Dukes

Every hotel needs a little reinvention now and again and Dukes has been steadily changing its image over the last few years. It has enjoyed a constant presence in St James's for over a century and traditionally had a clubby, very British feel but this has given way to a brighter, fresher look which seems to suit it equally well. What hasn't been lost is the discreet atmosphere which is largely down to the very central, yet surprisingly quiet, location. The basement restaurant, which looks out at street level thanks to the vagaries of local topography, now offers an ambitious, modern menu with dishes that are original in look and elaborate in construction. The comfortable sitting rooms still do a brisk trade in afternoon tea but there is now also an outside cigar lounge. The bar is a London landmark and was reputedly one of Ian Fleming's old haunts - martinis are a speciality. Bedrooms are devoid of chintz and come in warm, calming colours; they have smart marble bathrooms and are decently proportioned.

Egerton House

17-19 Egerton Terr ⊠ SW3 2BX
☎ 020 7589 2412
www.egertonhousehotel.com
⊖ South Kensington

28 rm – ♦**£295/425** ♦♦**£295/425**, ☕ **£29**

Egerton House

In challenging economic times hotels can either panic and cut staff and rates – a course of action which usually ends in ruin – or they can hold their nerve and provide greater value for their guests. Anyone wondering what more a hotel can do should get along to Egerton House. This is a townhouse whose decorative style is at the lavish end of the scale; the fabrics are of the highest order and the colours neatly coordinated. The ground floor Victoria and Albert Suite comes with its own little decked terrace and a row of filled decanters for company. All the rooms are slightly different; the marble bathrooms are very neat and the hotel has made the best use of limited space – ask for one of the quieter rooms at the back overlooking the little garden. What really makes this little place stand out, though, is the service and the eager attitude of the staff. Lots of hotels spout tosh about being 'a home from home' but here they do make a genuine effort to make their guests feel part of things by, for example, arranging complimentary admission to events at the V&A.

Four Seasons

Hamilton Pl, Park Ln ⊠ W1J 7DR
℡ 020 7499 0888
www.fourseasons.com/london
⊖ Hyde Park Corner
⚘ **Amaranto** *(See restaurant listing)*

193 rm – ♦£330/630 ♦♦£330/630,⊽ £30 – 33 suites

Four Seasons

These days competition is pretty fierce at the luxury end of the hotel market so, to stay ahead of the game, contenders need to do more than just tinker with the cosmetics. The Four Seasons, which was the group's first hotel outside the US, closed for a couple of years and in that time was stripped right back, before being put together again. The result is that Park Lane now has a hotel that's really raised the bar in the comfort stakes. The bedrooms, trimmed with plenty of walnut, sycamore, marble and shiny steel, are particularly striking and come with all the latest wizardry like self-regulating ambient heating. They also occupy impressive square footage, as do the suites, the number of which has been greatly increased. Dining is a flexible feast – Amaranto is divided into a three areas: a bar, restaurant and lounge and you can eat what you want, where you want it, and that includes on the secluded outdoor terrace. The stunning top-floor spa, with its fantastic views, caps off this hotel's dazzling renaissance.

45 Park Lane

Mayfair ▶ Plan II

G4

45 Park Ln ✉ W1K 1PN
℘ 020 7493 4545
www.45parklane.com
⊖ Hyde Park Corner
✗ **Cut** *(See restaurant listing)*

46 rm – †£495/695 ††£495/695, ☕ £21 – 10 suites

45 Park Lane

It was the original site of the Playboy Club and has also been a car showroom but now 45 Park Lane has been reborn as The Dorchester's little sister and, lit up at night, her art deco façade makes her look rather cute. The style is certainly different from her famous sibling but the quality and depth of service come from the same top drawer. On each floor you'll find the work of a different contemporary British artist as well as a couple of hosts to take care of everything from unpacking your bags to booking you a restaurant. The bedrooms, which all have views over Hyde Park, are wonderfully sensual, with velvet walls, leather-wrapped doors and warm, heavy fabrics and the marble bathrooms are beautiful. Suites take up great positions on the corners of the building and have the best views, while the penthouse occupies the entire top floor. The red leather makes the cocktail bar on the mezzanine level a very sexy spot, while on the ground floor sits Wolfgang Puck's glamorous restaurant, Cut, which specialises in steaks.

Goring

15 Beeston Pl ⊠ SW1W 0JW
☏ 020 7396 9000
www.thegoring.com
⊖ Victoria
☆ **Dining Room at The Goring** *(See restaurant listing)*

69 rm⌂ – ♦£335/615 ♦♦£380/710 – 8 suites

The Goring

In 2015, for the first time in over 100 years, The Goring actually closed its doors for a few weeks. Fortunately this was only done so that the finishing touches to the lobby restoration could be completed, the last piece in the jigsaw of the hotel's renovation programme. What was so clever about all the work undertaken was that it brought the hotel up-to-date while respecting its traditions, atmosphere and pervading sense of Britishness. The hotel is under the stewardship of the great grandson of the founder but it has never traded on former glories. Instead it has constantly updated and reinvented itself by recognising the myriad differing needs of the modern traveller. The bedrooms are all about comfort thanks to the wonderful fabrics and handmade furniture – but all the mod cons are there if you look closely. The lounge is a popular place for place for drinks, snacks and afternoon tea and opens onto the Veranda overlooking a surprisingly large enclosed garden. The Dining Room is warm and welcoming and continues the theme of updated tradition.

Halkin

5 Halkin St ⊠ SW1X 7DJ
☏ 020 7333 1000
www.comohotels.com/thehalkin
⊖ Hyde Park Corner
⚡ **Ametsa** *(See restaurant listing)*

41 rm – ♦£300/420 ♦♦£400/500,☕ £30 – 6 suites

Halkin

There may be glossier and glitzier hotels around these days but there aren't many that can be considered quite as dapper as The Halkin. When it opened back in the early '90s, its boutique style and modern design were considered quite ground-breaking as the majority of London hotels at that time were still exhibiting a feverish devotion to all things chintz. In the intervening years the hotel has retained its reputation as a preferred London address of those who like a little comfort and calmness to go with the cool. The hotel is big enough to provide all the desired services yet small enough to feel familiar. The bedrooms have an enduring quality and hide their technology well – touchscreen panels control everything from the curtains to the temperature; those rooms overlooking the garden at the back are particularly quiet. The Armani-clad staff glide around the place with calm assurance and know all their regulars well, while Ametsa, with its modern Spanish food, is the latest in a long line of impressive restaurants to grace the ground floor.

Ham Yard

1 Ham Yard, ✉ W1D 7DT
📞 020 3642 2000
www.firmdalehotels.com
⊖ Piccadilly Circus
🍴 **Ham Yard** *(See restaurant listing)*

91 rm – ♦£260/380 ♦♦£260/380,☺ £14 – 2 suites

Ham Yard

Ham Yard is the thoroughfare that links Denman and Archer streets and having lain empty for years is now home to this stylish hotel from the Firmdale group. The U-shaped building is set around a tree-lined courtyard which is a little haven of tranquillity bang in the middle of the West End. Unsurprisingly, the hotel itself is very pleasing on the eye and, with decorative influences ranging from Africa to India, there's a talking point at every turn. Each of the very luxurious and generously proportioned bedrooms is different – one can be lime green, the next bright red – but the best ones are those with floor to ceiling windows overlooking the courtyard. That said, you can't go wrong with any of the rooms – the emphasis here is very much on comfort. Along with a large restaurant is a basement 'Dive Bar', a terrific rooftop terrace with a little vegetable garden, a 190-seater theatre and even a four-lane bowling alley; the fully stocked library and drawing room is for the exclusive use of hotel residents.

1 Suffolk Pl. ✉ SW1Y 4HX
☎ 020 7470 4000
www.haymarkethotel.com
⊖ Piccadilly Circus
🍴 **Brumus** *(See restaurant listing)*

50 rm – ♛£230/320 ♛♛£230/1,395,☕ £15 – 3 suites

Firmdale

Created out of one of the finest examples of a John Nash building and next to his celebrated Haymarket Theatre Royal is this elegant hotel from the Firmdale group. The contemporary interior provides a striking contrast to the traditional Regency façade and is its most arresting feature. It was a gentleman's club for a while – a Shooting Gallery once used by chaps checking their aim is now a private dining room – but there is certainly nothing fuddy or even duddy about the place these days. An eclectic collection of artwork and furniture runs throughout and the bedrooms are spacious, designed with an eye for detail and decorated with a contemporary palette – they are also very well soundproofed but ask for one overlooking the inner courtyard if you're a light sleeper. Brumus manages the trick of feeling like an independent restaurant rather than a hotel dining room and does a roaring trade pre- and post-theatre. The huge pool and bar in the basement doubles as a great party venue.

Hazlitt's

6 Frith St ✉ W1D 3JA
✆ 020 7434 1771
www.hazlittshotel.com
⊖ Tottenham Court Road

30 rm – ♦£210/235 ♦♦£300/650,⌣ £12

Hazlitt's

Dating from 1718, the former house of essayist and critic William Hazlitt still welcomes many a writer today in its role as a charming townhouse hotel. It is bursting with character, from the wood panelling and busts to the antique beds and Georgian fixtures, and all the mod cons have been carefully secreted to retain the period look. Duke of Monmouth is the most striking room: it's spread over two floors and has its own terrace with a retractable roof. Madam Dafloz, named after another of Soho's roguish former residents, is also appealing, with its sultry, indulgent feel. Many hotels have a bar called The Library but this one actually contains books; it also has an honesty bar and is a popular place for an evening drink. There is a charming little sitting room; the staff are delightful; and the location, in the heart of Soho, is hard to beat. As there is no restaurant this is one of the few hotels where breakfast in bed really is the only option – and who is going to object to that?

K + K George

1-15 Templeton Pl ⊠ SW5 9NB
℡ 020 7598 8700
www.kkhotels.com
⊖ Earl's Court

154 rm – ∗£119/330 ∗∗£119/350, ⊊ £18

K&K Hotels

There's more to this hotel than meets the eye: it occupies seven houses of an eye-catching, stucco-fronted terrace yet, in contrast to its period façade, its interior is stylish, colourful and contemporary. It is set on one of the quieter residential streets in Earl's Court but is still close to the Tube, and although it is part of an international chain, its style is very much in keeping with the local area. Perhaps its most surprising feature is its large, well-kept rear garden where you can enjoy breakfast on the terrace in the summer – sitting here it's hard to believe that you're in one of the busiest areas of London. Other places in which to dine include a comfortable bar/lounge and a spacious restaurant that serves a wide-ranging menu. Like the rest of the hotel, bedrooms are smart, warm and modern with up-to-date facilities including full minibars and underfloor heating in the bathrooms; rooms facing the rear have the garden outlook. Staff are welcoming, professional and eager to please.

Knightsbridge

10 Beaufort Gdns ✉ SW3 1PT
☎ 020 7584 6300
www.knightsbridgehotel.com
⊖ Knightsbridge

44 rm – †£215/275 ††£235/445,⬄ £14

Firmdale

Firmdale Hotels all seem so quintessentially British and The Knightsbridge, converted from a row of Victorian terraced houses in an attractive square, is another typical example of what they do so well: it proves style and comfort are not mutually exclusive and that a hotel can be fashionable without being fuzzy. The work of British artists, such as Carol Sinclair's slate stack and Peter Clark's dog collages, sets the tone and the bedrooms are constantly being refreshed and rearranged. Those facing the square on the first floor benefit from floor to ceiling windows, while the Knightsbridge Suite stretches from the front to the back of the building. All rooms are so impeccably tidy and colour coordinated it'll make you question your own dress sense. The Library Room differs from many similarly named hotel sitting rooms by actually containing books, along with an honesty bar which holds everything from fruit and snacks to champagne and ice cream.

Langham

1c Portland Pl, Regent St ✉ W1B 1JA
📞 020 7636 1000
www.langhamhotels.com
⊖ Oxford Circus
🍴 **Roux at The Landau** *(See restaurant listing)*

380 rm – ♦£360/960 ♦♦£360/960, ⬜ £32 – 24 suites

Langham

The Langham was one of Europe's first purpose-built grand hotels when it opened in 1865. Since then it has been owned by all sorts, including at one stage the BBC – they used it as their library and it was where 'The Goon Show' was recorded. A few years ago, it emerged from an extensive refurbishment programme that didn't provide much change from £80 million and has been competing with the big boys ever since. Pride of place must be the Palm Court, a twinkling ersatz art deco space, which serves light meals and afternoon teas. The Artesian bar is a stylish affair and does interesting things with gin; there's a small courtyard terrace named in honour of a BBC radio gardener; and the striking restaurant is under the aegis of the Roux organisation. The bedrooms have personality and, for a change, the furniture is free-standing rather than fitted; the boldly decorated Club rooms are particularly distinctive. The health and fitness club is impressively kitted out and includes a swimming pool in what was once a bank vault.

Hyde Park Corner ✉ SW1X 7TA
✆ 020 7259 5599
www.lanesborough.com
⊖ Hyde Park Corner
🍴 **Céleste** *(See restaurant listing)*

93 rm – ♦£500/740 ♦♦£500/740,☕ £38 – 30 suites

The Lanesborough

A multi-million pound refurbishment and a change of management have catapulted The Lanesborough back up into the top tier of London hotels, its Regency splendour now rightfully restored. The top-to-toe transformation was overseen by the late Alberto Pinto and shows remarkable attention to detail, from the sumptuous Withdrawing Room and the luxurious Library Bar with its vast selection of cognacs, to opulent restaurant, Céleste, which serves rich French cooking under a domed glass roof. Four floors of bedrooms are dressed in an elegant Georgian style, with bespoke furniture, hand-stencilled wooden panels, beautiful fabrics and marble bathrooms; while 21st century technologies offer tablet control of temperature and lighting, and enable you to call the 24 hour butler, who will attend to your every whim. Rooms are triple-glazed to ensure your night's sleep is a peaceful one; ask for a room facing Hyde Park and, though you may not be able to hear much of the outside world, you can enjoy some pretty terrific views.

The Levin

28 Basil St. ✉ SW3 1AS
☎ 020 7589 6286
www.thelevinhotel.co.uk
⊖ Knightsbridge

12 rm 🛏 – **♦£248/382 ♦♦£255/389**

The Levin

Its bigger sister, The Capital, is a few strides down the road and may be better known, but The Levin still does the (Levin) family proud. Here you'll find a different decorative style but still the same level of care and enthusiasm in the service. The eye-catching fibre optic chandelier dominates the staircase, while the collection of Penguin paperbacks reminds you that this is a fundamentally British hotel. All 12 bedrooms are light and fresh-feeling; there are subtle nods in the direction of art deco in the styling but these are combined with a cleverly contemporary look which blends in well with the building. The best room is the top floor open-plan suite. Mini-bars are stocked exclusively with champagne - along with some helpful hints on how to prepare an assortment of champagne cocktails. In the basement you'll find Le Metro which provides an appealing, all-day menu with everything from quiche and salads to shepherd's pie and sausage and mash, along with selections from the family estate in the Loire.

Mandarin Oriental Hyde Park

F4

66 Knightsbridge ✉ SW1X 7LA
☎ 020 7235 2000
www.mandarinoriental.com/london
⊖ Knightsbridge
Bar Boulud and Dinner by Heston Blumenthal *(See restaurant listing)*

194 rm – †£600/1,020 ††£600/1,020, ☕ £26 – 25 suites

Mandarin Oriental Hyde Park

Mandarin Oriental is one of the great hotel companies of the world and, to ensure their reputation remains as such, the company is constantly making improvements to their landmark London property which dates from 1889. The best of the most recent changes has been the creation of The Rosebery, a charming salon where the original cornicing and plasterwork are juxtaposed with some vivid modern art. It is here where afternoon tea and evening cocktails are served and the room is proving a much admired addition to the hotel, which already boasts Heston Blumenthal's enigmatically named 'Dinner' restaurant, along with Daniel Boulud's downstairs 'Bar Boulud'. The other major development has been the improvements made to the spa; it is now spread over two floors and includes a new gym and a 17m pool under One Hyde Park. Upstairs, the suites have been redecorated and the next stage is the refurbishment of the bedrooms which are currently decorated in an English country house style. One appealing feature here has always been the standard of the service and this remains as strong as ever.

The Milestone

D4

1-2 Kensington Ct ⊠ W8 5DL
℘ 020 7917 1000
www.milestonehotel.com
⊖ High Street Kensington

62 rm⊑ – ∱£348/480 ∯£400/1,000 – 6 suites

The Milestone

Behind the striking Gothic red-brick façade is a little gem of a hotel. Fashioned out of three houses dating from the 16C, which were joined together early in the 20C, The Milestone is discreet, cosy and sumptuously decorated. It is also very well soundproofed so you can enjoy the location opposite Kensington Gardens without being disturbed by the traffic on Kensington Road. There's a thoroughly British feel to the hotel, especially the sitting room where you can have afternoon tea beneath a painting of a youthful Noel Coward. The Jockey Bar is so named because this was where the horses were once stabled and the basement leisure club is a useful little facility for those who like to exercise their way out of jetlag. For others, there's the wood-panelled Cheneston's restaurant for modern British food. Entry level bedrooms can be a little on the small size but there's impressive attention to detail in all the rooms, especially the suites which display greater levels of whimsy. Every room has enough Penhaligon's toiletries to stock a small shop.

Number Sixteen

16 Sumner Pl. ⊠ SW7 3EG
☎ 020 7589 5232
www.firmdalehotels.co.uk
⊖ South Kensington

41 rm – †£150/190 ††£235/340,⌷ £14

Firmdale

Number Sixteen opened back in 2001 and was the first one in Tim and Kit Kemp's Firmdale Group of hotels not to have its own restaurant. This actually suits it because it feels more like a private house than the others and, with repeat business standing at around 55%, they've clearly got it right. Attention to detail underpins the operation, whether in the individual styling of the bedrooms or the twice-daily housekeeping service. Breakfast is in the conservatory overlooking the little garden – don't miss the smoothie of the day – and is served until midday: welcome acknowledgement that not every guest has an early morning meeting. Firmdale also operates its own laundry service which explains how the bed linen retains such crispness. Rooms 2 and 7 have their own private patio terrace and all the first floor rooms benefit from large windows and balconies. The drawing room, with its plump sofa cushions and pretty butterfly theme, is a very charming spot and there's the added bonus of a nearby honesty bar.

One Aldwych

1 Aldwych ✉ WC2B 4BZ
☎ 020 7300 1000
www.onealdwych.com
⊖ Temple

105 rm – †£387/770 ††£387/770, ☕ £19 – 12 suites

One Aldwych

Things have gone all green down at One Aldwych. The hotel is hoping to take a lead within the hospitality industry on matters environmental (without, of course, neglecting its duties as a luxury hotel) and has appointed a 'green team' to oversee and coordinate procedures. The swimming pool is chemical and chlorine free; bath products are organic; and the chocolate on your pillow has been replaced by a book called 'Change the World'. As far as guests are concerned though, it's business as usual, which means extremely comfortable bedrooms and plenty of polished staff. Fruit and flowers are changed daily in the rooms, which are awash with Bang & Olufsen toys and also come with Frette linen; deluxe rooms and corner suites are particularly desirable. First floor Indigo offers a light, easy menu, while Eneko serves modern Basque dishes from acclaimed Spanish chef, Eneko Atxa. The lobby of the hotel is also a well-known feature; not only does it double as a bar surprisingly successfully but it also changes its look according to the seasons.

The Pelham

15 Cromwell Pl ⊠ SW7 2LA
✆ 020 7589 8288
www.pelhamhotel.co.uk
⊖ South Kensington

51 rm – †£180/335 ††£260/480,⊽ £18 – 1 suite

The Pelham

If museum visiting is high on your London agenda then you'll find The Pelham's South Kensington location hard to beat. Owned by the people who have The Gore in Queensgate, the hotel boasts a stylish look derived from juxtaposing the feel of a classic English country house with the contemporary look of a city townhouse. Made up of three houses, the hotel has a pleasing lack of conformity in its layout and, although it may not be looking quite as crisp and debonair as it did a few years back, the bedrooms are all a little different and are warm and comfortable. Spend too long in the panelled sitting room or library, with all those cushions, an honesty bar and a fridge full of ice cream and the world outside will seem positively frenzied. Downstairs you'll find Bistro Fifteen, a relaxed all-day affair which becomes a cosy and romantic dinner spot and offers a menu of largely Mediterranean persuasion – a nod perhaps to the high number of French émigrés in this neighbourhood.

Ritz

150 Piccadilly ⊠ W1J 9BR
℘ 020 7493 8181
www.theritzlondon.com
⊖ Green Park
⚘ **Ritz Restaurant** *(See restaurant listing)*

136 rm – ♦£355/875 ♦♦£430/1,130,⌷ £35 – 24 suites

The Ritz

Henry James considered that, "There are few hours in life more agreeable than the hour dedicated to the ceremony known as afternoon tea". Such is the popularity of Tea at the Ritz, which is served daily in the grand surroundings of the Palm Court, that the ceremony begins at 11.30 am – an hour before lunch is served in their restaurant – and doesn't cease until 7.30pm. Meanwhile, the rest of the hotel, built in 1906 in the style of a French chateau, remains in fine form thanks to constant re-investment by its owners, the Barclay Brothers. The William Kent Room must be the most ornate private dining room in London and the bedrooms are all immaculately kept. The Royal and Prince of Wales Suites both have enormous square footage and are often booked for long stays by those for whom the credit crunch is no more than a mild irritant. The Ritz Restaurant, with its dinner dances, lavish surroundings and brigades of staff, evokes images of a more formal but more glamorous age and the art deco Rivoli bar remains a veritable jewel.

The Rookery

12 Peters Ln, Cowcross St ✉ EC1M 6DS
✆ 020 7336 0931
www.rookeryhotel.com
⊖ Farringdon

33 rm – ♦£195/225 ♦♦£265/650,⌂ £12

The Rookery

The mere fact that the original opening of the hotel was delayed because the owner couldn't find quite the right chimney pots tells you that authenticity is high on the agenda here. Named after the colloquial term for the local area from a time when it had an unruly reputation, the hotel is made up of a series of Georgian houses whose former residents are honoured in the naming of the bedrooms. Its decoration remains true to these Georgian roots, not only in the antique furniture and period features but also in the colours used; all the bedrooms have either half-tester or four-poster beds and bathrooms have roll-top baths. However, with the addition of all the mod cons, there is no danger of the hotel becoming a twee museum piece; Rook's Nest, the largest room, is often used for fashion shoots. Breakfast is served in the bedrooms and there is just one small sitting room which leads out onto a little terrace - its mural of the owner herding some cows goes some way towards blocking out the surrounding sights of the 21C.

St James's Hotel and Club

H4

7-8 Park Pl. ✉ SW1A 1LS
☎ 020 7316 1600
www.stjameshotelandclub.com
⊖ Green Park
🍽 **Seven Park Place** (See restaurant listing)

60 rm – †£265/550 ††£265/550,☕ £23 – 10 suites

St James's Hotel & Club

The liveried doorman and a plethora of concierges immediately tell you that this is a hotel with an eye for service. Staff make concerted efforts to note down guests' preferences for future visits and the housekeeping department ensure that bedrooms are so immaculate you feel you're sullying the room just by being in it. The building dates from 1892 and there can be few better positions for a London hotel: it is bang in the heart of the metropolis and yet because Park Place is a cul-de-sac, it's very quiet. For those who like a little exercise, there's a cut-through to get to Green Park. Before being a hotel this was a private club and there remains a discernible clubby feel. Granted, it's quite a compact place but they've made good use of the space – the bar doubles as a simple brasserie and this leads into the intimate, gilded restaurant. However, perhaps the greatest aspect is the vast collection of art from the Rosenstein collection scattered around the building and covering the 1920s to the 1950s.

St Martins Lane

45 St Martin's Ln ⊠ WC2N 3HX
☎ 020 7300 5500
www.morganshotelgroup.com
⊖ Charing Cross

206 rm⚏ – †£199/500 ††£199/500 – 2 suites

St Martins Lane

If you're uncomfortable with the idea of hotel staff calling you by your first name or have never considered working out in a gym wearing a pair of stilettos then St Martins Lane is probably not the hotel for you; nor you the right guest for them. Philippe Starck's design of the modern juxtaposed with the baroque creates an eye-catching lobby. The bedrooms are decorated in a blizzard of white, although you can change the lighting according to your mood. The views get better the higher you go but all have floor to ceiling windows. Thanks to the paparazzi, readers of the more excitable magazines will be familiar with Bungalow 8: Anne Sacco's London outpost of her hip New York club is a favoured hang-out for the already-famous, the would-be-famous and the related-to-someone-famous-famous. Asia de Cuba is Scarface meets Dr No: fiery Floridian Cuban mixed with teasing influences from across Asia – dishes are designed for sharing. The Light Bar is sufficiently hip and the Gymbox is a branded gym with a nightclub vibe – what else?

Sanderson

50 Berners St ⊠ W1T 3NG
☎ 020 7300 1400
www.morganshotelgroup.com
⊖ Oxford Circus

150 rm – †£234/538 ††£234/538,⊊ £18

Sanderson

The Sanderson has always worn its exclusivity with confidence but now there's some substance to it. When it was converted from the Sanderson fabric factory it was Philippe Starck's vision and design which really made it so different. Since then other designers have been engaged here but his influence is still very much in evidence. The bedrooms remain crisp, bright and artfully arranged and, although they are a little less idiosyncratic these days, they are now a little warmer in their colour schemes. The bars have always been the hotel's strong suit: on the ground floor the Purple Bar has over 75 different vodkas, miniature chairs and a selective door policy; the Long Bar is a little more accessible. When it comes to restaurants, competition is a little fiercer in this neck of the woods these days – this is where the hotel has yet to make its mark or settle for a particular style or cuisine, so you're better off taking your pick from the various places that lie within walking distance.

Savoy

Strand ✉ WC2R 0EU
☎ 020 7836 4343
www.fairmont.com/savoy
⊖ Charing Cross

267 rm – †£420/1,500 ††£420/1,500,⌷ £35 – 45 suites

The Savoy

The Savoy is one of the grande dames of the London hotel scene and its understated elegance has been attracting legions of regulars to this spot on the north bank of the Thames for over a century. The lobby offers a welcoming air and creates a sense of expectation, with plenty of staff on hand to offer help or directions. Bedrooms remain true to the hotel's origins, with either an Edwardian or an art deco style; the hotel was originally built in 1889 and extended in the 1920s, when the iconic entrance on the Strand was also added. Signature suites pay homage to famous past guests including Monet, Charlie Chaplin, and Richard Harris, while the Royal Suite offers the ultimate in luxury as well as stunning river views. Afternoon tea is served in the Thames Foyer, complete with a live pianist and there is also a choice of two bars: the world famous American Bar and the Beaufort Bar which occupies the space from which the BBC once broadcast. Informal Kaspar's is a seafood bar and grill – tables here are easier to secure than those in the famous Savoy Grill.

Shangri-La

M4

The Shard, 31 St Thomas St ✉ SE1 9QU
✆ 020 7234 8000
www.shangri-la.com/london
⊖ London Bridge

202 rm – †£350/575 ††£350/575, ☕ £32 – 17 suites

Shangri-La

When your hotel occupies floors 34-52 of The Shard, you know there's already plenty of wow factor. Shangri-La was the most eagerly anticipated hotel opening of 2014 and when one considers how much marble they've used, it's a wonder Renzo Piano's iconic building is still upright. Due to the building's shape and configuration, the bedrooms vary in size, although the hotel judges the best ones – ergo, the most expensive ones – to be those facing north across the river. Modern Chinese abstracts and calming shades feature throughout the hotel; London's highest swimming pool is on level 52 and sits alongside the Gong bar where one side serves champagne, the other cocktails. Lang is a small all-day patisserie at ground level and Ting is the comfortable restaurant where classic British dishes with the odd Asian twist are made using plenty of produce from nearby Borough Market. This fusion of East and West extends to afternoon tea, where you have a choice of traditional English or Asian-style with dim sum.

Soho

4 Richmond Mews ✉ W1D 3DH
𝒞 020 7559 3000
www.sohohotel.com
⊖ Tottenham Court Road
✗ **Refuel** *(See restaurant listing)*

96 rm – †£235/340 ††£285/540, ⌣ £14 – 7 suites

Firmdale

It's almost as if they wanted to keep it secret. The hotel is on a relatively quiet mews – not something one readily associates with Soho – and, even as you approach, it gives little away. But inside one soon realises that, if it was a secret, it wasn't very well kept as it's always buzzing with people. Their guests' every dietary whim or food mood should find fulfilment in 'Refuel', the restaurant with its own bar as a backdrop. Whether your diet is gluten-free, vegetarian, vegan, carnivorous or organic you'll discover something worth ordering and, if you're off out, you'll find the early dinner menu a steal. It's also worth checking out the Film Club for a meal and a movie in the screening room. Upstairs, the bedrooms are almost celestial in their cleanliness. From jazzy orange to bright lime green, from crimsons to bold stripes, the rooms are vibrant in style and immaculate in layout; those on the top floor have balconies and terraces. Add infectiously enthusiastic service and it's little wonder the hotel has so many returning guests. And to think this was once an NCP car park.

South Place

3 South Pl ⊠ EC2M 2AF
☎ 020 3503 0000
www.southplacehotel.com
⊖ Moorgate
⅍ **Angler** *(See restaurant listing)*

80 rm – †£185/350 ††£185/350,⊑ £17 – 1 suite

South Place

Restaurant group D&D's first venture into the hotel business is a very stylish looking affair, and for that credit goes to their erstwhile boss, in the shape of Conrad & Partners, who designed the interior. The bedrooms are a treat for those with an eye for aesthetics and a great advert for how design can enhance one's mood. They are understated, uncluttered and cool yet no detail has been forgotten, from blackout blinds to all manner of high-tech gizmos; contemporary artwork lines the walls and the bathrooms are a great balance between form and function. On the food front you have a choice of two restaurants: 3 South Place is a bustling bar and grill on the ground floor, with a good range of modern brasserie dishes and food-inspired pop art on the walls; Angler, a more formal seafood restaurant is on the top floor. The hotel is actually fashioned out of two former offices but you wouldn't know it from the exterior – the atmosphere is relaxed yet animated, helped along by service that is discreet and professional.

Stafford

16-18 St James's Pl. ⊠ SW1A 1NJ
☏ 020 7493 0111
www.thestaffordlondon.com
⊖ Green Park

104 rm – ♦£350/535 ♦♦£350/535,⟉ £25 – 15 suites

Stafford

The Stafford has, for a few years, been a mix of the new and the more traditional. The owners have injected considerable amounts of money into its upkeep and redecoration; something which no doubt terrifies many of its loyal and long-standing guests who appear to like things just the way they are. Thanks to some judicious lighting, the lobby and lounge are now brighter and more inviting. The dining room opens out more into the drawing room and is named Lyttleton after a family who once lived here - it specialises in traditional British food, and also boasts an impressive cellar. The relatively recently created suites in the Mews House, a converted office block in the rear courtyard of the hotel, are the most impressive of all the bedrooms. What will never change at The Stafford is the celebrated American Bar, which is festooned with an impressive collection of assorted ties, helmets and pictures and is one of the best in London for those who like their bars with chairs and without music.

Town Hall

✉ E2 9NF

✆ 020 7871 0460

www.townhallhotel.com

⊖ Bethnal Green

 Typing Room and Corner Room *(See restaurant listing)*

98 rm⌂ – †£162/429 ††£186/452 – 57 suites

Town Hall

What used to be the civic headquarters for the borough of Bethnal Green was converted into a hotel in 2010, and whilst the hotel is stylish, relaxed and trendy with a capital T, the conversion has cleverly managed to retain or restore much of the architectural splendour of this historic building. The Grade II listed town hall was originally built in 1909 but was added to in the 1930s, so as well as the Edwardian grandeur of features like the magnificent marble staircase, you can admire art deco details such as the stunning stained glass and the original wood-panelled council chamber, which is now used as conference space. The striking, individually decorated bedrooms come with retro furnishings, modern bathrooms and frequently changing art. Most have a separate sitting room and a hidden kitchen – while the light-filled De Montfort Suite has to be one of the biggest in London. There are two impressive restaurants – the Typing Room and the Corner Room – as well as a nicely kitted out gym and a 50ft swimming pool.

Twenty Nevern Square

20 Nevern Sq. ⊠ SW5 9PD
☎ 020 7565 9555
www.twentynevernsquare.co.uk
⊖ Earl's Court

20 rm⌂ – †£99/249 ††£119/299

Michelin

Waking up in a faceless corporate hotel with no obvious association to the city in which you're in can be a dispiriting affair. Twenty Nevern Square gives you the opportunity to stay in an affordable, discreet and comfortable townhouse overlooking a classic Victorian Square which, in turn, will make you feel a little like a Londoner. Ten of the bedrooms overlook the square, which is something of an oasis in bustling Earl's Court yet is still close to the Tube. All the rooms come with a good mix of the traditional and the modern; some have balconies and those on the higher floors tend to be a little smaller – the biggest are Ottoman and Pasha. Attractive hand-carved Indonesian furniture adds personality and the owners, who are very hands-on, are always refreshing and refitting their hotel. Breakfast can be taken in your room or in the conservatory; and if you don't have the will to venture out for dinner in the evening, a couple of local eateries now deliver their fare to your room.

The Wellesley

11 Knightsbridge ⊠ SW1X 7LY
☎ 020 7235 3535
www.thewellesley.co.uk
⊖ Hyde Park Corner

36 rm – ⸙**£350/599** ⸙⸙**£350/599,**☕ **£34 – 14 suites**

The Wellesley

It may once have been one of the entrances to Hyde Park Corner Tube, but for nearly three decades this site was occupied by the legendary Pizza on the Park, which was celebrated by its fans less for the pizzas and more for being a great venue for live jazz. It was subsequently gutted and rebuilt and emerged at the very end of 2012 as this very stylish, intimate boutique hotel named after Sir Arthur Wellesley, the first duke of Wellington. The owners were not blind to the building's past: not only are some of the decorative features inspired by the jazz age but live music is also performed in the Jazz Lounge. The discreet restaurant serves modern Italian food and, in perhaps another nod towards the appetite of your typical jazz fan, the hotel has a great cigar lounge and a bar with a superb selection of whiskies and cognacs. The smart, elegant bedrooms have been beautifully finished and come with every conceivable facility, including full butler service; those most in demand are the ones facing the park.

Westbury

Bond St ✉ W1S 2YF
℘ 020 7629 7755
www.westburymayfair.com
⊖ Bond Street
⚘ **Alyn Williams at The Westbury** *(See restaurant listing)*

246 rm⛄ – ♦£263/599 ♦♦£263/599 – 13 suites

Westbury

The Westbury opened in the 1950s and caused quite a commotion with its New York sensibilities. Over recent years, considerable funds have been spent restoring it to its former glory, with the result that this is now one of Mayfair's more comfortable hotels. It is traditional without being staid and discreet without appearing precious; the staff are suitably enthusiastic and clearly proud of their hotel. There is no doubt that its location is also a huge draw: there are enough exclusive brands just outside the front door to satisfy even the most committed disciple of Edina and Patsy. The bedrooms are sleek and comfy and each floor is decorated with photos from the corresponding decade (so 1960s style icons adorn the 6th floor). The suites are particularly smart, especially those with art deco styling. The iconic Polo bar is elegantly dressed in Gucci and Fendi and its celebrated cocktail list ensures it's busy at night. Along with a sushi bar the hotel offers sublime dining courtesy of chef Alyn Williams' creative and elaborate cuisine.

Zetter

K1

St John's Sq, 86-88 Clerkenwell Rd. ✉ EC1M 5RJ
✆ 020 7324 4444
www.thezetter.com
⊖ Farringdon

59 rm – †£150/498 ††£150/498, ☕ £14

The Zetter

It doesn't matter how good looking and coolly dressed you are – if you never crack a smile no one will want to know you. What makes the Zetter more than just another hip hotel lies in the friendliness of its staff: instead of checking their pose or practising their pout they'll actually greet you with a warm smile and this is one of the reasons why guests keep returning. The main part of the hotel is within a converted Victorian warehouse, although the bistro on the ground floor adds a little continental element. Not only does the hotel have impressive eco-credentials – it bottles the water from its well – it also comes with some nice touches, like affordable vending machines on each floor; you can even borrow a folding bike from reception, complete with helmet and map. The rooms in this part of the hotel are understated and come with a cool retro edge. The more idiosyncratic Clerkenwell Townhouse across the road acts as an overflow, with more colourfully decorated rooms and a cocktail bar that has become a destination in its own right.

F1

28-30 Seymour St ✉ W1H 7JB
℘ 020 7324 4544
www.thezettertownhouse.com
⊖ Marble Arch

24 rm – †£290/480 ††£290/480,⊊ £14

Zetter Townhouse

Like its Clerkenwell sister, this boutique hotel is sumptuous and stylish with friendly, professional staff and impressive eco-credentials. Whereas the Clerkenwell Townhouse represents the home of a fictional Great Aunt, Wilhelmina, this is the property of Wicked Uncle Seymour, a man who obviously has a taste for the good things in life, and though the entrance to this mid-terrace Georgian townhouse is ultra-discreet, the interior is lavishly decked out with a quirky, clubby feel. The lounge & cocktail bar is based on Sir John Soane's Museum with dark, rich décor and an inviting open fire; nibbles like potted shrimps or a charcuterie board are available but cocktails are the main focus and come with quirky names like Turf Club, Valais Fizz and The Last Laugh. Bedrooms are beautifully appointed and furnished with antiques and curios. All come with reclaimed beds and Egyptian cotton linen; the best is called Lear's Loft – after Edward Lear, whose home this once was – which is accessed via its own staircase and features a roll-top bath on its rooftop terrace.

MICHELIN IS CONTINUALLY INNOVATING FOR SAFER, CLEANER, MORE ECONOMICAL, MORE CONNECTED... BETTER ALL-ROUND MOBILITY.

Tyres wear more quickly on short urban journeys.

TRUE!

You tend to accelerate and brake more often when driving around town so your tyres work harder!
If you are stuck in traffic, keep calm and drive slowly.

Tyre pressure only affects your car's safety.

FALSE!

Driving with underinflated tyres (0.5 bar below recommended pressure) doesn't just impact handling and fuel consumption, it will shave 8,000 km off tyre lifespan.
Make sure you check tyre pressure about once a month and before you go on holiday or a long journey.

Fitting **2 winter tyres** on my car guarantees maximum safety.

?

FALSE!

In the winter, especially when temperatures drop below 7°C, to ensure better road holding, all four tyres should be identical and fitted at the same time.

2 WINTER TYRES ONLY = risk of compromised road holding.

4 WINTER TYRES = safer handling when cornering, driving downhill and braking.

If you regularly encounter rain, snow or black ice, choose a **MICHELIN Alpin tyre**. This range offers you sharp handling plus a comfortable ride to safely face the challenge of winter driving.

MICHELIN

MICHELIN
IS COMMITTED

▶ MICHELIN IS **GLOBAL LEADER IN FUEL-EFFICIENT TYRES** FOR LIGHT VEHICLES.

▶ **EDUCATING OF YOUNGSTERS IN ROAD SAFETY,**
NOT FORGETTING TWO-WHEELERS. LOCAL ROAD SAFETY CAMPAIGNS WERE RUN IN **16 COUNTRIES** IN 2015.

QUIZ

1 TYRES ARE BLACK SO WHY IS THE MICHELIN MAN WHITE?

Back in 1898 when the Michelin Man was first created from a stack of tyres, they were made of natural rubber, cotton and sulphur and were therefore light-coloured. The composition of tyres did not change until after the First World War when carbon black was introduced. But the Michelin Man kept his colour!

2 FOR HOW LONG HAS MICHELIN BEEN GUIDING TRAVELLERS?

Since 1900. When the MICHELIN guide was published at the turn of the century, it was claimed that it would last for a hundred years. It's still around today and remains a reference with new editions and online restaurant listings in a number of countries.

3 WHEN WAS THE "BIB GOURMAND" INTRODUCED IN THE MICHELIN GUIDE?

The symbol was created in 1997 but as early as 1954 the MICHELIN guide was recommending "exceptional good food at moderate prices". Today, it features on the MICHELIN Restaurants website and app.

If you want to enjoy a fun day out and find out more about Michelin, why not visit the l'Aventure Michelin museum and shop in Clermont-Ferrand, France:
www.laventuremichelin.com

Index & Maps

Alphabetical list of restaurants

Alphabetical list of restaurants

483

Map Index

Central London

Greater London

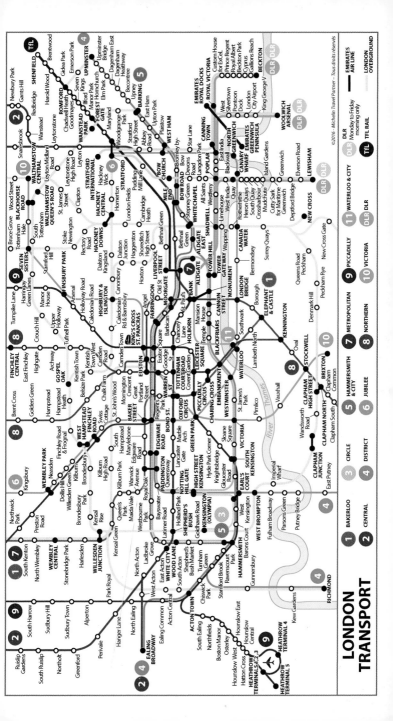

LONDON TRANSPORT

 Notes…

Notes…

Notes...

Michelin Travel Partner

Société par actions simplifiées au capital de 11 288 880 EUR
27 Cours de l'Ile Seguin - 92100 Boulogne Billancourt (France)
R.C.S. Nanterre 433 677 721

© **Michelin, Propriétaires-Éditeurs**

Dépôt légal August 2016

Printed in Italy - August 2016
Printed on paper from sustainably managed forests

Compogravure: Nord Compo à Villeneuve d'Ascq (France)
Impression et Finition: Lego Print (Lavis)